Abandoning Their Beloved Land

Abandoning Their Beloved Land

THE POLITICS OF BRACERO MIGRATION
IN MEXICO

Alberto García

UNIVERSITY OF CALIFORNIA PRESS

University of California Press
Oakland, California

© 2023 by Alberto García

Portions of chapters 1, 2, and 5 were first published in Alberto García, "Regulating Bracero Migration: How National, Regional, and Local Political Considerations Shaped the Bracero Program," *Hispanic American Historical Review* 101, no. 3 (2021): 433–60. Copyright 2021, Duke University Press. All rights reserved. Reprint by permission of the copyright holder.

Library of Congress Cataloging-in-Publication Data

Names: García, Alberto, 1983- author.
Title: Abandoning their beloved land : the politics of bracero migration in Mexico / Alberto García.
Description: Oakland, California : University of California Press, [2023] | Includes bibliographical references and index.
Identifiers: LCCN 2022024992 (print) | LCCN 2022024993 (ebook) | ISBN 9780520390225 (cloth) | ISBN 9780520390232 (paperback) | ISBN 9780520390249 (ebook)
Subjects: LCSH: Seasonal Farm Laborers Program. | Agricultural laborers—Political aspects—Mexico—20th century. | Agricultural laborers—Mexico—History—20th century.
Classification: LCC HD1531.M6 G355 2023 (print) | LCC HD1531.M6 (ebook) | DDC 331.7/630972—dc23/eng/20220907
LC record available at https://lccn.loc.gov/2022024992
LC ebook record available at https://lccn.loc.gov/2022024993

32 31 30 29 28 27 26 25 24 23
10 9 8 7 6 5 4 3 2 1

Para mi familia

CONTENTS

List of Illustrations viii
Acknowledgments ix
Abbreviations xiv

Introduction 1

1 · "The Urgent Need to Regulate Departures":
Federal-Level Administration of the Bracero Program 14

2 · "According to the Jurisdiction's Necessities": State-Level
Administration of the Bracero Program 43

3 · "Long-Standing Political and Religious Differences":
Political-Religious Conflicts and Bracero Migration in
the Greater Bajío 68

4 · "Lack of Work and Lands to Sow": The Agrarian Reform
and Bracero Migration in the Greater Bajío 98

5 · A "Mockery of Responsibility": Municipal-Level
Administration of the Bracero Program 121

Conclusion 149

Notes 157
Bibliography 215
Index 235

ILLUSTRATIONS

MAPS

1. States of Aguascalientes, Guanajuato, Jalisco, Michoacán, and Zacatecas   2
2. The Greater Bajío (southern Guanajuato, northern Michoacán, and northeastern Jalisco)   7
3. The Greater Bajío (southwestern Aguascalientes and southern Zacatecas)   8
4. Contracting center sites   40

FIGURE

1. Changuitiro bracero David Maldonado Mendoza   94

ACKNOWLEDGMENTS

I am fairly certain that I am not the first author to realize during the writing process that referring to "my" book was something of a misnomer, since it would have been impossible to write it without the generous support of numerous individuals and institutions. Bringing this book to completion was a collective effort, though I alone am responsible for any errors or omissions in the pages that follow.

Writing this book required extensive archival and library research, and that extensive research required significant financial support. I would like to thank the University of California, Berkeley, Graduate Division, the University of California Institute for Mexico and the United States, and the San José State University Research Foundation for providing the funds that facilitated my research trips. Once I was at the archives and libraries, I was fortunate enough to count on the support of a host of talented, enthusiastic, and dedicated archivists and librarians. The personnel at the Archivo General de la Nación, the Archivo Histórico del Estado de Aguascalientes, the Archivo Histórico del Archivo General del Poder Ejecutivo de Guanajuato, the Archivo Histórico del Estado de Jalisco, the Archivo General e Histórico del Poder Ejecutivo de Michoacán, the Archivo Histórico Municipal de Irapuato, the Archivo Municipal e Histórico de Tepatitlán de Morelos, the Archivo Histórico del Municipio de Zacatecas, the Bancroft Library, and the Nettie Lee Benson Latin American Collection were unfailing in their determination to locate any and all relevant primary documents, monographs, and journal articles. Just as important, their friendliness and generosity made the archives feel like a second home during lengthy research trips. I would also like to recognize Diana Ávila Hernández, Jayson Porter, and Naomi Sussman, all of whom conducted research on my behalf in Mexico City when it was not possible for me to travel there personally.

This book grew out of an impromptu conversation that I had with Margaret Chowning toward the end of my first semester as a graduate student at UC Berkeley. I was beginning to think about a research seminar paper that I had to write during my second semester, but I did not have a topic beyond "the twentieth century." Because she already knew that my family was originally from Michoacán, Margaret suggested that I research my family's hometown, Changuitiro, and that I should perhaps pay attention to factors that could explain why it became a migrant-sending community. Thankfully, I followed her advice, and that seminar paper helped generate the research questions that inspired my dissertation, which in turn inspired this book. In the years since that conversation, Margaret has been everything I could have asked for in an academic mentor: keen-eyed, constructively critical, and, most important, kind. Her feedback has made this book better; her unceasing kindness has given me an example to strive for as I continue my career as a scholar and teacher.

Margaret was not the only outstanding scholar I had the great fortune to learn from and alongside while I was at UC Berkeley, and each of them helped make this book a reality. Mark Healey has been a constant source of enthusiastic support and valuable feedback since I was an admitted graduate student visiting Berkeley's campus, and the way he has embraced and championed my work, as well as my family's corner of the Mexican Republic, has meant a great deal to me. Brian DeLay's scholarly rigor and generosity are second to none, and I will forever be grateful for his unwavering belief that my work could reach the highest standard possible. Elena Schneider's insightful questions when I presented my research at the Berkeley Latin American History Working Group helped me clarify my thinking and refine some of the finer points of my argument. Mark Brilliant taught me the importance of both the wide and long views. And of course, I have to thank my graduate colleagues who were enduring sources of inspiration, comradery, and support: Rebecca Herman, Germán Vergara, Lynsay Skiba, Sarah Hines, Sarah Selvidge, Pablo Palomino, David Tamayo, Andra Chastain, Craig Johnson, Amada Beltrán, Clare Ibarra, Natalie Mendoza, Maggie Elmore, Bathsheba Demuth, Peggy O'Donnell, Rhiannon Dowling, Sam Robinson, Jason Rozumalski, Katie Harper, Tehila Sasson, Chris Casey, Erica Lee, Andrea Horbinski, Gillian Chisom, and Michel Estefan.

Once my time at UC Berkeley came to an end, I spent a year as a research fellow at the University of Texas at Austin's Institute for Historical Studies.

The institute was the ideal setting to begin revising my dissertation into this book, and I would like to thank Matthew Butler, Madeline Hsu, Miriam Bodian, Titas Chakraborty, Eyal Weinberg, Jennifer Jones, Henry Wiencek, Elizabeth O'Brien, and Courtney Meador for welcoming me with open arms and providing invaluable suggestions that ensured that this book was in much better shape when I left UT Austin than it was when I arrived.

After leaving central Texas, I returned to the San Francisco Bay Area to join the faculty at San José State. My colleagues Glen Gendzel, Michael Conniff, Libra Hilde, Xiaojia Hou, Allison Katsev, Patricia Hill, Bruce Reynolds, and Leslie Corona have been generous with their encouragement as I approached the finish line. I would also like to thank the Division of Research and Innovation for granting the course releases that gave me the time I needed to complete the book.

In the months before I submitted my manuscript for initial review, three colleagues and mentors gave me the opportunity to present my research, and the questions, comments, and suggestions I received during these presentations proved invaluable during the final stages of the writing process. Lorena Ojeda Dávila, who I first met when she was a visiting scholar at UC Berkeley, invited me to deliver a lecture to her students and colleagues at the Universidad Michoacana de San Nicolás de Hidalgo in summer 2019; my thanks to her for that invitation, as well as for all her kind support throughout the years. Chuck Walker invited me to return to my undergraduate alma mater, the University of California, Davis, and participate in its history department's Annual Colloquium Series in fall 2019. I also need to note that without Chuck's mentorship and encouragement, this book would not exist: Chuck was the first person who pushed me to consider attending graduate school and making history my profession, and for that I will always be indebted to him. And last, Julia Young invited me to make a presentation at a special conference that was cohosted by Georgetown University, the Catholic University of America, and the Mexican Cultural Institute of Washington, DC, in fall 2019. I first met Julia when Margaret Chowning introduced us, and she has been a wonderful source of support and feedback since then. In addition to asking me to present a paper at one of the most fantastic conferences I have ever been a part of, Julia graciously read this book's third chapter and provided key suggestions that greatly improved it.

I could not have found a better home for this book than the University of California Press. Kate Marshall and Enrique Ochoa-Kaup are brilliant, thoughtful, and caring editors who patiently guided me through the publication process in the midst of a global pandemic that affected every aspect of our lives. I also have to thank Paul Gillingham, Mireya Loza, and an anonymous reader for reviewing the book and giving me critiques that ultimately strengthened my arguments and narrative structure.

I have also been incredibly fortunate to count on a group of close friends who have been, and I am certain will continue to be, extremely generous with their intellectual and emotional support. These friends were always willing to look over a draft or help talk me out of argumentative and narrative corners that I had written myself into. Just as important, I could always count on them to join me for hikes, good meals, long conversations about Bay Area sports, celebrations of professional and personal milestones, and marathon viewings of *The Simpsons*, *Brooklyn Nine-Nine*, the latest HBO series, Marvel movies, college football, and international soccer tournaments. For this and for so much more, I will always be grateful to Zoe Griffith, Marcus Johnson, Chris Bovbjerg, Giuliana Perrone, Javier Cikota, Irina Popescu, Olivia Benowitz, Bobby Lee, Dorothee Unger-Lee, Eric Johnson, Lauren Chiarulli, Lily Pearl Balloffet, Ben Pearl, Yael Schacher, Jessica Meinke, Matt Countryman, Jay Shuttleworth, Megan Annis, Kendra Chan, Elliot Blair, Rachel Cajigas, and Costanza Rampini.

I have saved the last words of these acknowledgments for my family, to whom this book is dedicated. I must begin with my maternal great-grandparents, Teófilo Fuentes Fajardo and Julia Aguilar Guzmán, whose stories of a Mexico that used to be first inspired my interest in studying the past. My paternal grandparents, Leopoldo García Guillén and María de Jesús Maldonado Fuentes, bequeathed me a legacy of strength and tenacity. My maternal grandmother, Bernardina Fuentes Aguilar, has been a never-ending source of wisdom and inspiration. And though he passed away before I was born, my maternal grandfather, David Maldonado Mendoza, has left an indelible mark on my life: he was among the first to leave Changuitiro as a bracero, and I hope that my work does justice to his experiences. My niece, Julia Escamilla, and my nephews, Diego Escamilla, Jordan García, and Julián García, have helped keep my spirit young and reminded me how important it is to step away from work every now and then to enjoy the little things in life. My brother-in-law, Jesús Escamilla, gave me an early boost when he handed down his Mexican history textbooks to me, and he has been a constant source of support through the years. My sister-in-law, Kristen García, has never failed to put a smile on my face or make me laugh during family gatherings. But far more important, Jesús and Kristen have brought joy to my siblings, Lucila Escamilla and Javier García. Lucila and Javier have been my most unfailing cheerleaders since they helped me learn how to read and write, drove me to doctor's appointments, and taught me how to swing a baseball bat. They have always been in my corner, pushing me to strive higher, even during moments when I doubted myself. Simply put, they were my first heroes, and they always will be. And last but by no means least, my parents, Francisco García Maldonado and Amparo Maldonado Fuentes. Like millions of others during the twentieth century, they made the decision to leave Mexico for the United States when they were young. They spent countless hours in the fields, orchards, and packing plants of California's Central Valley, all so they could make a better life for themselves and their children. In that, they succeeded. Although my siblings and I did not grow up in luxury and still had to contend with structural barriers that affect the Mexican-origin community living in the United States, our parents' tireless efforts created untold opportunities for us. Their sacrifices and dedication to their family lie at the heart of every success I have enjoyed. There are no words that can fully capture how grateful I am for all that they have done for me, or how proud I am of all that they have accomplished during their lives. That being the case, I will have to make do with the following: gracias, y los quiero mucho.

ABBREVIATIONS

CNC	Confederación Nacional Campesina
CTM	Confederación de Trabajadores de México
DIPS	Departamento de Investigaciones Políticas y Sociales
PAN	Partido Acción Nacional
PRI	Partido Revolucionario Institucional
SEP	Secretaría de Educación Pública
SNOCIAS	Sindicato Nacional de Obreros y Campesinos de la Industria Azucarera y Similares
STIASRM	Sindicato de Trabajadores de la Industria Azucarera y Similares de la República Mexicana
UCC	Unión Cívica Calvillense
UNS	Unión Nacional Sinarquista

Introduction

IN 1942 US OFFICIALS APPROACHED their Mexican counterparts with a novel proposal: they suggested that the two governments cooperate on a program that would allow Mexican men to work in the United States as seasonal contract farmworkers, or braceros. These braceros would replace the young Americans mobilizing to fight in World War II, as well as satisfy the demands of farm owners in states like California and Texas who wanted access to a labor force that could be used to undercut farmworkers' unions.[1] Despite a history of publicly discouraging migration to the United States and concerns that migratory departures would harm domestic agricultural production, Mexican authorities accepted the proposal after concluding that a guest worker program would help them place some limits on departures and that braceros' earnings and acquired knowledge could advance development in rural Mexico.[2] The Bracero Program, the unofficial name given to the bilateral initiative, was and remains unprecedented, the only instance when the Mexican and US governments formally reached an accord that aimed to manage the Mexico-US migratory flow.[3] And while the program was initially conceived as a wartime measure, it would continue through the end of 1964. All told, a total of 4.6 million bracero contracts were granted to Mexican workers during the program's duration.[4] Mexican federal officials earmarked a disproportionate share of these contracts, at least 44 percent, for distribution in Aguascalientes, Guanajuato, Jalisco, Michoacán, and Zacatecas, five states in the center-west and center-north that were home to one-fifth of Mexico's total population. Contract allocations for these states are given in table 1.[5]

The Bracero Program's impact on Mexico-US migration patterns, the lives of braceros and their families, Mexico-US diplomatic relations, and US politics, society, and economics has been well documented in historical and

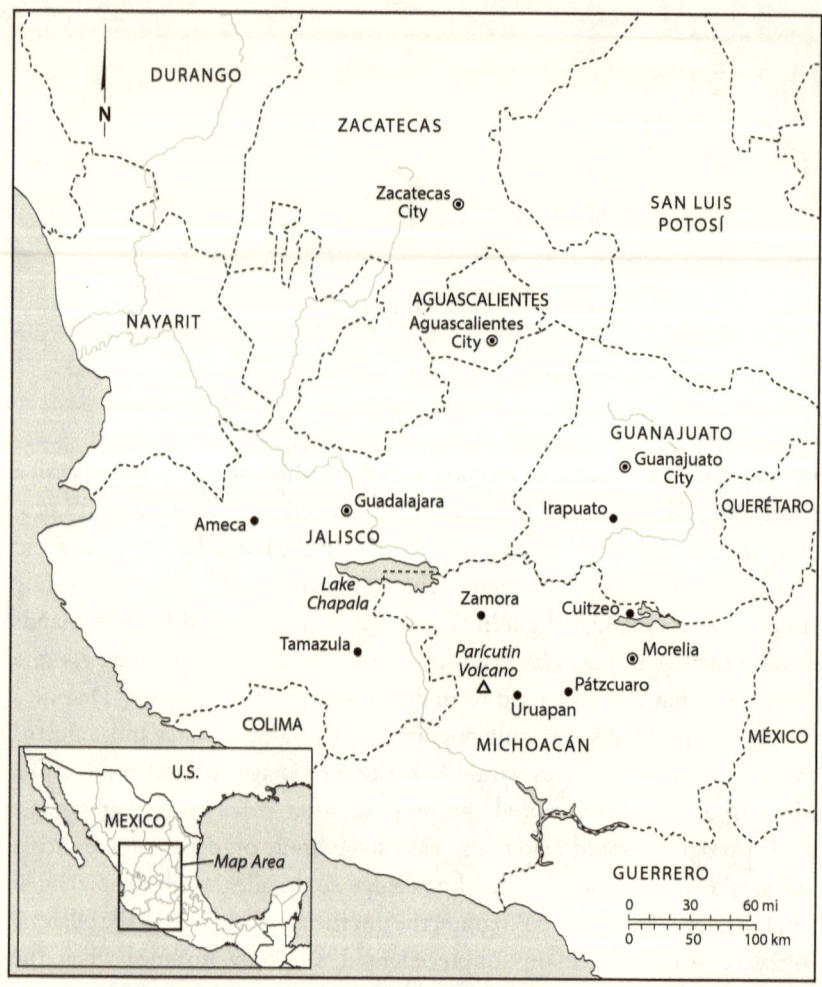

MAP 1. States of Aguascalientes, Guanajuato, Jalisco, Michoacán, and Zacatecas. Map by Bill Nelson.

social scientific studies. In the United States, the bilateral initiative prompted the development of punitive immigration and border policing policies that targeted undocumented Mexican immigrants, spurred a reshaping of Mexican American and Chicana/o ethnic and political identities, motivated farm labor activists and organizers, and helped advance the interests of commercial-scale farm owners who rely on underpaid Mexican immigrant labor.[6] And it was the US government that generally held the stronger hand and extracted favorable concessions during the periodic bilateral negotiations

TABLE 1 Contracts allotted to the states of Aguascalientes, Guanajuato, Jalisco, Michoacán, and Zacatecas

State	Bracero Contracts Allotted	Percentage of Total Bracero Contracts
Aguascalientes	90,101	1.9
Guanajuato	590,652	12.7
Jalisco	463,915	10.0
Michoacán	504,927	10.9
Zacatecas	407,360	8.8

SOURCE: González Navarro, *Población y sociedad en México (1900–1970)*, vol. 2, chart between pp. 146 and 147.

that renewed the terms of the agreement that authorized the Bracero Program.[7] As for the braceros themselves, they engaged in transnational labor activism, refashioned their own ethnic and sexual identities, confronted anti-Mexican discrimination, and earned moneys that they invested in their home communities, all while their families adapted to their seasonal absences.[8] And significantly, the braceros established a web of transnational social and financial networks that their younger relatives and acquaintances used to facilitate their migratory journeys to the United States during the final decades of the twentieth century, which helps explain why a similarly disproportionate share of post–Bracero Program Mexican immigrants—between 39 and 51 percent—were from Aguascalientes, Guanajuato, Jalisco, Michoacán, and Zacatecas.[9] My own parents, who are both natives of Changuitiro, a rural community in northern Michoacán, are among those who used these transnational networks: my father, who began migrating seasonally to the United States during the mid-1960s, is the younger brother of a bracero; he married my mother, the daughter of a bracero, in the late 1960s, and they decided to settle permanently in California's Central Valley, where numerous Changuitiro braceros had worked, during the late 1970s.

Abandoning Their Beloved Land examines bracero migration from the states of Aguascalientes, Guanajuato, Jalisco, Michoacán, and Zacatecas. It shifts away from the focus of previous studies to explore how the Bracero Program functioned within Mexico *before* braceros reached the United States, and it pays special attention to the political factors that undergirded both the administration of the bracero selection process and individual decisions to migrate. It thus addresses underexplored questions about the bilateral initiative whose answers cast light on the full array of factors that shaped Mexico-US migration patterns during the pivotal years of the Bracero Program, as well as the internal mechanics of the postrevolutionary (1940–76) Mexican state and the ruling Partido Revolucionario Institucional (PRI; Institutional Revolutionary Party). What were the politics of the program's administration at the federal, state, and municipal levels? Why did federal authorities allocate a disproportionate share of contracts to the center-northern and center-western states? How did state governments distribute contracts within their jurisdictions? What role did local-level authorities play? How did officials select individual braceros, and why? What were the politics of bracero decision making? What political factors motivated *campesinos* (rural workers) from Aguascalientes, Guanajuato, Jalisco, Michoacán, and Zacatecas to seek out and accept bracero contracts? How did aspiring braceros engage with the officials who determined who would have the opportunity to migrate?

I argue that bracero migration was a deeply politicized process shaped by a complex web of national, regional, and local factors. Put another way, bracero migration cannot be fully explained as a strictly socioeconomic phenomenon wherein Mexican officials dispassionately identified impoverished campesinos who stood to benefit materially from migrating. I do not discount socioeconomic factors such as landlessness, unemployment, and low wage levels as the proximate cause that prompted individual decisions to migrate as braceros, nor do I dismiss the federal government's belief that braceros' earnings would boost development levels in rural Mexico. But as this book shows, the individual political allegiances of aspiring braceros—for example, whether they supported official initiatives such as land redistribution or opposed such measures because of their religious beliefs—contributed directly to the socioeconomic marginalization that fueled the elevated popular demand for bracero contracts in the center-north and center-west. Simultaneously, powerful political factors—such as official concerns that unregulated migration would lead to agricultural production declines, the implementation of competing rural development initiatives, the working relationship between federal and state administrations, the lobbying efforts of rural labor unions, and the personal alliances and rivalries of municipal authorities—influenced the decisions of the federal and state officials who crafted bracero eligibility guidelines and allocated contracts, as well as the actions of the municipal authorities who selected individual braceros.

This book's argument is based on unexplored and underexplored document collections stored in the federal archives of Mexico City; the state archives of Aguascalientes, Guanajuato, Jalisco, and Michoacán; and the municipal archives of local jurisdictions like Zacatecas City; as well as a small number of interviews. The Mexican government's active intervention in the migratory process during the years of the Bracero Program produced a wealth of documents. A significant portion of the available documents were drafted by the officials administering the program: memoranda that detailed bracero eligibility guidelines and selection instructions; correspondence between federal, state, and municipal administrations in which officials relayed instructions and expressed their concerns about how the program was unfolding; domestic intelligence reports compiled by agents of the federal Departamento de Investigaciones Políticas y Sociales (DIPS; Political and Social Investigations Department) who were dispatched to monitor contract distribution sites; and officially compiled lists of aspiring and selected braceros. Alongside these officially produced documents is a treasure trove of written contract requests, nearly three thousand, in which aspiring braceros, or relatives and allies who were writing on their behalf, explained to government officials why they were interested in migrating to the United States. And there are numerous letters in which aspiring braceros and others denounced officials whose corruption and inefficiency were affecting the program's administration.

A close reading of the written contract requests and other documents that detail on-the-ground conditions in bracero-sending communities—such as federal decrees that sanctioned the redistribution of privately owned lands and security reports compiled by community leaders, labor union officials, and military officers—reveals the close links between individual political allegiances and the socioeconomic marginalization that aspiring braceros cited as the primary reason they wanted to migrate. These documents show that the socioeconomic standing of numerous prospective braceros had been adversely affected by local-level political conflicts. Some of these conflicts involved progressive and conservative factions that were struggling for control of rural labor union locals in the sugar-producing zones of central and southern Jalisco, which led to workers who had been dismissed or blacklisted seeking out bracero contracts. Others pitted community-level factions of conservative Catholic partisans who opposed official anticlericalism, land redistribution, and secular public education against their neighbors who supported these government initiatives. The roots of these religious-political conflicts date to the 1920s, when tens of thousands of conservative Catholic partisans took up arms against the federal government during the Cristero War (1926–29).[10] Jean Meyer has calculated that nearly two-thirds of the Cristeros were from Aguascalientes, Guanajuato, Jalisco, Michoacán, and Zacatecas.[11] And many former Cristeros then joined Catholic opposition organizations and political parties like the Unión Nacional Sinarquista (UNS; National Synarchist Union) and the Partido Acción Nacional (PAN; National Action Party) during the late 1930s and early 1940s; the UNS had slightly more than 300,000 members by the time the Bracero Program began, and nearly two-thirds of them were from the center-north and center-west.[12] Other recent studies of post–Cristero War Catholic activism have shown that violent community-level clashes between conservative Catholic partisans and their pro-government rivals persisted into the years of the Bracero Program.[13] What this book establishes is that in many cases these endemic conflicts led directly to the landlessness, unemployment, and low wage levels that aspiring center-western and center-northern braceros mentioned in their contract requests.

The written contract requests also demonstrate that there was another group of prospective braceros whose socioeconomic fortunes had been negatively affected by political considerations: *ejidatarios* (beneficiaries of the agrarian reform) and those whose desire to become ejidatarios had been frustrated by a conservative shift in federal agrarian policy.[14] Officials redistributed 5.5 million hectares of land among 399,829 Aguascalientes, Guanajuato, Jalisco, Michoacán, and Zacatecas ejidatarios between 1915, when the first law that sanctioned the redistribution of privately owned lands went into effect, and 1940.[15] But the guidelines that structured the establishment and governance of *ejidos* (agrarian reform communities) routinely saddled ejidatarios with poor-quality or insufficient lands, restricted their access to credit sources, and prohibited the subdivision, sale, or leasing of their holdings. And because the conservative federal administrations of the postrevolutionary period did not prioritize land redistribution like their counterparts from previous decades had, the agrarian reform process slowed considerably during the years of the Bracero Program.[16] Only 3.5 million hectares were redistributed among 61,625 center-northern and center-western ejidatarios between 1940 and 1964, which meant that a rapidly growing population—the combined population of Aguascalientes, Guanajuato, Jalisco, Michoacán, and Zacatecas increased from 4.4 million in 1940 to 7.1 million in 1960—had decreased access to land.[17] Thus, like their counterparts whose fortunes had been affected by local political conflicts, campesinos who were frustrated with the agrarian reform's flawed implementation turned to the Bracero Program for relief.

MAP 2. The Greater Bajío (southern Guanajuato, northern Michoacán, and northeastern Jalisco). Map by Bill Nelson.

The influence that local religious-political conflicts and the agrarian reform's shortcomings had on bracero migration was most evident in the Greater Bajío, the name I use to refer to the contiguous lands of southern Guanajuato, northern Michoacán, northeastern Jalisco, southwestern Aguascalientes, and southern Zacatecas. This was because the Greater Bajío was one of the principal bastions of conservative Catholic opposition to government policies, the amount of land redistributed in the region prior to the Bracero Program, and the dramatic slowing of the agrarian reform there after 1940, which coincided with a significant demographic expansion rate. Greater Bajío jurisdictions like Pénjamo (Guanajuato), Tepatitlán (Jalisco), and Zamora (Michoacán) were among the earliest and most enduring sites of Cristero, Sinarquista, and PAN activity.[18] And while 1.9 million hectares were redistributed among 191,357 Greater Bajío ejidatarios before 1940, only 397,596 hectares were redistributed among 18,962 ejidatarios in the region during the years of the Bracero Program.[19] At the same time that the land redistribution

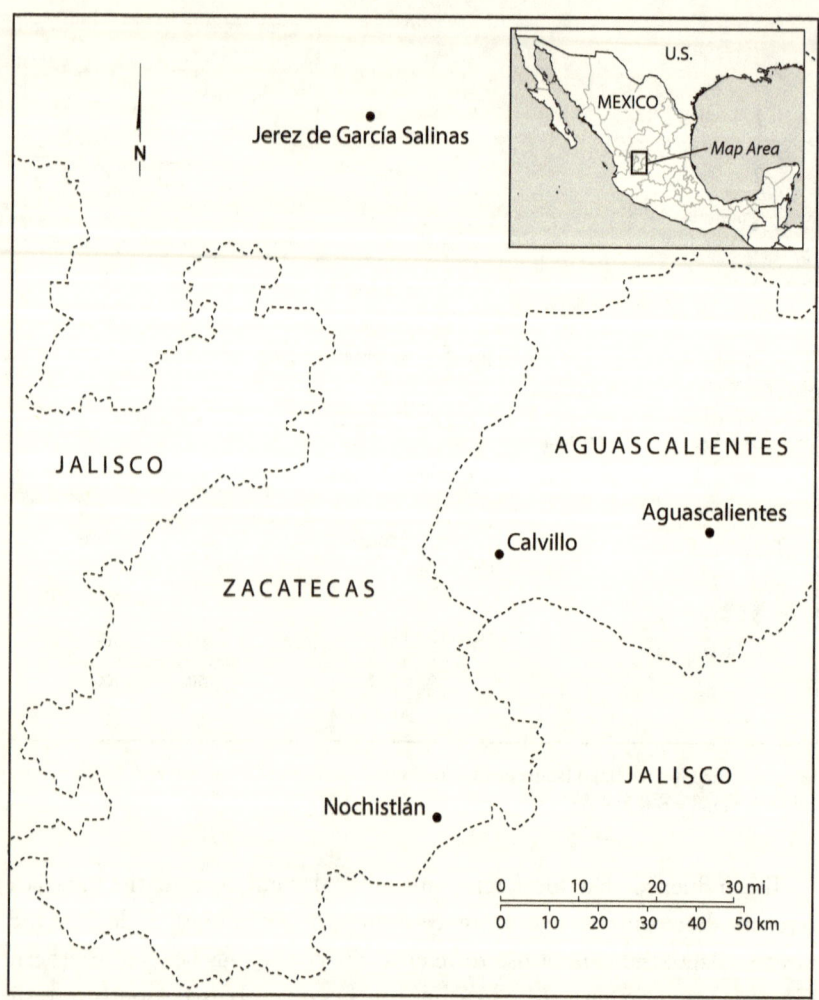

MAP 3. The Greater Bajío (southwestern Aguascalientes and southern Zacatecas). Map by Bill Nelson.

process slowed to a crawl in the Greater Bajío, the region's population grew from 2.2 million in 1940 to 3.5 million in 1960.[20] The combined impact of these pressures—campesinos who had lost their lands or their jobs because of ongoing religious-political conflicts, ejidatarios hampered by the agrarian reform's administration, and a growing population of disenchanted would-be ejidatarios with dim prospects for acquiring redistributed lands—was reflected in the written contract requests sent from Greater Bajío communities, which accounted for 64 percent of those I examined during my research.

Where written contract requests shed light on the political factors that motivated campesinos' decisions to migrate as braceros, official documents reveal the myriad political considerations that shaped the contract distribution and bracero selection processes. The authorities who crafted eligibility guidelines, allocated contracts, and selected individual braceros based their decisions on a political calculus that accounted for the concerns of officials who worried about bracero migration harming domestic agricultural production, the lobbying efforts of rural labor unions, the need to respond to natural disasters like the Parícutin Volcano eruption in central Michoacán, the status of other development initiatives, and regional and local alliances and rivalries, as well as gauges of popular demand for contracts. This calculus also reflected the relative autonomy that state and municipal governments enjoyed during bracero selection periods. The official documents that detail the Bracero Program's administration show that Mexican federal authorities, like their counterparts in the United States, played a less prominent role in that process as the program progressed into the 1950s and 1960s. But whereas in the United States this retreat from administrative duties involved an increased deferment to the interests of farm owners who employed braceros (as well as agricultural guest workers from Caribbean islands like Jamaica) and reduced oversight of bracero work and housing sites, in Mexico it was marked by the deliberate delegation of bracero selection responsibilities to state governments following a failed attempt to centralize that process in Mexico City.[21] Once the federal government divorced itself from direct participation in the bracero selection process, it focused its administrative efforts on dividing contract allocations among the states. For their part, the governments of Aguascalientes, Guanajuato, Jalisco, Michoacán, and Zacatecas had broad latitude to distribute contract allotments as they saw fit within their jurisdictions and to craft eligibility requirements that coexisted alongside but did not supersede federal ones. State authorities generally earmarked the majority or plurality of their contract allotments for distribution in Greater Bajío municipalities, but they occasionally carved out special contract allocations for aspiring braceros who had been affected by organized labor conflicts or natural disasters. However, cautious state officials did not want to overextend their governments, even in those instances when they set aside contracts for specific groups of campesinos. As a result, they decentralized the bracero selection process even further by delegating the authority to choose individual migrant workers to municipal governments and exercising minimal oversight of their local counterparts.

The decentralization of the bracero selection process and the absence of any significant oversight made municipal officials the Bracero Program's ultimate power brokers within Mexico. Municipal authorities essentially had free reign to choose braceros however they pleased, and they routinely ignored federal- and state-level eligibility guidelines and their constituents' genuine needs so that they could enrich themselves and meet their own political ends. In addition to selling contracts, municipal officials used the bracero selection process to solidify their local political standing by favoring their allies who were interested in migrating, freezing their rivals out of the program, and temporarily removing campesinos who were deemed threats during critical electoral cycles. In several instances, the aspiring braceros who were targeted by local authorities were the conservative Catholic and pro-government partisans who were involved in the religious-political conflicts that were destabilizing center-western and center-northern communities; which specific faction was graced with bracero contracts often depended on the political inclinations of individual municipal officials. What this shows is that, counter to Harry Cross and James Sandos's assertion in their 1981 study that federal officials used the Bracero Program to remove members of organizations like the UNS, it was municipal authorities who used bracero migration as a safety valve to ease the political pressures that resulted from the conservative Catholic opposition's outsized presence in the center-north and center-west.[22]

This book's finding that municipal governments wielded such power in the bracero selection process broadens our understanding of both the Bracero Program's administration and the Mexican state's internal mechanics during the mid-twentieth century, specifically, the decades after 1940, the year that Manuel Ávila Camacho's conservative presidential administration succeeded Lázaro Cárdenas's progressive one. The traditional idea of the PRI as a "leviathan" that successfully centralized political power at the federal level, reduced regional and local officials to dutiful vassals who enacted directives issued in Mexico City, and used violence to stifle resistance and impose its will after 1940 has been gradually undermined by several waves of historiography in recent decades.[23] These revisionist studies have provided a more nuanced interpretation that recognizes the PRI's monopolization of national-level political offices and its regular use of repressive violence—violence that assumed a distinctly harder edge during Adolfo López Mateos's presidency (1958–64) and that was increasingly directed at both rural and urban leftists during the presidencies of Gustavo Díaz Ordaz (1964–70) and Luis

Echeverría (1970–76)—but also effectively highlights how "messiness, ambiguity, contradiction, and diversity" were hallmarks of Mexican state building during the mid-twentieth century, as well as how "considerable cultural, local, and ethnic autonomies" and "salient popular bargaining and veto power" softened the ruling party's governing style and prompted strategic concessions to regional and local actors, particularly during the 1940s and 1950s.[24] The Bracero Program did not generate the kind of radical political activism that became the target of state-sanctioned repression campaigns during the bilateral initiative's later years. But this study of its administration casts light on how haphazard the policy-making process could be during the middle decades of the twentieth century, and it also reveals a significant instance of high-level officials conceding tangible power to local-level authorities. This concession is all the more striking because it was largely a response to the federal government's failure to tightly control the bracero selection process and the state governments' fear that they would overextend their administrative capacities, not popular protests or pressure from municipal officials who wanted to play a greater role in the Bracero Program's administration.

STRUCTURE

This book's narrative begins with a top-down perspective that examines federal and state policies and eligibility guidelines, the failed attempt to centralize the bracero selection process in Mexico City during the Bracero Program's earliest years, and the decision to delegate bracero selection responsibilities to local authorities. It then shifts to a local lens that explores the political factors that fueled popular demand for bracero contracts and the way in which municipal officials used the bracero selection process to advance their own distinct agendas. Chapters 3 and 4 focus specifically on the Greater Bajío; chapters 1, 2, and 5 examine the entirety of the center-north and center-west. Each chapter covers the Bracero Program's entire duration.

Chapter 1 examines the federal administration of the Bracero Program. Believing that tight control and close oversight of the bracero selection process would minimize domestic agricultural production declines and undocumented migration, federal officials initially required all aspiring braceros to travel to Mexico City and implemented a host of restrictions. But multiple setbacks hampered this attempt at centralization, and federal authorities gradually reduced their oversight responsibilities and delegated the task of choosing individual braceros to state governments. Chapter 2 focuses on the state governments of Aguascalientes, Guanajuato, Jalisco, Michoacán, and Zacatecas. Unlike their federal counterparts, center-northern and center-western state officials never seriously considered centralizing the bracero selection process in their jurisdictions and quickly decentralized that process even further. However, state authorities did draft eligibility parameters that granted preference to aspiring braceros who had been affected by natural disasters or whose employment had been disrupted by organized labor conflicts.

Chapters 3 and 4 explore the factors that generated demand for bracero contracts in the Greater Bajío. Chapter 3 focuses on how endemic intracommunity conflicts between conservative Catholic opposition factions and pro-government ones influenced individual decisions to seek out bracero contracts. These ongoing clashes contributed directly to landlessness, unemployment, and low wage levels, which in turn generated demand for bracero contracts. Chapter 4 examines ejidatarios and aspiring ejidatarios who wanted to migrate as braceros. Although they had nominally benefited from the agrarian reform, ejidatarios found that the policies that structured the land redistribution process, particularly those that detailed which lands could be redistributed and what ejidatarios could do with their holdings, ultimately constricted their socioeconomic opportunities. At the same time, a growing population of young men found their access to lands blocked by conservative federal administrations that slowed the pace of land redistribution during the years of the Bracero Program. Both frustrated ejidatarios and would-be ejidatarios turned to the Bracero Program for relief.

Chapter 5 returns to an administrative focus, albeit a local one. Municipal officials wasted little time turning control of the bracero selection process to their political and financial advantage. They extorted bribes in exchange for contracts, granted contracts to their local allies, or deprived their rivals of the opportunity to migrate as braceros. In numerous instances, these allies and rivals were embroiled in the intracommunity conflicts that are the focus of chapter 3. Above all, municipal officials prioritized using the Bracero Program to meet their own ends, and they zealously guarded their power whenever there was popular pushback from constituents who were unhappy with how the bracero selection process was being corrupted.

Together, these chapters tell a new and richly detailed story of Mexican migration to the United States during the years of the Bracero Program, one that has been obscured by contemporary discourses that tend to portray past and present Mexican immigrants as primarily socioeconomic actors—that is, as impoverished individuals who come to the United States in search of higher wages and either fulfill a vital role in the US economy or "take" jobs from American workers—and distill the politics of the Mexico-US migratory process to the rhetoric and policy positions of high-level officials.[25] *Abandoning Their Beloved Land* shows us that bracero migration was more than a socioeconomic phenomenon. It reveals that the Bracero Program was shaped by the political calculations of the officials who administered it *and* the campesinos who decided to migrate; that in addition to being transnational actors, Mexican officials and aspiring braceros from Aguascalientes, Guanajuato, Jalisco, Michoacán, and Zacatecas made decisions in deeply interconnected national, regional, and local political contexts; and that the center-west's and center-north's migratory tradition is inextricably linked to both the revolutionary agrarian reform's flaws and the region's status as the epicenter of conservative Catholic opposition to government initiatives during the revolutionary and postrevolutionary periods.

ONE

"The Urgent Need to Regulate Departures"

FEDERAL-LEVEL ADMINISTRATION OF THE BRACERO PROGRAM

IN EARLY MARCH 1942, the Mexican consul in McAllen, Texas, contacted his superiors in Mexico City after touring the Lower Rio Grande Valley. During his tour, the consul had witnessed firsthand that harvesting and packing, which was mostly performed by Mexican immigrants, had already started on local vegetable farms and citrus orchards. Since the consul did not observe any evidence of labor shortages in the valley, he believed that additional Mexican migration to the United States was unnecessary and would only harm the interests of Mexican nationals who were already living and working there. The Foreign Relations Secretariat sent a summary of the consul's report and recommendations to the federal Interior Secretariat. And on March 3, Interior Undersecretary Adolfo Ruiz Cortines forwarded that summary to the state governors and instructed them to publicize it and urge their constituents to stay in their home communities.[1] Ruiz Cortines's and the diplomatic corps' actions—publicly discouraging migration to the United States without explicitly prohibiting it—were well in line with the "limited engagement" emigration policy, to use Alexandra Délano's term, that Mexican officials had practiced since the turn of the twentieth century.[2]

Two months after Ruiz Cortines forwarded the consular summary report to the governors, President Manuel Ávila Camacho initiated a sea change in Mexican emigration policy. On May 4, the president convened a special, federal-level Inter-Secretariat Commission to consider the US government's formal request that Mexican men be allowed to migrate north as seasonal contract laborers, or braceros, to replace the young American farmworkers who were mobilizing to fight in World War II. The American request had highlighted the "urgent need to regulate" the departure of US-bound Mexican workers. But the commission, which brought together high-ranking representatives from the Interior, Foreign Relations, Labor and Social Welfare, and Agriculture and Development Secretariats, as well as the Public Health Department, was divided on the critical question of whether cooperating with the US government was the best means of regulating the migratory flow. Interior Secretary Miguel Alemán and Agriculture and Development Secretary Marte R. Gómez openly worried that a guest worker program would lead to domestic labor shortages that would harm agricultural production. Foreign Relations Undersecretary Jaime Torres Bodet sensed an opportunity to improve the bilateral relationship with the United States, which remained tenuous after the 1938 nationalization of the Mexican oil industry. Torres Bodet and other like-minded commission members also supported the initiative because they subscribed to the anthropologist Manuel Gamio's argument that remittances and the acquired knowledge and work habits that returning migrant workers could apply in their home communities would modernize rural Mexico. The commission also had to consider popular opposition from progressives, who denounced a guest worker program as a betrayal of economic nationalism, and conservatives, including Catholic clergy, who worried that braceros would indulge in vices and be exposed to Protestantism while in the United States.[3] Ultimately, the commission determined that cooperation was the best option because there were no effective means of fully preventing US-bound migration, and it recommended that the government sanction the departure of braceros. The administration decided to participate in the Bracero Program on July 23, and Ávila Camacho expressed his hope that official intervention in the bracero selection process would limit migration-related damage to the Mexican economy and "clandestine" migration.[4]

This chapter explores the federal government's frustrated attempt to regulate the departure of braceros via its direct management of the bracero selection process and the establishment of eligibility restrictions. Because they shared their revolutionary predecessors' ambitions of centralizing political power, federal authorities initially attempted to tightly control the bracero selection process by choosing migrant workers at a contracting center in Mexico City exclusively, and they unilaterally crafted eligibility guidelines that restricted broad groups of campesinos from migrating while granting preference to others.[5] Numerous political considerations—such as the status of other officially sanctioned rural development initiatives, official concerns that bracero migration would lead to regional agricultural production declines, the official response to natural disasters, the working relationship between federal and state administrations, and the demands of labor unions—conditioned federal-level decisions regarding which campesinos were allowed to migrate as braceros and which were excluded from participating in the program. But aspiring braceros who exploited eligibility loopholes or ignored official mandates and entered the United States as undocumented workers, as well as corrupt and incompetent federal personnel, quickly undermined this centralization effort and sparked chaos in Mexico City and at the US border. The federal government closed the Mexico City Contracting Center in favor of centers in provincial cities, relaxed some of its most significant eligibility restrictions, and delegated the critical responsibility of selecting braceros to state governments within the first five years of the Bracero Program. However, federal officials retained the power to divide bracero contracts among the state governments, which they used to pressure recalcitrant governors who had crossed the ruling PRI's national leadership and solidify their patronage networks. And they periodically renegotiated the terms of the bilateral agreement with US officials who often resorted to unilateral pressure to exact favorable concessions regarding the location of the provincial contracting centers. All told, the Bracero Program's federal-level administration was a politicized process marked by frustrated ambitions, on-the-fly policy adjustments, and the deliberate and calculated delegation of responsibilities that federal authorities proved unable to effectively manage.

THE BEGINNING OF THE BRACERO PROGRAM

The Ávila Camacho administration's decision to simultaneously sanction and manage migration to the United States was unprecedented and represented a significant break with previous policy. While the departure of hundreds of thousands during the early twentieth century prompted Mexican officials to worry that migration to the United States would lead to domestic labor shortages, they imposed few exit restrictions because they believed that Mexican citizens had the right to move freely across international borders and they did not want to alienate US administrations that, at least until the Great Depression sparked an increase in official and popular nativism, welcomed Mexican immigrant labor. Even during an informal guest worker program that ran from 1917 to 1921—informal because US authorities relaxed entry restrictions for Mexican contract laborers without pursuing a bilateral agreement—Mexican officials limited their actions to vouchsafing the rights of immigrant workers via the consular corps and publicly discouraging permanent residence in the United States.[6] But the Ávila Camacho administration's decision to participate in the Bracero Program would require a new degree of federal intervention in the migratory process. As it had been during the late 1910s and early 1920s, the Foreign Relations Secretariat was responsible for monitoring the living and working conditions of braceros in the United States. The novel responsibility of administering the bracero selection process fell to the Interior and Labor and Social Welfare Secretariats, as well as the Public Health Department. The Interior Secretariat was instructed to liaise with state and municipal governments and coordinate a publicity campaign that would inform aspiring braceros about the program's protocols and the contract eligibility requirements; it was hoped that this publicity campaign would channel all US-bound migration through the Bracero Program. Labor and Social Welfare personnel were charged with screening aspiring braceros, securing any necessary cooperation from labor unions, and monitoring the departure of braceros so as to prevent domestic labor shortages. They also established an ill-fated and short-lived Bracero Savings Fund that collected 10 percent of each bracero's earnings in the federally administered Banco Nacional de Crédito Agrícola (National Agricultural Credit Bank). (The fund was abandoned in 1946 after corrupt bank personnel refused to make payouts to braceros; later attempts to revive it also faltered.) Public Health doctors would examine selected braceros before they left for the United States.[7]

The Interior Secretariat was the first domestic regulatory agency to mobilize. Although the Ávila Camacho administration agreed to participate in the Bracero Program on July 23, it did not officially announce its decision until August 21, the day the president's decree was published in the *Diario Oficial de la Federación*, the federal newspaper that printed executive declarations and approved legislation.[8] That same day, Interior Undersecretary Ruiz Cortines sent out a circular that made clear the administration's goal of dictating the terms of bracero migration. The circular officially informed the state governors about the guest worker initiative. It also stressed that it was critical for workers to acquire a contract so they could claim certain protections and guarantees, a likely reference to clauses that safeguarded braceros from anti-Mexican discrimination and mandated that they be paid wages comparable to those of US-born workers. Ruiz Cortines asked the governors to forward the circular to the municipal authorities in their jurisdictions and to use whatever means they deemed convenient so that residents knew about the Bracero Program. Any and all program-related announcements had to warn aspiring braceros that attempts to enter the United States without a contract would be thwarted by either Mexican or American immigration authorities.[9]

To further its ambitious goal of controlling the migratory flow, federal authorities declared that all workers who were interested in acquiring a bracero contract, regardless of their state of origin, had to travel to Mexico City and apply for one at the Labor and Social Welfare Secretariat's offices. But the vetting process was rather simple in summer and fall 1942. The Ávila Camacho administration did not declare any specific groups of campesinos ineligible to receive bracero contracts when the program began, and Labor and Social Welfare personnel had full discretion during the selection process. As a result, aspiring braceros were only asked about their age, their employment status, and where they were from. Those who were selected were given physical examinations to confirm that they were fit before they boarded the special trains that transported them to the US border.[10] It was only then that a restriction went into effect: because of concerns that braceros would be victims of extreme anti-Mexican discrimination there, they were not allowed to work in the states of Arkansas, Missouri, and Texas.[11]

However, the Interior Secretariat's publicity campaign quickly proved ineffective. Within one week of the Bracero Program's official announcement, hundreds of would-be braceros from central and southern Mexico had traveled to the border cities of Mexicali and Ciudad Juárez with the hope that they would be given contracts there.[12] It soon became apparent that aspiring braceros flocked to the border because media reports about the Bracero Program reached them before official pronouncements regarding the selection procedure did. In a September letter to President Ávila Camacho, Mariano González noted that he and forty-nine others from Jalisco had trekked to the border city of Tijuana after reading about the Bracero Program in nationally circulated newspapers, not an official government source.[13] That same month, Nogales's municipal president, Anacleto Olmos, reported that the hundreds of aspiring braceros who were straining resources in his border jurisdiction knew about the guest worker initiative from media reports.[14] And in October undocumented workers who were awaiting deportation hearings in San Diego, California, told consular officials that they had become aware of the Bracero Program via press reports.[15]

THE OPENING OF THE MEXICO CITY CONTRACTING CENTER AND THE FIRST ELIGIBILITY RESTRICTIONS

Despite these initial hiccups, the Ávila Camacho administration remained committed to tightly controlling the contract distribution and bracero selection processes in 1943, the first full year of the Bracero Program. All prospective braceros were still required to travel to Mexico City that year. And Labor and Social Welfare Secretariat personnel still determined who would receive a bracero contract. But rather than report to the Labor and Social Welfare Secretariat's offices, aspiring braceros would now go to a contracting center that federal authorities established at the National Stadium. Sebastián Ortiz, a Labor and Social Welfare official, told Matías Michel, a would-be bracero who wrote from Tijuana to inquire about the contract distribution process, that the Mexico City Contracting Center had been opened so that the Mexican government could abide by the terms of the bilateral agreement and ensure that every bracero was "duly protected" by a contract. Furthermore, Ortiz explained that the Ávila Camacho administration had found it "impossible" to open a contracting center in another region of the country.[16] The implication was clear: the federal government wanted to ensure that all braceros left on the terms it dictated.

However, the contracting center was immediately beset with inefficiencies that frustrated aspiring braceros and Mexico City residents. In March a prospective bracero who only identified himself as "a spokesperson" for the more than two thousand hopefuls who were gathered at the National Stadium complained to Ávila Camacho about the situation there. The spokesperson claimed that Labor and Social Welfare Secretariat personnel distributed just two hundred contracts per day, all in the space of a few hours in the morning. This led to daily chaos as would-be braceros scrambled to get in line when the contracting center staff arrived and local police attempted in vain to impose some semblance of order. Aspiring braceros spent their nights sleeping on the streets near the stadium, presumably because they could not afford lodging or because they wanted to increase their odds of receiving a contract. And they often went hungry, since a small fruit stand was the only food source that was readily available near the stadium.[17] The anonymous spokesperson's claims were corroborated by Mexico City residents who decried the "lamentable spectacle" of hungry prospective braceros wandering aimlessly through the city and the "inhumane scene" of would-be braceros sleeping on the sidewalks near the stadium.[18]

The spokesperson and the complaining residents asked Ávila Camacho to either increase the number of personnel assigned to the contracting center or open the stadium at night so that aspiring braceros could sleep there. But rather than assign more personnel to the stadium or provide aid to those who were there to acquire a contract, federal authorities began dissuading hopeful braceros from traveling to Mexico City. In July Sebastián Ortiz, the same official who declared that it was impossible to establish a contracting center outside of Mexico City, told a group from the northeastern state of Nuevo León that a trip to the capital would be pointless because the number of aspiring braceros there was greater than the number of available contracts. Ortiz then recommended that the group avoid "serious discomforts and deprivations" and remain at home.[19] Two months later, Ortiz's colleague Luis Fernández del Campo used the same language when he urged José Terriquez Martínez to stay at home.[20] Fernández del Campo apparently failed to note that Terriquez Martínez, a native of Jalisco, was already in Mexico City when he wrote to the president's staff to ask for help securing a contract.[21] This oversight indicates that either Fernández del Campo did not read carefully the correspondence forwarded to him or that the Labor and Social Welfare Secretariat had a standardized response to any queries regarding the bracero contract distribution process by September 1943.

Nineteen forty-three also saw the federal government's first attempts at barring certain rural workers from receiving bracero contracts, ostensibly to safeguard domestic agricultural production. The first campesinos declared ineligible for bracero contracts were ejidatarios, campesinos who had received access to lands through the revolutionary agrarian reform program.[22] (All the available evidence indicates that this ban remained in place for the remainder of the Bracero Program.) The restriction made practical sense because the ejido sector represented a vital part of the agrarian economy, and their depopulation could have had disastrous consequences for domestic agricultural production. Between 1915, when the first revolutionary law sanctioning land redistribution was issued, and 1940, 1.6 million ejidatarios received access to 30.4 million hectares.[23] And according to the 1940 Agrarian and Ejido Censuses, half of the nation's maize and 55 percent of its wheat were produced on ejidos.[24]

But the ejidatario ban also reflected the political influence and modernizing agenda of Agriculture and Development Secretary Marte R. Gómez, who, as discussed earlier, was one of the federal officials who worried that bracero migration would have a negative impact on Mexico's agrarian economy. Gómez was a longtime champion of land redistribution—his administration sanctioned the expropriation and redistribution of nearly 650,000 hectares when he governed the northeastern state of Tamaulipas during the 1930s—who was appointed to Ávila Camacho's cabinet because he shared the president's goal of boosting domestic agricultural production.[25] Given his background, Gómez likely believed that allowing ejidatarios to migrate as braceros could tacitly signal that a cornerstone revolutionary policy that he promoted had failed. But just as important, the Bracero Program clashed with another transnational initiative that Gómez spearheaded: the Oficina de Estudios Especiales (Special Studies Office, known in the United States as the Mexican Agricultural Program), a federal-level partnership with the US-based Rockefeller Foundation that was established in 1943 and sought to increase production on existing ejidos via agricultural research and extension work.[26] Since Gómez and the Agriculture and Development Secretariat were pursuing the modernization of ejidos through an avenue that was distinct from the Bracero Program—as noted earlier, Mexican officials believed that returning braceros would use their earnings and acquired knowledge to modernize rural Mexico—it makes sense that the Ávila Camacho administration barred ejidatarios from migrating so that they could benefit from the Oficina de Estudios Especiales' initiatives.

The ejidatario restriction also benefited the Ávila Camacho administration because it allowed it to better balance itself on the "strategic tightrope," to borrow Tore Olsson's term, of postrevolutionary agrarian policy and rhetoric. Federal authorities considerably slowed the pace of land redistribution after 1940: Ávila Camacho's government redistributed only 7.3 million hectares during his term (1940–46), fewer than half the 18.8 million hectares redistributed during Lázaro Cárdenas's presidency (1934–40).[27] Ávila Camacho also had an increasingly strained relationship with campesino activists, like Morelos's Rubén Jaramillo, who supported the agrarian reform and were frustrated with the conservative turn in federal agrarian policy.[28] But as Olsson noted, the Ávila Camacho administration engaged in a rhetorical campaign that aimed to convince rural constituents that, despite slowing the land redistribution process, it was fully dedicated to supporting existing ejidos and ensuring their success through other initiatives, such as the Oficina de Estudios Especiales.[29] Federal authorities could thus cite the ejidatario ban as further proof of its commitment to already established ejidos, since it was blocking even the temporary departure of the men who worked redistributed lands.

Despite the ban, ejidatarios remained interested in migrating and used subterfuge to evade it. Without divulging how exactly the failure was discovered, Labor and Social Welfare Secretary Francisco Trujillo Gurría informed the state governors in June 1943 that some ejidatarios had received bracero contracts, despite the "meticulous nature" of the vetting process at the contracting center. He then announced a new policy that would take effect in July: aspiring braceros had to present letters from their respective municipal governments that certified their status as non-ejidatario campesinos.[30] This was a curious policy adjustment since it ran counter to the federal government's stated desire to closely manage the bracero selection process and since the agrarian reform was a federally coordinated initiative, which meant that the national government maintained records of who had benefited from the land redistribution process. Unfortunately, no available record casts light on why federal officials turned to their municipal counterparts rather than rely on their own records. But whatever the Ávila Camacho administration's motives, the new requirement failed to prevent the departure of ejidatarios. Before July was out, ejidatarios from the southern Guanajuato municipality of Pénjamo were crossing into the neighboring northern Michoacán municipalities of La Piedad, Numarán, and Penjamillo and acquiring letters that identified them as non-ejidatario residents of those jurisdictions. Pénjamo's municipal government and Guanajuato's Labor Secretariat were incensed when they learned that the effort to prevent ejidatarios from abandoning their lands had been undermined, and they lodged a complaint with Michoacán governor Félix Ireta. Guanajuato officials did not accuse their Michoacán counterparts of corruption, claiming instead that Pénjamo ejidatarios had taken advantage of the "kindness" of local authorities in the neighboring state.[31] For its part, Michoacán's government told La Piedad, Numarán, and Penjamillo officials that they would be held responsible if they continued to issue certifying letters to campesinos who did not live in their jurisdictions.[32]

One day after they lodged their complaint with Michoacán's governor, Guanajuato officials openly worried that the Bracero Program was contributing to production declines and the depopulation of the state's primary agricultural zones.[33] The Ávila Camacho administration, which had declared in 1942 that one of its priorities was minimizing negative Bracero Program–related economic effects, responded to these concerns in early August and declared that all campesinos from Guanajuato, as well as Jalisco and Michoacán, were ineligible to migrate as braceros, whether or not they were ejidatarios.³⁴ Federal authorities told their center-western state counterparts that the ban had been put into effect because their jurisdictions had already sent enough braceros to the United States.³⁵ There was truth to this claim. According to official counts, 52 percent of the braceros who were selected in 1942 and 1943 were from Guanajuato, Jalisco, and Michoacán.³⁶ This despite the fact that according to the 1940 Population Census, these states accounted for only 19 percent of the national population.³⁷ The ban would thus give federal officials an opportunity to simultaneously craft more balanced bracero departure patterns and placate center-western officials who had started to sour on the Bracero Program.

But the Ávila Camacho administration inadvertently undermined its restriction when it created an exploitable loophole in its response to the Parícutin Volcano eruption. The volcano was born on February 20, 1943, in the Sierra Purépecha, the mountainous central region of Michoacán. That afternoon, a smoking fissure opened in a field that Dionisio Pulido and Demetrio Toral were plowing in Parícutin, a village 25 kilometers west of Uruapan. The earth then started quaking and the fissure widened, and by evening a small mountain that hurled "lava bombs" had emerged.³⁸ Two days later Michoacán interior secretary Luis Marín Pérez informed President Ávila Camacho that the volcano had already grown to a height of 200 meters and that it was continually ejecting lava and ash.³⁹ Up to 15 centimeters of ash were falling daily in the eruption zone in late March, and researchers stationed in Uruapan calculated that the eruption's ash column had reached an elevation of 6,000 meters above the crater.⁴⁰ In mid-June the state government relocated all 186 Parícutin families to lands that it expropriated just outside of Uruapan.⁴¹ Four months later residents from the villages of San Juan Parangaricutiro and Zirosto began moving to expropriated lands in the Tierra Caliente, the semiarid lowlands immediately south of the Sierra Purépecha.⁴²

Eruption zone residents began requesting bracero contracts shortly after Parícutin was evacuated. In late June Félix Anguiano Pérez wrote directly to Ávila Camacho on behalf of 135 rural workers from Peribán, 18 kilometers west of the volcano, who were interested in migrating as braceros. Anguiano Pérez described the prospective braceros as experienced and expert maize, wheat, and bean cultivators. The ash from the eruption had damaged their lands and ruined their harvests, and because they had nothing else to fall back on, the group wanted to migrate as braceros, though they were optimistic that they would be able to resume working their lands once they returned from the

United States. Anguiano Pérez also proposed that the federal response teams in the region perform the required medical exam and that the aspiring braceros be allowed to leave for the US border from the railroad station in Irapuato, Guanajuato. The would-be braceros were willing to travel to the Mexico City Contracting Center if departing from Irapuato was not an option, though they hoped any trips to the capital would be subsidized.[43]

Facing a significant natural disaster—and perhaps also behind-the-scenes pressure from former president Cárdenas, who, as Christopher Boyer noted, personally lobbied officials on behalf of those affected by the eruption—the Ávila Camacho administration ultimately opted to exempt Parícutin *damnificados* (victims) from the center-western ban.[44] But although federal authorities started openly discouraging prospective braceros from traveling to the contracting center in summer 1943, they were still unwilling to cede full control of the bracero selection process. They thus decided to vet Parícutin damnificados in Mexico City and give them their contracts there. Those who went to the contracting center had to have documents from both state- and municipal-level officials that certified them as residents of eruption zone municipalities like Cotija, Los Reyes, Parangaricutiro, Peribán, or Uruapan. The first groups of damnificados arrived at the National Stadium in early September.[45] One month later, contracting center personnel noticed that the signature of Los Reyes's municipal president varied from document to document. When pressed, the aspiring braceros who claimed to be from there admitted that they were Guanajuato and Jalisco residents who had paid as much as ten pesos for the forged documents.[46] In December officials from Jiquilpan, Michoacán, a municipality immediately northwest of the eruption zone, discovered that rural workers from that jurisdiction had acquired authentic victim certificates.[47] That discovery prompted the state government to order local officials in the eruption zone to stop issuing victim certificates to campesinos who did not live there.[48]

Federal officials came to regret their decision to have aspiring Parícutin braceros travel to Mexico City. And for the first time since the Bracero Program began, they openly considered decentralizing the selection process. In October, the same month that Guanajuato and Jalisco campesinos were found using forged documents to pass as eruption damnificados, federal Labor and Social Welfare Secretariat official, Luis Padilla Nervo, wrote to Michoacán's governor, Félix Ireta, and proposed modifying how Parícutin braceros were selected. Padilla Nervo wanted to send personnel directly to the eruption zone to screen and select prospective braceros. Those who were chosen would still have to travel to the Mexico City Contracting Center to receive their contracts, but they would not be questioned further there. Padilla Nervo believed that this would facilitate the contracting process, especially since the eruption had deprived a "high number" of Michoacán rural workers of their livelihoods.[49] Left implied was the presumption that the policy adjustment would neutralize non-Parícutin damnificados' ability to exploit the exemption to the center-western ban. Unfortunately, there is no available record of how Governor Ireta responded to Padilla Nervo's proposal, nor is there evidence that suggests that Parícutin braceros were screened in the eruption zone.

DECENTRALIZATION

The Mexico City Contracting Center was still operating at the beginning of 1944, but official corruption sparked the violent event that ultimately prompted the initial decentralization of the bracero selection process. On January 5 a local police commander assigned to the contracting center arrested a man who had aroused suspicion when he and eighteen aspiring braceros had gone directly to the front of the contract distribution line. The police commander searched the detainee and found a letter from a Labor and Social Welfare Secretariat attorney. The letter instructed the contracting center personnel to give contracts to the eighteen would-be braceros, all of whom were then discovered to have paid a bribe.[50] Two weeks later an agent from the Departamento de Investigaciones Políticas y Sociales (DIPS; Political and Social Investigations Department), one of Mexico's federal-level domestic intelligence agencies, visited the National Stadium and reported that unscrupulous individuals had pocketed as much as 50,000 pesos by selling authentic and forged contracts to "humble, hungry, and miserable" workers.[51] Carlos Madrazo, who represented Mexico City in the federal Chamber of Deputies and was arrested for trafficking bracero contracts, alleged that Labor and Social Welfare Secretary Francisco Trujillo Gurría was fully aware of and profiting from the illicit activities at the contracting center. (Madrazo maintained his innocence and claimed that he was scapegoated because of political disagreements with the Ávila Camacho administration; he was eventually released from prison and resumed his political career.)[52]

The situation at the contracting center reached its nadir on February 15. At noon that day, an unnamed former federal legislator and four prospective braceros who were with him were allowed into the stadium without having to wait in line. The two thousand campesinos who had been in line since the morning were infuriated and forced their way into the stadium to complain. The police officers on the scene were quickly overwhelmed, and two Labor and Social Welfare Secretariat employees, Ángel Avaytua González and Manuel Hernández, intervened and ordered the frustrated crowd to exit the stadium. When the aspiring braceros refused, Avaytua González and Hernández drew out handguns and began pistol-whipping the disgruntled workers. The Labor and Social Welfare employees eventually pushed part of the crowd back through the stadium entrance, and they then opened fire. Three prospective braceros were wounded, although their injuries were non-life-threatening. Once the dust settled, three hundred would-be braceros, including those who had been injured, marched to the Labor and Social Welfare Secretariat's offices. Labor and Social Welfare Undersecretary Jorge Medellín greeted the protesters, and he assured them that Avaytua González and Hernández would be "severely punished" and removed from their posts.[53] However, there is no record of what consequences, if any, the pair faced.

The violence at the National Stadium marked the beginning of the end of the federal government's direct intervention in the bracero selection process. On March 1, Interior Secretary Miguel Alemán announced that contract distribution was temporarily halted, and he asked state and municipal governments to publicize the hiatus via broadsides, radio announcements, and the press.[54] This did not stop workers from traveling to Mexico City. In late April, Estela Merino and other women who lived near the National Stadium complained that aspiring braceros were using the streets as a public rest room and making life difficult for local schoolchildren.[55] In May, federal authorities implemented a bracero selection process that closely resembled the one they had suggested to Michoacán's government in fall 1943 and that also served as a tacit declaration that they no longer prioritized closely managing that facet of the Bracero Program. Prospective braceros would now be screened in precontracting centers that were established in provincial cities like Irapuato and Zacatecas City. And state-level officials there were charged with selecting braceros, which meant that Guanajuato non-ejidatarios were once again eligible to receive contracts.[56] Those who were selected at the precontracting centers would then go to the Mexico City Contracting Center but only to undergo a medical examination before receiving their contracts and departing for the United States.[57]

The opening of the precontracting centers prompted political skirmishes that partially checked federal prerogatives when state governors who wanted to limit the number of bracero departures from their jurisdictions, like Zacatecas's Pánfilo Natera, pushed back against the Ávila Camacho administration's desires. Federal officials initially allotted two thousand contracts to Zacatecas in spring 1944. However, the Labor and Social Welfare Secretariat asked Natera if he would sanction the departure of an additional 1,140 Zacatecas braceros after the US government requested more braceros in late May. The governor was only willing to allow 300 newly selected braceros to leave, but federal authorities disregarded his wishes and instructed the precontracting center's personnel to select 621 additional braceros. When Natera discovered this, he dispatched state Interior Secretariat personnel to the precontracting center and had them shut it down, though not before 436 of the 621 additional braceros had been screened. Labor and Social Welfare and US personnel who were in Zacatecas City then personally beseeched the governor to reopen the precontracting center and approve the selection and departure of the remaining 185 braceros. Natera remained steadfast; he told the Labor and Social Welfare and US officials that he could not allow the state to be stripped of its agricultural workforce and that he was willing to accept the consequences of his resistance. Ultimately both camps contacted federal officials in Mexico City and argued their respective cases. After being reminded that the Bracero Program was part of the broader war effort, Governor Natera—who took this opportunity to boast that he would be the first to report to the front lines if Mexican soldiers were ever needed to fight in the war—agreed to a compromise that allowed the departure of the 436 braceros who had been vetted before the state government closed the precontracting center.[58]

While Zacatecas's government challenged federal authorities, Jalisco and Michoacán campesinos, who were still ineligible to receive bracero contracts in 1944, found a new means of evading the restrictions placed on them: provisional passports, state government–issued travel documents that were recognized as valid tourist visas. Foreign Relations Secretary Ezequiel Padilla raised the alarm about aspiring braceros using these documents to enter the United States without contracts in June, and the practice soon led to interstate government recriminations.[59] In July, residents of the northeastern Jalisco municipality of San Diego de Alejandría were found to have crossed into neighboring Guanajuato and acquired Guanajuato-approved provisional passports. Jalisco governor Marcelino García Barragán concluded that San

Diego de Alejandría workers were attempting to circumvent the bracero ban, and he demanded that Guanajuato authorities stop issuing passports to his constituents.[60] Guanajuato's interior secretary, Fausto Villagómez, vehemently denied the allegations, and he told García Barragán that Guanajuato officials would take no action unless they were shown definitive proof that they had issued travel documents to Jalisco residents.[61]

The federal Interior Secretariat weighed in on the matter of provisional passports in October. Officials from that agency opined that aspiring braceros had taken advantage of the "good faith" of state governments when they applied for provisional passports under false pretenses. They then announced a three-prong strategy that they hoped would simultaneously curb the use of provisional passports and undocumented departures, which numbered in the tens of thousands—the INS apprehended a combined 34,478 undocumented Mexican workers in 1943 and 1944—during the Bracero Program's initial phase.[62] First, state governments were ordered to restrict the number of provisional passports they issued and thoroughly vet those who applied for that type of travel document. Applicants who were determined to be aspiring braceros were to be denied a passport. Second, border state governors and municipal officials were asked to help federal migration offices establish an effective surveillance system across the entire border region. And third, all state governments had to issue publicity materials that warned campesinos that undocumented workers could not claim the wage protections included in bracero contracts and that they would be subject to immediate deportation.[63] The increased scrutiny of provisional passport applicants seems to have had its desired effect, as there is no more recorded mention that prospective braceros were using these documents to enter the United States without contracts. But the measures designed to curb undocumented departures proved ineffective. In late November, a DIPS agent stationed in Baja California reported that at least four thousand would-be braceros were gathered near Mexicali and that an indeterminate number were crossing the US border without contracts every day.[64]

Once the calendar turned to 1945, federal authorities further decentralized the bracero selection process and fully delegated that responsibility to their state counterparts, thus effectively conceding that they were unable to control the selection process the way they desired. In February, Labor and Social Welfare Secretariat official Luis Fernández del Campo informed the governors that the Mexico City Contracting Center would be shuttered and replaced by several contracting centers in provincial cities. Fernández del

Campo expressed the federal government's desire that this major policy adjustment would free Mexico City of the "multiple harms"—likely a reference to the violence that had occurred at the National Stadium and the deplorable living conditions that the Labor and Social Welfare Secretariat's own inefficiency and corruption had exacerbated—that occurred when aspiring braceros traveled there.[65] Broadsides informed prospective braceros of the change and warned them that trips to the capital would be useless.[66] Several of the precontracting centers, including Irapuato's, were upgraded to full contracting centers.[67] A contracting center was also opened in Uruapan, which meant that Michoacán non-ejidatarios were eligible for contracts once again.[68] And while federal personnel and Public Health Department doctors were assigned to the contracting centers, the burden of selecting the rural workers who received their contracts there fell squarely on the shoulders of state-level officials.[69]

THE END OF THE JALISCO BAN

Although the Ávila Camacho administration allowed Michoacán non-ejidatarios to resume migrating as braceros in 1945, Jalisco non-ejidatarios remained ineligible to receive contracts. The ban's continuation did not sit well with aspiring Jalisco braceros, particularly those who worked in the sugar mills concentrated in the sierras south of Lake Chapala and the valleys west of Guadalajara. Many of these mill workers belonged to locals of the Sindicato de Trabajadores de la Industria Azucarera y Similares de la República Mexicana (STIASRM; Mexican Sugar Industry Workers Union), a union that was a member of the Confederación de Trabajadores de México (CTM; Mexican Workers Confederation), the national-level labor confederation that was formally affiliated with the ruling PRI. In early June, Salvador Guzmán and other seasonally unemployed members of STIASRM Local 81, which represented workers in Tamazula's Santa Cruz Mill, wrote to President Ávila Camacho expressing their interest in migrating as braceros.[70] Later the same month, another group of unemployed Tamazula mill workers requested contracts and expressed their bewilderment that federal officials would deny them the "right" to migrate while their compatriots from other states, presumably a reference to Guanajuato and Michoacán non-ejidatarios who no longer faced restrictions in 1945, were free to leave.[71]

The Ávila Camacho administration's dedication to upholding the Jalisco ban ended in January 1946 when Labor and Social Welfare Secretariat personnel identified that state as one of the five where popular interest in migrating as braceros was highest (Aguascalientes, Guanajuato, Michoacán, and Zacatecas were the others).[72] Two months later, Labor and Social Welfare Secretary Francisco Trujillo Gurría contacted Jalisco's governor, Marcelino García Barragán, and asked him how many campesinos could leave that state as braceros. The governor answered that he wanted his state to be completely excluded from the Bracero Program because he wanted to maximize local agricultural production.[73] Trujillo Gurría acknowledged García Barragán's worries when he replied in late April. But he informed the governor that President Ávila Camacho had decided to override those concerns and grant contracts to 545 sugar mill workers who had been members of the Sindicato Nacional de Obreros y Campesinos de la Industria Azucarera y Similares (SNOCIAS; National Industrial and Rural Sugar Workers Union). The union had folded at the end of 1945, but Ávila Camacho decided to fulfill a promise he had made to its membership that some of them would be allowed to migrate as braceros.[74] Despite his stated worries about safeguarding Jalisco's agricultural production, García Barragán did not openly object to the president's decision because the SNOCIAS members had also approached him with their desire to migrate and because he determined that these workers' absence would not harm Jalisco's economy.[75]

García Barragán reacted with far more hostility when the Ávila Camacho administration expanded Jalisco's bracero contract allocation in May. That month, federal authorities earmarked 2,000 bracero contracts for Jalisco sugar mill workers who were represented by the STIASRM.[76] Ultimately, 1,732 STIASRM members from throughout Jalisco were selected as braceros during a June 10 drawing that was held in Ameca, a sugar-growing community west of Guadalajara.[77] Eleven days after the STIASRM braceros were chosen, García Barragán wrote to Ávila Camacho to express his displeasure. The governor told the president that he had only begrudgingly allowed the departure of STIASRM members because the union's leadership had bypassed him and taken their pleas directly to federal authorities. He then told the president that he was renewing his opposition to Jalisco's participation in the Bracero Program, and he demanded that no other rural workers from his jurisdiction be allowed to migrate.[78] But federal officials organized the selection of the 545 SNOCIAS members on June 24 in Guadalajara.[79] Incensed that Ávila Camacho had ignored his demands, García Barragán refused to send any state government personnel to assist with or oversee that selection drawing.[80]

The Ávila Camacho administration's actions regarding the departure of Jalisco braceros in 1946 raise a number of questions. Why did federal officials specifically favor organized sugar mill workers? Why did they intervene so directly in the bracero selection process given their full delegation of that responsibility in 1945? And why did federal authorities openly disregard Governor García Barragán's objections, especially as they simultaneously proved sensitive to Michoacán officials' request that that state's bracero contract allotment be as small as possible in 1946?[81]

The answers to those questions are manifold and demonstrate the extent to which the bracero migratory process was politicized. First, favoring Jalisco's organized sugar mill workers afforded Ávila Camacho an opportunity to present himself as a president who fulfilled his promises and who was sensitive to the needs of unemployed union members who wanted to migrate. Second, as Michael Snodgrass effectively argued, the contracts allotted to organized sugar mill workers allowed the federal government to solidify its patronage networks and reward union members who were loyal to the PRI, an argument that is corroborated by the fact that the only braceros who left Michoacán in 1946 were five hundred STIASRM members from Los Reyes.[82] There may well have been an expectation that this extension of patronage would lead to votes for PRI candidates in future elections. This would have benefited the ruling party since, as Paul Gillingham demonstrates, elections, particularly local ones, remained relatively competitive until at least the early 1950s.[83] (The 1946 presidential election was held after the STIASRM and SNOCIAS braceros were selected, so it is not clear if those chosen would have been able to vote in that election.) And third, sending contracts to Jalisco's organized sugar mill workers gave Ávila Camacho an opportunity to exact a measure of retribution against García Barragán after the latter backed General Miguel Henríquez Guzmán's failed bid to become the PRI's presidential candidate. As Jaime Sánchez Susarrey and Ignacio Medina Sánchez note in their study of mid-twentieth-century Jalisco state politics, this move damaged the governor's working relationship with Ávila Camacho, who supported the ultimately successful candidacy of his interior secretary, Miguel Alemán, and the president chipped away at the governor's power whenever he could.[84] The departure of braceros did not deliver a fatal blow to García Barragán's government. But it undermined his authority, explicitly reminded him of his place in the PRI's hierarchy, and likely weakened his standing among union members who would have reasonably thought of federal officials like Ávila Camacho as the ones who were most responsive to their needs.

UNDOCUMENTED MIGRATION AND THE NORTHERN CONTRACTING CENTERS

Lifting the restrictions on Jalisco's aspiring braceros was the Ávila Camacho administration's final significant action concerning the Bracero Program. Miguel Alemán, who had publicly expressed reservations about participating in the Bracero Program when the United States first proposed the bilateral initiative, succeeded Ávila Camacho in December 1946. And once in office, the onetime Bracero Program skeptic found himself in the curious position of supporting the program's continuation. With World War II over, many US officials believed that the Bracero Program was no longer necessary. But as Alexandra Délano notes, the Alemán administration wanted to continue the program for two reasons: to ease rural unemployment pressures; and to maintain a healthy bilateral relationship with the United States at a moment when commercial ties between the two countries were deepening. The Alemán administration's willingness to continue participating in the Bracero Program, as well as the lobbying efforts of American farm owners who desired continued access to bracero labor, convinced the US government to renew the bilateral agreement, the terms of which were subject to periodic renegotiation.[85]

Once the program was renewed, Alemán convened the Interior, Labor and Social Welfare, and Foreign Relations Secretariats and formed a new Inter-Secretariat Commission that would consider means to reduce undocumented migration. The INS had apprehended a combined 155,058 undocumented Mexican workers in 1945 and 1946, almost double the 81,497 braceros who were hired during those years.[86] And as Richard Craig has noted, the high number of rural workers willing to migrate outside the parameters of the Bracero Program had become a source of frustration for federal officials.[87] The commission ultimately proposed that braceros should finally be allowed to work in Texas and that undocumented workers who were already in the United States should be given the opportunity to regularize their migration status. The US government agreed with these proposals, and the commission opened offices in the border cities of Mexicali, Ciudad Juárez, and Reynosa. Undocumented workers were instructed to ask their employers to formally request their services in writing and then travel to the commission office nearest them, where they would be issued bracero contracts. These contracts stipulated that the formerly undocumented workers had to return to their home communities once they expired. Interior Secretariat officials echoed previous ambitions when they expressed their belief that this clause would help Mexican authorities tighten their control of the migratory flow, since returning braceros would presumably go through the formal contracting process if they wanted to work again in the United States.[88] According to Manuel García y Griego's calculations, 55,000 undocumented workers normalized their migration status at commission offices.[89] But these efforts did not curb undocumented migration: the INS apprehended 182,986 undocumented Mexican workers in 1947.[90]

Even though tens of thousands of formerly undocumented workers received bracero contracts at the Inter-Secretariat Commission's offices in 1947, the US government still requested twenty thousand braceros who would receive their contracts at the provincial contracting centers that spring.[91] The Alemán administration could have used this relatively small request as an opportunity to reassert federal control of the bracero selection process. But the newly-inaugurated president, who had been one of the federal officials involved in the decision to decentralize the bracero selection process, seemed comfortable maintaining the decentralized status quo, and there is no available evidence indicating that his government ever seriously entertained reclaiming the responsibilities that Ávila Camacho's had delegated.

Simultaneously, past experience and changing official state-level attitudes regarding the Bracero Program influenced the Alemán administration's decision to abstain from imposing eligibility restrictions that barred all campesinos from specific states from migrating. In stark contrast to its immediate predecessor, which temporarily banned all bracero migration from Guanajuato, Jalisco, and Michoacán in order to craft more balanced departure patterns, the Alemán administration relied heavily on these three states, as well as Aguascalientes and Zacatecas, to fulfill the US government's bracero requests. As I discuss in more detail in chapter 2, 91 percent of the 20,000 contracts distributed at the provincial contracting centers in 1947 went to braceros from Guanajuato, Jalisco, and Michoacán.[92] And at least 48 percent of the braceros selected from 1948 through 1952 were from Aguascalientes, Guanajuato, Jalisco, Michoacán, and Zacatecas, the states that federal officials identified in early 1946 as the ones where popular demand for bracero contracts was highest.[93] The Alemán administration likely determined that attempting to block the departure of aspiring braceros from these states was a fool's errand, especially since those from the center-west had a demonstrated willingness and ability to circumvent any restrictions placed on them. Perhaps just as important, officials from these states dropped their opposition to bracero migration during Alemán's presidency because they also began thinking of the program as a means of ameliorating rural crises. Guanajuato governor Nicéforo Guerrero explicitly requested a bracero contract allocation in 1947 so that his government could provide relief to campesinos who had been affected by the loss of livestock during a foot-and-mouth disease outbreak.[94] And in July 1950, Jalisco's interior secretary, Carlos Guzmán, told federal officials that the Bracero Program had not led to rural labor shortages that year, thus tacitly signaling that that state government welcomed the departure of more braceros.[95] Given these shifting attitudes, bracero contract allocations became signs of federal goodwill and attentiveness to state government's desires, not antagonism and fractured working relationships, during the late 1940s and early 1950s.

The center-western state governments may have stopped pushing back against federal-level Bracero Program policy during the late 1940s and early 1950s. But the US government began exerting unilateral diplomatic pressure during this period. And because the Alemán administration prioritized maintaining a legally sanctioned migratory channel, US pressure ultimately led to the contracting centers being moved from central Mexico to the border states. After receiving numerous reports that braceros working in Texas had been mistreated or cheated of their wages, President Alemán reimplemented the provision that barred braceros from working in that state in May 1948.[96] Mexican officials proposed lifting the ban in the fall on condition that Texas farm owners accepted new wage levels. But in stark contrast to their counterparts in the Arkansas Delta—who, as Julie Weise has detailed, agreed to pay braceros their promised wages so that they could avoid being placed on a blacklist that was kept by the Mexican consul in Memphis, Tennessee—Texas farm owners rejected the proposal in October.[97] And with the help of US Border Patrol agents who responded to farm owner pressure and opened the Ciudad Juárez–El Paso crossing, they hired as many as eight thousand Mexican workers who did not have bracero contracts.[98] Alemán denounced this flagrant violation of the bilateral agreement, and President Harry Truman formally apologized, though some US officials maintained that their Mexican counterparts were wholly responsible for the impasse.[99]

With the El Paso events still fresh in mind, representatives of the Mexican and US governments met in January 1949 to begin renegotiating the terms of the bilateral agreement. The two sides reached a preliminary accord in early February. The US government pledged to monitor braceros' working conditions, enforce provisions that mandated their wages be comparable to those of US-born workers, and regularize the status of undocumented workers who were in the United States when the new terms of the agreement became effective. The US delegation also proposed moving the contracting centers from central Mexico to the border cities of Mexicali, Ciudad Juárez, and Nuevo Laredo. This was done to save US farm owners money, since the new agreement made them responsible for paying braceros' round-trip transportation costs from the contracting centers to their work sites.[100] The Mexican government had opened a contracting center in Guaymas, a coastal town in the border state of Sonora, in 1948, but they balked at the idea of moving the centers to border cities.[101] Mexican officials feared that such a move would spark social and economic chaos at the border and limit their ability to enforce a new provision that barred the residents of border communities from receiving bracero contracts. The Mexican delegation counter-proposed moving the contracting centers to Hermosillo, Torreón, and Monterrey, cities in the border states of Sonora, Coahuila, and Nuevo León, respectively, but not on the border proper.[102] Ultimately, the Mexican and US delegations opted for a compromise solution: new contracting centers were opened in Hermosillo, Chihuahua City, and Monterrey, and there were also centers in Irapuato and the Guadalajara suburb of Tlaquepaque.[103]

This compromise upset Sonora's government, but the Alemán administration proved willing to risk the discontent of Sonoran officials if it meant that the Bracero Program would continue. As soon as news of the preliminary agreement reached him in early February, Governor Horacio Sobarzo wrote to President Alemán and Interior Secretary Ruiz Cortines and begged them to reconsider their decision. The governor's primary concern was that the contracting center would strain local resources that had already been stretched thin by a series of severe floods.[104] But Alemán and Ruiz Cortines were unmoved, and thousands of aspiring braceros began arriving in Hermosillo in early August, one month before the contracting center was set to open. Sobarzo openly worried that city would not survive the "alarmingly large" crowds that had gathered there, and he renewed his plea that the contracting center be moved.[105] By that point the governor also had an explicitly political concern: he alleged that Jacinto López—a member of the left-wing Partido Popular (Popular Party) who had lost Sonora's recent gubernatorial election—was attempting to recruit the would-be braceros in Hermosillo to his cause so he could use them to disrupt the formal transfer of powers, which was scheduled for September 1.[106] On August 25, federal officials ordered that the prospective braceros in Hermosillo be vacated to Guadalajara by railroad but only until the new governor was inaugurated.[107]

Diplomatic tensions regarding the location of the contracting centers persisted into Adolfo Ruiz Cortines's presidency (1952–58), and his administration's continued attempts to find a middle ground resulted in another confrontation between the Mexican and US governments. In 1953 centers were opened in the central cities of Irapuato and Tlaquepaque and the northern cities of Chihuahua City and Durango City.[108] However, US officials were not satisfied with this arrangement. When the two governments met at the end of the year to renegotiate the terms of the bilateral agreement, the US delegation insisted that the Monterrey Contracting Center be reopened.[109] Mexican officials refused to consider the idea, as well as ones that would have lessened the protections granted to braceros, and they broke off negotiations. The end of the negotiations sparked a burst of patriotic sentiment and cooperation pledges among the governors of the primary bracero-sending states. Jalisco's Agustín Yáñez celebrated the Ruiz Cortines administration's actions as a noble defense of braceros' rights and dignity.[110] And Aguascalientes's Benito Palomino Dena convened a special state-level commission and tasked it with organizing a campaign that would inform would-be braceros of the new status quo and prevent departures from the state, though it is not clear what steps if any this commission took.[111]

But US officials did not share the sending-state governors' enthusiasm, and they decided to exert unilateral pressure to renew the bilateral agreement with terms to their liking. In January 1954, the US State, Labor, and Justice Departments announced that bracero contracts would be given to any Mexican workers who successfully crossed the border. This led to a series of violent confrontations in Mexicali in late January and early February as Mexican soldiers tried to block thousands of would-be braceros from entering the United States. Nearly ten thousand aspiring braceros managed to cross the border before overwhelmed US officials declared a moratorium on entries.[112] Although US authorities had lost control at the border, their actions ultimately had their desired effect. The bilateral negotiations resumed in the middle of February, and Mexican officials agreed to open contracting centers in the northern cities of Chihuahua City, Mexicali, and Monterrey, as well as Irapuato.[113]

The bilateral agreement's new terms went into effect in March, two months before retired US Army general Joseph Swing became the commissioner general of the INS. Swing, as Mae Ngai and Adam Goodman have noted, had a goal that had eluded Mexican officials since the beginning of the Bracero Program: the curbing of undocumented migration. Undocumented migration had eclipsed formal bracero migration in the years since the 1947 Inter-Secretariat Commission allowed undocumented workers to regularize their migration status. From 1948 through 1953, the INS apprehended 2.8 million undocumented Mexican workers, more than triple the 800,325 braceros who entered the United States during the same period.[114] National Mexican newspapers like *El Universal* and *Excélsior* reported that many of these undocumented workers were campesinos from bracero-sending states like Guanajuato, Jalisco, and Michoacán who had essentially transformed Guadalajara into the central hub of undocumented departures and that they were willing to cross the border without contracts because there were numerous farm owners in the United States who were willing to hire them.[115] The Alemán and Ruiz Cortines administrations were seemingly out of ideas to prevent these types of departures, save for dispatching DIPS agents to the principal sending states and having them post broadsides that asked campesinos to stay at home if they did not have contracts.[116]

Swing wasted little time once he was in office, and while his measures did not completely eliminate undocumented migration, they remarkably reduced it. In June 1954, the INS launched "Operation Wetback," which took its name from the derogatory term used to describe undocumented Mexican immigrants who crossed the Rio Grande into Texas. The operation—which targeted the agricultural production zones of California and Texas, as well as cities like Los Angeles, San Francisco, and Chicago—was a mass deportation campaign that relied on workplace raids and publicity campaigns that urged undocumented Mexican immigrants to leave the United States before immigration authorities apprehended them.[117] All told, the INS recorded 1.1 million apprehensions in 1954, the highest single-year total during the Bracero Program. Swing also successfully secured an increase in the number of braceros the US government requested each year so as to reduce American farm owners' need to hire undocumented workers. From 1955 through 1964, an average of 331,724 braceros entered the United States each year, up from an annual average of 102,228 entries during the period 1942–54. Concurrently, the annual average number of apprehensions fell from 356,226 to 60,471.[118]

Operation Wetback led to chaos and calamity on the Mexican side of the border that the Ruiz Cortines administration accepted as the price of curbing undocumented migration. In Nuevo Laredo there were reports that deportees were being transported in trucks "like cattle" and left in the desert miles from the border. More than eighty died of sunstroke near Mexicali after they were detained and deported in 112-degree weather. And thousands of deportees remained in border cities, where they quickly strained local resources.[119] But Ruiz Cortines's government raised no objections and appeared satisfied with the actions that the US government had taken. In his annual address to the federal legislature in September, the president assured legislators that the "effective measures" that US officials were using had limited and would continue to limit undocumented departures. Ruiz Cortines also noted that there were not enough permanent employment opportunities in rural communities to entice aspiring braceros to stay at home, a tacit declaration that his administration viewed the Bracero Program as a necessity.[120] The implications of these statements were clear: federal authorities' principal priority was keeping a legally sanctioned migratory channel open, not the defense of braceros' rights that bestirred Aguascalientes and Jalisco officials in early 1954. And after years of frustration, they were willing to defer to the US government on the question of undocumented migration and ignore the sometimes-fatal consequences of mass deportation campaigns.

Federal officials also welcomed the US government's escalation of deportations because it benefited them financially. As Adam Goodman has detailed in his study of American deportation policy and practices, US immigration officials contracted with two Mexican shipping companies to transport deportees from Texas to Veracruz between September 1954 and August 1956. During this period, individual ships that were approved to carry as many as eight hundred deportees made seventy-six deportation runs after delivering export cargo like bananas to Texas. Interior Secretariat official, José Rocha, owned stock in Transportes Marítimos Refrigerados (TMR; Refrigerated Maritime Transports), the shipping company that gained exclusive control of the deportation route in December 1955. As such, Rocha personally profited from the deportation boatlifts, which netted TMR between US$8 and US$9 per deportee. The Ruiz Cortines administration continued to approve the boatlifts despite deportees' complaints about the abysmal conditions—exposure to inclement weather, cramped living quarters, lack of adequate bedding, the serving of underprepared or spoiled food—on board the ships. (US officials hoped that these conditions would convince deportees that the risks of being apprehended and possibly being deported by boat again outweighed the benefits of recrossing the border without authorization.) The boatlifts were only terminated after deportees aboard the SS *Mercurio* mutinied in August 1956 while the ship was docked in the Tamaulipas port of Tampico.[121]

While the deportation boatlifts made their initial journeys across the Gulf of Mexico, Ruiz Cortines's government turned its attention once again to the location of the contracting centers. In October 1954 federal officials announced plans to reopen the Hermosillo Contracting Center the following year. The announcement immediately reminded the leaders of the Hermosillo Medical Association of the "serious problems" that had afflicted the city when a contracting center was first opened there in 1949, and other local business and financial leaders were quick to make their objections known.[122] The United Merchants Corporation worried that a contracting center would prompt local campesinos to abandon the state, and the Regional Cereal Producers Association feared that the center would undermine their efforts to recruit internal migrants for the cotton harvest.[123] And Alfonso Almada, chair of the National Chamber of Industry's Sonora chapter, told the president that it would be unfair to reopen the Hermosillo Contracting Center since that city and the surrounding region were not home to many braceros, nor had it traditionally been a stopping point for braceros who were heading to the US border. Almada also reminded Ruiz Cortines that "bracerismo" did not exist in Sonora and that "it would be lamentable to promote such a habit among us."[124]

Federal officials disregarded these concerns and moved forward with their plans to reopen the Hermosillo Contracting Center.[125] However, Sonoran fears that the state would be depopulated ultimately proved unfounded. Much like its immediate predecessor, Ruiz Cortines's administration relied heavily on Aguascalientes, Guanajuato, Jalisco, Michoacán, and Zacatecas during bracero selection periods: at least 39 percent of the braceros chosen during Ruiz Cortines's presidency were from these five states; by contrast, only four-tenths of 1 percent were from Sonora.[126] According to a 1956 Foreign Relations Secretariat report, this disproportionate allocation pattern was a response to elevated seasonal unemployment that coincided with bracero selection periods and drought conditions in the center-west and center-north.[127] The allocations also reflected the efforts of governors like Guanajuato's Jesús Rodríguez Gaona and Zacatecas's José Minero Roque who openly lobbied for bracero contract allotments that would be distributed in rural communities that had suffered severe crop losses.[128]

The reopening of the Hermosillo Contracting Center in 1955 ultimately served as a prelude to the permanent shifting of the contracting centers to Chihuahua City, Monterrey, and Empalme, a Sonora railroad depot

MAP 4. Contracting center sites. Map by Bill Nelson.

near Guaymas, in 1956.[129] This shift ultimately benefited the northern cotton producers who had previously worried that the contracting centers would undermine their efforts to recruit internal migrants during harvest seasons. With the federal Interior Secretariat's direct approval, cotton producers in the northern states where the contracting centers were located, as well as Tamaulipas, were allowed to hire aspiring braceros who were waiting to receive their contracts. In exchange, the prospective braceros who worked in northern cotton fields received assurances that they would be given their contracts before those who did not participate in this new initiative.[130] Permanently shifting the contracting centers to the states of Sonora, Chihuahua, and Nuevo León thus provided two boons to the Ruiz Cortines administration: it appeased US officials who had been lobbying for all the contracting centers to be moved to border states since the late 1940s; and it helped secure seasonal labor for domestic cotton producers.

• • • •

Definitively moving the contracting centers to the northern states in 1956 was the federal government's final significant Bracero Program–related policy adjustment. And there were no further serious diplomatic confrontations with the United States after the one in early 1954. Adolfo López Mateos's government (1958–64) maintained the decentralized bracero selection process first implemented in 1945, and Interior Secretariat officials explicitly reminded aspiring braceros who sent written contract requests to federal authorities that they had "nothing whatsoever" to do with the selection of individual migrant workers.[131] The López Mateos administration also continued to allocate a significant number of contracts to Aguascalientes, Guanajuato, Jalisco, Michoacán, and Zacatecas: 44 percent of the braceros chosen during the Bracero Program's final years were from those states.[132]

The bracero selection and contract distribution process in place during the program's final years—federal officials assigning contract allotments and delegating selection responsibilities to state governments, and chosen braceros then traveling to contracting centers in border states to receive their contracts—was far removed from the one Ávila Camacho's administration implemented when it agreed to participate in the Bracero Program. The latter government believed that centralization was the key to channeling the migratory flow through the Bracero Program, so it assumed the responsibility of selecting braceros, mandated that all aspiring migrant workers travel to Mexico City for their contracts, and unilaterally declared large segments of the country's rural population ineligible for contracts. But centralization led to chaos, both in Mexico City, where official corruption and inefficiency contributed to violence and deteriorating living conditions, and at the border, where tens of thousands gathered and then entered the United States without contracts. All the while, many of the campesinos who were barred from receiving contracts acquired them by exploiting loopholes or paying bribes. Ávila Camacho's government desperately scrambled to make policy adjustments that would help it regain control of the migratory process. But the administration conceded defeat when it shuttered the Mexico City Contracting Center, lifted most of the eligibility restrictions it had implemented, and shifted the burden of selecting braceros to state governments. After that, federal officials' primary domestic responsibility was deciding which states could send migrant workers north, a power it used to punish wayward governors, show favor to key constituencies, and generate goodwill among governors who wanted braceros chosen in their jurisdictions.

But the deliberate delegation of bracero selection responsibilities did not entirely free the federal government from outside pressure that forced it to make policy adjustments. From the late 1940s through the mid-1950s, the US government enacted unilateral measures to extract favorable concessions during bilateral negotiations and curb undocumented migration. The administrations of Miguel Alemán and Adolfo Ruiz Cortines responded to this unilateral pressure by shifting the contract distribution sites from provincial cities in central Mexico to ones in northern border states—something that the US government wanted to happen so that American farm owners would not have to pay as much to transport braceros from Mexico to their job sites—and not objecting when US immigration authorities launched a mass deportation campaign that led to the death of numerous deportees.

Because federal officials allotted a disproportionate number of bracero contracts to the states of Aguascalientes, Guanajuato, Jalisco, Michoacán, and Zacatecas, the governments there were heavily involved in the bracero selection process. But as I show in the following chapter, sending-state officials never seriously entertained closely managing the selection process the way their federal counterparts had during the Bracero Program's initial phase. They limited themselves to dividing their contract allotments within their jurisdictions—a process that political considerations influenced—and they further decentralized the bracero selection process when they delegated that task to local-level authorities who regularly flouted state-level eligibility directives.

TWO

―――

"According to the Jurisdiction's Necessities"

STATE-LEVEL ADMINISTRATION OF
THE BRACERO PROGRAM

SHORTLY AFTER FEDERAL OFFICIALS DELEGATED bracero selection responsibilities to state governments and announced that precontracting centers—where aspiring braceros would be vetted before traveling to Mexico City to receive their contracts—would be established in provincial cities in spring 1944, more than four thousand prospective Guanajuato braceros flocked to Irapuato, site of that state's precontracting center, even though the center had yet to formally open. This "breakneck mobilization" worried Governor Ernesto Hidalgo, who bemoaned the "very serious problems" that it was causing in Irapuato. In early June, the governor instructed the state's municipal presidents to remind aspiring braceros that they needed to stay in their home communities until told otherwise.[1] Two weeks later, Hidalgo's administration designed a decentralized bracero selection process that relied heavily on municipal officials and that they believed would simultaneously safeguard regional agricultural production and lower the likelihood of "hasty journeys" that resulted in "inconvenient agglomerations" of aspiring braceros in Irapuato. The state interior secretary, Fausto Villagómez, instructed Guanajuato's municipal authorities to compile lists of healthy non-ejidatario campesinos who were interested in migrating and to determine how many of them could leave without harming agricultural production in their jurisdictions. State officials would then use that information to decide how many bracero eligibility cards they would send to each municipal government, though no available record details precisely how Guanajuato's government distributed eligibility cards in 1944. Once local governments received their allotment of cards, they had to organize a random drawing to determine who would receive them. Those selected in the drawings would then present their cards at the Irapuato Precontracting Center.[2]

As this chapter shows, the calculated caution that Guanajuato officials displayed when they deliberately delegated bracero selection responsibilities in 1944 became a hallmark of the Bracero Program's state-level administration there and in Aguascalientes, Jalisco, Michoacán, and Zacatecas. Because they prioritized maintaining a semblance of order at the cities chosen as the sites of precontracting and contracting centers over asserting full control of the migratory flow, sending-state governments abstained from intervening directly in the bracero selection process. Instead, state officials focused their administrative efforts on dividing contract allocations within their jurisdictions. State authorities usually divided contracts among municipal governments, though there were years when contracts were allotted to state legislative districts and rural labor unions. And state governments transferred the responsibility of choosing individual braceros to municipal presidents primarily but also to state legislators, union local leaders, and officials of the Liga de Comunidades Agrarias (League of Agrarian Communities), an organization whose state chapters represented ejidos. This delegation of authority was ostensibly done because officials with local ties were better positioned to determine which prospective braceros would benefit most from migrating. But this also shifted the administrative burden of selecting braceros from state governments which were never interested in managing that facet of the Bracero Program and confined domestic Bracero Program–related political conflicts to the local level, thus shielding state governments from possible political fallout. And by insulating themselves from negative consequences and ensuring that the contract distribution sites remained free of strife, state governments could uphold one end of the mid-twentieth-century "pragmatic pact," to borrow Rogelio Hernández Rodríguez's term, that existed between federal and regional officials: namely, the latter would do their best to maintain political and social stability in their jurisdictions.[3]

State-level disinterest in administering the bracero selection process does not mean that state officials were always apolitical bystanders during contracting periods. There were years when pressure from both federal officials and aspiring braceros prompted state authorities to carve out contract allocations for specific groups, such as the victims of natural disasters, union members whose socioeconomic fortunes had been affected by labor disputes, and, despite the federal statute prohibiting their departure as braceros, ejidatarios. But these instances were exceptional. In most years, sending-state governments based their eligibility card distribution patterns on popular demand levels or information they gathered from municipal officials, which usually resulted in the bulk of the eligibility cards being allotted to municipalities in the Greater Bajío. And even when they decided to grant preference to specific aspiring braceros, state authorities refused to manage the selection process directly or exercise strict oversight, which in turn afforded ground-level officials the opportunity to openly disregard state-level directives. Thus, much like their federal counterparts, state officials were ultimately unable to enforce the politically motivated bracero eligibility guidelines that they enacted.

FROM PRECONTRACTING TO CONTRACTING CENTERS

As I noted in chapter 1, federal authorities opened a precontracting center in Zacatecas City in spring 1944. In May, a DIPS agent stationed there reported that Governor Pánfilo Natera's administration had delegated bracero selection responsibilities to the state's municipal governments.[4] Unfortunately, there is no available evidence aside from this domestic intelligence report that gives further details of how Zacatecas's government managed the Bracero Program in 1944. But the DIPS agent's report clearly demonstrates that Zacatecas officials, like their counterparts in Guanajuato, did not want to choose individual braceros themselves.

The provincial precontracting centers were replaced by full contracting centers after federal officials shuttered the Mexico City Contracting Center in early 1945. In Guanajuato, state officials maintained their cautious course and did not significantly alter the bracero selection procedure they first used in 1944. Municipal authorities were again asked to determine the number of campesinos who could leave their jurisdictions without "damaging the economy and normal agricultural activities of that region."[5] Once state officials reviewed these numbers, they "proportionally" distributed eligibility cards that chosen braceros would exchange for contracts; that is, the municipal governments that reported they could spare more rural workers were instructed to select more aspiring braceros via random drawings than those governments that stated they could spare fewer. Thus Pénjamo's municipal government, which reported that 500 braceros could leave the jurisdiction, selected 250 prospective braceros.[6] And in San Miguel de Allende, where only 20 to 30 rural workers could be spared, local authorities selected 10 aspiring braceros.[7] The reports submitted by municipal officials stated that 85 percent of the 7,830 rural workers who could leave Guanajuato were from the southern municipalities that fall within the Greater Bajío. Ultimately, 81 percent of the 4,100 braceros who were selected in February were from that region of the state.[8]

Nineteen forty-five also saw the opening of a contracting center in Uruapan, Michoacán. And though Governor José María Mendoza Pardo's administration never publicly expressed concern regarding "inconvenient agglomerations" of aspiring braceros, like its counterpart in Guanajuato did in 1944, it emulated the selection system implemented in the neighboring state. However, Michoacán's government divided its eligibility cards among the eleven districts that made up the state's unicameral legislature, the Chamber of Deputies, and it was state deputies who were charged with selecting the prospective braceros who would travel to the Uruapan Contracting Center. There is no record that the Mendoza Pardo administration asked state legislators to supply it with information regarding how many braceros could leave their jurisdictions without affecting local agricultural production. Instead, the available evidence suggests that Michoacán authorities linked the distribution of eligibility cards to popular demand. At least 72 percent of the written contract requests that Michoacán's aspiring braceros made in 1945 were sent from communities in the northern municipalities that form part of the Greater Bajío, and 73 percent of the four thousand eligibility cards allocated to the state government in February went to legislative districts that included Greater Bajío municipalities.[9]

The decentralized bracero selection process in Michoacán immediately went awry, as state deputies used the process to enrich themselves or reward their political allies, which in turn stoked local political tensions. For example, José Garibay Romero, a member of the ruling party's progressive wing whose Jiquilpan-based district included rural communities affected by the still-erupting Parícutin Volcano, disregarded Parícutin damnificados' desire to continue migrating as braceros, which they had been doing since federal authorities favored them in fall 1943. Instead, he openly flouted the federal government's guidelines and personally distributed eligibility cards among ejidatarios who had supported his candidacy.[10] Zacán's community leaders beseeched Garibay Romero in February to change course and choose their constituents as braceros because of how dire their situation was after two years of continual eruptions: a thick layer of ash, they said, had "covered our cultivable lands, destroyed our fruit trees, and ruined everything else that helped us provide for our families"; livestock had perished because of the lack of feed; the price of daily consumables like maize, rice, sugar, and cooking lard had skyrocketed; and local children had been reduced to a state of "near nakedness."[11] Simultaneously, Abelino Torres Herrera and other aspiring braceros from Los Reyes told Garibay Romero that they wanted bracero contracts because they had not harvested any crops since the volcano started erupting in 1943.[12] But these pleas failed to make Garibay Romero reconsider his politically motivated course.

In the neighboring district of Zamora, Procopio Valadéz, who identified himself as a resident of the district seat, alleged in February that state deputy Ignacio Torres Espinosa and his alternate, Antonio Loera, had "shamelessly" exploited aspiring braceros by selling them eligibility cards for upwards of 150 pesos. Valadéz then suggested to Governor Mendoza Pardo that it would be better to entrust the responsibility of choosing braceros to Zamora's municipal authorities in future selection periods.[13] However, Zamora's municipal president told the governor that Valadéz had no standing to make his accusations because he was not a Zamora resident and that Valadéz was likely an operative working on behalf of "dissident elements" who wanted to sow discord in Torres Espinosa's district.[14] And the secretary general of Zamora's Campesino Union dismissed Torres Espinosa's critics as "irresponsible individuals" who were "envious" of the state legislator.[15] For his part, Loera denied the accusations and assured the governor that they were the work of "deposed leaders" (*líderes caídos*) who were upset that that they would not be able to reward their partisans with bracero contracts.[16] Another allegation of Bracero Program–related malfeasance soon followed, however. In March, Acuitzeramo's community leaders accused Torres Espinosa of conspiring with Tlazazalca's municipal president to sell eligibility cards for 304 pesos, an exorbitant sum that none of Acuitzeramo's aspiring braceros could afford to pay.[17]

But the state government's disinterest regarding the bracero selection process extended to exercising oversight of the individuals it had instructed to choose individual braceros. Frustrated Parícutin damnificados asked federal authorities to intervene on their behalf and grant them the eligibility cards that state deputies like José Garibay Romero had denied them. Although federal officials forwarded those complaints to Governor Mendoza Pardo, there is no record that the governor ever asked eruption zone legislators to favor damnificados or that he disciplined Garibay Romero for giving eligibility cards to ejidatarios, who were barred from migrating.[18] As for the accusations lodged against state deputy Torres Espinosa, state officials were content with conducting a pro forma investigation. The state's interior secretary, Luis Moreno, informed the state's attorney general, Francisco Mora

Plancarte, about the allegations that Torres Espinosa and his alternate had sold eligibility cards in Zamora, and Mora Plancarte then asked Zamora's judicial authorities to inquire into the matter.[19] That marked the extent of the Mendoza Pardo administration's intervention, and Torres Espinosa was presumably cleared of any wrongdoing, since, as I discuss later, he was still in office in 1947. The governor did personally approve an investigation of the sale of bracero eligibility cards in Coalcomán, in Michoacán's coastal sierra, which resulted in an official recommendation that Coalcomán's municipal president and secretary be sanctioned for violating state-level directives. But Mendoza Pardo only launched this inquiry because his hand was forced: he and his chief of staff had witnessed the irregularities firsthand while visiting Coalcomán, which meant that they could not soft-pedal the allegations or sweep them under the rug like they did others.[20]

In Aguascalientes, it was Governor Jesús Rodríguez's administration itself that openly flouted federal directives when it permitted ejidatarios to migrate as braceros in 1945, provided that there was someone who could work their lands during their absence. Since agrarian reform beneficiaries would be migrating, Rodríguez's government delegated bracero selection responsibilities to the state's chapter of the Liga de Comunidades Agrarias, an organization that represented all of Aguascalientes's ejidos and was formally linked to the ruling PRI.[21] The delegation of responsibility also meant that it was the Liga, not the state government, that had to deal firsthand with the frustrations that the bracero selection process generated. In a March 28 letter, Juan Morán, secretary general of Aguascalientes's chapter, informed the governor that choosing braceros was such a "laborious" task that the Liga had neglected all other business during the March 16–26 selection period. And it was a task that was ultimately left unfinished. When the 3,500 eligibility cards—51 percent of which were earmarked for aspiring braceros from the southwestern municipalities that fall within the Greater Bajío—allotted to the state dwindled to 114, desperate ejidatarios who wanted to ensure that they had an opportunity to migrate stormed the selection site in Aguascalientes City, which prompted Liga personnel to withdraw. Despite this, Morán declared that the Liga was "satisfied" with its work, and he did not express any desire to distribute the remaining eligibility cards.[22] There is no record that state officials asked Morán to restart the selection process.

Why did Aguascalientes's government disregard federal mandates and favor ejidatarios during the 1945 bracero selection period? There are several plausible explanations. The Rodríguez administration may have wanted to generate goodwill among agrarian reform beneficiaries or fashion a patron-client relationship with the Liga. Perhaps Aguascalientes officials determined that it was better to facilitate ejidatarios' departure as braceros since it would be impossible to prevent them from migrating. Or maybe Rodríguez reasoned that he would not suffer any tangible consequences for his transgression because he was in sufficiently good standing with the federal government. Indeed, while the federal Interior Secretariat official Benito Coquet lamented in a May 1946 circular that he sent to all the state governors that some regional and local authorities had encouraged ejidatarios to migrate as braceros, he did not single out Rodríguez by name.[23] Nor is there any record that indicates that federal officials reprimanded Rodríguez or threatened to withhold bracero contract allocations as punishment.

THE TARGETED DISTRIBUTIONS OF 1947

Of the twenty thousand newly contracted braceros requested by the US government in 1947, the vast majority of the contracts, 91 percent, went to aspiring braceros from Guanajuato, Jalisco, and Michoacán. (The remaining braceros were from the center-western state of Querétaro.)[24] Regional political considerations and natural disasters prompted center-western state officials to craft eligibility card distribution patterns that favored specific groups of rural workers. But one federal desire did influence how Michoacán officials distributed a portion of their eligibility cards. In an April 12 communiqué, Arcadio Ojeda García, an official with the federal Interior Secretariat, assured Michoacán's governor, José María Mendoza Pardo, that his administration would be able to select braceros "according to the jurisdiction's necessities," but he also expressed his hope that state officials would reserve some contracts for campesinos who lived near Parícutin, which was still erupting.[25] Michoacán authorities opted to heed their federal counterparts' suggestion, and they set aside fifteen hundred eligibility cards for eruption zone damnificados.[26] The revival of this preferential treatment was almost certainly welcomed by eruption zone rural workers like Angahuan's Miguel Bravo Cortés and Bonifacio Bravo Soto, who requested contracts in February because a thick layer of ash made it impossible for them to plant and harvest crops.[27]

More localized political concerns influenced the Mendoza Pardo administration's decision to have a civilian select Parícutin braceros in 1947. State authorities delegated that responsibility to Rafael Hinojosa Torres, an

Uruapan resident who was not an active government official.[28] Tapping Hinojosa Torres to lead the selection process reflected the state government's desire to avoid further inflaming political tensions in the area. As Verónica Oikión Solano has discussed in her study of mid-twentieth-century Michoacán state politics, the state legislative election scheduled for 1947 had caused Governor Mendoza Pardo's relationship with Uruapan's middle-class organizations and labor unions that were affiliated with the Confederación de Trabajadores de México to deteriorate. Mendoza Pardo backed the primary candidacy of a former Uruapan municipal president whom many denounced as a corrupt and "despotic" official, and middle-class groups and labor unions mobilized to block the governor's nomination.[29] Had Michoacán's government given the responsibility of selecting braceros to a local official who supported Mendoza Pardo's position, it would have further antagonized those who were already unhappy with and actively working against the governor. The decision also precluded the possibility that a local official who was sympathetic to Uruapan's labor and middle-class organizations would be able to benefit from the bracero selection process.

Michoacán's government also directed Pátzcuaro's municipal president, Luis Ortiz Lazcano, to select fifteen hundred landless Indigenous braceros from his jurisdiction, immediately east of the Sierra Purépecha and the Parícutin eruption zone.[30] This was a curious allocation, since Pátzcuaro was largely unaffected by either the volcano or the foot-and-mouth disease outbreak (discussed later in this chapter), and there was little documented popular demand for bracero contracts there. There is only one available written contract request sent to state officials from that municipality in 1947, and it was made by a group of unemployed railroad workers who did not identify themselves as either landless or Indigenous.[31] Furthermore, the municipal president had a strained relationship with Pátzcuaro's Indigenous communities. As Christopher Boyer has noted in his study of revolutionary agrarian politics in Michoacán, Ortiz Lazcano—scion of a prominent landowning family that had settled in the Pátzcuaro area during the mid-nineteenth century—had denounced Indigenous peoples in the early 1920s as naturally lazy individuals who never worked of their own accord.[32]

The likeliest explanation is that Michoacán officials designed the Pátzcuaro accommodation in order to modernize Indigenous workers by exposing them to US technology and labor practices, a goal that, as Mireya Loza and Deborah Cohen have noted in their transnational studies of the Bracero Program, influenced Mexican officials' decision to participate in the guest worker initiative.³³ The Mendoza Pardo administration likely felt a renewed urgency to modernize its Indigenous constituents because the Tepalcatepec River Commission began its work in 1947. The commission, which remained active until 1961, funded the construction of irrigation canals, reservoirs, hydroelectric dams, and paved roads, which in turn led to tens of thousands of hectares being opened to cultivation in the Sierra Purépecha and the Tierra Caliente, the semiarid lowlands immediately south of Pátzcuaro. Former president Cárdenas, who served as the commission's chair, promoted its works as a means of reviving land redistribution in Michoacán and providing jobs for local campesinos.³⁴ Furthermore, many of the lands the commission opened were eventually dedicated to the production of cash crops like cotton and citrus, crops that the US farm owners who employed braceros also cultivated, and they were worked by internal migrants from Michoacán's Indigenous communities.³⁵ And as Guillermo de la Peña has demonstrated, officials prioritized incorporating Indigenous peoples who lived near large-scale development projects into broader economic and cultural systems—such as regional and national markets and the increased use of the Spanish language—during the late 1940s and early 1950s.³⁶ In light of all these factors, Michoacán authorities likely determined that sending Pátzcuaro's Indigenous population north to work in putatively modern US fields and orchards was the ideal means to prepare them for the types of jobs that would soon become available in the Tierra Caliente. According to Mireya Loza's study, these efforts bore some fruit. As she details, while Hispanized mestizo braceros—people of mixed Indigenous and European descent— often discriminated against their Indigenous counterparts in the United States, many members of the latter group, including Purépechas from Michoacán, improved their Spanish-language skills and gained valuable work experience.³⁷

The remainder of Michoacán's contract allotments and the entirety of Guanajuato's were used as a response to an outbreak of foot-and-mouth disease (*aftosa*), a highly infectious viral malady that causes fevers and blistered mouths and feet in cattle, sheep, goats, and pigs and leads to the death or permanent debilitation of infected animals. The outbreak began in the Gulf Coast state of Veracruz in December 1946.³⁸ By March 1947, the disease had spread as far west as Zamora, and livestock owners in northwestern Michoacán worried that more than a hundred thousand head of cattle were imperiled.³⁹ As Mary Mendoza and C. J. Alvarez have noted, the US government was anxious to prevent the spread of the disease north, so it agreed to form a bilateral commission to address the outbreak in early 1947. The Mexico–United States Commission for the Eradication of Foot-and-Mouth Disease began its work in March. Its affiliated agencies recruited thousands of American veterinarians and ranch hands to travel to Mexico and help with the implementation of quarantine measures designed to confine the outbreak to central and southern Mexico; it also adopted the *rifle sanitario* (sanitizing rifle), a strategy that called for the immediate slaughter of infected animals.[40]

But the commission's measures worsened the situation and influenced the decision to use the Bracero Program as a response to the outbreak in Guanajuato and Michoacán. Guanajuato governor Nicéforo Guerrero visited the state's southeastern municipalities in late March and sent a grim report to President Alemán. Two thousand head of cattle had already been slaughtered in the area, and an additional thirty thousand head were at risk of becoming infected unless they were transported away. The mules that federal officials had promised as replacements for destroyed work oxen had not yet arrived, thus delaying preparations for the upcoming agricultural cycle. The quarantine measures had already led to a scarcity of basic goods, and merchants told the governor that their sales had declined by 50 percent. Guerrero concluded his report by asking Alemán to allocate bracero contracts to Guanajuato so that some relief could be provided to those affected by the outbreak.[41] Within one month of Guerrero's report, a group of sixty aspiring braceros from the northern Michoacán municipality of Penjamillo, immediately across the border from Guanajuato, exhorted the state government there to favor them with eligibility cards because the outbreak had cost them their jobs and they had no hope of finding work in the foreseeable future.[42]

In Michoacán, state officials reserved 4,500 contracts for rural workers affected by the outbreak. That allocation was split evenly between Cuitzeo, immediately north of Morelia, and Zamora.[43] The Mendoza Pardo administration had Francisco Núñez Chávez and Enrique Bravo Valencia—who represented Morelia and Zamora, respectively, in the federal Chamber of Deputies—administer the selection of aftosa braceros, though both men ultimately delegated that responsibility to municipal officials in Cuitzeo and Zamora.[44] A budget shortfall that affected the upkeep of the Guanajuato state government's archives in 1947 means that we cannot know precisely how Guerrero's administration distributed its allotment of 7,000 contracts throughout the state that year. But the governor told the state legislature in a September address that preference had been given to municipalities impacted by the aftosa outbreak. This indicates that Greater Bajío municipalities like Celaya, Moroleón, and Pénjamo, which Guerrero identified as the ones most affected in that same address to the state legislature, were likely home to the majority of the state's braceros. As in previous years, the task of choosing braceros was delegated to Guanajuato municipal authorities.[45]

Because the aftosa outbreak did not reach crisis levels in Jalisco until after the bracero selection period had ended, Governor Jesús González Gallo's recently inaugurated administration decided to distribute the bulk of its contract allotment in a liberal manner, distinguishing it from its immediate predecessor (which had fiercely opposed the departure of braceros from Jalisco) and likely generating goodwill among campesinos who had been denied the opportunity to migrate as braceros since summer 1943.[46] Three thousand eligibility cards were sent to municipal officials, who were simply instructed to select non-ejidatario campesinos. Virtually all the state's municipalities, 122 of 124, sent braceros north. The plurality of these cards, 25 percent, went to jurisdictions in the highlands of northeastern Jalisco, the region of the state that forms part of the Greater Bajío.[47]

González Gallo's government used the remainder of its contract allotment to ameliorate the effects of an intraunion conflict that, according to federal deputy Vidal Díaz Muñoz, had left twelve hundred members of the STIASRM, one of the sugar workers' unions that federal authorities favored with contracts in 1946, unemployed and eager to migrate.[48] The conflict began as a dispute between Filemón Avalos Osorio and Francisco González, two veteran leaders of STIASRM Local 2, which represented workers in Ameca's San Francisco Mill. The two had been active labor organizers in that mill since the 1930s, but they began clashing in 1943 when González joined a "dissident" local that Avalos Osorio opposed.[49] The split was part of a broader labor conflict within Jalisco that escalated during the mid-1940s, as unions and their members affiliated themselves with one of two competing factions of the state-level labor confederation: a progressive "Authentic" one and a conservative "Loyal" one, which counted González as one of its principal officers.[50] The conflict escalated in December 1946, when González and his allies reported that a combined five hundred members of Local 2, Local 3 (in Acatlán's Bella Vista Mill), and Local 25 (in Tala's Tala Mill) had been unjustly fired and that Local 2's "perverse" leaders had sided with management and permanently blacklisted an unspecified number of mill workers.[51] For their part, Local 2's leaders held González responsible for spreading "anarchy" in Jalisco's sugar mills by aligning himself with municipal governments like Villa Corona's, which was antagonizing members of Local 66.[52]

After STIASRM leader Félix Ponce approached the state government and suggested setting aside eligibility cards for unemployed union members, state authorities decided to send 777 eligibility cards to eighteen STIASRM locals, including Locals 2, 3, 25, and 66; union local leaders were also allowed to select 123 alternates.[53]

But because state governments remained unwilling to choose braceros themselves, the individuals tapped to coordinate the selection process disregarded the specialized eligibility guidelines so that they could achieve their own financial and political ends, which ultimately rendered the Bracero Program a mostly ineffective response to natural disasters and labor disputes. For example, Michoacán officials' decision to have a nominally politically neutral civilian select Parícutin eruption zone braceros backfired. In April, a group of Uruapan labor leaders set aside their grievances with Governor Mendoza Pardo and wrote to him to complain about how Hinojosa Torres was choosing braceros. The complainants noted that Hinojosa Torres had given eligibility cards to his "protectors" among Uruapan's merchant class and to others who were not from that region. The group also reported that Hinojosa Torres had flagrantly lied to them by claiming that he was merely following the state government's instructions. The labor leaders then betrayed their own self-interest when they asked the governor to immediately intervene in the selection process but on behalf of members of the unions they represented, not the Parícutin damnificados who were supposed to have received eligibility cards in the first place.[54] There is no record that the state government took any action on the matter.

While Hinojosa Torres was favoring his commercial contacts, the selection drawing in Zamora descended into violent chaos. As noted earlier, federal deputy Enrique Bravo Valencia delegated the responsibility of choosing braceros to Zamora's municipal government. But the municipal president, Francisco Cristóbal Ruiz, had no interest in using the Bracero Program as a response to the aftosa outbreak, which is the reason that Michoacán officials had allocated eligibility cards to Zamora. The bracero selection drawing was held in April in Zamora's main plaza, and Ruiz and three men who accompanied him exchanged eligibility cards for bribes in full view of the assembled crowd, without ascertaining if those who paid bribes had been affected by the aftosa outbreak. State deputy José Garibay Romero and former Zamora municipal president Vicente Chávez, who were there monitoring the proceedings alongside members of a campesino union who were interested in acquiring eligibility cards, confronted Ruiz and objected to his flagrant corruption. But Ruiz and the men who were with him physically assaulted Chávez, drew firearms, and threatened to shoot if the state legislator and the former municipal president persisted in their objections. The selection drawing immediately descended into pandemonium, and state deputy Torres Espinosa, who was also on hand, took advantage of the confusion and stole sixty eligibility cards. By the time authorities tracked down Torres Espinosa in Morelia, the state legislator, who had been accused of trafficking bracero cards in the past, had already sold the cards he had stolen.[55]

In Jalisco's sugar-growing communities, the special allotment granted to the STIASRM deepened the intraunion divide when Avalos Osorio and his partisans in the locals that received eligibility cards gained control of the selection process. In late May, Francisco González, Avalos Osorio's rival within the union, and the leaders of eight STIASRM locals that had not received bracero cards traveled to Mexico City. The group wanted to meet personally with President Alemán so that they could explain that they had been cheated. The complainants were certain that the STIASRM's national leadership had conspired with Avalos Osorio to deprive them of the opportunity to migrate, and they wanted federal authorities to intervene in the matter.[56] But unlike 1946, when the deteriorating relationship between President Ávila Camacho and Governor García Barragán influenced the former's decision to personally favor Jalisco STIASRM members with bracero contracts, President Alemán had no motive or desire to intervene. As a result, the Alemán administration remained on the sidelines in 1947.

Although local-level irregularities disrupted their designs in 1947, Guanajuato, Jalisco, and Michoacán officials still reaped several political benefits from the bracero eligibility card distribution patterns they crafted that year. First, incidents of violence were confined to locales like Zamora and Salvatierra, Guanajuato—where municipal authorities detained aspiring braceros in the municipal government's offices in order to extort bribes from them—not the sites of the contracting centers.[57] Second, while complaints were sent directly to the center-western governors, the ire and frustration in these letters were primarily aimed at the local officials who had selected braceros. And third, the governors could still claim a rhetorical moral high ground and argue that rogue local authorities had undermined their selfless attempts to assist those affected by natural disasters or labor disputes. This is essentially what Guanajuato's Nicéforo Guerrero did in a September address to the state legislature when he lamented that some municipal officials had behaved "clumsily or in bad faith" and defrauded aspiring braceros.[58]

GROWING RELIANCE ON MUNICIPAL GOVERNMENTS

In the years immediately following 1947, sending-state officials shifted to relying more heavily on their municipal counterparts during bracero selection periods, which resulted in some aspiring braceros losing the favor they had enjoyed during previous years. Jalisco's government summarily ended the STIASRM's special allocation in May 1948 when it distributed an allotment of 4,000 eligibility cards exclusively among the state's municipal governments. (A small plurality of these cards, at least 22 percent, went to northeastern Jalisco municipalities.)[59] The state government's decision caught STIASRM leaders, who had requested 3,000 eligibility cards in April, and their federal legislative allies by surprise, and they soon sought redress. After no members of Local 47, which represented workers in Tecalitlán's La Purísima Mill, were chosen in a selection drawing that was held in May, Local 47 secretary general Roberto Ramírez wrote to Governor Jesús González Gallo to complain about the new status quo. But Ramírez made sure to note in his letter that his dissatisfaction would be placated if Tecalitlán's municipal government included Local 47 members in future selection drawings.[60] There is no record of how the governor responded to Ramírez's complaint, but Tecalitlán's municipal president defended his actions by claiming that he had only excluded STIASRM members from the selection drawing because he assumed that they would once again be given a "special place" in Jalisco's bracero contingent.[61] Four months later, federal deputy Vidal Díaz Muñoz blasted González Gallo's "disgraceful" behavior in a message he sent to President Alemán, and he then asked the president to supersede the governor and order the federal Interior Secretariat to grant contracts to 1,500 unemployed Jalisco sugar mill workers.[62] But just as it did in 1947 when Francisco González and his partisans requested federal intervention after they failed to receive bracero cards, the Alemán administration opted not to intercede.

The sudden termination of the STIASRM's allotment of bracero cards reflected the broader conservative shift in official labor policy that occurred during the late 1940s. As Jaime Sánchez Susarrey and Ignacio Medina Sánchez have detailed in their study of mid-twentieth-century Jalisco state politics, Governor González Gallo's priority with regard to organized labor was to foster a spirit of "cordial collaboration" between workers, employers, and the state government that would minimize strife.[63] Since the STIASRM allotment had exacerbated rather than alleviated intraunion conflicts in

1947, the state government likely determined that continuing the allocation could further destabilize the state's sugar mills. The end of the special allotment also helped the González Gallo administration align itself with its federal counterpart. It was in 1948 that Alemán's presidential administration started moving against national-level leftist union leaders and replacing them with *charros,* conservative labor leaders who shared the president's anticommunism and view on limiting strike activity. The ascension of the charros ushered in a period of depressed labor militancy when Priísta officials punished activism and generally treated unions as little more than vote-delivering vehicles.[64] Excluding STIASRM members from the Bracero Program would have signaled to federal officials that Jalisco's government was taking steps to assert greater control over regional labor organizations and ensure that union members would be in Mexico during electoral cycles, which remained relatively competitive, at least at the local level, during the late 1940s.[65]

At the same time in Aguascalientes, Governor Jesús Rodríguez's administration stopped allowing ejidatarios to migrate as braceros after reaching the limits of the federal government's patience. In April 1948, federal Interior Secretariat official, Horacio Terán, informed Rodríguez that two thousand bracero contracts had been allotted to Aguascalientes. Terán pointedly reminded the governor in the same message that ejidatarios were ineligible to receive contracts, thus implying that the state government had continued to flout federal directives in the years since 1945, and he told Rodríguez that he should work with municipal officials during the upcoming selection period.[66] Aguascalientes officials heeded Terán's recommendations, and they instructed the state's municipal presidents to begin compiling lists of aspiring braceros in early May.[67] The state government ultimately distributed 2,086 eligibility cards, though the available evidence does not indicate if this was the result of an administrative error or the federal government increasing Aguascalientes's bracero contingent. The Rodríguez administration allotted 65 percent of these cards to the southwestern municipalities that fall within the Greater Bajío.[68]

The braceros who left Aguascalientes in 1948 presented their eligibility cards at a contracting center that opened in Aguascalientes City in early May.[69] And events that transpired at that contracting center ultimately demonstrated to Aguascalientes officials how quickly the contract distribution sites could become political and social powder kegs. The root cause of the problems that affected the Aguascalientes City Contracting Center in 1948 was a federal policy that declared residents of the Distrito Federal (which included Mexico City) eligible to receive bracero contracts, so long as they were unemployed, could demonstrate that they had no job opportunities in Mexico, and prove at a contracting center that they were capable of performing agricultural work; left implied in these guidelines was that aspiring Distrito Federal braceros would only be considered after their counterparts from other jurisdictions had been vetted.[70] Would-be braceros from the Distrito Federal rushed to Aguascalientes City once the contracting center there opened, hoping that they would be able to acquire contracts. But when their efforts failed, they organized public demonstrations to voice their displeasure and threatened to hunger strike, which prompted Governor Rodríguez to contact the federal Interior Secretariat and request military intervention to "resolve this conflict."[71] Interior officials responded to the governor and assured him that they had instructed the federal personnel assigned to the contracting center to take steps "to avoid the disruption of public order."[72] However, whatever steps if any the contracting center personnel took proved ineffective, as state officials informed their federal counterparts in late May that aspiring braceros from the Distrito Federal had started their hunger strike.[73] Unfortunately, the available documentary evidence does not reveal how long the hunger strike lasted or how it was resolved. But it served as a reminder of how quickly conditions at the contracting centers could deteriorate. And that Aguascalientes's governor would request military intervention to end the aspiring braceros' demonstrations shows that sending-state officials prioritized maintaining social order at the contracting sites.

Four years after the hunger strike, Guanajuato officials took advantage of the Irapuato Contracting Center's continued operation to further reduce their administrative burden during bracero selection periods. Perhaps because they reasoned that Irapuato municipal president Florentino Oliva's physical proximity to the contracting center made him an ideal candidate to coordinate the selection process, Guanajuato authorities made Oliva one of the state's lead Bracero Program administrators in 1952. State officials still determined how many braceros would be selected in each municipality—and the vast majority of the eligibility cards, as many as 89 percent during the April 1952 selection period, were still sent to southern municipalities—during the random drawings.[74] But it fell to Oliva to relay that information to his fellow municipal presidents, inform them of the dates selected campesinos needed to be in Irapuato, and then ensure that aspiring braceros received their contracts.[75] This system remained in place through the end of 1955, the final year that Irapuato was the site of a contracting center.[76]

While Guanajuato's government was elevating municipal officials to key administrative positions, Jalisco's maintained the course it first charted in 1948. González Gallo's administration once again sent bracero eligibility cards only to its municipal counterparts in 1952.[77] And in stark contrast to four years earlier, when the STIASRM and its allies protested the end of that union's special allocation, the union did not express any frustration at being shut out of the Bracero Program. In fact, popular interest in migrating had become virtually nonexistent in Jalisco's sugar-growing communities by 1952. STIASRM members made only one documented written bracero contract request that year, and that request is the last available one that members of that union sent to state officials during the Bracero Program.[78] Absent any calls to favor specific groups of aspiring braceros, Jalisco's government simply opted to maintain the status quo.

But why did popular demand for bracero contracts in Jalisco's sugar-growing communities, where organized mill workers had been lobbying for contracts since the Bracero Program's initial phase, decline so precipitously during the early 1950s? One possibility is that STIASRM members had resigned themselves to the reality that Jalisco's government would no longer favor them during bracero selection periods. Michael Snodgrass has offered another explanation in his examination of mid-twentieth-century union politics: namely, that STIASRM leader José María "Chema" Martínez secured significant eligibility card allocations, presumably through his official connections, for southern Jalisco sugar-growing municipalities like Tamazula.[79] Southern Jalisco STIASRM members may not have felt it was necessary to make individual contract requests if Martínez was indeed working on their behalf behind the scenes, although, because full eligibility card distribution patterns from the 1950s and 1960s are not available, it is difficult to ascertain how successful the union leader's efforts may have been.[80] And while southern Jalisco STIASRM members could apparently count on an advocate like Martínez, those who worked in the mills west of Guadalajara lost many of theirs during a bloody intraunion dispute at the turn of the 1950s. Avalos Osorio, the prominent member of Local 2 in Ameca who had gained control of the 1947 STIASRM bracero card allotment, was murdered on April 3, 1950.[81] The STIASRM's national leadership hired two Mexico City–based investigators, who concluded that Félix Ponce, another union leader who had fallen out with Avalos Osorio two years earlier, and his allies ordered the murder to prevent Avalos Osorio from being elected Local 2's secretary general. Ponce and his collaborators, including Dionisio Ahumada, were all detained by local authorities two weeks after the murder.[82] Avalos Osorio's and Ponce's roles in previous bracero selection periods were detailed earlier. But Ahumada had also lobbied on behalf of STIASRM members who aspired to be braceros during the 1940s.[83] The sudden absence of union leaders who had encouraged and facilitated the migration of STIASRM members likely also contributed to the depressed bracero contract demand levels in Jalisco's sugar-growing communities during the 1950s.

THE FINAL YEARS

The evidence from Aguascalientes and Michoacán, the states with the most available records from the Bracero Program's final decade, indicate that the program's state-level administration was relatively stable from the mid-1950s through the end of the guest worker initiative in 1964. Officials in both states continued to allocate eligibility cards among municipal governments and instruct their local counterparts to select individual braceros.[84] Michoacán authorities fully embraced this system in part because they calculated that local officials were better positioned to determine who would benefit most from migrating. In 1959 the state government instructed its municipal counterparts to favor the "most needy" (*más necesitados*) aspiring braceros in their jurisdictions when compiling the lists of names that would be included in the selection drawings.[85] And four years later, Michoacán officials decreed that four ground-level agents who were presumably knowledgeable about local agrarian conditions and employment levels—the *ayuntamiento* (municipal council) chair, a campesino representative, the state tax collector assigned to that area, and an "honorable resident" of the municipal seat—had to draft the lists of aspiring braceros in each municipality; municipal presidents would still organize and host the selection drawings proper.[86]

Aguascalientes's government briefly deviated from this course in fall 1959 when it explicitly allowed ejidatarios to receive bracero eligibility cards. This return to a practice from the mid-1940s was the result of pressure from the state's chapter of the Liga de Comunidades Agrarias. In July 1959 Aguascalientes Liga secretary general Alberto Alcalá de Lira denounced municipal officials who were selecting braceros who lived in other states and excluding from the selection drawings ejidatarios who no longer had access to lands in their respective ejidos. Alcalá de Lira then urged Aguascalientes interior secretary Carlos Salas Calvillo to either allocate half the state's eligibility cards to ejidatarios or mandate that a campesino representative had to be physically present at the selection drawings to ensure that they were conducted equitably.[87] Until that point in 1959, state authorities had simply informed municipal officials how many aspiring braceros they needed to choose.[88] But beginning in September, state officials told their municipal counterparts that half their eligibility card allocations would be fulfilled by aspiring braceros selected by Liga personnel.[89] However, the Liga's revived participation in Aguascalientes's bracero selection process was short lived. When the 1960 selection cycle began in February, state-level instructions no longer included any mention of a special allocation for Liga-selected braceros, and those directives remained unaltered through the entirety of that year.[90]

Because they did not want presumably landless and unemployed aspiring braceros returning empty-handed from the contracting centers and causing unrest like would-be braceros from the Distrito Federal had done in 1948, Aguascalientes officials also began sending representatives to monitor the centers during the late 1950s and early 1960s.[91] These representatives' primary responsibility was to inform state authorities about delays that prevented Aguascalientes braceros from successfully exchanging their eligibility cards for contracts. For example, Amador Guerrero, the representative assigned to the Monterrey Contracting Center in 1960, told the state government on August 11 that the contract distribution process unexpectedly halted while three hundred Aguascalientes braceros were still waiting for their contracts.[92] That same day, Governor Luis Ortega Douglas contacted the federal Interior Secretariat and urged it to resume distributing contracts so that these would-be braceros whose "situations were truly sad and desperate" would be able to leave as soon as possible.[93] Whether or not this pressure influenced their federal counterparts, Aguascalientes officials could claim that they were actively working on behalf of constituents who were interested in migrating and simultaneously minimize the possibility that aspiring braceros who had been denied the opportunity to work in the United States would target the state government with recriminations. But this apparent selflessness came at a cost for aspiring braceros: each selected bracero had to pay between 1.20 and 5 pesos to subsidize the representative.[94]

Another trend that continued into the later phase of the Bracero Program was state governments allocating the bulk of the eligibility cards to Greater Bajío municipalities. For the period 1958–60, I was able to document how Aguascalientes officials distributed 11,109 bracero cards; 60 percent went to the southwestern municipalities that form part of the Greater Bajío.[95] In

Michoacán, I was able to document how state authorities allocated 16,128 eligibility cards during the period 1959–64; 70 percent went to the northern municipalities that fall within the Greater Bajío.[96]

At first glance, the eligibility card distribution patterns from the late 1950s and early 1960s suggest that Michoacán officials tied the bracero card allocations to popular demand levels, since at least 70 percent of the available written contract requests that Michoacán aspiring braceros sent to federal and state authorities from 1959 through 1964 were from Greater Bajío communities.[97] However, Michoacán's government undercut the Sierra Purépecha, a region that both federal and state authorities had favored with bracero card allocations during the 1940s because of the Parícutin volcanic eruption, which ceased in 1952.[98] At least 12 percent of the available written contract requests from 1959 through 1964 were sent from Sierra Purépecha communities, but state authorities only sent 9 percent of the aforementioned 16,128 eligibility cards to Sierra Purépecha municipalities.[99]

Why did Michoacán's government reduce the Sierra Purépecha's bracero card allotment to below popular demand levels during the later years of the Bracero Program? It is possible that state officials reasoned that the need to migrate from the Sierra Purépecha was not as pressing as it was in the Greater Bajío, especially as the Parícutin eruption had finally ended. Although the eruption had ceased, the motives aspiring braceros from the Sierra cited in their requests during the Bracero Program's final years were similar to those mentioned by their Greater Bajío counterparts, and they proved willing to bend the rules to acquire eligibility cards. For example, a group of seasonally unemployed campesinos from Los Limones, in the municipality of Los Reyes, requested contracts twice in spring 1962 because they simultaneously feared that the "specter of hunger" would soon visit their homes and wanted to contribute financially to the construction of a new schoolhouse.[100] And in February 1962 and April 1963, aspiring braceros from Nurío, in the municipality of Paracho, asked for contracts because a communal boundary dispute with San Felipe de los Herreros and San Bartolomé Cocucho, two communities in the neighboring municipality of Charapan, had prevented them from working their lands.[101] Furthermore, Rubén Ochoa Zambrano, a landless prospective bracero from Los Reyes who wrote to the state government in June 1962, reported that individuals from that region were acquiring eligibility cards in other states, presumably after paying bribes.[102]

It was political considerations that prompted Michoacán officials to temper the number of eligibility cards they allotted to Sierra Purépecha municipalities and overlook the reports of aspiring braceros from those jurisdictions traveling to other states to acquire cards. First, the departure of Sierra Purépecha braceros posed a threat to other regional development initiatives. As Boyer has detailed in his study of twentieth-century forestry policies and practices, federal officials exempted Sierra Purépecha campesinos who had been affected by the Parícutin eruption from logging bans and then encouraged them to sell their lumber to local sawmills, as well as tree resin to turpentine distilleries. Officials hoped that this policy would spur the post–Parícutin eruption economic recovery, integrate Sierra Purépecha campesinos into broader regional and national markets, and foster forestry management practices that would preserve woodlands for sustained use and exploitation.[103] Thus it made sense for state authorities to limit bracero migration from the Sierra so that local rural workers could stay in their home communities and harvest raw materials for the timber industry.

Second, facilitating the departure of Sierra Purépecha braceros would have interfered with official efforts to resolve intercommunity boundary disputes in that region. Unlike the conflicts in the Greater Bajío that I examine in chapter 3—which dated to the 1920s and involved internal community factions that either supported or opposed revolutionary policies like land redistribution, secular public education, and official anticlericalism—clashes in the Sierra often dated to the colonial period, and they involved landowning Indigenous communities that were competing for access to or control of agricultural and forest lands.[104] In a September 1955 open meeting held in Uruapan, the Tepalcatepec River Commission's administrators identified "centuries-long" conflicts between Indigenous communities as one of the principal obstacles to the region's economic progress. To resolve those conflicts, the commission enlisted individuals like Felipe Chávez, a Purépecha-speaking lawyer who hailed from Parícutin and attended the Uruapan meeting, to travel to Sierra communities as dispute mediators. Chávez began his work in November 1955, and he set about informing Sierra rural workers about the agrarian statutes that applied to communal holdings, examining legal documents generated by the conflicts, and attempting to foster goodwill between feuding communities by promoting commercial relations. The lawyer admitted in a September 1956 report that he sent to Governor David Franco Rodríguez that there were still many disputes left to resolve. But he noted happily that he had helped negotiate accords in the municipality of Chilchota—one between Carapan and Urén and another between Carapan and Ichán—and that Nurío, San Felipe de los Herreros, and San Bartolomé

Cocucho were actively negotiating an end of hostilities.[105] Even though, as touched on previously, Chávez's efforts in the latter conflict ultimately proved unsuccessful, state officials were likely wary of upsetting the commission's campaign with significant bracero card allocations. Michoacán authorities knew that the bracero selection process could exacerbate local-level political tensions, especially if competing groups were interested in acquiring eligibility cards. And since intercommunity clashes in the Sierra Purépecha were deemed a threat to a regional development project, Michoacán's government had a vested interest in reducing the number of possible motives for clashes.

Third and last, the state government, particularly during Franco Rodríguez's administration (1956–62), may have wanted to punish aspiring braceros whose loyalty to state officials was suspect. For example, Luis González Nava made three contract requests on behalf of aspiring braceros from San Lorenzo, an Indigenous community in the municipality of Uruapan, in 1959 and 1960. (These three requests represent half of the available ones sent from that municipality between 1959 and 1964.) González Nava explained in these requests that he and his fellow prospective braceros were landless and unemployed rural workers who could not provide "even the most indispensable things for our families."[106]

González Nava and the others from San Lorenzo were likely landless because they had backed the wrong political horse in the lead-up to Michoacán's 1956 gubernatorial election. In April 1955, González Nava alleged in messages sent to President Ruiz Cortines and former president Cárdenas—who was still active in Michoacán state politics as chair of the Tepalcatepec River Commission—that Santiago Vargas Reyes, a San Lorenzo community leader, was corruptly administering the communal treasury and allowing outsiders to tap tree resin in community-owned woodlands.[107] But one month later, the secretary general of the officially sanctioned Regional Campesino Committee counteralleged that González Nava and his partisans were members of the conservative Catholic opposition Partido Acción Nacional and that González Nava had no standing to make his accusations because he was a native of the municipality of Paracho.[108] San Lorenzo residents seconded these accusations, but they also claimed that González Nava was collaborating with Victoriano Anguiano, a federal judge and native of the Sierra Purépecha who was attempting to build an independent electoral base that would allow him to compete in state-level elections, like the gubernatorial election that was scheduled for 1956; the residents were certain that

González Nava's ultimate goal was to gain political control of the community so that he could then deliver its votes to Anguiano.[109] However, González Nava's attempt to formally unseat Vargas Reyes failed after he lost a federally supervised community plebiscite in September 1955, and Anguiano's electoral ambitions ended when the state PRI united behind Franco Rodríguez's gubernatorial candidacy.[110]

Whether or not the Franco Rodríguez administration was aware that González Nava had made his requests in 1959 and 1960—federal authorities did forward contract requests to their state counterparts, but there is no record that they forwarded González Nava's—state officials likely knew that Sierra Purépecha aspiring braceros who cited landlessness in their contract requests may have once been among Victoriano Anguiano's supporters.[111] Thus limiting the number of bracero cards allotted to Sierra municipalities afforded the state government a means of exacting a small measure of retribution for the transgression of backing Anguiano's electoral ambitions. State officials could not absolutely ensure that aspiring braceros like Luis González Nava would be denied the opportunity to migrate as municipal authorities were still the ones who chose individual braceros. But Michoacán officials could at least lessen the likelihood that those with suspect loyalties could achieve their goal of migrating as braceros. And since González Nava made multiple contract requests, it appears that the state government's effort was at least partially successful.

. . .

During the 1954 bracero selection cycle, a Zacatecas Interior Secretariat official, Salvador Ibarra, traveled through rural communities in Villanueva, a municipality in the southern region of the state. In El Vergel, Ibarra met with Eduardo de Santiago, who had recently assumed a leadership position within that community after moving there from Jomulquillo, a rural community in the neighboring municipality of Jerez. After they became reacquainted—de Santiago recalled in interviews from 2003 and 2005 that he and Ibarra attended primary school together in Jerez—Ibarra asked de Santiago to give him a list of campesinos from El Vergel who wanted to migrate as braceros. When de Santiago replied that he did not have such a list ready, Ibarra gave him time to choose those rural workers who stood to benefit from participating in the Bracero Program. Ultimately, de Santiago gave Ibarra a list of twenty names, including his own, and all those named in the list were then instructed to travel to the Chihuahua City Contracting Center.[112]

The remaining available evidence does not cast any light on why Ibarra visited rural communities in 1954 and personally asked for and received lists of aspiring braceros. Perhaps federal officials unexpectedly allotted additional contracts to the state of Zacatecas and asked that aspiring braceros from there report to the contracting centers as soon as possible, thus prompting quick and immediate action from the state government. Or Ibarra may have intervened personally in Villanueva because of his personal ties to that region of the state. Or he may have been trying to bypass a municipal government that had ignored previous selection instructions. Whatever Ibarra's motives, his behavior indicates that he had no interest whatsoever in actually selecting individual braceros. Ibarra merely relayed instructions to his childhood classmate and then accepted and approved the list that was given to him. He did not try to influence the drafting of the list by suggesting or removing names, nor did he tell de Santiago that he expected a favor in exchange for sanctioning the departure of braceros from El Vergel.

Ibarra's disinterest in choosing individual braceros was emblematic of the deliberately cautious approach that authorities in the principal bracero-sending states of Aguascalientes, Guanajuato, Jalisco, Michoacán, and Zacatecas adopted during bracero selection periods. When state governments who had never asked for that responsibility were entrusted with the task of choosing individual braceros in the mid-1940s, they immediately delegated that duty to local officials with close ties to bracero-sending communities, such as municipal presidents, union local leaders, and state legislators. This decision shifted the administrative burden of selecting braceros and shielded state authorities from Bracero Program–related political fallout. But state officials were not merely passive bystanders during bracero selection periods. Although ground-level authorities chose migrant workers, state-level personnel allocated the eligibility cards within their jurisdictions. While state authorities often based bracero card allocation patterns on popular demand levels or data that their municipal counterparts compiled, political factors similar to the ones that federal administrations considered when they crafted eligibility guidelines and restrictions—such as the need to respond to natural disasters, the status of other rural development initiatives, organized labor disputes, the lobbying efforts of campesino organizations, and the political loyalties of aspiring braceros—also influenced decisions regarding which communities would have the opportunity to send braceros north or which local officials would be choosing migrant workers.

However, while bracero eligibility card distribution patterns could be malleable, sending-state governments consistently allocated a significant number of cards to municipalities in the Greater Bajío. Although eligibility card distribution patterns from Zacatecas are not readily available, officials in the other states regularly allotted a plurality or a clear majority of their bracero cards to Greater Bajío jurisdictions. As discussed previously, these allocations partly reflected municipal reports that highlighted Greater Bajío communities as the ones with the most available aspiring braceros. And popular demand corroborated official conclusions: 64 percent of the available written contract requests that aspiring braceros from Aguascalientes, Guanajuato, Michoacán, Jalisco, and Zacatecas made during the entirety of the Bracero Program were sent from Greater Bajío communities. The national-, regional-, and local-level political factors that contributed to these elevated demand levels are the focus of the next two chapters.

THREE

"Long-Standing Political and Religious Differences"

POLITICAL-RELIGIOUS CONFLICTS AND BRACERO MIGRATION IN THE GREATER BAJÍO

ON THE MORNING OF MARCH 6, 1930, Guanajuato governor Agustín Arroyo Ch., General Juan Domínguez, and Director of Education Eduardo Zarza arrived in Cupareo, a rural community in the southern municipality of Salvatierra, to preside over the inauguration of a new primary school. More than five thousand campesinos attended the ceremony, which culminated with a banquet and a speech delivered by the governor.[1] One year later, the inspector for the federal Secretaría de Educación Pública (SEP; Public Education Secretariat), José Macías Padilla, visited Cupareo and reported that the community's residents greeted him warmly and were "enamored" with the school.[2] But by 1933, the condition of the school and local attitudes toward it had changed dramatically. When a different SEP inspector, Roberto Oropeza Nájera, traveled to Cupareo in February, he discovered that "long-standing political and religious differences" had produced a "deep division" between two factions fighting for control of the community. The conflict had hindered the day-to-day operations of the school, which had started falling into disrepair due to lack of regular maintenance. After unsuccessfully attempting to mediate a resolution between the parties, the SEP official instructed the teacher assigned to Cupareo to maintain neutrality and work with both factions, and he urged parents to continue to send their children to class and organize a campaign to make the necessary repairs to the schoolhouse.[3] There is no record of Cupareo's residents taking any concrete steps to make the needed repairs until February 1956, however, when a group that gathered at the schoolhouse decided that it would be better to replace it with a new one and drafted a letter to President Ruiz Cortines asking him to send an allotment of bracero cards to that community. If their request was approved, each bracero who left

Cupareo pledged to contribute 150 pesos toward the construction of the new schoolhouse.[4]

This chapter explores how "long-standing political and religious differences," like the ones that divided Cupareo, influenced demand for bracero contracts in the Greater Bajío. Before it became the epicenter of popular demand for bracero contracts, the Greater Bajío was the epicenter of conservative Catholic opposition to the revolutionary state. In the 1920s and 1930s, devout Greater Bajío parishioners protested anticlerical measures that reduced the number of active priests in their communities; rejected an agrarian reform process that granted beneficiaries usufruct rights to—but not individual ownership of—expropriated lands on the grounds that this was a violation of the sanctity of private property; and denounced a socialist public education curriculum that aimed to cultivate socioeconomic class consciousness among students and included units on family planning as an ideological assault that would lead to the moral corruption of their children.[5] Conservative Catholic partisans known as Cristeros mobilized twice against the federal government: first during the Cristero War, a sustained conflict that began in 1926 and ended with a ceasefire agreement in 1929 and that, as Julia Young has shown, contributed to US-bound migration from Greater Bajío states; and then again during La Segunda (the Second War), a series of more sporadic guerrilla uprisings that began in the early 1930s and spiked during the first half of Lázaro Cárdenas's presidency (1934–40).[6] Although the Cristeros were active throughout Mexico, their actions were concentrated in Aguascalientes, Guanajuato, Jalisco, Michoacán, and Zacatecas: 63 percent of the fifty thousand Cristeros who were active in 1929 were from these states, and Greater Bajío municipalities such as Pénjamo (Guanajuato), Tepatitlán (Jalisco), Zamora (Michoacán), Valparaíso (Zacatecas), and Calvillo (Aguascalientes) were Cristero strongholds during both conflicts.[7] Many former Cristeros then joined two conservative Catholic opposition organizations that were established in the Greater Bajío during the late 1930s: the UNS, which was established in León, Guanajuato, in 1937 and eschewed electoral politics in favor of direct action until the mid-1940s; and the PAN, which was established in Morelia, Michoacán, in 1939 and immediately committed itself to gaining power through the electoral arena. The UNS had 307,365 active members by 1943, the first full year of the Bracero Program, and 64 percent were from Aguascalientes, Guanajuato, Jalisco, Michoacán, and Zacatecas. And PAN and UNS-supported candidates launched competitive and successful local electoral campaigns during the mid-1940s.[8]

The growth of the UNS and the PAN in the Greater Bajío states coincided with the subsiding of national-level religious-political tensions. Manuel Ávila Camacho declared himself "a believer" and repealed the socialist public education curriculum during his presidency (1940–46), while the PRI's post-1940 embrace of anticommunism led to a reconciliation between senior ruling party and ecclesiastical leaders.[9] Greater Bajío UNS and PAN members did not mobilize in great numbers during the "last Cristiada," a failed 1962 attempt to incite a conservative Catholic uprising against the federal government that, as Benjamin Smith noted, enjoyed its most significant popular support in Oaxaca's Mixteca Baja.[10] But the reconciliation of high-ranking political and religious leaders and the lack of support for an anti-national government rebellion did not mean that the Greater Bajío was free of political violence that involved conservative Catholic partisans during the years of the Bracero Program. Priísta officials may have been on better terms with senior church leaders, but they opposed the UNS and the PAN and cracked down on the two organizations, with the most notable incident being a January 1946 state government–sanctioned attack that resulted in the death of twenty-six individuals who were protesting against Guanajuato governor Ernesto Hidalgo after he had refused to recognize the UNS-supported candidate's victory in León's municipal elections.[11] Greater Bajío Sinarquistas also clashed with the federal personnel who were enforcing the anti-aftosa outbreak measures (see chap. 2), and a June 1947 confrontation in Senguío, Michoacán, ended with the death of one veterinarian, one official, and six soldiers.[12]

Most significantly, community-level conflicts that began during the Cristero War and pitted conservative Catholic partisans against those who supported government initiatives like the agrarian reform continued into the years of the Bracero Program. And it was conflict-related landlessness and unemployment that prompted numerous Greater Bajío campesinos to seek out socioeconomic relief through the Bracero Program. As I discuss later, the specific contours of each conflict varied from community to community. In some, such as Santa Elena, Jalisco, conservative Catholic partisans who enjoyed the support of sympathetic local officials went on the offensive and successfully pushed their rivals off their lands. In others, like Presa del Aguacate, Guanajuato, it was the supporters of land redistribution who reinitiated hostilities and put the competing faction on the defensive. And in Changuitiro, Michoacán, a violent stalemate developed after residents who had refused redistributed lands on religious grounds attempted to gain control of the community. In these and other cases that this chapter explores, it was members of the losing faction that most often sent written bracero contract requests to federal and state officials.

THE GREATER BAJÍO'S CONSERVATIVE CATHOLIC ROOTS

Why did the Greater Bajío emerge as a bastion of conservative Catholic opposition to revolutionary policies during the 1920s and 1930s, which in turn set the stage for the community-level conflicts of the 1940s, 1950s, and 1960s? Two factors contributed to the conservative Catholic opposition's strength in the region. The first was the Catholic Church's deeply rooted institutional presence in the Greater Bajío. Parishes, convents, and missionary colleges established during the colonial era influenced the development of a largely Hispanized and patriarchal regional culture, and Catholicism became so entwined with daily life that, as John Tutino has stated, it "centered discussions of production and state powers, ethnic roles and rights, and patriarchal relations" and became "the primary language of morality in the Bajío before 1810."[13] During the nineteenth century, as Margaret Chowning, Brian Stauffer, and others have effectively argued, new lay associations like the Vela Perpetua, popular mobilizations against Liberal anticlericalism, and the work of "intransigent" bishops and priests who established new parishes and denounced Marxist-inspired ideologies as threats to Hispanic Catholic identity reinforced the church's social and cultural standing in the Greater Bajío.[14] By 1900, the Greater Bajío states all ranked in the top third nationally in terms of Catholic priests per capita, and some parish priests enjoyed as much social prestige in their communities as elected local leaders during the revolutionary period.[15] Thus devout Greater Bajío parishioners reacted with hostility when regional and national leaders who viewed the Catholic Church as a cultivator of popular "fanaticism" that threatened to impede the revolutionary agenda enacted measures that restricted the number of priests that could minister in individual states and established a federal-level clerical registry.[16]

The second factor was Social Catholicism, which emerged during the late nineteenth and early twentieth centuries. This doctrine acknowledged that capitalist production had contributed to income inequality and the abuse of workers. But it rejected the Marxist argument that socioeconomic class conflict was necessary to establish more egalitarian societies. Instead, Social Catholicism argued that socioeconomic class cooperation and the respect of private property rights would improve the lives of workers and lead to more harmonious and just societies. The spread of Social Catholicism contributed to the establishment of Catholic labor unions and lay associations that focused on charitable giving during the late Porfiriato and the early revolutionary period.[17] And the doctrine's emphasis on preserving private property rights resonated in a region where commercially oriented, privately owned agricultural estates—most notably, small to midsize ranchos, which as late as 1930 outnumbered large-scale haciendas by a ratio of 629 to 2 in Greater Bajío municipalities like Tepatitlán—had been the most common form of land tenure since the colonial period.[18] Thus, as Matthew Butler, Jennie Purnell, and others have noted, many in the Greater Bajío interpreted the revolutionary agrarian reform—which called for the federal government to distribute use rights to expropriated lands that it retained ultimate ownership of—as a threat to their material interests as landowners, estate administrators, tenant farmers, sharecroppers, and resident estate laborers, as well as their spiritual interests as devout Catholics who believed that private property was the foundation of a divinely ordained status quo.[19] This combination of spiritual and material anxieties also prompted conservative Catholic partisans to reject a socialist public education curriculum that aimed to "defanaticize" students, portrayed rural Mexicans as members of an oppressed socioeconomic class, championed land redistribution, and promoted family planning.[20]

Opposition to official anticlericalism, land redistribution, and secular public education put Greater Bajío conservative Catholics in direct conflict with "village revolutionaries," to use Boyer's term, such as schoolteachers and *agraristas*, rural workers who supported the agrarian reform. As Boyer, Paul Friedrich, and others have shown, agraristas engaged with revolutionary ideology and, to varying degrees, began thinking of themselves as members of a distinct socioeconomic class of campesinos who would benefit materially from the implementation of revolutionary policies, particularly land redistribution.[21] In the early 1920s, Greater Bajío governors like Michoacán's Francisco Múgica (1920–22) provided firearms to community-level agrarista militias and encouraged them to invade privately owned estates.[22] Federal authorities then called on these militias to serve as auxiliaries who could effectively combat Cristero units that adopted guerrilla tactics. And though many agraristas were themselves practicing Catholics, they answered the call because their faith was not the defining factor of their political, social, and cultural identities and because they came to see the Cristeros as direct threats to their interests. As scholars of the Cristero War have shown, the bloody clashes between agraristas and Cristeros divided families and communities, and they fueled political polarization, as both sides accused the other of "fanaticism" while claiming to be the true representatives of campesino interests.[23]

INTRACOMMUNITY CONFLICTS IN NORTHERN MICHOACÁN

Intracommunity political conflicts whose roots can be traced to the 1920s had a lasting impact that influenced individual decisions to migrate as braceros. Clashes between agraristas and conservative Catholic partisans first flared up in the northern Michoacán municipality of Puruándiro during the early 1920s, when Governor Múgica began actively promoting the creation of ejidos in that state and arming community-level agrarista militias. The municipality then fell under the sway of the Zacapu-based Cristero leader Ramón Aguilar during the Cristero War.[24] Unfortunately, the available documentary evidence does not cast much light on what transpired in the municipality during the 1930s. But the evidence does show that intracommunity clashes between Puruándiro's conservative Catholic partisans and supporters of the agrarian reform resumed in 1944 when individuals who were members of or sympathetic to the UNS gained control of the municipal government. In early January, the leadership council of Galeana's ejido accused members of the local administration of aiding and abetting individuals who were antagonizing the ejidatarios there.[25] Two months later, José Medrano of Villalongín informed Governor Félix Ireta that an unspecified number of ejidatarios had been murdered in that community and that he and other agrarian reform beneficiaries had sought refuge in Mezquite Gordo after being forcibly driven off of their parcels.[26] By May, the conflict in Rodeo de San Antonio had become so intense that Michoacán's interior secretary, Luis Marín Pérez, asked the commanding officer of the 21st Military Zone to send soldiers there so they could disarm the parties that were attacking the ejidatarios.[27] Tensions were ratcheted higher in November when prominent local Sinarquistas were chosen to fill two vacant ayuntamiento seats on a provisional basis, an act that drew immediate condemnation from the leaders of one dozen Puruándiro ejidos.[28] One of the Sinarquistas who received a provisional ayuntamiento appointment was ultimately sworn in as a permanent council member on New Year's Day 1945, though his oath of office had to be administered in a private residence because a group of "rebels" who opposed him had occupied the municipal government's offices.[29]

San José Huipana (hereafter Huipana), where clashes between agraristas and conservative Catholic partisans first began in 1921, was one of the Puruándiro communities that became embroiled in the renewed conflicts.[30] Huipana's agraristas formally requested ejido lands for their community in February 1931, and the Cárdenas administration approved their petition in June 1935. Cárdenas's decree granted 305 Huipana campesinos use rights to 2,342 hectars that had once formed part of the Santa Ana Mancera Hacienda.[31] But the agrarian reform's apparent triumph in Huipana proved fleeting. Huipana's Donato Silva was one of the local ejido leaders who protested when Sinarquistas were appointed to Puruándiro's ayuntamiento in late 1944.[32] And Huipana's conflict acquired a new wrinkle in 1946 when rural workers from the neighboring Guanajuato municipality of Valle de Santiago intervened and allied themselves with the conservative Catholic faction.[33]

The clashes in Huipana ultimately endured into the 1960s and heavily influenced the desire of locals to migrate as braceros. In March 1953, Huipana's Ángel Guevara wrote to federal officials to request a bracero contract.[34] It was the first of twenty petitions for socioeconomic aid that either Guevara or his wife, Teresa Ceballos, sent to federal authorities during Ruiz Cortines's presidency (1952–58), and they requested a bracero contract in ten of them.[35] The missives the married couple sent in 1953 and 1954 simply stated that their family was impoverished, without offering any details explaining the root causes of their marginalization. However, after more than two years of fruitless attempts to secure federal assistance, a frustrated Guevara offered a deeper account of his family's circumstances in an October 1955 letter he addressed directly to Ruiz Cortines. Since the previous decade, when Sinarquista activity in the municipality spiked, a group of armed individuals with ties to the hostile parties from Valle de Santiago had continually terrorized and threatened Guevara and other Huipana residents. The hostilities had resulted in numerous deaths, including the death of one of Guevara's brothers, which in turn led to a growing population of widows in the community who had no means of providing for their families. By the time Guevara wrote in fall 1955, the situation in Huipana had deteriorated to such a degree that he and many others were afraid to leave their houses because they believed that they would become the next victims, and he opined that military intervention might be necessary to restore the peace in the community.[36]

Guevara's circumstances and conditions in Huipana continued to worsen after the October 1955 message. In a July 1956 letter, Guevara noted bitterly that direct attacks against him had increased after he had openly supported Ruiz Cortines's presidential candidacy, and he also reported that he and his surviving brothers had been "dispossessed of our lands, our homes, and the barest minimum of our material interests." They had all relocated to the municipal seat after being forced off of their lands, and there they were enduring a "lamentably appalling situation" since they no longer had any means of providing for their children. Guevara then begged the president to send aid and to intervene directly with Puruándiro's municipal authorities so that the "persecutions" in Huipana would end.[37] But his plea went unheeded. Guevara sent his final recorded letter to Ruiz Cortines in May 1957. He and his family were still living in the municipal seat, deprived of their "agrarian rights," a term often used by ejidatarios to describe the usufruct rights they enjoyed in their respective ejidos, and "suffering through the most abysmal conditions."[38]

Huipana's more conservative and devout residents also expressed an interest in migrating, though their requests were made from a position of relative strength that reflected how the specific course of intracommunity political conflicts affected aspiring braceros' motives. In February 1962, Father Tomás Flores requested an unspecified number of contracts for Huipana residents who lacked the means to "make progress on the construction of local infrastructure" and wanted to use their earnings to build potable water and electricity systems, a schoolhouse, and, most important to them, a new parish church.[39] The priest conspicuously omitted any mention of bloody intracommunity political clashes, which, according to a November 1963 request for military assistance that Huipana's *comisariado ejidal* (ejido president) and *encargado del orden* (keeper of the peace) made, persisted into the early 1960s and robbed the community of any semblance of "peace, tranquility, and order." (The community officials even noted that the factions that were fighting in 1963 were the same ones that had been at odds with each other since 1921.)[40] Father Flores's silence regarding Huipana's endemic violence, coupled with the aspiring braceros' stated desire to invest their earnings in infrastructure projects, indicated that the conservative Catholic faction still enjoyed the upper hand in the community. Unlike those who were driven off of the ejido's lands during the 1950s, the aspiring braceros Father Flores wrote on behalf of did not view migration as an avenue that would ensure their basic survival. To them it was a means of improving the community's material conditions and building a house of worship that would serve as a testament to their faith.

A conflict similar to Huipana's unfolded to the south, in Comanja, a rural community in the municipality of Coeneo, though in this case neither faction was able to secure a definitive victory. A relatively small ejido was established in Comanja in 1921, when 137 campesinos received access to 417 hectares.[41] Comanja's ejidatarios formally requested an ejido expansion in October 1925, but that petition was not approved until September 1936, when the Cárdenas administration allotted 953 additional hectares to 78 ejidatarios.[42] During that interregnum, the Cristero War divided communities throughout the Greater Bajío, including those in Coeneo; in March 1927, officials seized Comanja's and Zipiajo's parish churches and converted them into public schoolhouses.[43] And though records from the 1930s are scarce, Coeneo's municipal authorities reported during the late 1940s that conflicts between factions "that have always been at odds with each other" had resumed in communities like Santiago Azajo.[44]

Comanja's intracommunity political conflicts were reignited during the 1950s after the municipal government intervened there on behalf of conservative Catholic partisans who wanted to disrupt the ejido's administration. After an October 1950 firefight in Comanja that left one dead, Coeneo's municipal president removed the community's *jefe de tenencia* (community chief) from office, despite the protests of community-level organizations like the Women's League.[45] It soon became evident that Coeneo's municipal president had instigated the fatal shootout so that he would have a pretext to appoint two personal allies of his, Melecio Juárez and Alfredo Hernández, to jointly hold the position of community chief. The dual appointment immediately elicited a complaint from Comanja's residents. A group wrote to the governor in November, accusing Juárez of supplying ammunition to the parties involved in the October firefight. The complainants also noted that Hernández owned a "scandalous" bar where Comanja's most "disorderly" residents regularly consumed to excess and wildly fired their guns.[46] A follow-up investigation by state authorities in early 1951 revealed that Hernández had ties to known members of the PAN, the conservative Catholic political party that opposed the agrarian reform. State officials ultimately determined that tensions in Comanja would likely subside if Emigdio Cervantes Calixto, a "well-regarded and hard-working" ejidatario who enjoyed substantial popular support within the community, replaced Hernández, and they urged Coeneo's municipal authorities to make the change.[47]

But David Herrera Tapia, who was sworn in as municipal president in early 1951, refused to countermand his predecessor's appointment. Herrera Tapia defended his intransigence by informing the state government that two competing factions had started fighting in Comanja. He asserted that both Hernández and Juárez had been appointed because they were honorable men who did not have a stake in the conflict, not because of any ties to the previous municipal administration. Furthermore, Herrera Tapia was certain that putting Cervantes Calixto in Hernández's place would exacerbate Comanja's internal tensions.[48] A group of Comanja residents enthusiastically seconded Herrera Tapia in a January 1951 letter. Though the writers described themselves as neutral parties, they heartily endorsed Hernández, and they claimed that an outside "agitator" who "actively fomented a constant state of conflict" whenever he visited his relatives in Comanja was responsible for the community's ills.[49] With Hernández and his official and popular supporters digging in their heels, state authorities contacted the commanding officer of the 21st Military Zone in February and asked him to monitor the situation in Comanja until the internal conflict there was resolved.[50]

However, military surveillance did not prevent the conflict from escalating, nor did it stop Comanja's municipal government-supported community leadership from antagonizing local ejidatarios. In October 1951, Comanja comisariado ejidal Aurelio Cervantes Calixto (who was likely the brother of the would-be community chief Emigdio Cervantes Calixto) complained to Governor Dámaso Cárdenas that community officials had found an innovative means of interfering with the agrarian reform community's everyday activities: an indifference that had robbed the community of "authorities who could protect even the most basic rights of its residents." Despite the constantly recurring shootouts between members of the opposing factions, the community chiefs—who were presumably still Melecio Juárez and Alfredo Hernández—were not opening their office or attending to their constituents. Furthermore, they refused to meet with a member of the federal Agrarian Department who was visiting the area. The Agrarian Department official was there to conduct a census of the ejidatarios and, if necessary, reallocate the use rights to individual ejido parcels. But the community chiefs had to formally sign documents in order for the survey and reallocation process to move forward, and they made it known that they would not provide their signatures so long as they were in power. As a result of Juárez's and

Hernández's tactics, the ejido's lands had slipped into a bureaucratic limbo that stymied the ejidatarios.[51]

Coeneo's municipal government continued to stoke bloody political conflicts in Comanja through the 1950s: in 1957, Comanja's ejido leadership council, Women's League, and Sociedad de Padres de Familia, an officially sanctioned parent-teacher association–style organization, together complained about the "impositions that have harmed our personal interests and robbed our households of their tranquility," and they explicitly told state government officials that municipal officials had inflamed tensions and were directly responsible for all bloodshed that had occurred and was likely to continue occurring.[52] By the 1960s, the endemic conflict had pushed Comanja's rural workers to want to migrate as braceros. In May 1963, Andrés Sandoval Castillo wrote to the state government and requested bracero eligibility cards for himself and nineteen others.[53] Sandoval Castillo did not elaborate on why he and others were interested in migrating in his May letter, but he provided more details when he wrote directly to Governor Agustín Arriaga Rivera in August to renew his request. Comanja's aspiring braceros were rural workers who had been declared eligible to use ejido parcels; however, conditions in Comanja had prevented them from gaining physical access to their parcels, despite orders issued by the Agrarian Department.[54] Sandoval Castillo would ask for bracero eligibility cards once again in May 1964, presumably because conflict-related landlessness persisted in Comanja.[55] Thus, while neither Comanja faction managed to gain definitive control of the community and its lands as in Huipana, the factional conflict affected local ejidatarios to such a degree that would-be agrarian reform beneficiaries looked to the Bracero Program to alleviate their marginalization.

INTRACOMMUNITY CONFLICTS IN SOUTHERN GUANAJUATO

Intracommunity conflicts in the southern Guanajuato municipality of Pénjamo, which was one of the first jurisdictions in that state to experience Cristero activity in 1926, also influenced individual decisions to migrate as braceros.[56] Local political tensions resurfaced in 1931, two years after the Cristero War, when agraristas from nine Pénjamo communities accused the municipal president, Juvencio Reyes, of naming prominent former Cristeros to key local administrative posts and governing as a champion of the landed elite.[57] Reyes denied the allegations, but the renewed tensions soon escalated into clashes that would mark rural Pénjamo for the next two decades, although, unlike in Coeneo and Puruándiro, in most instances it was agraristas and ejidatarios who initiated the hostilities.[58] In April 1932, the agrarista militias from nine communities, including five of the ones that had accused Reyes of harboring Cristero sympathies, attacked a *guardia blanca*—community militia that fought on behalf of conservative Catholic landowners—that was based in Potrerillos and had received weapons from sympathetic military officers.[59] Simultaneously, Potrerillos's ejidatarios launched a series of land invasions, one of which lasted until at least 1958.[60] Las Cuevas's ejidatarios complained in November 1942 that reserve soldiers were funneling weapons to their conservative opponents, who had already used them to murder three agrarian reform beneficiaries.[61] In October 1945, San Antonio de Aceves's agraristas openly threatened to kill estate administrators who interfered with their attempts to displace sharecroppers who were working lands they wanted for their ejido grant.[62] Rural violence was so commonplace in Pénjamo by March 1948 that municipal president Jesús Govea casually informed Governor Jesús Castorena that a spate of "bloody events" that had occurred in Corrales earlier that year were nothing more than the latest manifestation of the "ancient battle between ejidatarios and non-ejidatarios."[63] Govea himself instigated a land invasion in Capilla de Márquez the following year, which prompted a conflict that military authorities stationed in the region were certain would end like the ones in numerous other Pénjamo communities: in "blood, death, and the destruction of entire families."[64]

Although the clashes in Presa del Aguacate were not as deadly as others in Pénjamo, they nevertheless contributed to the desire to emigrate from that community. The agraristas there formally requested ejido lands in February 1931, though the request languished in bureaucratic limbo until the mid-1930s. Once federal agrarian authorities reviewed the petition, they determined that they could satisfy it by expropriating lands from the Presa del Aguacate Rancho and the Corralejo Hacienda. But Eusebio Vergara, Presa del Aguacate's owner, challenged the federal government's findings by claiming that he had subdivided his estate by selling separate portions of it to thirteen individuals, a process formally known as a *fraccionamiento,* and that his remaining holdings and the newly created ones were small enough to be exempt from expropriation. However, because the sale receipts were dated after the agraristas had filed their formal ejido request, the Agrarian

Department dismissed this challenge as a cynical attempt to use bureaucratic chicanery to stifle the land redistribution process. The Cárdenas administration authorized the creation of Presa del Aguacate's ejido in April 1936. The decree granted seventy-two campesinos use rights to 821 hectares; 465 of those hectares had belonged to Vergara.[65]

The newly minted ejidatarios went on the offensive almost immediately after their request was approved. In June 1936, Eligio León complained that a group of individuals was using threats to demand that rural workers from Presa del Aguacate and neighboring Cañada de Corralejo abandon the homes and small orchards that were their "sole possessions."[66] Four months later, Pénjamo's municipal president, Cayetano Quiles, confirmed that the aggressive individuals were Presa del Aguacate's ejidatarios. By the time Quiles sent a report on the situation to Governor Enrique Fernández Martínez in October, the agrarian reform beneficiaries had set their sights on three fruit orchards and a building lot (*solar*) that Florentino Rosas owned. Quiles was incensed that the ejidatarios were behaving as if they, and not agrarian officials, had the authority to expropriate lands, and he described their actions as a "truly unjust attempt to swallow up properties that were not included in their ejido grant."[67] Ricardo Acosta, a federal survey engineer, corroborated the claims of a land invasion shortly after Quiles wrote to the governor. Acosta acknowledged that Rosas had purchased 16 hectares from Eusebio Vergara six months after Presa del Aguacate's agraristas had formally asked for ejido lands. However, he had determined that that particular sale had been made in good faith, and as a result Rosas's holdings were not part of the ejido grant.[68] But the land invasion continued until the 1940s, prompting Rosas to hope for federal intervention while he and his wife and their seven children relied on agricultural day labor to sustain themselves.[69]

Presa del Aguacate's comisariado ejidal responded to the accusations against his constituents in April 1944. He did not offer even a cursory denial, and he claimed that Rosas was the one threatening the ejidatarios' interests. According to the ejido president, Rosas's allegations were little more than "machinations" designed to dispossess the agrarian reform beneficiaries of orchards that belonged to their grant. This supposed conspiracy was even more galling because Presa del Aguacate's ejidatarios had officially requested an expansion of their ejido after determining that the original grant was insufficient to meet their needs.[70] Left implied in this message was the comisariado ejidal's belief that land invasions were a justifiable means to achieve the end of acquiring more land for the ejido he led.

The available documentary evidence does not make clear if the landowners that Presa del Aguacate's ejidatarios targeted were conservative Catholic partisans who had fought as Cristeros or were members of either the UNS or the PAN. However, it is plausible to conclude that they were, given Pénjamo's polarized political climate and the overt hostility that Presa del Aguacate's ejidatarios displayed. Regardless of their personal religious and political convictions, the private Presa del Aguacate smallholders who had been put on the defensive during the mid-1940s came to see the Bracero Program as their only means of relief by the late 1940s. In July 1948, Cleofas Cervantes Hernández and Alberto Rodríguez, two self-described "poor campesinos who earn our living exclusively from what we produce on our lands," informed federal agrarian authorities that Presa del Aguacate's ejidatarios had invaded 27 hectares that they owned. The pair lamented that rural insecurity and the actions of "ejidatarios who already have sufficient lands but nevertheless have dedicated themselves to antagonizing their neighbors who own small private properties" had made it impossible for them to provide for their families. And the invasion and "mutilation" of their holdings had only served to worsen their already precarious socioeconomic standing. Given the scale of the losses they had suffered at the hands of Presa del Aguacate's ejidatarios, Cervantes Hernández and Rodríguez had sadly concluded that they would have no choice but to "abandon their dearly beloved land" and migrate to the United States as braceros.[71]

VIOLENCE AND LANDLESSNESS IN NORTHEASTERN JALISCO

Religiously inspired violent opposition to land redistribution also profoundly shaped agrarian conditions in northeastern Jalisco and contributed to individual decisions to migrate as braceros. As early as spring 1921, conservative Catholics in municipalities like Arandas, Atotonilco el Alto, and Tepatitlán were denouncing supporters of the agrarian reform as "misbegotten agitators" whose unconstitutional and unpatriotic assault on private property rights would lead to the ruin of agricultural production and every level of Mexican society.[72] The region then went on to become one of the "most solidly" Cristero ones in Mexico, and the Cristeros scored one of their most significant victories against federal forces in Tepatitlán.[73] Cristero resistance became so intense in northeastern Jalisco that federal authorities conducted aerial bombings there in order to flush the Catholic rebels out of their rural strongholds.⁷⁴

Cristero resistance resurged in northeastern Jalisco when the Cárdenas administration began promoting land redistribution and secular public education on a national scale during the 1930s. Broadsides posted in Tepatitlán in 1936 called on locals to join those fighting against "revolutionary mercenaries" and "for liberty and the fatherland in the mountains of Jalisco and Zacatecas, the twisting sierras of . . . Guanajuato, [and] the virgin forests of . . . Michoacán."⁷⁵ These proclamations also reflected the influence of Social Catholicism—which identified private property rights as one of the cornerstones of a just and harmonious society—and highlighted that conservative Catholic partisans interpreted their defense of private property as a both a spiritual and material matter. Their drafters argued that private property was the key to "social peace, social justice, social cooperation, and economic wellbeing," vilified the proponents of land redistribution as "criminals who were corrupting the morals of the rural working class," and denounced revolutionary leaders as demagogues whose "misguided fanaticism" had ravaged the countryside "like an apocalyptic hurricane that had left the smoking ruins of our culture and traditions behind its wake." Given that Jalisco's conservative Catholic partisans viewed revolutionary policies and their supporters as all-encompassing threats that endangered every facet of Mexican society, they felt that they were obligated to "match force with force" and violently fight in the name of the "sacred cause of liberty."⁷⁶

Northeastern Jalisco's conservative Catholic partisans continued to violently oppose the agrarian reform during the 1940s, but like their counterparts in northern Michoacán analyzed earlier, their strategies and tactics changed during this decade. First, their attacks were focused primarily on preventing the establishment of new ejidos or undermining existing agrarian reform communities, not toppling the national government. Second, they partnered with conservative municipal presidents, legislators, judges, ground-level agrarian authorities, and military officers who either had a lukewarm relationship with or were outright hostile to agraristas and ejidatarios. And third, they affiliated themselves with the UNS, which began to hold public demonstrations in former Cristero strongholds like Tepatitlán.⁷⁷

The hostilities in northeastern Jalisco municipalities like Atotonilco returned to a fever pitch in 1945. José Valle Padilla, whose hacienda had been partially expropriated when Santa Elena's ejido was established in 1938, was accused of ordering the April 1945 murder of Cornelio Flores, a Santa Elena agrarista who remained an active promoter of land redistribution.[78] And Manuel Hernández, whose lands had been expropriated to form part of the Atotonilco ejido of El Alacrán in 1937, found sympathetic state district court judges who accepted his arguments that his lands had been unjustly expropriated and then ordered the arrest of sixteen ejidatarios.[79] This ruling worried the national-level leadership of the Confederación Nacional Campesina (CNC; National Campesino Confederation), the umbrella campesino union that was formally affiliated with the PRI, which warned President Ávila Camacho that northeastern Jalisco's judicial, civil, and military authorities were antagonizing agraristas and ejidatarios there.[80] For his part, Atotonilco municipal president Pedro Valle dismissed any concerns and asserted that the arrests were legally justified.[81] The municipal president further burnished his anti–agrarian reform credentials the following spring when he began harassing and extorting Santa Elena's agraristas.[82]

Conservative Catholic landowners and local authorities received high-level official support in summer 1945, when Fidencio Vázquez Cerda, who represented one of northeastern Jalisco's districts in the federal Chamber of Deputies, started actively intervening in the region's agrarian affairs. According to the leadership councils of seven Atotonilco ejidos, including Santa Elena, who opposed Vázquez Cerda, the federal deputy had made common cause with "criminals and murderers who have destabilized and caused untold difficulties in agrarian reform communities." One of these "criminals" was Carlos Trujillo, who became the secretary general of northeastern Jalisco's Regional Agrarian Committee in July 1945. This appointment shocked Atotonilco's agraristas and ejidatarios because Trujillo had led "a Cristero unit that murdered numerous comrades who were fighting to acquire lands" during the 1920s, and he remained an "absolute enemy" of land redistribution and its proponents. The former Cristero immediately set about interfering in the internal affairs of numerous ejidos and attempted to install conservative leadership councils that would be friendlier to him and Vázquez Cerda. When Trujillo and his allies—including the ejido promotion delegate assigned to the neighboring municipality of Ocotlán—targeted the Atotonilco ejido of Margaritas during spring 1946, the sitting leadership council refused to step down. That standoff prompted a series of firefights between the ejidatarios and Trujillo's partisans, one of which led to Trujillo's death. Incensed that his efforts to gain a foothold in Atotonilco's ejidos had been frustrated, Vázquez Cerda had three ejidatarios from Milpillas arrested and charged with murdering Trujillo. Atotonilco's ejido leadership councils concluded that the federal deputy ordered the arrests because he hoped that arbitrarily directing his reprisals against innocent parties would fracture inter-ejido solidarity in the municipality. But Margaritas's and Milpillas's leadership councils remained united in their opposition to Vázquez Cerda, and they held him responsible for initiating the chain of events that ended with Trujillo's death.[83]

While the agrarian conflicts in Atotonilco escalated, some Santa Elena agraristas sought relief through the Bracero Program. Although the vast majority of Jalisco campesinos were still ineligible to receive contracts in 1946, Bartolo Lomelí Anguiano wrote to Governor Marcelino García Barragán in May and asked him to make an exception for an unspecified number of Santa Elena rural workers who had been forced off of their lands and left with no means to earn a living by factors that were beyond their control.[84] Lomelí Anguiano made no mention of Santa Elena's ejido leadership council in his request, thus indicating that despite their leaders' proclamations of unity, there were rank-and-file agraristas and ejidatarios in northeastern Jalisco willing to break ranks and remove themselves from the conflict, at least for as long as a bracero contract would allow.

Community-level clashes also resumed in the municipality of Tepatitlán during the mid-1940s when conservative Catholic landowners moved against agraristas in communities where ejidos had not been established. In August 1946, private landowners who feared that their lands would be expropriated attacked rural workers in Plan del Sabino. The violent confrontation ended with the death of two Plan del Sabino residents, and the survivors of the confrontation requested permission from the commanding officer of the 15th Military Zone to form a Rural Defense Corps, the title given to officially recognized community militias, so they could defend themselves.[85] But these pleas ultimately fell on unsympathetic ears. Seven months after the clashes in Plan del Sabino, Commander Felipe González Gallo was ordered to investigate allegations that armed parties had assaulted agraristas in Mezcala. But González Gallo dismissed the accusations out of hand because Mezcala's agraristas had a "poor history of atrocious behavior."[86] The commander's attitude is not entirely surprising; as Thomas Rath has detailed in his study of the mid-twentieth-century military, army units during the 1940s and 1950s often operated as police units that targeted perceived threats to national political stability, including the proponents of land redistribution.[87] With the military deciding to look the other way, the conflict in Mezcala continued. A series of "armed scandals" in the community left one dead and three wounded in early October 1947, and municipal president Manuel González Vargas informed the state government that the wounded had successfully evaded apprehension.[88]

Tepatitlán's conservative Catholic landowners prolonged their offensive through the end of the 1940s. In November 1948, San José de Gracia's agraristas, who had been lobbying for lands since 1940, organized an assembly where a census that would formally register every individual interested in petitioning for an ejido would be carried out. (This San José de Gracia should not be confused with the one in Michoacán that Luis González y González studied.) But an armed party of landowners and their partisans, some of whom appeared to be inebriated, interrupted the meeting and threatened to murder the gathered agraristas. The aggressors ultimately backed down because the agraristas were also armed, but their intervention successfully prevented the completion of the census, which meant that San José de Gracia's agraristas could not formally request ejido lands at that time. When San José de Gracia's agraristas began preparations for another census assembly in late February 1950, they asked the commanding officer of the 15th Military Zone to send a detachment of soldiers to guarantee the peace during the proceedings.[89] However, this request for military assistance, like earlier ones sent from northeastern Jalisco, went unheeded. Two weeks after San José de Gracia's agraristas wrote to the military authorities, municipal president Zenaido González Ruvalcaba informed the governor that a number of "scandals and acts of bloodshed" had occurred in that community and that the municipal police force lacked the manpower to effectively respond to the clashes. He then asked the governor to intervene with federal officials and secure the deployment of troops to San José de Gracia, but there is no evidence that indicates that this request was fulfilled.[90]

The violence Tepatitlán's conservative Catholic landowners unleashed during the 1940s and early 1950s served its intended purpose. Only one ejido, Loma Larga, was established in the municipality between 1915, when the first revolutionary law authorizing land redistribution went into effect, and 1964, when the Bracero Program ended. By contrast, during that same period, 17 were established in Atotonilco, 28 were established in Coeneo, 53 were established in Puruándiro, and 141 were established in Pénjamo, despite the fierce opposition to land redistribution there.[91]

Landless rural workers from Tepatitlán communities where violence had prevented the establishment of ejidos began leaving that municipality as braceros. In June 1953, municipal president Miguel Navarro Castellanos reported that San José de Gracia was the rural community with the most aspiring braceros, forty, in his jurisdiction; it was followed by Mezcala, with twenty-nine. Together, these two communities accounted for 49 percent of the prospective braceros who lived outside of the municipal seat.[92] Among those who emigrated as braceros from San José de Gracia were Pedro Carmona Vera and Antonio Nuño Gonzáles. Though Carmona Vera did not refer to the internal conflict in San José de Gracia when he was interviewed for the Bracero History Archive in May 2006, he noted that he received his first bracero contract in 1948, the same year that landowners blocked the completion of the community's agrarian census, and he continued to migrate as a bracero through the early 1960s.[93] In a July 1960 contract request he sent to President Adolfo López Mateos, Carmona Vera explained that he wanted to continue migrating because he was a landless day laborer who could only find work two to three days per week at grain- and citrus-producing estates that were increasingly far from his home.[94] Like Carmona Vera, Nuño Gonzáles, who migrated five times as a bracero between 1958 and 1963, did not mention the agrarian conflicts that divided San José de Gracia when he spoke with an interviewer in November 2008. But he did state that before he began migrating to the United States, his family only had access to land when his parents entered into sharecropping agreements with local landowners; Nuño Gonzáles also recalled that landowners collected half the family's maize harvest as payment for the use of their lands.[95] The available evidence does not indicate what either Carmona Vera's or Nuño Gonzáles's attitude regarding land redistribution were. But whether or not they supported the agrarian reform, their socioeconomic opportunities as landless rural workers in San José de Gracia were limited to low-wage day labor and exploitative sharecropping arrangements because the opponents of land redistribution had successfully stymied the attempt to create an ejido there.

STATE GOVERNMENT HOSTILITY AND LANDLESSNESS IN SOUTHERN ZACATECAS

Unfortunately, there is little available evidence that documents community-level political conflicts in southern Zacatecas, which was an epicenter of Cristero activity and the site of pitched confrontations between agraristas and Catholic landowners in the 1920s and 1930s, during the bracero era.[96] But previous studies and aspiring braceros' written contract requests suggest that official, state-level opposition to the agrarian reform influenced such individuals' decisions. As César Ramírez Miranda, Ramón Vera Salvo, and Pedro Gómez Sánchez have noted in their examination of mid-twentieth-century Zacatecas agrarian policies and practices, Governors Pánfilo Natera (1940–44) and Leobardo Reynoso (1944–50) both encouraged municipal governments to move against campesinos who advocated for land redistribution and openly antagonized agraristas and ejidatarios.[97] One of the agraristas the state government targeted was Benigno Hurtado, who was elected Jerez's municipal president in 1941. But as Sandra Nichols has pointed out in her study of twentieth-century emigration from the Jerez community of El Haro to California's Napa Valley, Governor Natera refused to recognize Hurtado's victory. Rather than risk violent confrontations between his supporters and opponents of the agrarian reform who enjoyed the governor's backing, Hurtado decided to end his bid for the municipal presidency and retreated from local politics. Despite this, Hurtado and his family still received death threats, and in 1944 he and one of his sons began to migrate as braceros. The Hurtados were not the only ones who followed that route. According to Nichols, fear of political reprisals prompted other Jerez agraristas to abandon the cause of land redistribution, and some of these former agraristas migrated as braceros with the hope that they would earn enough money to purchase privately owned parcels.[98]

Simultaneously, there were others from Jerez communities who requested contracts because they did not want to sell lands that they already owned. In January 1958, Daniel Bautista García wrote to President Ruiz Cortines from El Durazno—where an ejido had been established in 1931—and requested a contract so that he could provide for his eight children.[99] Bautista García elaborated on his motives when he renewed his petition the following month. He owned five hectares that he had considered selling because the lack of irrigation infrastructure made it difficult to produce harvests. But he had a change of heart when he realized that whatever money he earned from the sale would not last long. Bautista García then decided that supplementing his income as a bracero would allow him to keep his lands, support his children, and send his children to school.[100] Like the aspiring braceros from San José de Gracia, Jalisco, discussed previously, the available evidence does not shed light on what opinion if any Bautista García had regarding land redistribution. But I believe we can reasonably conclude that the violent stifling of the agrarian reform in Jerez during the 1940s influenced Bautista García's behavior and decisions during the 1950s. Absent an active land redistribution process, private ownership was the aspiring bracero's only means of having access to his own lands, and he was determined to stay out of the ranks of landless rural workers.

Other contract requests that aspiring braceros from southern Zacatecas municipalities, including Jerez, made lend credence to Nichols's argument that official, state-level opposition to the agrarian reform created a class of landless campesinos who decided that migration afforded them the best opportunity to improve their socioeconomic standing. Of the available eighty-seven written contract requests that prospective braceros from southern Zacatecas sent to federal authorities during the entirety of the Bracero Program, 64 percent came from communities that never had access to ejido lands.[101] Some of these would-be braceros, like Francisco Durán Ortega, who represented groups from the Nochistlán community of Los Cárdos that requested braceros contracts in September 1953 and February 1959, explicitly noted that they were unemployed non-ejidatarios.[102] While the available evidence does not cast light on the political inclinations of these aspiring braceros or the status of political conflicts within their communities, we know that the state government's opposition to land redistribution limited the socioeconomic opportunities for all landless rural workers in southern Zacatecas, much like the armed conservative Catholic opposition did in northeastern Jalisco municipalities like Tepatitlán.

VIOLENCE AND THE BRACERO SELECTION PROCESS IN SOUTHWESTERN AGUASCALIENTES

As in the case of southern Zacatecas, primary evidence that documents the specific course of bracero-era intracommunity political conflicts in southwestern Aguascalientes municipalities like Calvillo—a jurisdiction that the Cristeros managed to fully control on several occasions during the Cristero War—is scarce compared to northern Michoacán, southern Guanajuato, and northeastern Jalisco.[103] But Miroslava Chávez-García's study of her family's emigration from Calvillo to California, which uses personal correspondence and oral interviews, suggests that local violence did influence bracero migration there, as her father and paternal uncles began migrating as braceros because of the Cristero War's lasting impact on their socioeconomic fortunes.[104] Furthermore, the available archival evidence indicates that the bracero selection process itself became a factor that prompted clashes between conservative Catholic partisans and supporters of the agrarian reform. This was in part because Aguascalientes's government regularly defied federal directives and encouraged ejidatarios to migrate as braceros, and state officials sometimes asked the Liga de Comunidades Agrarias to help coordinate the bracero selection process. Thus Aguascalientes ejidatarios had a reasonable expectation that they would have an opportunity to migrate as braceros, which contributed to local political tensions during selection periods.

In June 1956, Félix de Loera, the municipal government's delegate in the Calvillo ejido of El Terrero, wrote to President Ruiz Cortines to complain about the arbitrary administration of criminal justice in that area of the state. De Loera alleged that only local impoverished peoples were accused and jailed as "bandits," while (presumably better-connected and relatively wealthier) individuals who had murdered multiple victims had never been imprisoned. The local official then claimed that three men had been killed in the ejido he represented and that no one had been held accountable. De Loera ended his letter by discussing a seemingly unrelated matter: the practice of aspiring braceros paying as much as 300 pesos for the documents they needed to secure their entry into the United States. He admitted that it was naive of him to ask the president to weigh in on and resolve that particular issue.[105] But the fact that de Loera implicitly linked rural violence and bracero migration suggests that the Calvillo rural workers paying for bracero eligibility documents may have been seeking to escape local clashes that had already claimed the lives of numerous ejidatarios, just like their counterparts in other Greater Bajío jurisdictions.

Further evidence emerged the following year that the bracero selection process had become another facet of the conflicts between conservative Catholic partisans and supporters of the agrarian reform. In August 1957, Aguascalientes Liga secretary general, Alberto Alcalá de Lira, wrote to Governor Luis Ortega Douglas to complain that Calvillo's municipal government had not chosen any local ejidatarios as braceros. He then asked the governor to intervene directly and allocate at least five bracero eligibility cards each to eight Calvillo ejidos: the municipal seat, El Terrero, La Labor, Presa de los Serna, El Huarache, El Terrero del Refugio de los Serna, Las Tinajas, and El Chiquihuitero.[106] There is no record of an ejido ever having been established in the latter two communities, but there was an active agrarista group in Las Tinajas, as Camilo López Gómez wrote to President Ruiz Cortines in January 1953 to express that community's interest in acquiring ejido lands.[107] Alcalá de Lira's August 1957 letter was not the first time that

Liga personnel had lobbied on behalf of Calvillo ejidatarios who wanted to migrate as braceros. In 1953, then Aguascalientes Liga secretary general José Esparza Díaz forwarded bracero contract requests from El Terrero and La Labor to the state government. But in those instances, Esparza Díaz simply stated that La Labor's ejido lands were no longer sufficient for the number of people who lived there and that El Terrero's ejidatarios had suffered crop losses.[108]

Other available documents suggest that Calvillo officials were sympathetic to local conservative Catholic partisans during the late 1950s, which lends credence to the Liga's allegations that municipal authorities were antagonizing agraristas and ejidatarios by denying them bracero contracts and ignoring violence that targeted them. In October 1957, Juan Pablo Monreal Buendía, who owned a billiards hall in Malpaso, complained that the municipal government had arbitrarily closed his business at the behest of the local parish priest. Monreal Buendía alleged that the priest wanted to tightly control social and leisure life in Malpaso and had successfully turned the community against him. Shortly before Monreal Buendía sent his complaint to Governor Ortega Douglas, a group of apparently inebriated Malpaso residents initiated a verbal altercation with the priest. The individuals who accosted the priest were immediately jailed. The priest then told the municipal government that Monreal Buendía had incited the confrontation, which led to the closure of the billiards hall. Monreal Buendía admitted that he had been present when the argument occurred, but he claimed that he was nothing more than a bystander and that local authorities had not even bothered to investigate whether he had actually exchanged words with the priest before they shuttered his establishment.[109] The municipal government's sensitivity and prompt acquiescence to the priest's demands, combined with the impunity enjoyed by the parties that had attacked El Terrero's ejidatarios the previous year and the Liga's allegations that ejidatarios had been frozen out of the Bracero Program, indicates that hostilities between conservative Catholic partisans and supporters of the agrarian reform had resurfaced in Calvillo and that local authorities had sided with the Catholic faction.

But the local political tides turned in 1963 when Camilo López Gómez, the agrarista leader from Las Tinajas, became Calvillo's municipal president. Though his efforts to secure ejido lands for Las Tinajas failed, he had remained active in regional agrarian politics and was appointed the campesino representative to the State Agrarian Commission in 1958.[110] And once López Gómez attained local power, members of the Unión Cívica Calvillense (UCC;

Calvillense Civic Union), a local conservative Catholic group, explicitly accused him of Bracero Program–related malfeasance and implicitly alleged that he was encouraging rural violence in the municipality. In August 1963, UCC member Salvador Martínez López accused López Gómez of being a cacique, or local strongman, who had defrauded numerous aspiring braceros, and he asked President López Mateos to investigate and punish the municipal president.[111] In another message sent later that month, Martínez López alleged that López Gómez had been liberally selling firearms permits throughout the municipality, and he renewed his call for federal intervention that would lead to the removal of the "bad official."[112] By September, the UCC was organizing public demonstrations to protest against López Gómez.[113]

Given López Gómez's history as both a local agrarista and a state agrarian official, it is likely that Calvillo's conservative Catholic partisans would have levied accusations against him regardless of his actions and policies. But that the UCC complained specifically about the bracero selection process and the proliferation of firearms in the jurisdiction (much as had happened during the 1950s when a municipal government that appeared to be more sympathetic to conservative Catholic partisans was in power) suggests that López Gómez decided to use his position as municipal president to settle scores with those who opposed land redistribution and extort any who might seek relief through the Bracero Program. If López Gómez was indeed encouraging violence in Calvillo's rural communities while simultaneously extracting bribes from or denying bracero contracts to conflict participants who wanted to migrate, it demonstrates that local conflicts and bracero migration had become as deeply intertwined in southwestern Aguascalientes as it had in northern Michoacán, southern Guanajuato, northeastern Jalisco, and southern Zacatecas.

REFUSING THE REVOLUTION IN NORTHERN MICHOACÁN

There were aspiring braceros in the Greater Bajío who also wanted to migrate because their religious beliefs prompted them to reject the agrarian reform grants. For example, J. Guadalupe Castro and fifteen others from Romero de Torres—a community in the Michoacán municipality of Zamora where a relatively small ejido (379 hectares) was formed in 1935—wrote to Governor José María Mendoza Pardo in March 1945 and requested bracero contracts.[114]

The group explained that they were resident estate laborers who could no longer provide for their families with the low wages they received.[115] Castro renewed the petition one month later. This time he noted that he and the other would-be braceros had refused to join Romero de Torres's agraristas when they petitioned for ejido lands out of respect for the landowner who would be affected. But Castro and the other aspiring braceros had come to regret their decision. The group had attempted to claim rights as sharecroppers in 1941, but the landowner used his wealth to frustrate their effort. By the time the group sought bracero contracts, Castro claimed, the landowner who employed them "either cannot or does not want to pay us more than three pesos per six-day workweek."[116]

It is possible that Castro and his fellow prospective braceros respected their local landowner because they had a good working relationship with him prior to the 1940s, or perhaps they feared him because he threatened reprisals if they joined the agrarista cause. But it is telling that when the group first came to regret their decision to reject the agrarian reform, they attempted to gain access to lands as sharecroppers, not as ejidatarios. This indicates that the group's respect for the landowner was rooted in their respect for private property rights. And as I discussed at the beginning of this chapter, respect for private property rights in the Greater Bajío was rooted as much in the Catholic belief that private property was sacrosanct and inviolable as it was in material concerns. Frustrated that their desire to work privately owned lands had not come to fruition, Castro and the others decided that migrating as braceros was preferable to upsetting what they interpreted as a divinely sanctioned status quo.

A similar situation unfolded in Changuitiro, a Michoacán community east of Romero de Torres in the municipality of Churintzio. In January 1937, one hundred Changuitiro campesinos received use rights to 1,220 hectares that had been expropriated from the Changuitiro and Torrecillas y Sanguijuelas Haciendas.[117] An additional 533 hectares were expropriated from the Changuitiro Hacienda and allotted to the ejido in January 1939; forty newly minted ejidatarios received use rights to these lands.[118] But according to the community's oral tradition, several of the original ejidatarios were agraristas from the municipal seat that Changuitiro's agraristas had recruited to bolster their petitions. Changuitiro's agraristas resorted to this strategy because the community's former Cristeros flatly refused to join the ejido, despite being eligible. Their refusal was based in their personal faith and the efforts of Churintzio's parish priest, who denounced land redistribution as theft and threatened to excommunicate anyone who "stole" from private landowners.[119] Available documents lend credence to this oral tradition. When Humberto Beltrán, a federal engineer, surveyed the lands that were included in Changuitiro's initial ejido grant, he noted that many local parents had not enrolled their children in the community's primary school and that numerous former Cristeros had implicitly threatened him by reminding him that they had fought under the command of the Zacapu-based Cristero leader Ramón Aguilar.[120] And as late as July 1945, Churintzio's parish priest was performing unauthorized outdoor religious ceremonies and inciting confrontations between "fanaticized elements" and less openly devout individuals.[121] While it is not clear if this parish priest is the same one who threatened to excommunicate Changuitiro campesinos who supported the agrarian reform in the 1930s, it is clear that local clerical leaders engaged in public activism.

Once the Bracero Program started, landless former Cristeros, like Ladislao Fuentes Fajardo, and the landless sons of those who opposed the agrarian reform, like David Maldonado Mendoza, began migrating as braceros.[122] Maldonado Mendoza was the son of Félix Maldonado, who was so opposed to land redistribution that he threatened to move to the municipal seat if an ejido was ever established in Changuitiro, and Josefa Mendoza, who convinced her husband to back down from his threat to leave Changuitiro when she told him that she would not be moving with him. Fuentes Fajardo joined the Cristero ranks when the tensions between conservative Catholic partisans and the federal government escalated into open hostilities in the mid-1920s. And like many of the Cristeros in Michoacán communities that Christopher Boyer, Matthew Butler, and Jennie Purnell have studied, Fuentes Fajardo had close relatives who fought on the federal government's side.[123] Two of his older brothers, Teófilo and Porfirio, fought in the Cristero War as agrarista militia members, and they joined the ejido when it was established.[124] Teófilo and Porfirio remained active in community- and municipal-level politics through the 1960s: both served stints as Changuitiro's encargado del orden, and Porfirio represented the community on Churintzio's ayuntamiento and served terms as comisariado ejidal.[125]

As community officials, Teófilo and Porfirio Fuentes Fajardo were on the front lines of a revived factional conflict that ultimately had fatal consequences. Changuitiro residents recall that many former Cristeros began attempting to forcibly gain control of the community's ejido lands during the mid-1940s.[126] Documents detailing the renewed hostilities are scarce, but available evidence

FIGURE 1. Changuitiro bracero David Maldonado Mendoza. Photo courtesy of/printed with permission of the author.

indicates that the resumption of the conflict coincided with rising religious-political tensions throughout the municipality. When Churintzio's parish priest was flouting official worship restrictions and instigating confrontations in summer 1945, municipal president Carlos Fuentes Aldama worried that those confrontations would escalate into "bloody clashes."[127] One year later, the PAN's congressional district leader was organizing secret meetings in the municipality with clergy members and active Sinarquistas.[128] And in October 1947, the PAN organized a public demonstration in Churintzio at which its partisans "insulted the Revolution and attacked the government in power."[129] Meanwhile, the situation in Changuitiro and other rural Churintzio communities continued to deteriorate. In July 1955, municipal president Abelino Heredia Herrera wrote to the commanding officer of the 21st Military Zone and asked him to send soldiers to the municipality to "disarm the individuals who use their firearms to cause scandals that have caused anxiety and alarmed the honorable and hardworking residents of the municipal seat and other communities in the jurisdiction."[130] Five months after Heredia Herrera's plea, a firefight between the factions in Changuitiro ended with three deaths.[131] The fatal clash marked the unofficial end of the conflict between Changuitiro's ejidatarios and their conservative Catholic opponents. And by 1963, some ejidatarios were flouting official restrictions and renting their parcels to their former rivals, much to the chagrin of Porifrio Fuentes Fajardo.[132] But though factional violence subsided in Changuitiro after 1955 and conservative Catholic partisans gained some measure of access to lands, young rural workers from that community continued to migrate as braceros until the program ended, as I explore in more detail in chapter 5.

. . .

In June 1947, while clashes between agraristas and conservative Catholic partisans were escalating in the northeastern Jalisco municipality of Tepatitlán, municipal president Manuel González Vargas responded to Governor Jesús González Gallo's request for a basic report on local demographics. The municipal president estimated that between 45,000 and 50,000 people lived in his jurisdiction, though he noted that it was difficult to provide a more precise number because of "frequent emigration." He also declared that Catholicism was the only religion practiced in Tepatitlán.[133]

Though González Vargas did not explicitly connect Catholicism and migration in his brief report, the Greater Bajío communities examined in this chapter demonstrate that the two were inextricably linked in that region. The contiguous lands of southern Guanajuato, northern Michoacán, northeastern Jalisco, southwestern Aguascalientes, and southern Zacatecas were the principal bastion of conservative Catholic opposition to revolutionary anticlericalism, land redistribution, and secular public education during the 1920s and 1930s. Opposition to the agrarian reform ultimately proved intractable, and community-level clashes between conservative Catholic partisans who rejected land redistribution and agraristas and ejidatarios who supported it continued into the 1960s. And these endemic conflicts contributed directly to the socioeconomic marginalization that prompted Greater Bajío rural workers' desire to migrate. Some, like Ángel Guevara (Huipana, Michoacán) and Andrés Sandoval Castillo (Comanja, Michoacán), had been forced off of or denied access to ejido lands by local conservative Catholic factions. Others, like Alberto Rodríguez and Cleofas Cervantes Hernández (Presa del Aguacate, Guanajuato), were landowners who had been targeted by ejidatarios. Pedro Carmona Vera (San José de Gracia, Jalisco) was a landless day laborer in a municipality where conservative Catholic landowners had violently stifled the land redistribution process. Daniel Bautista García (El Durazno, Zacatecas) wanted to migrate so that he could earn money that would allow him to keep his lands and thus avoid becoming landless in a jurisdiction where state and local officials were hostile to the agrarian reform. In Calvillo, Aguascalientes, conservative Catholic- and agrarista-sympathetic municipal administrations took turns antagonizing members of the competing faction who wanted to migrate as braceros. And Ladislao Fuentes Fajardo, a former Cristero from Changuitiro, Michoacán, became a bracero because his religious beliefs had prompted him to reject an agrarian reform grant.

Ladislao Fuentes Fajardo was joined by the young sons of Changuitiro conservative Catholics who had refused to join the ejido, such as David Maldonado Mendoza. But Ladislao's nephew, David Fuentes Aguilar—the son of Changuitiro ejidatario Teófilo Fuentes Fajardo—also left Changuitiro as a bracero.[134] And Ladislao's brother, the ejidatario Porfirio Fuentes Fajardo, also migrated at least once as a bracero, in 1945.[135] Although his father was an ejidatario, Fuentes Aguilar was too young to receive use rights when Changuitiro's ejido was established, and Changuitiro received no additional lands following the 1939 expansion. And while Porfirio Fuentes Fajardo's 1945 bracero contract coincided with the resumption of religious-political hostilities in Changuitiro, it also coincided with a punishing drought that led to crop losses in numerous Greater Bajío ejidos. The bracero journeys of

David Fuentes Aguilar and Porfirio Fuentes Fajardo point to factors that paralleled and existed independently of the community-level conflicts I examine in this chapter: the politicized implementation of the agrarian reform, which constrained Greater Bajío ejidatarios and prompted them to seek out bracero contracts. How the agrarian reform's institutional and structural shortcomings influenced bracero migration is the focus of the next chapter.

FOUR

"Lack of Work and Lands to Sow"

THE AGRARIAN REFORM AND BRACERO
MIGRATION IN THE GREATER BAJÍO

ON MARCH 10, 1939, campesinos from Jesús del Monte, a Michoacán community in the municipality of Maravatío, formally requested that an ejido be established there.[1] Exactly six years later, Ángel Sandoval Coronel wrote to Governor José María Mendoza Pardo and requested bracero contracts for himself and other landless Jesús del Monte campesinos who were still awaiting the official resolution of their ejido petition. Sandoval Coronel explained in his letter that state officials had told him and his fellow aspiring braceros in 1939 that survey engineers would soon arrive in Jesús del Monte and begin the land redistribution process. But the promised engineers had yet to arrive, and Sandoval Coronel told the governor that so long as their ejido petition remained mired in bureaucratic limbo, he and his neighbors had "no means to make a living." However, he believed that he and his fellow petitioners would be able to "remedy the disastrous economic situation" they were experiencing if they had the opportunity to migrate as braceros, which their counterparts in La Nopalera—a neighboring Maravatío community whose residents has also filed an unresolved ejido request—had recently done.[2] The available evidence does not make clear if any aspiring braceros from Jesús del Monte ever received contracts, but their ejido request was finally resolved in November 1951, albeit in a fashion that provided relatively few benefits to the community. Federal authorities expropriated 131 hectares to form Jesús del Monte's ejido. However, the lands lacked any access to irrigation water; and because federal officials determined that the lands they expropriated were insufficient to carve out individual-use parcels, they declared that Jesús del Monte's seventy-three ejidatarios would have to use the lands collectively.[3] Jesús del Monte's ejidatarios could perhaps take some solace that their situation was not as dire as that in La Nopalera, the community that had partly inspired Sandoval Coronel's 1945 bracero contract request: although they determined that eighty-eight La Nopalera campesinos were eligible to become ejidatarios, federal authorities denied that community's ejido request in March 1948 after concluding that there were no lands close enough to La Nopalera that were eligible for expropriation.[4]

This chapter examines how the politicized implementation of the agrarian reform motivated individual decisions to seek out bracero contracts in the Greater Bajío, a phenomenon that scholars like Jorge Durand, Douglas Massey, John Gledhill, and Gustavo López Castro have touched on but not explored deeply in their works.[5] Despite the fierce conservative Catholic resistance to land redistribution in the Greater Bajío, a significant amount of land was ultimately redistributed in the region during the decades preceding the Bracero Program. Between 1915, when the first revolutionary agrarian reform law went into effect, and the end of Cárdenas's presidency in 1940, federal administrations approved the redistribution of 1.9 million hectares among 191,357 Greater Bajío ejidatarios.[6] These figures represented 34 percent of the lands redistributed and 48 percent of the ejidatarios who received access to lands in Aguascalientes, Guanajuato, Jalisco, Michoacán, and Zacatecas during that period.[7]

However, the federal statutes that structured both the land redistribution process and the internal workings of ejidos, particularly the Agrarian Code that went into effect in March 1934, constrained ejidatarios' socioeconomic prospects as much as if not more than they boosted them. The 1934 Agrarian Code superseded all previous federal agrarian reform laws, made the president and the federal Agrarian Department the ultimate arbiters of the land redistribution process, delineated the procedure that communities interested in acquiring ejido lands had to follow, declared which privately owned lands were eligible for expropriation and redistribution, and explicitly prohibited ejidatarios from carrying out certain actions with respect to their holdings.[8] Just as important, the code became law at a critical juncture. Cárdenas, who championed agrarian reform as a means of fulfilling the 1910 revolution's promises and uplifting Mexico's rural communities, began his six-year presidential term the same year that the new Agrarian Code went into effect. The Cárdenas administration redistributed 71 percent of the lands that were redistributed in the Greater Bajío between 1915 and 1940, which meant that the code profoundly shaped that region's ejido sector on the eve of the Bracero Program.[9] The 1934 law's influence endured into the years of the program, since the Agrarian Codes of 1940 and 1942 mostly maintained the procedures and guidelines that were codified during the mid-1930s. (The 1940 Agrarian Code went into effect in September, two months before Cárdenas left office.)[10]

The 1934 Agrarian Code's specific provisions, which are discussed in detail in the next section, imposed limitations that prompted ejidatarios and aspiring ejidatarios to seek out bracero contracts, even after federal officials barred the agrarian reform beneficiaries from migrating as braceros in spring 1943. The code's application led to ejidatarios being allotted poor-quality lands that were susceptible to weather-related crop losses, left rural workers who were eligible to become ejidatarios landless because there were not sufficient lands available within the prescribed proximity to communities that filed ejido requests, created murky and contested boundaries between neighboring ejidos, and prohibited the subdivision of individual-use ejido parcels under any circumstances. After the Cárdenas administration established the federally backed Banco Nacional de Crédito Ejidal (National Ejido Credit Bank; hereafter Banco Ejidal) in December 1935, ejidatarios could only apply for and receive loans from that institution.[11] Furthermore, the presidency's paramount position in the land redistribution process allowed Cárdenas's more conservative successors to dramatically slow the pace of the agrarian reform during the years of the Bracero Program. Between 1940 and 1964, the administrations of Manuel Ávila Camacho, Miguel Alemán, Adolfo Ruiz Cortines, and Adolfo López Mateos redistributed a combined 397,596 hectares among 18,962 Greater Bajío ejidatarios.[12] Simultaneously, the Greater Bajío experienced a rapid demographic expansion: the region's population grew from 2.2 million in 1940 to 3.5 million in 1960, which meant that a growing population had decreased access to land.[13] The Greater Bajío ejidatarios who were denied lands, suffered crop losses on poor-quality lands, or faced the Banco Ejidal's onerous loan and repayment terms, as well as the young rural workers who came of age after the agrarian reform slowed to a crawl, ultimately joined their neighbors who were embroiled in community-level political conflicts in seeking relief through the Bracero Program.

THE BACKGROUND AND PROVISIONS OF THE 1934 AGRARIAN CODE

How did a land redistribution process that was supposed to benefit campesinos come to be designed in such a manner that it pushed many in the Greater

Bajío to consider migrating as braceros?[14] The answer lies in part in the political debates and factional revolutionary rivalries of the 1910s. As Emilio Kourí has noted, the Constitutionalist faction, which issued the first national-level agrarian reform law in January 1915, promoted the establishment of ejidos on federally expropriated lands as a means of undercutting their Zapatista rivals, who championed a community-led land redistribution process. At the same time, Constitutionalist intellectuals argued that it was best for national authorities to grant ejido lands to communities because they believed that rural Mexicans were more familiar with and socially suited to working communal-level holdings.[15] Debates over the mechanics and ultimate goal of the land redistribution process continued after the Constitutionalists secured their military victory and the agrarian reform was enshrined in the 1917 Constitution in article 27.[16] While relatively autonomous regional leaders like Yucatán's Felipe Carrillo Puerto pursued the collectivization of ejido holdings during the 1920s, national leaders like Presidents Álvaro Obregón (1920–24) and Plutarco Elías Calles (1924–28) advocated the creation of individual-use ejido parcels that would be privatized after an unspecified period, during which ejidatarios would learn how to become efficient producers.[17] But while the progressive Cárdenas administration supported the creation of individual-use parcels—Cárdenas had promoted this type of land redistribution when he governed Michoacán between 1928 and 1932—its belief that private property regimes contributed to the oppression of rural workers made it hostile to the idea that individual private ownership should be the end goal of the agrarian reform, so it abandoned its predecessors' plans for the privatization of ejido holdings. As a result, ejidos whose cultivable lands were divided into inalienable individual-use parcels that the federal government retained de facto ownership of became the definitive form of land redistribution in most of the nation during the 1930s.[18] (Cárdenas's government did establish collectivized ejidos in areas dedicated to the production of export crops, such as the henequen-growing zones of Yucatán and the cotton-producing lands of the Comarca Lagunera.)[19]

Thus the 1934 Agrarian Code's provisions and statutes—which privileged federal authority, clearly delineated how ejidos would be established, and placed limits on individual ejidatarios' autonomy—reflected the debates of the 1910s and 1920s, as well as the Cardenistas' ideological prerogatives. The land redistribution process began with interested communities, not individual aspiring ejidatarios, sending a formal written request for ejido lands to their respective state governments. State authorities then formally recognized ejido petitions by publishing them in the state government's official newspaper. Once a petition was published, local-level Agrarian Commissions dispatched personnel who conducted a census that determined which community residents were eligible to join the ejido; surveyed adjacent privately owned lands to confirm that they could be expropriated; and demarcated the tentative boundaries of the ejido, its individual-use parcels, and communal livestock grazing and woodland plots. Individual-use parcels that had access to irrigation water had to measure 4 hectares, while parcels that only had access to seasonal rainwater (*temporal*) had to measure 8 hectares. (These measurements were increased to 6 and 12 hectares, respectively, in the 1942 Agrarian Code.) Both landless men and landless women were eligible to join ejidos, but the code granted preference to men. Landless men could become ejidatarios when they reached sixteen years of age or were married, whichever occurred first. Landless women who joined ejidos had to have children and to be either widowed or unmarried. As for the privately owned lands that would be expropriated to form ejidos, they had to be within a 7-kilometer radius of the petitioning community, presumably so that ejidatarios could access their holdings as easily as possible. Privately owned holdings that measured 150 or fewer irrigable hectares or 300 or fewer temporal hectares were exempted from expropriation, even if they were within the prescribed 7-kilometer radius. (The 1940 Agrarian Code amended this statute so that privately owned holdings that measured 100 or fewer irrigable hectares or 200 or fewer temporal hectares were exempted from expropriation.)[20]

This first phase of the land redistribution process featured several of the principal pitfalls that prompted frustrated and aspiring ejidatarios to request bracero contracts. Many of these flaws grew out of the directive that ejido lands had to be within 7 kilometers of the community that requested them. While this meant that ejidatarios did not have to travel extensive distances to reach their parcels, it also meant that they had to settle for whatever lands were within the prescribed radius, regardless of their quality. And the quality of those lands, specifically if they had access to irrigation water, determined the finite number of individual-use parcels that would be created in each ejido. Furthermore, the 7-kilometer radiuses of neighboring ejidos that were in close enough proximity to each other could and did overlap, which led to the drawing of contested boundaries. Another pitfall was the creation of a category of smallholdings that were shielded from expropriation. As I discussed in chapter 3, small to midsize estates known as ranchos were the most common form of private land tenure in the Greater Bajío municipalities before the acceleration of the agrarian reform during the Cárdenas presidency. For example, according to the 1930 Agrarian Census, 91 percent of the 621 privately owned holdings in Abasolo, Guanajuato, measured 200 hectares or fewer; 96 percent of the 2,525 privately owned holdings in Tepatitlán, Jalisco, measured 200 hectares or fewer; and 97 percent of the 485 privately owned holdings in La Piedad, Michoacán, measured 200 hectares or fewer.[21] (Unfortunately, I cannot determine the percentage of holdings 300 hectares or fewer because the Agrarian Census grouped holdings that measured between 201 and 300 hectares in the "201 to 500 Hectares" category.) Thus Agrarian Commission survey engineers who were assigned to work in aspiring Greater Bajío ejidos were certain to survey significant portions of land that by law could not be expropriated to form agrarian reform communities.

The second stage of the land redistribution process began when Agrarian Commission personnel drafted a report that documented their census and land survey findings. These reports were sent to the state governors, who then had fifteen days to review them and render a provisional decision. Landowners who stood to lose lands if the governor approved the ejido request could make a formal challenge of the commission's conclusions during this fifteen-day window. If a governor approved the creation of an ejido, he decided how much land the ejido would be allotted and how many aspiring ejidatarios would receive access to individual-use parcels. If a governor failed to issue a decision within the fifteen-day window, it was assumed that the ejido request had been denied. However, the federal Agrarian Department reviewed all governors' decisions, including the tacit denials, as well as private landowners' challenges. Agrarian Department personnel worked with and answered directly to the president, and they had the authority to reduce or expand the size of provisionally approved ejidos, as well as overturn both explicit and tacit denials. The president's and the Agrarian Department's decisions regarding ejido requests were final and irrevocable, a power that allowed the progressive Cárdenas administration to countermand conservative governors who did not prioritize or were outright hostile to the agrarian reform.[22]

Like the initial steps of the land redistribution process, these intermediate ones could easily work against the interests of ejidatarios. As I detailed in chapter 3's analysis of intracommunity political conflicts in Pénjamo, Guanajuato, conservative Catholics who opposed the agrarian reform took advantage of their right to formally challenge the process by making spurious claims that they had sold enough of their holdings so that what remained in their possession was exempt from expropriation. Even when these challenges failed, they could slow the ejido creation process. And though state governors had to act within a well-defined time frame once they received Agrarian Commission reports, the Agrarian Code did not specify how quickly the Agrarian Department and the president had to review state-level provisional decisions. Because of this lack of specificity, conservative post-1940 federal administrations could stifle the agrarian reform by simply slowing their review process.

The final phase of the land redistribution process and its flaws were relatively straightforward. If federal officials sanctioned the establishment of an ejido, its external and internal boundaries were definitively set. The ejido leadership council, which was chosen via internal elections, would then assign parcels to individual ejidatarios using a random drawing. Perhaps to ensure that ejidatarios whose past employment opportunities had been more precarious benefited from the agrarian reform, individuals listed as *peones acasillados* (resident estate laborers) in the Agrarian Commission's census were assigned parcels after their neighbors, which put them at a distinct disadvantage in ejidos with a relatively small number of individual-use parcels. (The 1940 Agrarian Code terminated this guideline, and all ejidatarios were included in the random drawings.) It is possible that ejido leadership councils manipulated the drawings so that certain ejidatarios were allotted specific parcels, though I found no recorded evidence that this occurred in any of the ejidos I examined during my research. If the number of ejidatarios was greater than the number of available parcels, those who were excluded had three options: they could be granted access to unassigned parcels in a neighboring ejido; they could request an expansion of their ejido, which would require a new census and land survey; or they could request the establishment of an entirely new population center on vacant lands. Once ejidatarios were assigned a parcel, they were forbidden from subdividing it or transferring it to another individual's use via a sale, lease, or loan. And when an ejidatario died, only one individual—the widow (in the case of a male ejidatario), the oldest surviving child who was eligible to join the ejido, or, if the deceased ejidatario was unmarried or childless, the oldest surviving relative who was eligible to join the ejido—could inherit the parcel. These latter two provisions contributed to growing agrarian pressures when the Greater Bajío's population expanded during the years of the Bracero Program.[23]

INSUFFICIENT LANDS

The flaws inherent in the mandate that ejido lands had to be within 7 kilometers of the community that requested them became evident during the Bracero Program's earliest years, when landless campesinos who were eligible to become ejidatarios were denied lands because of that specific provision. In February 1930, campesinos from Isaac Arriaga (formerly Santa Ana Mancera), a community in the northern Michoacán municipality of Puruándiro, filed a formal request for ejido lands. The local Agrarian Commission did not conduct its land surveys and community census until September 1932, when it determined that 465 of Isaac Arriaga's 1,759 residents were eligible to become ejidatarios. However, no further official action was taken until Agrarian Department personnel exercised the powers that the 1934 Agrarian Code granted them and reviewed the case. It was during this review process that the Agrarian Department discovered a significant discrepancy in the reported census figures: only 321 individuals listed in the census met the eligibility criteria, and of those only 253 actually lived in Isaac Arriaga; the other 68 were from the neighboring communities of San José Huipana, La Soledad de Santa Ana, and Las Rosas. The Agrarian Department never explained why the census figures initially reported were erroneous, but federal officials decided that the mistake had been made in good faith and that the 321 campesinos who were eligible to become ejidatarios should receive access to lands. In July 1934, President Abelardo Rodríguez (1932–34) approved the expropriation of 2,290 hectares of the Santa Ana Mancera Hacienda to form Isaac Arriaga's ejido. All the 321 eligible rural workers listed in the census, including those who lived in neighboring communities, received access to an individual-use parcel in Isaac Arriaga.[24]

But Isaac Arriaga's residents were not satisfied with this resolution, and they formally requested an ejido expansion in February 1935. The Agrarian Commission determined that there were 195 Isaac Arriaga campesinos who were eligible to become ejidatarios but that only 314 hectares of the Santa Ana Mancera Hacienda could be earmarked for the expansion because of pending ejido requests from communities whose 7-kilometer radius overlapped with Isaac Arriaga's. The Agrarian Department reviewed the expansion request after Michoacán's governor failed to render a decision within the prescribed fifteen-day window, and while its personnel agreed that only 314 hectares could be allocated to Isaac Arriaga, it reduced the number of eligible ejidatarios to 194. President Cárdenas approved the ejido expansion in April 1936. However, only 59 individual-use parcels could be created within the newly expropriated lands, which meant that 135 aspiring ejidatarios were left landless. And though the president's official decision made no mention of the frustrated petitioners' occupation status, it is possible, perhaps even likely, that there were peones acasillados among the 135 who were denied lands, since they would only be assigned parcels after their neighbors.[25] Isaac Arriaga's landless rural workers formally requested a second ejido expansion in March 1938, but the Cárdenas administration denied it in April 1940 because there were no longer expropriation-eligible lands within 7 kilometers of the community. Perhaps because their neighbors realized that their prospects for a successful resolution were dim, only fifty-seven eligible aspiring ejidatarios attended the census meeting that the Agrarian Commission convened after the second expansion request.[26]

Nearly five years after the second ejido expansion petition was rejected, Isaac Arriaga's landless campesinos requested bracero contracts. In February 1945, Heliodoro Martínez Rangel, Isaac Arriaga's comisariado ejidal, wrote to Governor Mendoza Pardo, asking for an unspecified number of bracero eligibility cards that would be distributed among his community's landless campesinos. The ejido leader told the governor that there were approximately 300 "men in the community without an ejido parcel [who] thus find themselves in a most dreadful economic situation," but he was certain that they would be able to provide for their families if they were given the opportunity to migrate to and work in the United States.[27] The number of landless men that Martínez Rangel cited in his letter to the governor was significantly higher than either of the figures that the Agrarian Commission reported in the ejido expansion censuses, thus indicating that the census figures were inaccurate or that Martínez Rangel exaggerated his ejido's plight to curry sympathy with the state government. However, while he was apparently willing to stretch the truth in his request, he made no explicit mention of either the frustrated second ejido expansion or the initial ejido expansion that had failed to meet his constituents' needs. Perhaps he feared that state authorities would react with hostility if he highlighted that the application of official policies was one of the primary reasons that there were so many landless rural workers in Isaac Arriaga. But whatever reasons motivated Martínez Rangel's omission, the 1934 Agrarian Code's provisions regarding the proximity of ejido lands to the community that requested them clearly contributed to the landlessness phenomenon that the ejido president cited in his bracero contract request.

Isaac Arriaga's comisariado ejidal could at least take some solace from the fact that several hundred of his constituents did have access to an ejido parcel. That was not the case in La Quesera de Cortés, a community in the southern Guanajuato municipality of Pénjamo. La Quesera campesinos formally requested ejido lands in June 1932, but the local Agrarian Commission did not perform the community census and land surveys until December 1935. The commission's personnel registered eighty-six rural workers who were eligible to become ejidatarios. However, sixty-two of them were peones acasillados; and the only remaining privately owned holdings within 7 kilometers of La Quesera that had not already been earmarked for the formation of other ejidos were small enough to be exempt from expropriation. Guanajuato's governor explicitly denied La Quesera's request in September 1936 because there were not expropriation-eligible lands within the 7-kilometer radius. The Agrarian Department's review corroborated that there were no privately owned lands near enough to La Quesera that could be expropriated to form an ejido there. It also reduced the number of La Quesera residents who were eligible to join an ejido to twenty-three after revising the ages of those listed in the census and determining that the sixty-two listed peones acasillados had better standing to become ejidatarios in neighboring Las Liebres. Despite the lack of lands, the Cárdenas administration reversed the state government's decision and sanctioned the approval of La Quesera's ejido but only so that the twenty-three eligible campesinos would have legal standing to request the creation of a new population center on vacant lands.[28]

There is no record that La Quesera's landless rural workers ever petitioned for vacant lands elsewhere. Instead, they renewed their efforts to secure ejido lands near their home. Because federal authorities had approved their initial ejido request, they found themselves in the curious position of having to formally petition Guanajuato's government for the expansion of an agrarian reform community that only existed on paper. The state government published the undated request in the October 5, 1944, edition of its official newspaper, and the local Agrarian Commission submitted its report in late December of that year. The commission's census listed fifty eligible rural workers, but once again the land survey found that there were no privately owned lands within 7 kilometers of La Quesera that could be expropriated. Despite this, Governor Ernesto Hidalgo decided to give provisional approval to the expansion request, and he justified his decision by citing the fifty La Quesera residents who were deemed eligible to become ejidatarios.[29]

While La Quesera's aspiring ejidatarios awaited the federal government's final resolution, some decided to seek work in the United States as braceros. In June 1945, José Abundis, who identified himself as La Quesera's comisariado ejidal, asked Governor Hidalgo for six bracero contracts. Like his counterpart in Isaac Arriaga, Michoacán, Abundis noted that there were a significant number of landless rural workers, ninety, in the community he represented. Also like his counterpart, he omitted any mention that the strict application of the Agrarian Code had contributed to landlessness in La Quesera, perhaps because at that moment he still held out hope that federal authorities would find a means of building on the state government's provisional expansion approval and establish an ejido that existed outside the pages of official records.[30] Those hopes were dashed in July 1948, when President Miguel Alemán countermanded Governor Hidalgo's decision and denied La Quesera's request.[31]

POOR-QUALITY LANDS AND THE BANCO EJIDAL

Other Greater Bajío ejidatarios turned to the Bracero Program for relief because the only lands available within 7 kilometers of their ejidos were relatively poor-quality temporal ones that were extremely susceptible to crop losses during drought cycles, like the one that affected southern Guanajuato and northern Michoacán during the initial years of the guest worker initiative. In April 1936, President Cárdenas approved the expropriation of 576 hectares to form an ejido in Las Raíces, a community in the southern Guanajuato municipality of Valle de Santiago. The majority of the ejido's lands, 428 hectares, were cultivable, and the remainder were either for grazing livestock or building new housing; but the entirety of those cultivable lands were temporal.[32] In December 1944, Las Raíces's ejidatarios wrote to Governor Hidalgo and requested an unspecified number of bracero contracts. The aspiring braceros bluntly stated that they wanted to migrate "because of our absolute reliance on temporal lands," and they explained that "the lack of rains has led to the total loss of our maize and bean harvests, and the drought that is afflicting this region is so extreme that our livestock no longer have grass to feed on—our situation is, simply put, desperate, our families are on the brink of starvation because we do not have any maize or beans, the most indispensable elements that we need to live." The petitioners acknowledged their awareness of the federal directive that barred ejidatarios from migrating as braceros. But, in an echo of the Durango braceros that Deborah Cohen has studied—who stated in oral histories that one of the reasons they migrated as braceros was because they wanted to earn money that would help them fulfill their roles as patriarchal caregivers—Las Raíces's ejidatarios told Governor Hidalgo that they were fathers who could not "stand by with their arms crossed" while their families died of hunger, and they expressed confidence that he would surely find it in his heart to ignore federal mandates if he put himself in their shoes and imagined having to tell his children "with teary eyes" that there was no food to eat.[33] But these pleas failed to move state officials, who curtly informed Las Raíces's ejidatarios that their request for bracero contracts could not be fulfilled.[34]

Las Raíces's ejidatarios were not the only ones from Valle de Santiago who sought to ameliorate the socioeconomic impact of drought-related crop losses by migrating as braceros during the mid-1940s. Written contract requests sent from six other Valle de Santiago ejidos—El Salitre, Las Jicamas, Presa de San Andrés, Sanabria, San Antonio de Pantoja, and Santa Catarina—in 1944 and 1945 explicitly cited crop losses that drought conditions had caused as the reason rural workers from those communities wanted to migrate.[35] A review of their ejido grants, all of which were approved according to the 1934 Agrarian Code's provisions, shows that the lands these six communities had received left them especially vulnerable during drought cycles. The sizes of these ejidos ranged from 139 hectares (Santa Catarina) to 1,862 hectares (El Salitre). But only Santa Catarina, the smallest ejido of the six, featured lands that had access to irrigation water. (Forty-four hectares in Santa Catarina's ejido were irrigable.)[36]

The 1944–45 drought cycle also exacerbated the effects of other federal restrictions that applied to ejidatarios. As Boyer has written, the Cárdenas administration banned logging in Michoacán's Sierra Purépecha, immediately south of the state's Greater Bajío jurisdictions, in late 1937 to curb the feared overexploitation of the state's woodland resources. But while federal authorities allowed Parícutin eruption victims to resume logging during the mid-1940s, Greater Bajío ejidatarios remained subject to the proscription, therefore limiting how they could respond to the drought and pushing them toward the Bracero Program.[37] For example, the comisariado ejidal of Pretoria—an ejido in the northern Michoacán municipality of Coeneo, which is immediately north of the Sierra Purépecha—requested contracts on behalf of at least thirty ejidatarios from his community. Forty-three Pretoria ejidatarios had received a parcel when the ejido was established in August

1936; but federal authorities allotted the agrarian reform community just 152 cultivable hectares, and 70 percent of those cultivable lands were temporal.[38] The ejido president cited the drought's impact on Pretoria, which he described as the poorest ejido in Coeneo because of the meager quality of its lands, as one of the reasons he was contacting the governor. He also explained that Pretoria residents had supplemented their incomes and provided for their families in past lean years by traveling to nearby forested hillsides and logging small quantities of lumber. But since that avenue was now closed to them, Pretoria's ejidatarios had decided that migrating to the United States as braceros was the "only means of solving our difficult situation."[39]

Drought conditions also highlighted the pernicious nature of the Banco Ejidal, the federally backed bank that was ejidatarios' exclusive source of credit. In January 1944, José Rentería wrote to Guanajuato's governor from Rancho Nuevo de San Andrés (formerly Mogotes; hereafter Rancho Nuevo), another Valle de Santiago ejido that had recently experienced crop losses, requesting twenty-two bracero contracts.[40] Rentería did not explicitly cite the drought as the cause of the crop losses in his petition, but given the bracero contract requests from Valle de Santiago ejidos and the fact that all 976 hectares of cultivable land in Rancho Nuevo's ejido were temporal, it is reasonable to conclude that the scarcity of rains contributed to the community's plight.[41] Rentería renewed his petition one month later, only this time he asked the state government for sixty-five bracero contracts. In this second request, Rentería, who now identified himself as a member of the ejido leadership council, explained that the recent crop losses had dealt a particularly cruel blow to Rancho Nuevo's ejidatarios because many of them had liquidated their maize and bean reserves to repay debts that they owed to the Banco Ejidal. As a result, they had absolutely no food for their families, and they felt that they had little recourse but to seek employment in the United States.[42]

While Rancho Nuevo's ejidatarios sought out bracero contracts to ameliorate losses that the Banco Ejidal's repayment terms had exacerbated, ejidatarios from the Coeneo, Michoacán, ejido of Laredo asked for contracts to secure Banco Ejidal funds. Federal officials approved the establishment of Laredo's 694-hectare ejido in September 1934. The grant included 360 hectares of irrigable cultivable land (of a total of 384 cultivable hectares), a 70-hectare reservoir, and a canal system that measured 3 hectares.[43] But despite the relatively high quality of their lands, Laredo's ejidatarios wrote to Governor Mendoza Pardo to request thirty bracero contracts in March 1945. The aspiring braceros noted that the drought had been so severe that even their ejido had lost half of its most recent maize crop. The ejidatarios' initial response to their plight was to improve the ejido's irrigation system so that they could prevent crop losses during future drought cycles. But the personnel at the Banco Ejidal's Zacapu branch told them that the bank would provide a loan to fund the project only if they provided cash collateral. Without crops to sell, the ejidatarios reasoned that migration would afford them the opportunity to earn moneys that would allow them to secure the loan and finish a project that would "greatly benefit the community and the nation."[44]

The phenomenon of ejidatarios who only had access to cultivable temporal lands requesting bracero contracts was not confined to the mid-1940s: it reemerged during a drought cycle that affected southwestern Aguascalientes and southern Zacatecas during the late 1950s and early 1960s. In August 1957, the comisariado ejidal of Centro de Arriba, an ejido in Aguascalientes City's rural hinterland, wrote to the state government to ask for forty-five bracero contracts that would be distributed among ejidatarios "who are truly in utmost need of employment and who have not been able to sow their lands because of the lack of rains in this region."[45] Three years later, the ejido president of Ermita de Guadalupe, an agrarian reform community in the southern Zacatecas municipality of Jerez, asked federal authorities to consider the "urgent situation" in his community and allot it an unspecified number of bracero contracts that would go to those whose socioeconomic standing had worsened because of drought-related crop losses.[46] Like the Valle de Santiago ejidos discussed earlier, both Centro de Arriba and Ermita de Guadalupe were allotted cultivable temporal lands that were susceptible to losses during extreme weather conditions. Centro de Arriba's ejido had 2,977 hectares of communal-use livestock grazing lands and 852 cultivable hectares; all of the latter were temporal.[47] And in Ermita de Guadalupe—an ejido that was established according to the statutes of the 1927 Land and Water Grants Law, which also mandated that ejido lands had to be within 7 kilometers of the community that requested them—all of the ejido's 761 cultivable hectares were temporal, and the remaining 672 hectares were dedicated to livestock grazing.[48]

CONTESTED BOUNDARIES

The application of the 7-kilometer-radius provision led to infrastructure that had traditionally been used by one community being assigned to another's ejido, which resulted in agrarian pressures that prompted decisions to request bracero contracts. This is the situation that unfolded between the neighboring ejidos of La Luz and Presa de los Serna. La Luz, which is in the southern Zacatecas municipality of Huanusco, received its ejido lands in April 1940.[49] Federal authorities did not approve the creation of an ejido in Presa de los Serna, which is in the southwestern Aguascalientes municipality of Calvillo, until March 1957, nearly seventeen years after campesinos there had formally requested lands. And while seventy-two Presa de los Serna rural workers were deemed eligible to join the ejido, the land grant included only enough cultivable hectares to form sixteen individual-use parcels.[50] Six months after Presa de los Serna's ejido was established, Encarnación Flores wrote to Aguascalientes's governor from there and requested bracero contracts for five unemployed rural workers. Flores did not specify if these individuals had been denied lands in the recently created ejido. But he did note that drought conditions had delayed the flowering of local guava orchards, which he described as the principal source of rural employment in the community, and that the "lack of food, work, and even water to drink" had already caused fifteen families to leave Presa de los Serna in the hope that they would find better socioeconomic opportunities elsewhere. Furthermore, Flores claimed that conditions in Presa de los Serna had worsened after La Luz's ejidatarios had "stolen" a reservoir from the community.[51]

Flores did not elaborate on this alleged theft, but several of his neighbors did. One week before Flores sent his bracero contract request to the state government, five other Presa de los Serna residents lodged a complaint with Governor Luis Ortega Douglas. The five—Adolfo de la Serna, Cipriano Serna, Arturo Serna, Jesús Serna, and Rogelio Serna—accused La Luz's ejidatarios of invading lands that had belonged to Presa de los Serna residents since the late nineteenth century and seizing control of three small reservoirs "that our grandfathers built with much sacrifice and that we have maintained until the present day." The complainants alleged that Zacatecas state officials were aiding the invading ejidatarios' efforts, and they urged Ortega Douglas to intervene in the matter and ensure that Aguascalientes's state boundaries were respected.[52]

Governor Ortega Douglas forwarded the allegations to federal authorities, who dispatched Aureliano Guzmán Elías and Ricardo Becerríl López—the former represented the Agrarian Department; the latter, the Hydraulic Resources Secretariat, the agency responsible for maintaining water management infrastructure—to Presa de los Serna so they could investigate. The federal officials arrived in Presa de los Serna in October 1957 and immediately learned that the intercommunity conflict centered on access to one small reservoir (5,000 cubic meters of capacity) that Presa de los Serna residents had built. But federal authorities had included that reservoir in La Luz's ejido grant, and the complainants from Presa de los Serna wanted it returned to their community.[53] But Guzmán Elías, the Agrarian Department's representative, concluded that Presa de los Serna had no standing to reclaim the reservoir, which was primarily used for watering livestock. While he acknowledged that the reservoir was in Aguascalientes, it was also within 7 kilometers of La Luz, which meant that it could be part of the latter's ejido. Furthermore, Guzmán Elías reasoned, the president, by virtue of his office, had full legal authority to authorize ejido expropriations that crossed state lines. Guzmán Elías then spoke to La Luz's comisariado ejidal, who told him that his constituents had actually refrained from using the reservoir until 1957 and that they had only started exploiting it because of the severity of the drought cycle that was affecting southern Zacatecas and southwestern Aguascalientes. Ultimately, Guzmán Elías determined that there was no land invasion and that La Luz's ejidatarios were guilty of nothing more than using a resource that federal officials had allotted to them.[54]

The admission by La Luz's comisariado ejidal that ejidatarios in his community had not started using the contested reservoir until 1957, seventeen years after their ejido had been established, suggests an intriguing possibility—that La Luz's ejidatarios purposely instigated the dispute to secure a federal ruling that favored them. As noted previously, federal authorities did not approve the creation of Presa de los Serna's ejido until March 1957. It is possible that La Luz's agrarian reform beneficiaries were content to essentially ignore the reservoir so long as Presa de los Serna's residents did not have access to expropriated lands. But the establishment of the latter community's ejido changed the reality on the ground, and La Luz's ejidatarios may have felt that it was necessary for them to effectively assert their claim so as to prevent encroachments on their grant. If their sudden interest in the reservoir was a calculated gambit (as well as a response to the onset of another drought cycle), it paid dividends: federal authorities explicitly declared that the reservoir belonged to La Luz's ejido, and Aguascalientes officials informed the complaining parties in November 1957 that they would not be contesting the national government's ruling.[55] Without access to a sufficient number of individual-use parcels and deprived of a small but key piece of infrastructure, Presa de los Serna's campesinos continued to set their sights north. Nearly three years after he first requested bracero contracts, Encarnación Flores wrote to state officials once again and asked for contracts on behalf of four young rural workers who were in desperate financial need.[56]

THE CONSERVATIVE SHIFT IN AGRARIAN POLICY

While the enforcement of the Agrarian Code's provisions, particularly the mandate that ejido lands had to be within 7 kilometers of the community that used them, pushed ejidatarios to request bracero contracts, the slowing of the agrarian reform prompted younger non-ejidatarios who came of age after 1940 to set their sights north as well. As noted earlier, whereas federal administrations redistributed 1.9 million hectares among 191,357 Greater Bajío ejidatarios between 1915 and the end of Cárdenas's presidency in late 1940, they sanctioned the redistribution of only 397,596 hectares among 18,962 Greater Bajío ejidatarios between late 1940 and the end of the Bracero Program in 1964. And since the Agrarian Code explicitly stated that the president and the Agrarian Department were the nation's ultimate agrarian authorities, the conservative post-1940 presidential administrations stifled the land redistribution process by simply delaying the review of ejido petitions that state governments forwarded to them for final review. Concurrently, the region's population grew from 2.2 million in 1940 to 3.5 million in 1960.

Much like the 1934 Agrarian Code reflected the ideological and political debates that occurred during the decades that preceded its drafting, the slowing of the agrarian reform was indicative of the conservative leanings of Cárdenas's presidential successors. Ávila Camacho's administration of the early 1940s prioritized boosting production on existing ejidos over redistributing newly expropriated lands, and to achieve that end, his agriculture and development secretary, Marte R. Gómez, established the Oficina de Estudios Especiales, a transnational partnership with the US-based Rockefeller Foundation that introduced high-yield maize varieties via agricultural research and extension facilities. The administration could then point to this initiative when it argued that it was committed to strengthening the ejido sector, even if fewer lands were being redistributed. Alemán's government, which succeeded Ávila Camacho's, dispensed with even that rhetorical overture, as Alemán made no secret that he interpreted the agrarian reform as a source of rural insecurity and instability. His administration encouraged increased wheat cultivation and doubled down on the use of new maize varieties that had to be purchased from federal agencies. Furthermore, it established commissions that coordinated the construction of reservoirs, irrigation canals, paved roads, and hydroelectric infrastructure that in turn opened new lands to cultivation in river basins like the Tepalcatepec in central Michoacán and the Papaloapan in central Veracruz, eastern Oaxaca, and southeastern Puebla. It was hoped that these projects, which Alemán's successors continued during their administrations, would attract internal migrants from more densely populated regions, which would thus negate the need to expropriate and redistribute already existing private estates.[57]

There were already indicators by the mid-1940s that the conservative turn in national agrarian policy and demographic expansion were contributing to socioeconomic pressures that prompted individuals' decisions to migrate as braceros. On Christmas Day 1944, Gregorio Cervantes, comisariado ejidal of the Huanímaro, Guanajuato, ejido of San Cristóbal, wrote to Governor Hidalgo to request fifteen bracero contracts. Like his contemporary counterparts from neighboring Valle de Santiago, Cervantes noted that the community had suffered significant crop losses, presumably because of the drought that was afflicting the region. But he also mentioned that his constituents lacked seeds for the upcoming planting cycle, thus hinting that they may have started transitioning to the new varieties that federal officials were promoting. Cervantes then explained that the fifteen would-be braceros he was writing on behalf of were not ejidatarios. Rather, they were members of an "excessive group of young men who do not have access to an individual-use parcel because they were legal minors when the ejido grant was approved, but since many of them are now married, they have to fulfill their obligations . . . to the households that depend on them."[58] Forty-four San Cristóbal campesinos became ejidatarios when the Cárdenas administration approved their ejido request in November 1938. Federal authorities based their decision on a December 1933 Agrarian Commission census that listed 164 total residents in San Cristóbal.[59] But the 1940 Population Census showed that San Cristóbal's population had already grown to 232 by the eve of the Bracero Program, a harbinger of the demographic expansion that would occur throughout the Greater Bajío during the next two decades.[60]

The effects of the population boom and the agrarian reform's slowing on bracero migration patterns became more pronounced during the 1950s and 1960s. For example, in April 1953, 116 residents from eight ejidos in the northeastern Jalisco municipality of La Barca—El Gobernador, El Portezuelo, La Paz de Ordaz, Loreto Occidental, Salamea, San Antonio, San Francisco, and San Ramón—wrote to President Ruiz Cortines to request bracero contracts.

The petitioners noted that they had long lived "in the most frightful misery due to the lack of work and lands to sow, for we are members of the younger generations who did not benefit from the Agrarian Laws and the redistribution of the large estates (*latifundios*) because we were not old enough to be granted parcels, and now that we are old enough there are no longer lands that can be redistributed." These men worked as day laborers on unexpropriated private estates whenever they could. But, as they told the president, their wages were generally so low "that our families barely have enough to eat one daily meal and our children sometimes go to school without having eaten anything at all." The group also expressed certainty that there were privately owned lands in the municipality that could be expropriated. But since it appeared that federal authorities would no longer approve new redistributions, they asked for bracero contracts.[61] The aspiring braceros renewed their request two months later, and they explicitly noted that they were only interested in migrating as braceros because their desires to cultivate lands of their own had been frustrated.[62]

The spring 1953 bracero contract requests from La Barca reflected the dual impact of demographic expansion and the glacial pace of land redistribution after 1940. The eight ejidos that the petitioning group wrote from had all been established between November 1934 (San Antonio) and April 1938 (Loreto Occidental).[63] And the Cárdenas administration approved a modest expansion (264 hectares) of La Paz de Ordaz's ejido in May 1938.[64] It would be another decade before federal authorities approved the redistribution of newly expropriated lands in those eight ejidos. El Gobernador's ejidatarios formally requested an ejido expansion in October 1938; but while the Ávila Camacho administration approved the request, there were no expropriation-eligible lands within 7 kilometers of the community, so the ejido's size remained unchanged.[65] El Gobernador's agrarian reform beneficiaries filed another expansion request in January 1945 that the Alemán administration approved nearly five years later, in December 1949, though the ejido gained only 22 hectares.[66] The official resolution of El Gobernador's expansion request was lightning paced when compared to neighboring communities. Salamea's ejidatarios formally requested additional lands in March 1937, but federal authorities did not rule on their petition until November 1949; they denied the request on the grounds that there were no expropriation-eligible lands near enough to the community.[67] And it was not until October 1964, during the Bracero Program's final months, that federal officials approved an ejido expansion request that San Antonio's ejidatarios made in December

1948.[68] While these ejido expansion requests were either being rejected or collecting dust on the Agrarian Department's desk, the population in the eight petitioning ejidos grew. According to the 1950 Population Census, conducted three years before the group of 116 made their bracero contract requests, the combined population of El Gobernador, El Portezuelo, La Paz de Ordaz, Loreto Occidental, Salamea, San Antonio, San Francisco, and San Ramón was 6,926, up from 5,965 in 1940.[69]

The combination of demographic expansion and the slowed land redistribution process became particularly severe in the northern Michoacán municipality of Zacapu during the early 1960s. Zacapu was one of the cradles of the agrarian reform in the Greater Bajío. Primo Tapia, a native of the Zacapu community of Naranja who spent time working in the United States in the 1910s, became a leading popular proponent of land redistribution in Michoacán in the 1920s. Tapia helped establish ejidos in his native Naranja, the municipal seat, Tarejero, and Tiríndaro, and he was also the founding secretary general of the Michoacán chapter of the Liga de Comunidades Agrarias. Tapia was assassinated in 1926, but the land redistribution process continued in Zacapu in the decade after his death.[70] By the time Cárdenas's presidential term ended in late 1940, federal administrations had authorized the establishment of eighteen ejidos in the municipality and greenlit six ejido expansions.[71] However, much as it did in the rest of the Greater Bajío, the agrarian reform ground to a halt in Zacapu during the years of the Bracero Program. The only lands redistributed in the municipality during the Bracero Program were the additional 282 hectares that were allotted to Las Canoas in February 1950.[72] And federal officials never acted on formal requests for access to vacant lands, such as the ones Cantabría's landless campesinos made in November 1950 and March 1961.[73] Simultaneously, the municipality's demographic expansion rate exceeded the Greater Bajío's regional one. The jurisdiction's population more than doubled between 1940 and 1960, from 16,501 to 38,812.[74]

Bracero contract requests sent from Zacapu during the early 1960s reflected the population boom and the virtual end of the agrarian reform there. Of the twenty-two available written contract requests that Zacapu's aspiring braceros sent to state authorities during the Bracero Program's final three years, half cited landlessness, large families to provide for, or some combination of the two as the reason for wanting to migrate.[75] And in what may have been a bitter pill for the agrarian reform's initial popular supporters and their children to swallow, several of the requests noted that the aspiring braceros were the landless sons of ejidatarios, a demographic that had no hope of gaining access to newly redistributed lands or joining existing ejidos because the Agrarian Code barred their parents from subdividing their parcels under any circumstances. For example, in February 1964, Mateo Ambrís Constantino, comisariado ejidal of the municipal seat—where a combined 409 ejidatarios were granted access to a combined 1,714 hectares in the ejido's 1925 establishment and its 1935 expansion—wrote to Governor Agustín Arriaga Rivera to request contracts for forty-two landless sons of ejidatarios.[76] Perhaps to remind the governor of the pioneering role that Zacapu played during the agrarian reform's incipient years, Ambrís Constantino described the parents of the would-be braceros as "militant" ejidatarios. But the ejido president noted in his request that the aspiring braceros could no longer provide for themselves and their growing families by subsisting on what their parents harvested. Because of this, Ambrís Constantino urged the governor to look kindly on the aspiring braceros, all of whom had proven themselves to be hard workers, and allot them contracts so that they could live freer lives and cease burdening their "poor parents."[77]

Greater Bajío ejidos also suffered because conservative post-1940 federal administrations did not launch large-scale rural development initiatives in that region like they did in others. As I noted earlier, the Alemán administration established river basin commissions that aimed to open new lands to cultivation via the construction of irrigation infrastructure, hydroelectric dams, and paved roads. The river commissions also sought to control flooding in the regions they targeted, a goal that was deemed imperative after the Papaloapan River, which waters and drains the lands of southeastern Puebla, eastern Oaxaca, and central Veracruz, overflowed and flooded nearly 21,000 square kilometers in September 1944, leading to the death of several hundred residents.[78]

But because the federal government did not pursue hydraulic infrastructure initiatives in the Greater Bajío that were comparable to those of the Papaloapan River basin or the Tepalcatepec River basin in central Michoacán, Greater Bajío ejidos were as susceptible to flood-related crop losses during especially wet years as they were to drought-related crop losses during especially dry years. And much like their drought-affected counterparts, flood-affected ejidatarios turned to the Bracero Program for relief. During the 1963 rainy season, the Lerma River and its tributaries, which water and drain the lands of southern Guanajuato, northern Michoacán, and northeastern Jalisco before emptying into Lake Chapala, overflowed their banks and devastated agricultural production, particularly in northern Michoacán: twenty-one written bracero contract requests that northern Michoacán residents sent to state officials in 1963 cited flood-related crop losses as the reason for wanting to migrate.[79] For example, the ejido leadership council of Monteleón, in the municipality of Yurécuaro, wrote to the governor on August 9 to request an unspecified number of bracero contracts. The council members explained that their constituents wanted to migrate because heavy rains and floods washed away the maize that they had planted on 800 hectares.[80] Monteleón's ejido had 1,669 hectares of cultivable land, which meant that the floods had essentially destroyed half their maize harvest.[81] One week later, the leadership council of the Zamora ejido of La Sauceda requested bracero contracts for 70 ejidatarios—more than half the 123 ejidatarios who had use rights in the ejido—who could not work their flooded parcels and who had no other means of income to provide for their families.[82]

. . .

President Adolfo López Mateos's administration approved the expansion of the northeastern Jalisco ejido of San Antonio in October 1964. The decision was made nearly sixteen years after San Antonio's ejidatarios formally requested additional ejido lands and eleven years after young, landless rural workers from that ejido joined their neighbors and requested bracero contracts because federal officials had rebuffed their petitions for redistributed lands. But the expansion of San Antonio's ejido marked a hollow victory. Federal authorities added only 175 cultivable hectares to the ejido because those were the only privately owned lands that were within 7 kilometers of the community. And because the 175 hectares could not be divided into enough individual-use parcels to allot one to each of the 195 San Antonio campesinos who were eligible to join the ejido, federal authorities declared that the community would have to use the newly expropriated lands collectively.[83]

The ultimate fate of San Antonio's ejido expansion request was emblematic of the politicized shortcomings that plagued the land redistribution process in the Greater Bajío and contributed to popular interest in migrating as braceros. The 1934 Agrarian Code, which structured the establishment of the majority of the Greater Bajío's ejidos and reflected the ideological and political debates of the 1910s, 1920s, and 1930s—specifically, the concerns and prerogatives of the moderate Constitutionalist and progressive Cardenista factions—imposed guidelines and regulations that granted ejidatarios poor-quality lands that were close to their communities but susceptible to weather-related crop losses, limited what agrarian reform beneficiaries could do with their lands and where they could get credit from, and created a class of small private properties that were exempt from expropriation. When ejidatarios in Greater Bajío municipalities like Jerez, Zacatecas and Calvillo, Aguascalientes, suffered drought-related crop losses, or when individuals in jurisdictions like Puruándiro, Michoacán and Pénjamo, Guanajuato, were denied lands because there were no longer expropriation-eligible lands within 7 kilometers of their communities, they requested bracero contracts. Furthermore, because the Agrarian Code privileged federal power, the conservative presidential administrations of the post-1940 period—which prioritized increasing agricultural production on existing ejidos and opening new lands to cultivation via large-scale rural development initiatives like the Tepalcatepec and Papaloapan River Commissions—dramatically slowed the pace of the agrarian reform during the years of the Bracero Program. As a result, young rural workers with frustrated ambitions to become ejidatarios wrote to federal and state authorities from municipalities like La Barca, Jalisco and Zacapu, Michoacán, and asked permission to migrate as braceros.

Much like their neighbors who were embroiled in the community-level political conflicts that I examined in chapter 3, the actual and would-be agrarian reform beneficiaries who expressed an interest in migrating under the auspices of the Bracero Program directed their petitions to federal and state authorities. But the officials who actually wielded the power to select individual braceros were municipal ones. And, as I detail in the next chapter, these officials' primary interest was using the bracero selection process to meet their own political and financial ends, not ameliorate the socioeconomic marginalization of their constituents who were enmeshed in endemic community-level conflicts or whose interests had been undermined by the Agrarian Code's provisions or the post-1940 conservative turn in federal agrarian policy.

FIVE

A *"Mockery of Responsibility"*

MUNICIPAL-LEVEL ADMINISTRATION OF THE
BRACERO PROGRAM

IN MAY 1947, AN ANONYMOUS resident of the northeastern Jalisco municipality of La Barca wrote to Governor Jesús González Gallo to complain about how the municipal government there had selected braceros. The complainant, who did not reveal their name because they feared violent reprisals, alleged that the "thieving vampires" who made up La Barca's ayuntamiento had flagrantly disregarded the state government's instructions that only campesinos who were not ejidatarios be chosen as braceros. Instead, the ayuntamiento members had given bracero eligibility cards to relatives of theirs or individuals who were not campesinos, such as a confectioner, a shoeshine person, and a dredge operator who was actually a resident of the neighboring state of Guanajuato. The anonymous accuser claimed that some of those who had received eligibility cards had paid bribes for their documents and that the "scamming mafiosos" who administered the local government had openly boasted that they could do as they please during the bracero selection period because they did not answer to Governor González Gallo. The letter writer hoped that the governor would prove them wrong by citing the corruption of the bracero selection process as a motive to intervene in La Barca, dissolve the municipal government, and thus provide some relief to the jurisdiction's "unhappy" populace. But La Barca's ayuntamiento members were right to be confident of their impunity: there is no record that González Gallo's administration opened even a cursory investigation into the allegations.[1]

This chapter examines how municipal governments in the primary bracero-sending states of Aguascalientes, Guanajuato, Jalisco, Michoacán, and Zacatecas selected braceros and shows that episodes like the one involving the anonymous complainant were the norm during contracting periods.

Because of the federal government's failed attempt to closely manage the bracero selection process and state-level disinterest in intervening in that process, municipal officials were entrusted with the critical task of choosing which individuals received contracts for the vast majority of the Bracero Program's duration. And since federal and state authorities generally abstained from providing even minimal oversight, municipal governments essentially had free reign to distribute bracero eligibility cards as they pleased. Granted de facto autonomy, local officials corrupted the bracero selection process and routinely disregarded even the most basic directives issued by federal and state authorities. In most instances municipal authorities also proved utterly indifferent to the pressing socioeconomic marginalization that drove their constituents to seek bracero contracts.

Autonomy and corruption led to municipal officials reaping far more direct and tangible benefits from administering the Bracero Program than their federal- and state-level counterparts did. The most obvious benefit was financial. As soon as they became responsible for selecting braceros, local officials began enriching themselves by giving eligibility cards to anyone who was willing to pay a bribe, regardless of whether they met the established eligibility requirements. That practice continued until the Bracero Program ended, and some officials were alleged to have pocketed thousands of pesos. Moreover, controlling the bracero selection process yielded significant political rewards. Local authorities solidified their standing by giving eligibility cards to municipal personnel and employees, their allies in rural communities, or restive constituents who they wanted temporarily removed.

But the corruption of the bracero selection process cannot be simply ascribed to rogue officials who were operating in a vacuum. Put another way, the decision to use the Bracero Program as a means of achieving financial or political ends was deeply influenced by a web of local, regional, and national political factors that included but was not limited to the lack of meaningful federal and state oversight. Local officials who were sympathetic to or openly aligned with conservative Catholic opposition organizations like the UNS or the PAN, both of which drew most of their support from the primary sending states, gave eligibility cards as rewards to members of those groups. Those officials who were more hostile to the UNS and the PAN used the Bracero Program to neutralize their electoral strength by sending their partisans to the United States. Rural authorities whose treasuries were starved by federal taxation policy changes that centralized revenue collection and funneled funds to urban municipalities claimed that they were collecting bribes from aspiring braceros because they needed to finance their administrations, thus seeming to corroborate Smith's argument about rural governments resorting to bribery to recoup lost revenue streams.[2] And others, facing pressure from rural constituents who were expected to contribute monetarily to infrastructure projects like the electrification of their communities, behaved as "advocates"—to borrow the term María Teresa Fernández Aceves uses to describe Guadalupe Urzúa Flores, a Jalisco official who lobbied selflessly on behalf of her community of San Martín de Hidalgo—and asked higher-level officials for eligibility card allotments without any expectation of financial or political reward.[3]

Regardless of their motives, municipal officials were determined to maintain control of the bracero selection process and the benefits it yielded. This fierce commitment to maintaining the status quo sparked its own series of conflicts. Aspiring braceros were physically coerced into paying for their cards. The leaders of organizations that represented the interests of prospective braceros and highlighted municipal corruption, like the Alianza de Braceros Nacionales de México en los Estados Unidos de Norteamérica (Alliance of Mexican Braceros in the United States), were hounded and incarcerated. The few state-level officials who intervened directly during selection periods were violently confronted. And since the pleas of frustrated would-be braceros who denounced local corruption and asked that the selection process be modified went unanswered, those who wanted to migrate as braceros had little choice but to play by the rules that municipal governments established or attempt to enter the United States as undocumented workers.

THE EARLY SALE OF BRACERO ELIGIBILITY CARDS

Municipal officials in the primary bracero-sending states first became involved in the selection process when precontracting centers were opened in provincial cities like Zacatecas City and Irapuato, Guanajuato, in 1944. And they immediately corrupted the Bracero Program for their own financial gain. In May, a DIPS agent who was monitoring the Zacatecas City Precontracting Center overheard aspiring braceros from Morelos, a municipality immediately north of that city, discussing that they had paid local officials 5 pesos for their eligibility cards. The DIPS agent confiscated the cards and turned them over to Governor Pánfilo Natera, who pledged to investigate the matter.[4] Two months later, Ignacio Puente, a resident of the southern Guanajuato municipality of

San Francisco del Rincón, accused authorities there and in the neighboring jurisdiction of Purísima del Rincón of selling eligibility cards for between 50 and 100 pesos. Puente blamed a handful of "ill-intentioned individuals" who corrupted the "honorable" municipal president after the latter had registered those who were interested in migrating. He also expressed his dismay that the supposed "benefactors of the people" had turned out to be little more than men "without any kind of scruples who will find any pretext to exploit poor people who are trying to earn a living," and he asked the Ávila Camacho administration to intervene and put an end to the corruption. But federal authorities did little more than inform the state government about the accusations, and all state officials did was assure their federal counterparts that they had instructed municipal governments to distribute bracero eligibility cards free of charge.[5]

The men who paid Morelos, Purísima del Rincón, and San Francisco del Rincón officials for their eligibility cards were all presumably residents of those jurisdictions and met the eligibility requirements. But in other municipalities, local authorities profited by selling cards to nonresidents and men who did not meet the eligibility criteria. In early August 1944, Natividad Ortega Ramíres, a native and resident of the southern Guanajuato municipality of Pénjamo, traveled to neighboring Abasolo by bus because he hoped to acquire an eligibility card there. According to the statement Ortega Ramíres later gave to federal authorities, he was approached at the bus station by Ignacio Quiroz Ramírez. The latter had been selected during Abasolo's drawing, but he said that local authorities would give Ortega Ramíres his card in exchange for 25 pesos. The pair then went to the municipal government's offices, where Ortega Ramíres was given the card assigned to Quiroz Ramírez after paying the bribe. Ortega Ramíres also asserted that Abasolo authorities were selling other eligibility cards that had been distributed during the selection drawing, thus indicating that Abasolo's government had manipulated the drawing so that all the men who received cards were involved in the scheme to sell them. That same month, Leopoldo Torres Hernández—who was deposed on the same day and by the same federal officials who questioned Ortega Ramíres—left his native municipality of Tingüindín, in Michoacán's Sierra Purépecha, for Mexico City, where he hoped to acquire a contract. The train Torres Hernández was on made a stop in Irapuato, and he disembarked to purchase a meal. While he was on the platform, a man approached him and offered to sell him an eligibility card for 50 pesos. Torres Hernández agreed, and the man took the money and left.

Two hours later he returned with an eligibility card signed by Irapuato's municipal president.[6] (Although federal officials questioned both Ortega Ramíres and Torres Hernández, there is no record that municipal officials in Abasolo or Irapuato were punished for their actions.)

In the Guanajuato municipality of Romita, Zeferino Reyes Padilla, Ignacio Rodríguez Ramos, and Carlos Luna Rodríguez approached the municipal government after hearing about the 1944 contracting period. The municipal president, Daniel Vázquez, and an ayuntamiento member, David Rocha, told the three aspiring braceros that there was no need for them to register and enter their names in the selection drawing, so long as they paid 50 pesos. Although their financial resources were limited, the three would-be braceros decided to pay the bribe. But they were ultimately turned back at the precontracting center. Reyes Padilla and Rodríguez Ramos were too young to receive contracts, and Luna Rodríguez failed his medical exam. It was only after the three returned to Romita that they learned about the eligibility requirements and that the cards were supposed to be distributed free of charge. The desperate trio asked Vázquez to return their money, but Vázquez refused, which prompted the prospective braceros to take their pleas to Governor Hidalgo in late August.[7] Perhaps frustrated because they had to reissue the eligibility cards, state authorities instructed Vázquez to return the money.[8] However, Vázquez simply ignored the order. Reyes Padilla, Rodríguez Ramos, and Luna Rodríguez traveled to Guanajuato City in September to ask state officials to intervene more forcefully, but there is no evidence that Romita authorities suffered any consequences for their actions or that the aspiring braceros ever had their money returned to them.[9]

THE BRACERO SELECTION PROCESS AS A POLITICAL TOOL

Local officials quickly realized that they could also use the bracero selection process as a means of achieving political ends, such as favoring their home communities, repaying past favors, inducing rural constituents to participate in other government initiatives, or temporarily removing rural workers who posed an electoral threat. For example, the government of Dolores Hidalgo, in Guanajuato's northern highlands, received two hundred eligibility cards to distribute during the February 1945 contracting period.[10] The selection drawing was held on February 25. According to Sebastián Balderas and twelve others who wrote to the federal Labor and Social Welfare secretary the following day, at least three aspiring braceros were heard saying that they had paid for their eligibility cards. Balderas and his fellow would-be braceros also accused Eulalio Flores, the municipal government's delegate in Xoconoxtle el Grande, of tipping the scales in favor of his community. Flores was one of the local officials tasked with organizing the selection drawing, and he was ultimately the one who pulled names out of the pot. According to the group that wrote to the Labor and Social Welfare secretary, there were twenty-four prospective braceros from Xoconoxtle whose names were entered in the drawing. Twenty of them received eligibility cards, which meant that Xoconoxtle sent more braceros north that year than any other community in the jurisdiction. The complainants were certain that this was no mere coincidence, especially because they also heard Flores boasting during the selection drawing that he "knew how to get the job done."[11]

Members of local governments and friends of local officials were also the beneficiaries of municipal largesse during bracero selection periods. In May 1948, Domingo Álvarez, municipal president of Jesús María, Jalisco, decided to give eligibility cards to five "friends" who had loaned unspecified services to the municipal government without monetary compensation. One of these friends was an unemployed alternate member of the ayuntamiento. Álvarez went so far as to write to the state interior secretary, Carlos Guzmán, to ask that the municipality's allotment of eligibility cards be increased from twenty-six to thirty-one. Álvarez told Guzmán that he would only choose twenty-one braceros during the selection drawing and give the remaining five cards to his friends if his allotment was not increased, provided that the state government did not object.[12] State officials did not send Álvarez more eligibility cards, but there is no record that they openly opposed Álvarez's plan or explicitly instructed him against it. In early June, the municipal president informed Governor González Gallo that twenty-six aspiring braceros from his jurisdiction had received their eligibility cards.[13] His five friends were presumably among those who would be migrating.

Flores and Álvarez used the Bracero Program to meet relatively crude political ends. However, other municipal officials emulated the ones that Ana Elizabeth Rosas examines and decided to use the program as a means of advancing federal prerogatives. Rosas notes that local authorities in the western Jalisco municipality of San Martín de Hidalgo borrowed from the federal discourse that promoted the Bracero Program as a means to modernize rural Mexico when they encouraged middle-class constituents who were seen as being more likely to invest their earnings in entrepreneurial ventures to migrate during the 1940s.[14] And in spring 1946, municipal officials in Zacatecas City decided to use the Bracero Program to boost participation in a federal literacy campaign and only gave eligibility cards to campesinos who could prove that they had enrolled in the literacy drive.[15] The Ávila Camacho administration launched the national literacy campaign in August 1944 after the president declared that low literacy rates—the 1940 Population Census recorded that 45 percent of Mexicans six years or older could neither read nor write—represented the most dangerous "internal threat" to national unity and democratic participation.[16] But although Carmen Cosgaya and Dolores Uribe, two teachers employed by the SEP, designed the literacy curriculum, the federal government's campaign consisted of encouraging literate Mexicans via news and mass media to acquire curriculum workbooks and use them to teach their illiterate counterparts during their free time. Thus, as Cecilia Greaves has noted, state and local governments were essentially forced to take the lead and offered numerous rewards—reduced jail time for inmates who learned to read and write, scholarships for students who taught literacy, funding for infrastructure projects in communities that had high participation and success rates—to bolster participation.[17] Given the structure of the literacy campaign and the prominent role state and local administrations played in it, it is not surprising that Zacatecas City's municipal government offered bracero eligibility cards as a boon for those who learned to read and write.

But the decision to favor literacy campaign participants with bracero contracts reflected the failure and desperation of Zacatecas City's municipal government as much if not more than it did the federal government's relatively limited role in the literacy campaign. After meeting with teachers working in Zacatecas City's rural hinterland in early April 1945, SEP official Edmundo Gámez Orozco informed the municipal president, Luis de la Fuente, that for reasons that were not specified all the illiterate residents in the rural communities of San Blas and San Miguel had refused to enroll in the campaign.[18] De la Fuente immediately contacted the municipal government's representatives in both communities, urged them to convince the residents there to enroll in the campaign, and instructed them to warn those that still refused to participate that they could be subject to consequences.[19] Three months later, de la Fuente authorized punitive sanctions against rural constituents who did not enroll in the literacy campaign: either a one- to two-week jail sentence or a 5- to 50-peso fine.[20] The sanctions had a minimal effect on participation rates. Between October and November 1945, the number of the municipality's residents enrolled in the literacy program increased only slightly, from 711 to 776; the latter figure represented 10.2 percent of the municipality's registered illiterate population of 7,586.[21]

Since penalties had failed to boost participation in the literacy campaign, in 1946 de la Fuente's government shifted to offering bracero contracts as a reward to enrollees. But this strategy carried its own risks. The 1945 bracero contracting period had actually derailed the literacy campaign in La Escondida, one of the few rural communities in the municipality where residents had embraced the initiative. In the same report where he identified the resistance in San Blas and San Miguel, Gámez Orozco noted that the literacy campaign had been proceeding "satisfactorily" in La Escondida up until many residents departed as braceros. According to the SEP official, bracero migration deprived La Escondida of "competent authority" figures, and the community had plunged into a state of "disorder" marked by frequent household burglaries. As a result of the chaos, La Escondida's illiterate women refused to leave their homes to attend literacy classes, and others left the community for Zacatecas City (Gaméz Orozco did not specify if these moves were permanent or only until the braceros returned).[22] Despite the experience in La Escondida, de la Fuente's government decided that the benefits of using the Bracero Program as a reward to encourage participation in the literacy campaign outweighed the risks. Whether this strategy worked is unclear as I was unable to locate literacy campaign enrollment figures for 1946.

In Aguascalientes, municipal officials remained sensitive to the demands of that state's chapter of the Liga de Comunidades Agrarias, the organization that was directly involved in the bracero selection process in Aguascalientes on numerous occasions and continued to choose ejidatarios as braceros, despite the federal statute that barred ejidatarios from migrating. In May 1948, the Aguascalientes Liga secretary general, Juan Morán, informed the leadership of Viudas de Oriente, an ejido in the northeastern municipality of Asientos, that he had spoken with Asientos's municipal president and that the latter had agreed to select as braceros ejidatarios who lacked the credit and farm equipment to work their parcels. Morán also told the ejido leaders that because the Liga was not directing the selection process in Aguascalientes as it had in 1945, that arrangement marked the extent of his bracero-related influence that year.[23] But there is evidence that suggests that municipal governments continued to distribute bracero cards among Aguascalientes ejidatarios into the 1950s and that they may have expanded their efforts to include the recipients of loans issued by the Banco Ejidal. In April 1953, two Banco Ejidal employees reported to their superiors that an unspecified number of ejidatarios who had received loans to plant maize on irrigated parcels had migrated as braceros, and they wondered if it was wise to continue to extend credit to individuals who appeared more enthusiastic about migrating to the United States than working their lands in Mexico.[24]

The bracero selection process also became enmeshed in the ongoing community-level political conflicts between supporters of the agrarian reform and conservative Catholic opponents of land redistribution. As I noted in chapter 3, Puruándiro was one of the Michoacán municipalities where religious-political conflicts escalated during the early years of the Bracero Program, and active members of the UNS secured positions in the municipal administration there in early 1945. In February, Prisciliano Pérez, comisariado ejidal of Tres Mezquites, arranged for five aspiring braceros from his community to meet with Julio Torres, a state deputy who at the time was responsible for directing the bracero selection process in Puruándiro. (It is not clear if these aspiring braceros were ejidatarios.) The state deputy had no issue with the five Tres Mezquites workers leaving as braceros. But he had delegated the task of choosing braceros to municipal governments in his district, so he directed the prospective migrant workers to Puruándiro's municipal president, Martín Arroyo. But the would-be braceros' hopes were dashed when they learned that Arroyo was a UNS ally. The municipal president had asked the local Sinarquista chief Aristeo Aguirre to help with the bracero selection process. And the two of them had decided that they would give eligibility cards only to aspiring braceros who were also Sinarquistas. Since none of the five men from Tres Mezquites were active UNS members, they were denied eligibility cards. Arroyo told them that he was willing to reverse his decision if the prospective braceros swore allegiance to the Sinarquista cause, but Pérez implied in a letter he sent to Torres that his constituents had declined the opportunity.[25]

Irapuato Sinarquistas were also favored with bracero cards, although by a PRI municipal president who wanted to neutralize their electoral clout and forge something of a truce with them. Like numerous other religious-political conflicts in the Greater Bajío, the ones between Irapuato's conservative Catholics and proponents of the agrarian reform dated to the 1920s, when southern Guanajuato became an epicenter of the Cristero War.[26] And the Sinarquistas established a visible presence in the jurisdiction during the late 1930s and early 1940s. Pablo Serrano Álvarez documented twenty-four

Sinarquista demonstrations that were held in Irapuato between 1939 and 1943, which drew as many as twenty thousand participants.[27] The 1940s also witnessed a series of agrarian conflicts between ejidatarios and conservative landowners. In May 1942, clashes between San Miguel de Villalobos's ejidatarios and Roberto Vargas Cienfuegos ended with both parties involved burning their rivals' wheat harvests.[28] Laguna Larga's ejidatarios attacked and began destroying the main house of the former hacienda, which had not been included in their ejido grant, in July 1943.[29] And in February 1944, Ángela Contreras de Bustamante wrote to President Ávila Camacho to denounce a group of "depraved" ejidatarios who had invaded unexpropriated portions of the Santa Bárbara and Serrano Haciendas that she still owned and was trying to sell. (Contreras de Bustamante did not specify where the invading ejidatarios were from.) She then lamented her predicament, which in her view was "the bitter fruit of a wicked agrarian policy that had been imposed in the Republic and caused the complete ruin of the nation's agricultural production."[30]

Irapuato authorities remained relatively evenhanded as these conflicts unfolded, generally limiting themselves to filing reports with state government officials and asking them for guidance.[31] But local officials began showing themselves amenable to cooperating with the conservative Catholic opposition during the late 1940s. In October 1949, Higinio Bonilla, secretary general of Irapuato's Regional Agrarian Committee, reported that local law enforcement officials were strong-arming ejidatarios into supporting Antonio Ramírez's candidacy for municipal president and threatening them with "consequences" if they did not vote for him.[32] Bonilla did formally endorse Ramírez in November.[33] But in January 1950, shortly after Ramírez had been sworn in as municipal president, an anonymous complainant from Copalillo accused the local PRI of colluding with the PAN to "impose" the victorious candidate.[34] There were also allegations that Roberto Furber—a Ramírez ally and new ayuntamiento member who was also a member of a landowning family that had clashed with El Carmen's agraristas over water rights and hydraulic equipment in the late 1930s—was a foreign national and thus ineligible to hold office.[35] (Ramírez refuted both claims.)[36]

Whereas Ramírez was alleged to have collaborated with the PAN to secure his electoral victory, his successor, Florentino Oliva—who, as I noted in chapter 2, became one of Guanajuato's leading Bracero Program administrators in 1952—had a strained relationship with that party's members, whom he described as "eternal malcontents" in September 1952 after they accused him of using public moneys to purchase a car for his wife and turning a blind eye to multiple acts of corruption and violence, such as murder and assault, perpetrated by members of his administration.[37] Oliva, likely knowing that his relationship with Irapuato Panistas was beyond repair, decided to use the Bracero Program–related authority that the state government granted him to neutralize the electoral strength of and craft something of a peace with the Sinarquistas, the other wing of the conservative Catholic opposition. In June 1952, one month before that year's presidential election, DIPS agent Manuel Ríos Thivol visited Irapuato to gauge the political climate in that municipality. Ríos Thivol reported that Irapuato's rural population fully backed the PRI candidate, Adolfo Ruiz Cortines, whom rural workers held "in the highest regard." He cited the local campaign that municipal president Oliva and his staff coordinated as the primary reason Ruiz Cortines enjoyed such high levels of support in Irapuato's rural communities. Part of this campaign was a "determined effort" to ensure that Sinarquistas left the municipality as braceros, which meant that they were not in Irapuato to vote in the election.[38] This determined effort may explain why anonymous Irapuato residents complained later that summer that Oliva had been "wasting his time" every day with groups of aspiring braceros at the contracting center and leaving other important public matters unattended to.[39] Oliva admitted that he had spent considerable time at the contracting center, though he claimed that this was a result of his new administrative duties, which required him to prevent fraud and other irregularities.[40]

However, Ríos Thivol's intelligence report contained hints that the targeting of the Sinarquistas during the bracero selection period was not simply an electoral maneuver but also an effort to mend fences with at least one wing of the conservative Catholic opposition. The DIPS agent stated that Oliva viewed the Bracero Program as a means of changing Irapuato Sinarquistas' political inclinations. There is no evidence suggesting that Irapuato Sinarquistas who migrated as braceros returned as proponents of land redistribution or secular public education, two policies that UNS members vehemently opposed. But they appear to have thought positively of Oliva personally, likely because he gave them the opportunity to migrate and earn money in the United States, which would have bolstered their socioeconomic status as they very likely lacked access to ejido lands because of their religious opposition to the agrarian reform. Ríos Thivol reported that the municipal president was amicable with Irapuato Sinarquistas who did not migrate as braceros and that it was common to see local UNS members accompanying Oliva whenever he conducted official business throughout the municipality. He also noted that the local Sinarquista chapter did not object when Oliva ordered that UNS publicity materials be taken down and replaced with ones that supported Ruiz Cortines's presidential candidacy. If Irapuato's ejidatarios were concerned about their municipal president's seemingly cozy relationship with their long-standing rivals, they did not express it directly to Ríos Thivol, who noted that local ejidatarios' primary concern was arranging a meeting with Ruiz Cortines to profess their loyalty to him.[41]

The behavior of Irapuato's municipal president, Sinarquistas, and ejidatarios during the 1952 bracero selection period suggests the intriguing possibility that the municipal government and the UNS reached a quid pro quo agreement: the municipal president gave UNS members preference during the selection process in exchange for their nominal support of Ruiz Cortines's candidacy. If such an accord existed, no explicit written record is available. But there is other evidence that strongly points to Oliva using his administrative powers to forge such an arrangement. First, there is no record of the municipal president instructing municipal delegates to compile lists of aspiring braceros in 1952—which he did in 1953, when Oliva's administration also took the lead during the bracero selection process in Guanajuato—thus indicating that the municipal president personally decided which of his rural constituents would receive contracts.[42] Second, Oliva declared in 1952 that all prospective braceros who received their contracts in Irapuato had to be registered to vote, a policy that would have allowed him to know the political party affiliation of would-be migrant workers.[43] And third, the departure of thousands of aspiring braceros from other Guanajuato municipalities was delayed in April, much to the consternation of Oliva's counterparts in jurisdictions like Celaya (where 1,400 were waiting), León (where 2,000 were waiting), and Pénjamo (where 2,200 were waiting).[44] However, there are no recorded complaints that Irapuato prospective braceros were being forced to wait, thus demonstrating that Oliva likely prioritized their departure so that he could ensure they would be in the United States before that summer's election.

Oliva's actions during the 1952 contracting period, which were facilitated by a state government that granted him broad powers during the selection cycle, yielded numerous political dividends. He was assured that the local Sinarquistas would neither disrupt the upcoming electoral process nor be openly hostile to his government, like Panistas were. Furthermore, local ejidatarios were likely grateful to have a respite from their conflicts with the opposition. Oliva's decision to give preference to aspiring Sinarquista braceros also reflected a conservative shift among Irapuato officials, who were more concerned with quashing left-wing opposition groups and who were sensitive to the concerns of local Catholics. Oliva only documented "subversive" actions carried out by the supporters of Miguel Henríquez Guzmán, the left-leaning general who launched multiple failed bids for the presidency during the 1940s and 1950s, in a February 1954 report about political activities in his jurisdiction, and he told federal officials that his constituents wanted the political parties that supported Henríquez Guzmán to be proscribed.[45] One year later, Purísima de Temascatío's community officials complained that the municipal government's delegates there were in league with the local schoolteacher, a Seventh-Day Adventist who was attempting to convert her students and their parents.[46] Jesús Cervantes Reynoso, Oliva's successor as municipal president, responded by ousting the delegates.[47]

CONTROL AND COERCION

Flush with the political and financial benefits that controlling the bracero selection process afforded them and emboldened by federal- and state-level indifference, sending-state municipal authorities took coercive steps to ensure that they would continue to profit from the Bracero Program. These coercive steps and the attacks against any individual or organization that threatened municipal officials' control of the selection process sparked new political conflicts and influenced frustrated aspiring braceros' individual decisions to migrate as undocumented workers. One body that earned the enmity of local authorities was the Alianza de Braceros Nacionales de México en los Estados Unidos de Norteamérica. The Alianza was established in October 1943 in the Orange County, California, city of Fullerton.[48] That same month, Alianza's secretary general, José Hernández Serrano, told President Ávila Camacho that the organization's primary goal was to impress on its members that they were representatives of Mexico and that their behavior and work ethic should reflect well on their home country.[49] But it seemed that most of their efforts during the Bracero Program's initial years went to recruiting members in Mexico, drawing up lists of prospective braceros and submitting them for official consideration, and denouncing instances of Bracero Program–related corruption.[50]

Municipal officials did not look kindly on the Alianza's practice of drafting lists of aspiring braceros and refused to consider them. In July 1945, the

Alianza's Hernández Serrano complained that Tarimoro, Guanajuato's municipal government was ignoring an Alianza list, thus violating an agreement that the organization had reached with Governor Hidalgo regarding the selection of its members as braceros. The agreement was likely a reference to an Alianza list dated June 14 that state officials forwarded to their Tarimoro counterparts on June 18, though state authorities told the local government that they simply wanted to inform them about the interest in acquiring eligibility cards.[51] Hernández Serrano believed that Tarimoro's municipal president, Ernesto Santa Cruz García, did not want to grant Alianza members preference because he would then be deprived of the opportunity to sell eligibility cards to would-be braceros from other jurisdictions.[52] But Santa Cruz García accused the Alianza of acting in bad faith, disregarding state-level instructions, and exploiting aspiring braceros. In a letter to Hernández Serrano, the municipal president stated that he had rejected the Alianza list because it included ineligible ejidatarios, men who did not meet the age requirements, and residents from other municipalities. Santa Cruz García also claimed that Ricardo Aguado, the Alianza's representative in Tarimoro, was promising eligibility cards in return for membership dues; in contrast, Santa Cruz García stated, he had never taken money from prospective braceros.[53] Hernández Serrano fired back, noting that his organization's purpose was to vouchsafe the rights of braceros and protect them from official abuses. He also defended the Alianza's practice of collecting membership dues, which were used exclusively for the upkeep of the organization's offices and were never attached to a promise of receiving an eligibility card.[54]

The war of words between Santa Cruz García and Hernández Serrano soon escalated into open hostilities, and the former made clear that his authority regarding the selection of braceros was supreme. During the final week of July, immediately after Santa Cruz García had written to Hernández Serrano, the municipal president noted that "innumerable impoverished rural workers" from Tarimoro and the neighboring municipalities of Acámbaro, Jerécuaro, and Salvatierra were visiting Alianza representative Ricardo Aguado at his residence. The workers were foregoing meals and giving what little money they had to Aguado, who, according to Santa Cruz García, was still claiming that Alianza membership would guarantee them eligibility cards. The municipal president confronted Aguado and reminded him that drafting lists of aspiring braceros and distributing eligibility cards were the municipal government's exclusive responsibility. But the Alianza representative continued "deceiving" would-be braceros, and Santa Cruz García had the former arrested and jailed. Aguado was released after he paid a 25 peso fine, but he immediately resumed collecting membership dues for the Alianza and was imprisoned again. On August 9, Santa Cruz García traveled to Guanajuato City to discuss the matter personally with Governor Hidalgo. According to the municipal president, the governor disavowed the Alianza during this meeting; Santa Cruz García then told Secretary General Hernández Serrano that he should close the "illegal offices" the organization had opened in rural communities.[55] Hernández Serrano continued to defend the Alianza as a body that only had the best interests of braceros at heart, and he once again denounced Santa Cruz García's behavior and asked the governor to intercede in the matter of the incarcerated Aguado.[56] (Hernández Serrano himself was arrested and briefly jailed in March 1953 after officials in the western Jalisco municipality of Unión de Tula accused him of interfering in the bracero selection process there; he maintained that the accusations were retribution for his having highlighted Bracero Program–related corruption.)[57]

Municipal officials also targeted community-level authorities who denounced them. In April 1960, Rodolfo Mendoza, comisariado ejidal of San José del Río, in the northeastern Aguascalientes municipality of Asientos, complained to the state government that the municipal president, Gonzalo de la Torre, had not distributed bracero cards "equitably." Mendoza alleged that no one from San José del Río had been selected as a bracero because de la Torre had given eligibility cards to his "favorites" and to aspiring braceros from the neighboring state of Zacatecas.[58] De la Torre responded to the allegations after the Aguascalientes interior secretary, Carlos Salas Calvillo, forwarded the complaint to him. He denied that there was any truth to the "painful accusations" made by San José del Río's comisariado ejidal. De la Torre stated that he had only chosen braceros who lived in his jurisdiction and that the only reason that no rural workers from San José del Río had been selected was because the municipality had been allotted just seventy bracero cards so far that year, which made it impossible for him to meet popular demand. But de la Torre was not satisfied with simply claiming innocence. Due to the seriousness of Mendoza's allegations, de la Torre informed the state government, he was opening a judicial inquiry of the comisariado ejidal and was prepared to punish him and others for any Bracero Program–related crimes that they may have committed.[59] The available evidence does not make clear if de la Torre followed through with his promise to investigate

Mendoza. But that he would admit to state-level officials that he viewed anyone who challenged his prerogatives during bracero selection periods as criminals who needed to be punished indicates the lengths that sending-state municipal authorities were willing to go to defend their privileged position in the Bracero Program's administrative apparatus.

Other sending-state municipal officials transformed the local criminal justice system into a facet of their financial extortion schemes. In September 1959, Octavio Briseño and seventeen other campesinos from Juan Aldama, a municipality in northwestern Zacatecas, wrote to President Adolfo López Mateos. The writers told the president that "immoral" local authorities there were including "preferred persons who had no need to leave the country for work" on the eligibility lists and "denying all assistance to those who are truly in need." Those who did not have preference before the eligibility lists were compiled had to pay 215 pesos just to have their names included in the selection drawing. Would-be braceros from the jurisdiction had until the day of the drawing to pay the bribe. Several gathered the necessary money by selling their belongings or borrowing funds from individuals who were hoping to be repaid with US earnings. Others chose to travel to neighboring municipalities to see if they could be included in the drawings there. Those prospective braceros who failed to collect the 215 pesos but remained in Juan Aldama were arrested and incarcerated in the municipal jail. The imprisoned rural workers would only be released after paying fines that ranged between 25 and 50 pesos, thus ensuring that local authorities extracted as much profit as they could from aspiring braceros. The complainants noted that two hundred braceros ultimately received eligibility cards after paying the bribe, though they failed to mention how many were imprisoned and fined.[60]

Briseño and his fellow aspiring braceros, like others before them, begged federal officials to intervene and put an end to local-level corruption in the administration of the Bracero Program. But that plea went unheeded, and by the early 1960s some municipal officials were so confident in their impunity that they dispensed with the formality of compiling an eligibility list and hosting a selection drawing. In May 1960, Ernesto Robles and eight other prospective braceros from Luis Moya, a southeastern Zacatecas municipality, wrote to President López Mateos and accused the authorities there of committing a grave injustice. As had become customary by that year, the group had spent the spring anxiously awaiting the announcement of a new bracero contracting period. When they heard nothing from the local government, they investigated and learned that the municipal authorities had "hidden themselves away" and drawn up the eligibility lists in private homes. To make matters worse, the lists appeared to only include men who had agreed to pay at least 300 pesos for their eligibility cards or men who were not residents of the municipality. Robles and his fellow would-be braceros were disheartened because they were "humble" rural workers who depended on annual treks to the United States to supplement their income and provide for their families. The group then told the president that they were sending their complaint to him because they did not believe Zacatecas's state government would help them.[61] Federal Interior Secretariat official Rafael Velderrain responded to Robles in June but only to tell him that the federal authorities would need more "ample and precise" evidence of municipal wrongdoing before weighing in on the matter.[62]

Frustration with the tight control exercised by municipal officials during contracting periods and the rampant corruption and politicization of the selection process prompted demands that eligibility cards be sent directly to aspiring braceros in their home communities. Amador Magaña Valdovinos and thirteen other aspiring braceros from the Puruándiro community of Rincón de Don Pedro asked Michoacán governor Agustín Arriaga Rivera in May 1964 to send eligibility cards directly to their community because it would be "difficult" to acquire them through the municipal government.[63] The mention of difficulties was likely an allusion to deep-seated municipal corruption. A September 1964 local newspaper report alleged that José Vargas Rivera, the municipal president, and Abdías Liévanos Ríos, the municipal secretary, were promising eligibility cards to would-be braceros in exchange for 1,000 pesos. But Vargas Rivera and Liévanos Ríos were not giving the cards to those who had paid the bribe; instead, their allotment was going to relatives and friends who lived in the neighboring municipalities of Panindícuaro and Valle de Santiago (the latter municipality is in Guanajuato).[64] One month later, four members of Puruándiro's ayuntamiento wrote to the governor to confirm that the municipal president was selling eligibility cards and to report that he had pocketed 300,000 pesos from aspiring braceros since he assumed office in 1962. The council members—who, according to Vargas Rivera, were PAN members, thus indicating the continued active presence of conservative Catholic parties in the primary sending states—also admitted that they had initially approved of the municipal president's plan to sell bracero cards but only because he had told them that the moneys would be invested in local infrastructure projects.[65] Given that numerous Puruándiro officials had set aside their partisan differences so that they could be involved to some degree in the corruption scheme, Rincón de Don Pedro's prospective braceros were right to be wary of local officials.

In other instances, it was the female relatives of aspiring braceros who voiced their displeasure and asked for changes to the selection process. Ana Elizabeth Rosas notes in her study of braceros' families that although women were barred from migrating as braceros, they did attend town hall meetings in communities like San Martín de Hidalgo, Jalisco, where municipal officials touted the program as a boon that would provide tangible financial benefits to braceros and their loved ones.[66] The available evidence does not indicate if Coeneo, Michoacán's municipal authorities ever promoted the Bracero Program in the same manner as their counterparts in San Martín de Hidalgo. But whether or not Coeneo's authorities championed the financial rewards of bracero migration, women in that municipality viewed braceros' incomes as vital to their socioeconomic well-being, so they turned to the state government for redress when corrupt municipal officials blocked the departure of their male relatives. For example, on April 15, 1964, Juana Dimas Sosa, a widow from Santiago Azajo, wrote to Governor Arriaga Rivera to request eligibility cards on behalf of the nephews who had been supporting her financially since her husband's death. Dimas Sosa hoped that the governor would sanction her nephews' departure so that they could continue to assist her, a need she deemed especially pressing because she had failed to acquire a sewing machine through a state government–administered program.[67] Two weeks later, Dimas Sosa and eleven aspiring braceros who had been helping support her (seven of whom shared one of her surnames or that of her late husband's) traveled to Morelia to repeat their request in person. The state official they met with told them that eligibility cards would be sent to Coeneo's municipal government. But the widow wrote to the governor after the meeting and told him that municipal officials routinely mistreated her and others and that the prospective braceros she was representing had no hope of acquiring eligibility cards through the local government. She then asked the governor to give the cards to her, to no avail.[68]

Two months after Dimas Sosa's requests, María Guadalupe Gómez, who lived in the Coeneo community of San Pedro Tacaro, wrote to state staff secretary Leodegario López Martínez, asking that an unspecified number of eligibility cards be sent directly to that community for distribution. Gómez cited an earlier communication in which she and others had requested cards from the state government for their husbands and other male relatives, as well as an official reply in April that stated that no cards could be sent to Coeneo at that time. (Unfortunately, neither the request nor the official reply that Gómez mentioned in her June letter is available in the archive.) But Gómez asserted that Coeneo's municipal government had received an allotment of cards after the state government had replied to her and that Coeneo officials had not informed San Pedro Tacaro residents about the selection drawing. Furthermore, Gómez alleged that Coeneo authorities were selling some eligibility cards. She then told López Martínez that she would not be bothering him if Coeneo officials had not frozen San Pedro Tacaro's aspring braceros out of the selection process or if they could afford to pay the bribes the local government was demanding.[69] Unfortunately, there is no record of how or even if López Martínez replied.

Another avenue that prospective braceros could use to skirt municipal-level corruption was to migrate as undocumented workers. David FitzGerald, in his study of emigration from the northeastern Jalisco municipality of Arandas, reports speaking with twelve former braceros who all admitted that they had acquired their eligibility cards outside of the formal selection process, thus implying that they had paid bribes or had been the beneficiaries of political favoritism. But one Arandas rural worker who made nine trips to the United States during the Bracero Program's final decade told FitzGerald that he had been unwilling to pay municipal authorities a bribe for his eligibility card because it did not guarantee that he would actually receive one. Instead, this migrant worker hired the services of a "coyote"—a Mexican Spanish term for a smuggler who helps undocumented migrants enter the United States—who proved more reliable than the municipal government and was essentially offering the same service.[70] FitzGerald did not specify how many other campesinos left Arandas as undocumented migrants because they no longer wanted to treat with local authorities. However, it is plausible that discontent with sending-state municipal officials influenced people's decision to migrate without a bracero contract as much as American growers' willingness to hire them.

The activities of coyotes ultimately sparked political skirmishes with municipal officials who were intent on maintaining control of the Bracero Program. In October 1963, Abundio Medina Piñón, municipal president of Lagunillas, a Michoacán jurisdiction in the Pátzcuaro Basin, informed the state government that he had successfully weathered what he described as an attempted revolt. Medina Piñón admitted that his constituents' unhappiness with the recent selection of twenty-five braceros was the reason that they had openly turned against him. But he defended himself, claiming that he had chosen braceros in full accordance with the law. He also reported that the quarrelsome parties were being led by a group of local "agitators and malcontents" who were committed to toppling the duly elected ayuntamiento and were merely using the bracero selection process as a pretext to sow discord. According to Medina Piñón, one of the malcontents was Gregorio Meza, a known coyote who collected 1,300 pesos from each rural worker who hired him. Medina Piñón argued that Meza's actions damaged the municipality, and he asked state officials to intervene and take whatever actions they deemed convenient to put an end to his enterprise.[71]

Whether Medina Piñón was as honest during the selection drawing as he professed to be or he simply sensed an opportunity to rid himself of someone who was cutting into his Bracero Program–related benefits, his request for state assistance made him an exception. His counterparts in other municipalities were wary of officials connected to the state government, especially on the few occasions that they threatened the status quo of local control. As I noted in chapter 2, Michoacán's government instructed state tax collectors to help local governments compile the eligibility lists during the Bracero Program's final years, although municipal authorities remained responsible for the selection of braceros during the drawings.[72] On the morning of May 7, 1964, Manuel Cárdenas Mejorada, a state tax collector, traveled to the Pátzcuaro Basin municipality of Huiramba to fulfill his duty. Cárdenas Mejorada discovered on his arrival that no preparations had been made for the selection drawing and that it had not even been publicized. He and Sergio Maldonado Corral, an employee of an unspecified state agency who accompanied him, used a loudspeaker to announce that the selection drawing would be held that day and encourage would-be braceros to report to the municipal government's offices. Word quickly spread throughout the municipality, and 155 rural workers put their names on the list. The municipal secretary then chose forty to receive eligibility cards.[73]

While the selected rural workers were having their cards certified in the municipal government's offices, municipal president Manuel Rojas Segura returned from Morelia, where he had been during the selection drawing. According to Cárdenas Mejorada, the municipal president was clearly inebriated, and he angrily announced that an outsider had interfered in the bracero selection process. The municipal secretary assured Rojas Segura that he had personally inscribed all the required information on the eligibility cards. This led Rojas Segura to become less agitated, though he maintained that he had written orders from the state government that authorized him to declare the selection drawing null and void. When pressed, the municipal president refused to show anyone the orders he alleged having. What he did possess was a list of selected braceros dated before May 7, thus indicating that the municipal government had not publicized the selection drawing because he had already promised the eligibility cards to political favorites or those who had paid bribes. Rojas Segura then insisted on organizing a new drawing, but the municipal treasurer argued against this by noting that he, with the help of Cárdenas Mejorada, had already drafted official receipts that were given to the chosen braceros. Rojas Segura's temper reignited when he learned that Cárdenas Mejorada had assisted the treasurer, and he furiously shouted that the tax collector had no business "meddling" in municipal affairs. At that point Cárdenas Mejorada realized that there was no reasoning with Rojas Segura, and he left before his continued presence resulted in more serious consequences. The following day, Rojas Segura contacted the tax collector and assured him that he would respect the results of the selection drawing and certify the list of chosen braceros. But these assurances were little more than lip service, since Cárdenas Mejorada soon found that Rojas Segura issued eligibility cards to men who had not been selected during the drawing.[74]

ADVOCACY, PUBLIC WORKS, AND TAXATION

While Rojas Segura sought to maintain his corrupt hold on the bracero selection process in his jurisdiction, a significant number of his counterparts in Michoacán were behaving as advocates, to use Fernández Aceves's term.[75] During Adolfo López Mateos's presidency, Michoacán municipal presidents wrote to higher-level authorities and made fifty-five eligibility card requests on behalf of aspiring braceros from their jurisdictions, in apparent good faith and without any overt signs that they stood to gain financially or politically.[76] This represented a remarkable increase from all the previous years of the Bracero Program, when Michoacán municipal presidents combined to make three advocacy requests.[77] Many of these would-be braceros were landless, such as the 132 non-ejidatarios for whom Tangancícuaro's municipal president, Humberto Cerda Pimentel, wrote in February 1962.[78] Others, like the residents of four Ixtlán communities that the municipal president Carlos Tamayo Valladolid lobbied for in August 1963, had suffered crop losses due to inclement weather.[79] And some wanted to earn money to invest in infrastructure projects like schoolhouses, which, according to Ecuandureo's municipal president, Roberto Ángeles, is what La Soledad's prospective braceros wanted to do in March 1962.[80]

This boom in advocacy requests reflected the efforts of prospective braceros who began pressing local officials to lobby on their behalf. In a May 1963 request, Penjamillo's municipal president, David López Manriquez, admitted that he was writing because four hundred "completely impoverished, unemployed, and landless" aspiring braceros had approached him to ask for eligibility cards.[81] One month later, Churintzio's municipal president, Jesús Aguilar Naranjo, told state officials that he was writing on behalf of a group of rural workers from Changuitiro because their "repeated insistence" that he contact the state government had made it impossible for him to ignore their demand.[82] And in August, Benjamín García Guzmán, municipal president of Tarímbaro, told state authorities that would-be braceros from his jurisdiction were convening daily at the municipal government's offices and asking for eligibility cards. García Guzmán's constituents hoped that migration would improve their "truly depressing" socioeconomic status, so the municipal president decided to request eligibility cards for them.[83]

Beyond the direct pressure aspiring braceros applied to them, Michoacán municipal-level authorities were trying to keep from falling further behind community-level officials who themselves became increasingly vocal advocates during López Mateos's presidency. Michoacán comisariados ejidales, jefes de tenencia (community chiefs), and encargados del orden (keepers of the peace) made 217 written requests on behalf of prospective braceros from their communities during the Bracero Program's final years.[84] Such officials had made only thirty-five advocacy requests during the program's previous years combined.[85] These community-level advocates cited the same reasons for writing that their municipal-level counterparts did. Cornelio Maldonado Pulido, comisariado ejidal in Changuitiro, wrote to the state government on behalf of six landless non-ejidatarios in May 1963, one month before Churintzio's municipal president declared it impossible to ignore the pleas of that community's aspiring braceros.[86] In August of the same year, comisariado ejidal Carlos Esqueda requested eligibility cards for fifty rural workers who lost their maize harvests during floods in the Zamora community of Ario de Rayón.[87] And in February 1964, Ramón Vargas Mondragón, jefe de tenencia in the Zacapu community of Las Canoas, requested twenty cards so that the community could complete the construction of a potable water system.[88]

The advocates who highlighted landlessness as the motivation for their requests expressed their constituents' frustration with two trends that converged during the late 1950s and early 1960s: demographic expansion and a land redistribution process that slowed to a crawl after 1940 (see chap. 4). As for the advocacy requests that cited a desire to invest bracero earnings in material improvement projects, such as schoolhouses, potable water systems, and electrification, these were influenced by changes in taxation policy and revenue distribution patterns. As Luis Aboites Aguilar notes, the years of the Bracero Program were marked by "fiscal centralization," as municipal governments lost the ability to collect property taxes on lands that the federal government expropriated to establish ejidos, while Ávila Camacho's and Alemán's administrations (1940–46 and 1946–52, respectively) levied new commercial and industrial taxes that federal authorities collected directly. This fiscal centralization led to the federal government receiving an increasingly large share of total revenues. Between 1942 and 1965, the percentage of total tax revenues received by the federal government increased from 71.1 to 83.6. By contrast, the share municipal governments received during the same period declined from an already paltry 5.1 percent to a mere 1.5 percent, and state governments' share fell from 14.4 to 4.7 percent.[89] And since post-1940 federal administrations prioritized urban industrialization, they earmarked tax moneys to fund social services and infrastructure projects in cities, such as food price controls, subsidized housing, street paving, and sewage systems. Benjamin Smith has effectively argued that these allocations were also a means of quelling cross-class antitax protests that erupted in cities when urban property taxes were increased. Smith documented eighteen antitax movements between 1940 and 1955. Of these movements, four took place in sending-state cities: two in Aguascalientes City (1942 and 1948) and two in León (1946 and 1948).[90]

The emphasis on urban social services and infrastructure did not mean that federal officials were completely unwilling to spend on rural projects. But when they did, their contributions only partially covered the costs of the project, and community members were expected to contribute part of the remaining costs. For example, the Comisión Federal de Electricidad (CFE; Federal Electricity Commission) and Michoacán's state government approved the electrification of the Puruándiro community of San Nicolás in December 1962. The total cost of the project was determined to be 230,800 pesos. The CFE would contribute half that amount to the project. The remaining half would be divided between the state government and San

Nicolás's residents, which meant that the latter were responsible for 57,700 pesos.[91]

The electrification of San Nicolás was completed in spring 1964, and Governor Agustín Arriaga Rivera personally attended the inauguration of the new system. In May, J. J. Mejía and José Lemus, San Nicolás's comisariado ejidal and encargado del orden, respectively, wrote to the governor to thank him for visiting their community. They also asked for an unspecified number of bracero cards. These cards would go to the most impoverished residents of San Nicolás who, according to Mejía and Lemus, had so far been unable to gather their individual share of the 57,700 pesos the community needed to contribute to its electrification.[92] The same month, San Nicolás's school breakfast program director, María Pimentel, wrote to Governor Arriaga Rivera to thank him for supporting the electrification project. She also asked for bracero cards on behalf of relatives of hers who had "a tremendous need to emigrate to the United States" because they still "owed a great deal" of the costs associated with introducing electricity to her community.[93] There is no evidence that Michoacán's government took these requests into consideration when deciding how many eligibility cards would be allocated to Puruándiro. But if they did, San Nicolás's residents would have had to contend with a corrupt municipal president who, as noted earlier, was selling eligibility cards throughout the waning days of the Bracero Program.

Advocacy on behalf of prospective braceros expected to shoulder infrastructure-related financial burdens was not the only response to changes in revenue collection and distribution patterns. Smith argues that some rural governments used bribes to recoup lost revenue streams, keep their administrations afloat, and provide funding for local infrastructure works.[94] And some municipal officials did indeed justify the sale of bracero cards as an evil that was necessary to fund local treasuries and infrastructure projects like roads. Local authorities in Tacámbaro, a municipality in Michoacán's Tierra Caliente, went so far as to keep official records in which the bribes they collected were classified as "voluntary contributions" to local infrastructure improvements. The municipal president, Eduardo Chaparro Plata, used these records to safeguard against any "misinterpretations" and as proof that his government's intentions were aboveboard and benevolent, as asking for "voluntary contributions" saved his constituents from "traveling to distant parts of the country and uselessly spending money in a fruitless attempt to secure bracero contracts."[95]

Local officials in the southwestern Aguascalientes municipality of Calvillo also collected bribes that were supposedly destined to fund local infrastructure projects. In March 1954, Juan Hernández and other Calvillo residents wrote to Governor Benito Palomino Dena and told him that aspiring braceros there had been paying "significant sums" of money for their bracero cards since the previous decade and that local officials claimed that the bribes were being used to finance public works.[96] Three years later, Francisco Hernández Mota wrote to President Ruiz Cortines and reported that Calvillo's municipal president, Miguel González Hernández, was collecting 60 pesos from would-be braceros. González Hernández was telling Calvillo braceros that 10 pesos were to cover the administrative costs of issuing the eligibility cards and their receipts and the remaining 50 pesos were to "help" the municipal government. (Hernández Mota also noted that the municipal government in nearby Juchipila, Zacatecas, was collecting 200 pesos from prospective braceros, though he did not specify if authorities there were also claiming to be earmarking those moneys for public use.)[97] And in March 1962, Marcelino Hernández Díaz reported that Calvillo authorities were asking aspiring braceros to "voluntarily contribute" between 100 and 250 pesos to be used for "material improvements" in the municipality.[98]

A similar situation unfolded in the southern Zacatecas municipality of Valparaíso. In September 1960, an anonymous individual who deemed it "inconvenient" to reveal their true identity for fear of reprisals informed President López Mateos that Epimenio Talamantes, the municipal president, and Antonio Bañuelos, an alternate state deputy, had been collecting funds from braceros for several years. Talamantes and Bañuelos had justified the bribes in previous years by stating that the collected fees were being used to fund the construction of a paved highway to Fresnillo. By the time the anonymous complainant wrote the letter, Talamantes and Bañuelos were telling aspiring braceros that they needed the funds to organize and host a reception for President López Mateos, who was scheduled to visit the municipality to inaugurate the now-completed highway. The pair of officials had asked would-be braceros to pay 200 pesos to be considered for an eligibility card when the 1960 contracting period began. But they increased the payment to 500 pesos when they saw the high demand for eligibility cards. (The anonymous writer noted that Valparaíso's government had been allotted two hundred eligibility cards but failed to report how many local campesinos were interested in migrating.)[99]

However, the Calvillo and Valparaíso officials who claimed that they were putting prospective braceros' bribes to good use were using those justifications as a smokescreen to conceal their corruption. All the parties who wrote from Calvillo during the 1950s and 1960s reported that local officials were not spending the moneys they collected from aspiring braceros on any infrastructure projects. Juan Hérnandez and his group wanted to migrate in order to invest their earnings in a long-desired electrification project. But they asked the governor to send bracero cards directly to them because the Calvillo authorities always pocketed the bribes they collected from aspiring braceros instead of using them to develop local infrastructure, and they mentioned that they would entrust their earnings to the local priest to ensure that they would not be misused by any party.[100] Hernández's claims were corroborated by delays in the electrification of the municipal seat: while Calvillo's government had received numerous price estimates for electricity-generating equipment in 1953, one year before Hernández wrote to Governor Palomino Dena, it had seemingly made no progress on the project by 1957, when it was soliciting donations through a pro-electrification committee.[101] Francisco Hernández Mota noted in 1957 that although there had been preliminary discussions about building a reservoir that would have benefited local agricultural producers and reduced seasonal flooding, municipal officials had spent more money on hosting banquets for federal- and state-level planners who visited the jurisdiction than on furthering the reservoir's actual construction. He also stated that the municipal government had not hired enough construction workers for local road projects, despite press reports that there were sufficient funds in the budget to complete the work.[102] Hernández Díaz simply told federal authorities that the local government had not completed any recent infrastructure projects.[103]

The anonymous complainant who wrote to President López Mateos from Valparaíso in 1960 claimed that Talamantes and Bañuelos had blatantly lied about how they were using bracero bribes. The letter writer described Bañuelos as a "little cacique" who exploited the most impoverished segments of Valparaíso's population and controlled the "illiterate" Talamantes like a pawn. They also assured the president that a federal investigation would uncover the depths of the pair's Bracero Program–related corruption, depths that the state government was either unaware of or had willingly turned a blind eye to.[104]

. . .

In May 1963, Ezequiel Víctor, Luis Oseguera, and Mariano Martínez, who together formed the ejido leadership council of Las Fuentes, in the northern Michoacán municipality of Ecuandureo, complained to Governor Arriaga

Rivera about municipal president Miguel Arellano. The men accused Arellano of selling bracero cards to individuals who had no financial need to migrate and who were not even members of the ruling PRI. Víctor, Oseguera, and Martínez, who made sure to profess their loyalty to the party, felt betrayed by a man they had voted for because they believed he would honorably lead the municipality and provide some assistance to Ecuandureo's socioeconomically marginalized. Instead, he had defrauded them and made "a mockery of the responsibility" that the state government had entrusted him with.[105] Arellano's alleged behavior stood in stark contrast to that of his immediate predecessor, Roberto Ángeles, who, as mentioned earlier, had selflessly lobbied on behalf of aspiring Ecuandureo braceros who wanted to use their earnings to build new schoolhouses in their communities.

However, Arellano's selling of bracero cards and his granting preference to non-PRI members were perfectly aligned with what most of his sending-state counterparts practiced during the Bracero Program. Flagrantly self-interested financial and political corruption was the defining aspect of the Bracero Program's municipal-level administration from the moment local governments became responsible for selecting braceros in 1944 until the program ended twenty years later. A host of local-, regional-, and national-level political factors influenced this corrupt behavior: the indifference of federal and state authorities who did not want to intervene directly in the selection process; the strength and popularity of conservative Catholic opposition groups like the UNS in the primary sending states; the loss of revenues that resulted from fiscal centralization and the prioritization of spending on urban municipalities; and the slowing of the agrarian reform, which coincided with a demographic boom that exacerbated rural socioeconomic pressures. All the while, local officials proved ready to move violently against any individual or organization that threatened the status quo. This dogged determination to maintain their grip on the selection process put municipal authorities at odds with frustrated aspiring braceros whose denunciations and pleas for federal- and state-level intervention were met with a deafening silence that ultimately pushed many to seek the services of coyotes.

What this unchecked financial and political corruption shows is that in Mexico, municipal officials in the primary sending states of Aguascalientes, Guanajuato, Jalisco, Michoacán, and Zacatecas were the Bracero Program's ultimate power brokers. While federal and state authorities allocated bracero eligibility cards, local officials were the ones who actually decided which aspiring braceros received those cards. And municipal authorities parlayed that responsibility into an opportunity to enrich themselves, reward their local allies, neutralize electoral threats, advance other initiatives, and, in exceptional instances, behave as benefactors to their constituents. And since higher-level authorities refused to intervene in the bracero selection process after their disastrous mismanagement of the Mexico City Contracting Center during the Bracero Program's earliest years, municipal governments had aspiring braceros at their mercy. Those campesinos who were unable or unwilling to enter the United States as undocumented workers—which would have immediately left them vulnerable to apprehension and deportation by US immigration authorities—had no choice but to deal directly with local officials whose principal priorities were their own financial and political interests, not alleviating the socioeconomic marginalization that prompted rural Aguascalientes, Guanajuato, Jalisco, Michoacán, and Zacatecas workers' decisions to abandon their home communities and become braceros.

Conclusion

AT THE END OF 1964, Congress ceased the US government's participation in the Bracero Program. The unilateral termination of the decades-long bilateral initiative was a response to shifting political and social climates in the United States. The program had come under increasing fire from Mexican American farm labor unions and civil rights organizations that denounced employer abuses of braceros during the early 1960s.[1] Simultaneously, Congress was drafting and debating an immigration reform bill that, when it passed into law as the 1965 Immigration and Nationality Act, established a hemispheric quota system that placed a numerical ceiling on the number of Mexican immigrants who could enter the United States with residency visas each year.[2] Put another way, burgeoning social opposition to the Bracero Program and the legislative push to place limits on the number of Mexican immigrants who could enter the country made the continued involvement of the United States in the bilateral initiative untenable by the mid-1960s. Mexican workers who remained interested in migrating seasonally to the United States after 1964 were eligible to receive H2 visas, which authorized the temporary entry of guest workers. But unlike bracero contracts, H2 visas were available to workers from various nations, and their issuance was not regulated by a formal bilateral agreement between the Mexican and US governments.[3]

The end of the Bracero Program marked the end of a unique period in the history of the Mexico-US migration phenomenon, one where a formal bilateral agreement that aimed to manage the migratory flow was in place and Mexican officials actively chose those who would be able to migrate. I have shown in this book that bracero migration was a complex and profoundly political process that revealed the limits of the postrevolutionary Mexican state's administrative capacities and the broad array of political factors that prompted migratory departures; it was not a straightforward socioeconomic affair that could be easily regulated. When it agreed to participate in the Bracero Program in 1942, the Ávila Camacho administration was confident that its direct intervention in the bracero selection process would prevent undocumented departures and safeguard against agricultural production declines due to a lack of manpower. To that end, federal officials declared that all aspiring braceros had to travel to Mexico City to receive their contracts and declared broad groups of campesinos, such as ejidatarios, ineligible to migrate as braceros because their continued presence in Mexico was deemed critical to the success of the domestic agrarian economy. But the Ávila Camacho administration quickly lost control of the selection process, as official inefficiency and corruption plagued the contracting center established in Mexico City, while campesinos who were barred from migrating as braceros secured contracts through loopholes in the eligibility restrictions or simply entered the United States as undocumented workers. By 1945, federal officials had lifted many of the eligibility restrictions and fully delegated the duty of choosing individual braceros to their state-level counterparts. From that point forward, federal administrations focused their Bracero Program–related administrative efforts on dividing contract allocations among state governments and periodically renegotiating the terms of the bilateral agreement with the US government; they also deferred to US officials on the question of limiting undocumented migration, which was curbed significantly after the INS organized a mass deportation campaign in 1954 and then increased the number of available bracero contracts. For their part, state government officials in the principal sending states of Aguascalientes, Guanajuato, Jalisco, Michoacán, and Zacatecas handed off the responsibility of choosing braceros to municipal authorities because they feared the political consequences that could occur if they lost control of the selection process as the federal government had. This further decentralization of the bracero selection process made municipal officials the Bracero Program's ultimate power brokers. With few exceptions, municipal officials showed little regard for the genuine socioeconomic needs of aspiring braceros who were their constituents. Instead, they used the bracero selection process to enrich themselves and strengthen their local political standing by favoring their allies with contracts or depriving their rivals of the opportunity to migrate as authorized guest workers.

As for the center-northern and center-western campesinos who decided to navigate the politicized thicket of the selection process in order to migrate as braceros, landlessness, precarious employment opportunities, and low wage levels were indeed the proximate factors that influenced their desire for contracts. However, while braceros' socioeconomic marginalization could be the end result of factors that were beyond their control and had nothing to do with politics—for example, the Parícutin Volcano eruption that devastated central Michoacán during the Bracero Program's initial years—their individual political allegiances and the consequences of other official initiatives often contributed directly to their material insecurity. The official response to the foot-and-mouth disease outbreak that decimated livestock populations in southern Guanajuato and northern Michoacán during the late 1940s exacerbated the outbreak's effects and prompted victims to set their sights north. The braceros who left central and southern Jalisco's sugar-growing communities were mill workers who had been dismissed or blacklisted during a power struggle between progressive and conservative labor union leaders. And in the Greater Bajío, the contiguous lands of southern Guanajuato, northern Michoacán, northeastern Jalisco, southern Zacatecas, and southwestern Aguascalientes, endemic intracommunity conflicts and the shortcomings of the government-sanctioned agrarian reform combined to make that region the primary engine that drove popular demand for bracero contracts in the center-western and center-northern states. The community-level clashes between conservative Catholic partisans who opposed official programs like land redistribution and their neighbors who supported such measures, many of which had started in the 1920s during the Cristero War, forced campesinos off their lands or deprived them of the opportunity to acquire them. At the same time, the guidelines that structured the agrarian reform process during the 1930s left ejidatarios with poor-quality or insufficient lands, and landless campesinos who came of age during the 1940s, 1950s, and 1960s had their hopes of receiving redistributed lands dashed by conservative federal administrations that no longer prioritized the agrarian reform. Those whose fortunes had suffered because of the agrarian reform's mixed results and flawed implementation joined their neighbors who were embroiled in factional disputes in seeking relief through the Bracero Program.

These findings point to intriguing similarities that the Bracero Program shared with other twentieth-century guest worker initiatives. A full exploration of these similarities falls well beyond the scope of this book, but I believe that they merit a brief mention here, as well as more detailed analysis in future comparative studies. For example, the relatively short-lived Caribbean Farmworker Program (1943–47), which was authorized by a bilateral agreement between US and British colonial officials, granted seasonal entry to workers from the Bahamas and Jamaica, most of whom were then assigned to farms in southeastern states like Florida. Cindy Hahamovitch has found that the local officials who chose guest workers in Jamaica regularly favored those who they believed were more likely to vote for them in future elections, a practice that would not have seemed out of place in the rural municipalities of the Mexican center-north and center-west during bracero selection periods.[4] In West Germany, post–World War II reconstruction projects and a growing industrial economy resulted in elevated demand for labor, which in turn prompted officials to establish bilateral *Gastarbeiter* (guest worker) initiatives with multiple nations, including Turkey (1961–73). The selection process recalled by the former Turkish guest workers that Jennifer Miller interviewed for her study bears striking similarities to the chaotic scenes that unfolded at bracero contracting centers. The combination of high demand for Gastarbeiter contracts and the guidelines implemented by the West German officials assigned to oversee the selection process in Turkey led to bureaucratic delays that left applicants waiting for months to receive their contracts. However, both aspiring guest workers and their would-be employers found that they could accelerate the process by exploiting loopholes in the guidelines or simply forgoing some of the mandated procedures. This circumvention of the established rules led to confusion and disorder at the offices where Turkish Gastarbeiter were vetted and chosen, as West German officials, like their Mexican counterparts before them, struggled to maintain control of the selection process.[5]

More important, these findings provide nuance to an enduring but relatively simple narrative regarding the factors that fuel Mexican migration to the United States, one that treats the migration phenomenon as a straightforward socioeconomic affair that can be effectively managed via government intervention. This narrative has been promoted by high-ranking Mexican officials in the nearly sixty years since the Bracero Program ended, a period when the scale of Mexican migration to the United States, both authorized and unauthorized, expanded considerably against a backdrop of significant socioeconomic turbulence. Millions of Mexicans, many of whom knew that migration was a viable option because they were the younger relatives and acquaintances of former braceros, moved north in search of higher wages after inflation, currency devaluations, international debt defaults, and the implementation of macroeconomic structural reforms that slashed government spending on social programs, mandated the privatization of ejido parcels, and eliminated tariffs and other trade restrictions destabilized the

Mexican economy during the final three decades of the twentieth century.[6] The Mexican immigrant population living in the United States grew from 760,000 in 1970 to 9.2 million in 2000, and data from surveys that were administered during this period indicate that between 39 and 51 percent of these immigrants were from the principal bracero-sending states of Aguascalientes, Guanajuato, Jalisco, Michoacán, and Zacatecas.[7] But in the absence of a Bracero Program–style initiative that specifically facilitated the entry of Mexican workers, and despite the US government's enactment of punitive measures designed to deter unauthorized border crossings—such as increased budget allocations for immigration enforcement agencies like the Border Patrol, military-style blockades in and near border cities like San Diego and El Paso, the construction of new steel fencing on the border, and the passage of laws that denied social services to undocumented immigrants and mandated criminal penalties for those who were apprehended—the majority of Mexicans who entered the United States during the late twentieth century initially did so as undocumented immigrants.[8] Social scientists have estimated that there were a total of 36.5 million undocumented Mexican entries into the United States from 1965 through 1989, though 86 percent of these undocumented entries were offset by the return migration of those who worked in seasonal industries like agriculture.[9] And although 2.3 million undocumented Mexican immigrants became legal residents under the provisions of the 1986 Immigration Reform and Control Act, the INS estimated that 52 percent of the Mexican immigrant population in the United States at the turn of the twenty-first century were undocumented.[10] Since 2000, the Mexico-US migratory flow has slowed and then reversed, a trend that social scientists have attributed to declining birthrates in Mexico and the global recession caused by the 2008 financial crisis.[11] After tripling during the 1970s, doubling during the 1980s, and then doubling again during the 1990s, the Mexican immigrant population in the United States expanded at a relatively modest rate of 27 percent during the 2000s, growing from 9.2 million in 2000 to 11.7 million in 2010. The available data indicate that return migration to Mexico has outpaced outmigration to the United States since 2010, which has resulted in a slight decline of the Mexican immigrant population: there were 11.3 million Mexican immigrants living in the United States in 2017, roughly half of whom were undocumented.[12]

The undocumented departure of millions of Mexicans during the late twentieth and early twenty-first centuries renewed official fears in Mexico that uncontrolled migration was harming the domestic economy. These fears ultimately prompted three presidential administrations to seriously consider reviving the Bracero Program as a means of enacting some measure of control over the migratory flow. And it was during these episodes that Mexican officials betrayed their lack of institutional memory and their simplistic interpretation of the migration phenomenon. In May 1972, President Luis Echeverría told reporters that regulating the migratory process was necessary because of its socioeconomic impact and that his administration was interested in reaching a bilateral agreement with the United States that would authorize a new guest worker initiative.[13] But despite indications from Secretary of State Henry Kissinger that the US government was willing to set an annual bracero entry quota, Echeverría abandoned the effort to restart the Bracero Program in October 1974.[14] In public, the president declared that he had reversed course because he realized that sanctioning the departure of braceros would be an explicit admission that Mexican migration to the United States was inevitable; he elaborated that the "migratory problem" could only be resolved by investing more public resources in rural communities and that these investments would foster the kind of financial prosperity that would ultimately limit migration.[15] However, Echeverría's public statements, which were in line with his government's position that official intervention in the economy was the key to fueling growth and leveling socioeconomic inequalities, were a smokescreen.[16] As Ana Minian notes, the actual reason the Echeverría administration decided to stop pursuing the Bracero Program's revival was its internal conclusion that undocumented migration was a necessary evil that alleviated demographic and socioeconomic pressures.[17] But even this private conclusion betrays Echeverría's belief that socioeconomic factors were the primary ones driving migration to the United States.

The second presidential administration to pursue the Bracero Program's renewal was Vicente Fox's. Fox, a member of the conservative PAN who governed Guanajuato during the 1990s, became the first opposition candidate to win Mexico's presidency in seventy-one years when he was elected in 2000. During his presidential campaign, Fox pledged to address the needs of all Mexicans, including those who had migrated to the United States. Shortly after taking office, Fox's government sought to make good on the president's campaign promises and proposed a sweeping migration initiative. The central pillars of the Fox administration's proposal were a bracero-style program and regularizing the migratory status of the estimated 4.8 million undocumented Mexican immigrants who were living in the United States at that time. The proposal also included a plan to boost public and private investment in communities with high rates of outmigration, which would presumably curb the socioeconomic pressures that fueled the migration phenomenon. Mexican officials were optimistic that the United States would prove amenable to the proposal because of the increasingly close commercial ties between the two nations and the diplomatic goodwill generated by the democratic transfer of power in Mexico. Bilateral discussions on the matter began after Fox and US president George W. Bush met in February 2001. But the Fox administration's insistence that any accord had to include both a guest worker program and the granting of legal residency status to undocumented Mexican immigrants, as well as Fox's public declarations in early September 2001 that he wanted to set a firm deadline for the two nations to strike a deal, caused US officials to balk and lose interest in reaching an agreement. Thus, despite Mexican officials' continued interest in crafting an accord and presidential directives that instructed both governments to keep working toward an agreement, the negotiations regarding a new guest worker initiative effectively ended in fall 2001.[18]

Two decades after the bilateral discussions between the Fox and Bush administrations collapsed, Andrés Manuel López Obrador, who was elected Mexico's president in 2018 as the candidate of the center-left Movimiento de Regeneración Nacional (National Regeneration Movement), publicly announced his intent to formally propose the Bracero Program's revival. López Obrador made his declaration while he was visiting the state of Zacatecas in February 2021, shortly before he was scheduled to meet with Joe Biden, who had succeeded Donald Trump—an immigration hardliner whose signature campaign promise was forcing the Mexican government to fund the construction of a wall that would span the entirety of the US-Mexico border—as US president earlier that year.[19] The Mexican president highlighted how immigrant remittances had helped millions of Mexican families stay afloat financially during the COVID-19 pandemic, and he argued that because US industries like agriculture still relied on immigrant labor from Mexico, an agreement that authorized the entry of 600,000 to 800,000 seasonal guest workers each year would be "the best thing to do." López Obrador also stated that Central Americans should be allowed to make up part of the annual guest worker contingent, a novel wrinkle that reflected the growing number of Guatemalans, Salvadorans, and Hondurans who were migrating to the United States.[20] But aside from noting that a revamped Bracero Program would require negotiations with the US government, López

Obrador made no mention of how politics influenced Mexico-US migration.[21] And though the Biden administration expressed interest in cooperating with López Obrador's government on migration, as of this writing there has been no public progress made regarding the Bracero Program's revival.[22]

Despite their differing partisan allegiances and the decades that separated their respective administrations, two through-lines connected Echeverría's, Fox's, and López Obrador's interest in restarting the Bracero Program: their confidence that a bilateral guest worker initiative modeled on the mid-twentieth-century one would cleanly resolve the "problem" of unauthorized migration and allow the Mexican government to effectively regulate the pace and scale of departures; and their certainty that the migration phenomenon was primarily if not strictly a socioeconomic one. Perhaps this is not entirely surprising when one considers the socioeconomic crises that affected Mexico during the post–Bracero Program era, as well as the fact that while undocumented migration coexisted with bracero migration, the Bracero Program established an officially sanctioned channel that allowed millions of Mexican men to enter and work in the United States.

But the history of the Bracero Program's administration and the underlying factors that influenced individual decisions to migrate as braceros put the lie to Mexican officials' view that migration to the United States was a largely apolitical phenomenon that could be easily regulated. Managing the bracero selection process was a haphazard and politicized affair, one that federal officials quickly lost control of and that municipal officials corrupted so that they could achieve their own political ends. And the distinctly political actions that center-western and center-northern campesinos took during the 1920s and 1930s—such as becoming an ejidatario or violently opposing land redistribution because of their deeply held Catholic faith—had a direct influence on the socioeconomic marginalization that they cited when they explained to officials why they wanted to migrate as braceros during the 1940s, 1950s, and 1960s. Put another way, bracero migration was a socioeconomic *and* a political phenomenon. Recognizing that nuanced reality will help us better understand how the postrevolutionary Mexican state functioned and, just as important, why millions of Mexicans decided to abandon their beloved land.

NOTES

ABBREVIATIONS

AG	Fondo Agricultura y Ganadería
AGHPEM	Archivo General e Histórico del Poder Ejecutivo de Michoacán, Morelia
AGN	Archivo General de la Nación, Mexico City
AHAGPEG	Archivo Histórico del Archivo General del Poder Ejecutivo de Guanajuato, Guanajuato City
AHEA	Archivo Histórico del Estado de Aguascalientes, Aguascalientes City
AHEJ	Archivo Histórico del Estado de Jalisco, Guadalajara
AHEQ	Archivo Histórico del Estado de Querétaro, Santiago de Querétaro
AHMI	Archivo Histórico Municipal de Irapuato, Irapuato
AHMZAC	Archivo Histórico del Municipio de Zacatecas, Zacatecas City
ALM	Fondo Adolfo López Mateos
AMHTM	Archivo Municipal e Histórico de Tepatitlán de Morelos, Tepatitlán de Morelos
ARC	Fondo Adolfo Ruiz Cortines
DGIPS	Fondo Dirección General de Investigaciones Políticas y Sociales
GOB/SC	Fondo Gobernación sin Clasificar
LCR	Fondo Lázaro Cárdenas del Río
MAC	Fondo Manuel Ávila Camacho
MAV	Fondo Miguel Alemán Valdés

MO	Serie Movimientos Obreros
PB	Serie Programa Braceros
PD	Sección Primer Departamento
PE	Fondo Poder Ejecutivo
PEN	Serie Política Estatal y Nacional
SEGOB	Fondo Secretaría de Gobierno
SEP	Fondo Secretaría de Educación Pública
SGGOB	Fondo Secretaría General de Gobierno
TPS	Sección Trabajo y Previsión Social

INTRODUCTION

1. For the motives of both US officials and growers, see Richard B. Craig, *The Bracero Program: Interest Groups and Foreign Policy* (Austin: University of Texas Press, 1971), 36–52; Ernesto Galarza, *Merchants of Labor: The Mexican Bracero Story: An Account of the Managed Migration of Mexican Farm Workers in California, 1942–1960* (Santa Barbara, CA: McNally and Loftin, 1964); S. Deborah Kang, *The INS on the Line: Making Immigration Law on the U.S.-Mexico Border, 1917–1954* (New York: Oxford University Press, 2017), 87–99; Mae M. Ngai, *Impossible Subjects: Illegal Aliens in the Making of Modern America* (Princeton, NJ: Princeton University Press), 142–43.

2. For early twentieth-century Mexican emigration policy, which discouraged migration to the United States due to fears that it would cause domestic labor shortages, see Fernando Saúl Alanís Enciso, *El primer programa bracero y el gobierno de México, 1917–1918* (San Luis Potosí: El Colegio de San Luis, 1999); Alexandra Délano, *Mexico and Its Diaspora in the United States: Policies of Emigration since 1848* (New York: Cambridge University Press, 2011), 59–82; David FitzGerald, *A Nation of Emigrants: How Mexico Manages Its Migration* (Berkeley: University of California Press, 2009), 39–49. For the Mexican government's decision to participate in the Bracero Program, see Deborah Cohen, *Braceros: Migrant Citizens and Transnational Subjects in the Postwar United States and Mexico* (Chapel Hill: University of North Carolina Press, 2011), 21–42; Craig, *The Bracero Program*, 20–23; Natasha Iskander, *Creative State: Forty Years of Migration and Development Policy in Morocco and Mexico* (Ithaca, NY: ILR Press, 2010), 50; Mireya Loza, *Defiant Braceros: How Migrant Workers Fought for Racial, Sexual, and Political Freedom* (Chapel Hill: University of North Carolina Press, 2016), 23–60; Ana Elizabeth Rosas, *Abrazando el Espíritu: Bracero Families Confront the U.S.-Mexico Border* (Berkeley: University of California Press, 2014), 19–23; Michael Snodgrass, "The Bracero Program, 1942–1964," in *Beyond la Frontera: The History of Mexico-U.S. Migration,* ed. Mark Overmyer-Velázquez (New York: Oxford University Press, 2011), 83–88; Blanca Torres, *México y el mundo: Historia de sus relaciones*

exteriores: De la guerra al mundo bipolar (Mexico City: El Colegio de México, 2010), 36–39.

3. For studies of Mexico-US migration that highlight the Bracero Program's unprecedented nature, see Délano, *Mexico and Its Diaspora in the United States;* FitzGerald, *A Nation of Emigrants;* Overmyer-Velázquez, *Beyond la Frontera.*

4. Official US figures cited in Ngai, *Impossible Subjects,* 157.

5. The official Mexican figures are cited in Moisés González Navarro, *Población y sociedad en México (1900–1970),* vol. 2 (Mexico City: Universidad Nacional Autónoma, 1974), chart between pp. 146 and 147. However, González Navarro's figures only account for 4.5 million contracts allocated within Mexico. For population figures, see México, Dirección General de Estadística, *Sexto Censo de Población, 1940: Resumen General* (Mexico City, 1943), 1, 39; México, Dirección General de Estadística, *Séptimo Censo General de Población, 6 de Junio de 1950: Resumen General* (Mexico City, 1953), 26–27; México, Dirección General de Estadística, *VIII Censo General de Población—1960, 8 de Junio de 1960: Resumen General* (Mexico City, 1962), V–VI. Mexico's total population was 19.7 million in 1940, 25.8 million in 1950, and 34.9 million in 1960. The combined population of Aguascalientes, Guanajuato, Jalisco, Michoacán, and Zacatecas was 4.4 million in 1940, 5.4 million in 1950, and 7.1 million in 1960.

6. For how the Bracero Program furthered the development of large-scale, commercially oriented agribusiness that relies on low-wage Mexican immigrant labor in California and the Pacific Northwest, see Galarza, *Merchants of Labor;* Erasmo Gamboa, *Mexican Labor and World War II: Braceros in the Pacific Northwest* (Seattle: University of Washington Press, 2000); Mario Jiménez Sifuentez, *Of Forests and Fields: Mexican Labor in the Pacific Northwest* (New Brunswick, NJ: Rutgers University Press, 2016), 10–35. For the response of US farmworkers' unions, which generally opposed the Bracero Program because farm owners used braceros to depress the wages of US-born farmworkers and break strikes, see Mark Brilliant, *The Color of America Has Changed: How Racial Diversity Shaped Civil Rights Reform in California, 1941–1978* (New York: Oxford University Press, 2010), 147–56; Lori A. Flores, *Grounds for Dreaming: Mexican Americans, Mexican Immigrants, and the California Farmworker Movement* (New Haven, CT: Yale University Press, 2016). For how the Bracero Program sparked debates among members of the Mexican American community who welcomed immigrant workers and those who shunned them, see David G. Gutiérrez, *Walls and Mirrors: Mexican Americans, Mexican Immigrants, and the Politics of Ethnicity* (Berkeley: University of California Press, 1995), 133–78. For early Chicana/o activists and organizers who denounced how braceros were mistreated during the program's final years, see Lori A. Flores, "A Town Full of Dead Mexicans: The Salinas Valley Bracero Tragedy of 1963, the End of the Bracero Program, and the Evolution of California's Chicano Movement," *Western Historical Quarterly* 44, no. 2 (2013): 124–43. For administrative tensions and clashes between the US Department of Labor and the Immigration and Naturalization Service (INS), see Kitty Calavita, *Inside the State: The Bracero Program, Immigration, and the I.N.S.* (New York: Routledge, 1992). For how the efforts to

curb undocumented migration during the years of the Bracero Program prompted agencies like the Border Patrol and the INS to craft and implement policies that increasingly interpreted Mexican immigrants as a racialized class of deportable aliens, see Adam Goodman, *The Deportation Machine: America's Long History of Expelling Immigrants* (Princeton, NJ: Princeton University Press, 2020), 47–106; Kelly Lytle Hernández, *Migra! A History of the U.S. Border Patrol* (Berkeley: University of California Press, 2010), 103–217; Kang, *The INS on the Line,* 87–167; Ngai, *Impossible Subjects,* 127–66. For braceros who worked in the US railroad industry during World War II, see Erasmo Gamboa, *Bracero Railroaders: The Forgotten World War II Story of Mexican Workers in the U.S. West* (Seattle: University of Washington Press, 2016); Chantel Renee Rodríguez, "Health on the Line: The Politics of Citizenship and the Railroad Bracero Program of World War II" (PhD diss., University of Minnesota, 2013).

7. Délano, *Mexico and Its Diaspora in the United States,* 83–103; FitzGerald, *A Nation of Emigrants,* 48–55; Manuel García y Griego, "El comienzo y el final: La interdependencia structural y dos negociaciones sobre braceros," in *Interdependencia: Un enfoque útil para el análisis de las relaciones México–Estados Unidos,* ed. Blanca Torres (Mexico City: El Colegio de México; Centro de Estudios Internacionales, 1990), 87–117; Manuel García y Griego, "The Importation of Mexican Contract Workers to the United States, 1942–1964: Antecedents, Operation, and Legacy," in *The Border That Joins: Mexican Migrants and U.S. Responsibility,* ed. Peter G. Brown and Henry Shue (Totowa, NJ: Rowman & Littlefield, 1983), 49–98; Catherine Vézina, *Diplomacia migratoria: Una historia transnacional del Programa Bracero, 1947–1952* (Mexico City: CIDE; Acervo Histórico Diplomático, Estados Unidos Mexicanos, Secretaría de Relaciones Exteriores, 2017).

8. For braceros' lived experiences, including labor activism, the refashioning of their ethnic and sexual identities, how they used their earnings, and their response to official and popular anti-Mexican hostility, see Cohen, *Braceros;* Laura D. Gutiérrez, "A Constant Threat: Deportation and Return Migration to Northern Mexico, 1918–1965" (PhD diss., University of California, San Diego, 2016); Loza, *Defiant Braceros;* Julie M. Weise, *Corazón de Dixie: Mexicanos in the U.S. South since 1910* (Chapel Hill: University of North Carolina Press, 2015), 82–119. Weise also examines Mexican consular staff who worked to make sure that braceros were paid fair wages and were exempted from Jim Crow laws in southern US states like Arkansas. For how braceros' families responded to their absence and adopted new social and economic roles in their home communities, see Miroslava Chávez-García, *Migrant Longing: Letter Writing across the U.S.-Mexico Borderlands* (Chapel Hill: University of North Carolina Press, 2018), 99–129; Rosas, *Abrazando el Espíritu.*

9. There are numerous social scientific studies that highlight how transnational social and financial networks from the bracero era influenced late twentieth-century migration patterns. The works of Jorge Durand, Douglas Massey, and their academic partners are among the most noteworthy examples of this body of scholarship. See, e.g., Jorge Durand, "Guanajuato, cantera de migrantes," *Encuentro* 4, no. 4 (1990): 49–62; Jorge Durand and Douglas S. Massey, eds., *Crossing the Border:*

Research from the Mexican Migration Project (New York: Russell Sage Foundation, 2004); Douglas S. Massey, Jorge Durand, and Nolan J. Malone, *Beyond Smoke and Mirrors: Mexican Immigration in an Era of Economic Integration* (New York: Russell Sage Foundation, 2002); Douglas S. Massey et al., *Return to Aztlan: The Social Process of International Migration from Western Mexico* (Berkeley: University of California Press, 1987). See also Jesús Arroyo Alejandre, Adrián de León Arias, and M. Basilia Valenzuela Varela, *Migración rural hacia Estados Unidos: Un estudio regional en Jalisco* (Mexico City: Consejo Nacional para la Cultura y las Artes, 1991); Fernando Cámara and Robert Van Kemper, eds., *Migration across Frontiers: Mexico and the United States* (Albany: Institute of Mesoamerican Studies, State University of New York, 1979); María del Carmen Cebada, "La migración hacia Estados Unidos y dos comunidades de origen en el estado de Guanajuato," *Regiones* 1, no. 1 (1993): 73–87; Wayne A. Cornelius and Jorge A. Bustamante, eds., *Mexican Migration to the United States: Origins, Consequences, and Policy Options* (San Diego: Center for U.S.-Mexican Studies, University of California, San Diego, 1989); Ina R. Dinerman, *Migrants and Stay-at-Homes: A Comparative Study of Rural Migration from Michoacán, Mexico* (La Jolla: Center for U.S.-Mexican Studies, University of California, San Diego, 1982); Gustavo López Castro, *La casa dividida: Un estudio de caso sobre la migración a Estados Unidos en un pueblo michoacano* (Zamora: El Colegio de Michoacán; Asociación Mexicana de Población, 1986); Gustavo López Castro, ed., *Migración en el occidente de México* (Zamora: El Colegio de Michoacán, 1988); Joshua S. Reichert, "A Town Divided: Economic Stratification and Social Relations in a Mexican Migrant Community," *Social Problems* 29, no. 4 (1982): 411–23; Kenneth D. Roberts, "Agrarian Structures and Labor Mobility in Rural Mexico," *Population and Development Review* 8, no. 2 (1982): 299–322. These social scientific studies also identify the economic crises that affected Mexico after the Bracero Program ended as a factor that drove migration to the United States. For a general overview of how transnational social and financial networks influence migration patterns, see Douglas S. Massey et al., "Theories of International Migration: A Review and Appraisal," *Population and Development Review* 19, no. 3 (1993): 448–50. For the percentage of late twentieth-century Mexican immigrants who were from Aguascalientes, Guanajuato, Jalisco, Michoacán, and Zacatecas, see official Mexican and US figures cited in Jorge Durand, Douglas S. Massey, and René M. Zenteno, "Mexican Immigration to the United States: Continuities and Changes," *Latin American Research Review* 36, no. 1 (2001): 110–12.

10. For the causes and course of the Cristero War, see David C. Bailey, *¡Viva Cristo Rey! The Cristero Rebellion and the Church-State Conflict in Mexico* (Austin: University of Texas Press, 1974); Matthew Butler, *Popular Piety and Political Identity in Mexico's Cristero Rebellion: Michoacán, 1927–29* (Oxford: Published for the British Academy by Oxford University Press, 2004); Robert Curley, *Citizens and Believers: Religion and Politics in Revolutionary Jalisco, 1900–1930* (Albuquerque: University of New Mexico Press, 2018); Jean A. Meyer, *The Cristero Rebellion: The Mexican People between Church and State, 1926–1929*, trans. Richard Southern (Cambridge: Cambridge University Press, 1976); Alicia Olivera Sedano, *La guerra*

cristera: Aspectos del conflicto religioso de 1926 a 1929 (Mexico City: Fondo de Cultura Económica, 2019); Yolanda Padilla Rangel, *El Catolicismo social y el movimiento Cristero en Aguascalientes* (Aguascalientes: Instituto Cultural de Aguascalientes, 1992); Jennie Purnell, *Popular Movements and State Formation in Revolutionary Mexico: The Agraristas and Cristeros of Michoacán* (Durham, NC: Duke University Press, 1999).

11. Meyer, *The Cristero Rebellion*, 85.

12. For the UNS, see Jean A. Meyer, *El sinarquismo, el cardenismo y la iglesia: 1937–1947* (Mexico City: Tusquets Editores, 2003); Jean A. Meyer, *El sinarquismo: ¿Un fascismo mexicano?* (Mexico City: Editorial J. Mortiz, 1979); Pablo Serrano Álvarez, *La batalla del espíritu: El movimiento sinarquista en el Bajío (1932–1951)*, 2 vols. (Mexico City: Consejo Nacional para la Cultura y las Artes, 1992); Guillermo Zermeño P. and Rubén Aguilar V., *Hacia una reinterpretación del sinarquismo actual: Notas y materiales para su estudio* (Mexico City: Universidad Iberoamericana, Departamento de Historia, 1988). For the number of active UNS members, see Meyer, *El sinarquismo: ¿Un fascismo mexicano?*, 47. For the PAN, see Soledad Loaeza, *El Partido Acción Nacional: La larga marcha, 1939–1994: Oposición leal y partido de protesta* (Mexico City: Fondo de Cultura Económica, 1999).

13. Ben Fallaw, *Religion and State Formation in Postrevolutionary Mexico* (Durham, NC: Duke University Press, 2013); Enrique Guerra Manzo, *Del fuego sagrado a la acción cívica: Los católicos frente al estado en Michoacán, 1920–1940* (Zamora: El Colegio de Michoacán; Mexico City: Universidad Autónoma Metropolitana, Unidad Xochimilco; Itaca, 2015); Gema Kloppe-Santamaría, *In the Vortex of Violence: Lynching, Extralegal Justice, and the State in Post-Revolutionary Mexico* (Oakland: University of California Press, 2020), 40–62; Benjamin T. Smith, *The Roots of Conservatism in Mexico: Catholicism, Society, and Politics in the Mixteca Baja, 1750–1962* (Albuquerque: University of New Mexico Press, 2012), 246–93.

14. There is a wealth of historical studies that examine the implementation and shortcomings of the agrarian reform. For an overview of the political debates that influenced the specific style of agrarian reform that was implemented, see Emilio Kourí, "La invención del ejido," *Nexos* 37, no. 445 (January 2015): 54–61. For national-level overviews of the agrarian reform's implementation, see Óscar Betanzos, ed., *Historia de la cuestión agraria mexicana*, vol. 3: *Campesinos, terratenientes y revolucionarios, 1910–1920* (Mexico City: Siglo XXI, 1988); Enrique Montalvo, ed., *Historia de la cuestión agraria mexicana*, vol. 4: *Modernización, lucha agraria y poder político, 1920–1934* (Mexico City: Siglo XXI, 1988); Everardo Escárcega López, ed., *Historia de la cuestión agraria mexicana*, vol. 5: *El cardenismo, un parteaguas histórico en el progreso agrario nacional, 1934–1940* (Mexico City: Siglo XXI, 1990). For land redistribution in the center-north and center-west, see Christopher R. Boyer, *Becoming Campesinos: Politics, Identity, and Agrarian Struggle in Postrevolutionary Michoacán, 1920–1935* (Stanford, CA: Stanford University Press, 2003); Javier Colmenares López et al., *Historia de la cuestión agraria mexicana: Estado de Zacatecas*, vol. 2 (Mexico City: Juan Pablos Editor; Gobierno del Estado de Zacatecas; Universidad Autónoma de Zacatecas; Centro de Estudios Históricos del Agrarismo en México,

1992); Ann L. Craig, *The First Agraristas: An Oral History of a Mexican Agrarian Reform Movement* (Berkeley: University of California Press, 1983); John Gledhill, *Casi Nada: A Study of Agrarian Reform in the Homeland of Cardenismo* (Albany: Institute for Mesoamerican Studies, University at Albany, State University of New York; Distributed by University of Texas Press, 1991); Francisco Javier Meyer Cosío, *Tradición y progreso: La reforma agraria en Acámbaro, Guanajuato (1917–1941)* (Mexico City:: Instituto Nacional de Estudios Históricos de la Revolución Mexicana, Secretaría de Gobernación, 1993); Miguel Moctezuma Longoria, "La otra reforma agraria en Zacatecas (1917–1934)," in *Temas de historia, sociedad, política y cultura en Zacatecas,* ed. Alicia Bazarte Martínez and Eligio Meza Padilla (Zacatecas: Maestría en Ciencia Política, Universidad Autónoma de Zacatecas, 1998), 73–94; Beatriz Rojas, *La destrucción de la hacienda en Aguascalientes, 1910–1931* (Zamora: El Colegio de Michoacán, 1981). For regional studies that examine the agrarian reform in states outside of the center-north and center-west, see Adrián A. Bantjes, *As If Jesus Walked on Earth: Cardenismo, Sonora, and the Mexican Revolution* (Wilmington, DE: Scholarly Resources, 1998), 123–50; Ben Fallaw, *Cárdenas Compromised: The Failure of Reform in Postrevolutionary Yucatán* (Durham, NC: Duke University Press, 2001); Heather Fowler Salamini, *Agrarian Radicalism in Veracruz, 1920–1938* (Lincoln: University of Nebraska Press, 1978); Timothy J. Henderson, *The Worm in the Wheat: Rosalie Evans and Agrarian Struggle in the Puebla-Tlaxcala Valley, 1906–1927* (Durham, NC: Duke University Press, 1998); G.M. Joseph, *Revolution from Without: Yucatán, Mexico, and the United States, 1880–1924* (New York: Cambridge University Press, 1982), 122–49, 228–62; Mikael D. Wolfe, *Watering the Revolution: An Environmental and Technological History of Agrarian Reform in Mexico* (Durham: Duke University Press, 2017).

15. *Estadísticas históricas de México,* vol. 1, 4th ed. (Aguascalientes: INEGI, Instituto Nacional de Estadística, Geografía en Informática, 1999), 325, 327.

16. For the conservative turn in agrarian policy after 1940, see Sergio de la Peña, ed., *Historia de la cuestión agraria mexicana,* vol. 6: *El agrarismo y la industrialización de México, 1940–1950* (Mexico City: Siglo XXI, 1989); Julio Moguel, *Historia de la cuestión agraria mexicana,* vol. 7: *La época de oro y el principio de la crisis de la agricultura mexicana, 1950–1970* (Mexico City: Siglo XXI, 1988); Tore C. Olsson, *Agrarian Crossings: Reformers and the Remaking of the US and Mexican Countryside* (Princeton, NJ: Princeton University Press, 2017).

17. For the amount of land redistributed in the center-north and center-west between 1940 and 1964, see *Estadísticas históricas de México,* vol. 1, 325–28. For population figures, see México, Dirección General de Estadística, *Sexto Censo de Población, 1940: Resumen General,* 1, 39; México, Dirección General de Estadística, *VIII Censo General de Población—1960, 8 de Junio de 1960: Resumen General,* V–VI.

18. Meyer, *The Cristero Rebellion;* Olivera Sedano, *La guerra cristera;* Serrano Álvarez, *La batalla del espíritu.*

19. Padrón e Historial de Núcleos Agrarios, Registro Agrario Nacional, www.ran.gob.mx/ran/index.php/sistemas-de-consulta/phina.

20. See the following publications by México, Dirección General de Estadística: *Sexto Censo de Población, 1940: Aguascalientes; Baja California Territorios Norte y Sur* (Mexico City, 1943), 15; *Sexto Censo de Población, 1940: Guanajuato* (Mexico City, 1943) 13, 49, 85; *Sexto Censo de Población, 1940: Jalisco* (Mexico City, 1943), 13, 47, 77, 106, 133, 161; *Sexto Censo de Población, 1940: Michoacán* (Mexico City, 1943), 13, 46, 73, 102, 130, 160; *Sexto Censo de Población, 1940: Zacatecas* (Mexico City, 1943), 13, 45, 74; *VIII Censo General de Población—1960, 8 de Junio de 1960: Estado de Aguascalientes* (Mexico City, 1963), 1–2; *VIII Censo General de Población—1960, 8 de Junio de 1960: Estado de Guanajuato* (Mexico City, 1963), 25–34; *VIII Censo General de Población—1960, 8 de Junio de 1960: Estado de Jalisco* (Mexico City, 1963), 3–27; *VIII Censo General de Población—1960, 8 de Junio de 1960: Estado de Michoacán* (Mexico City, 1963), 3–25; *VIII Censo General de Población—1960, 8 de Junio de 1960: Estado de Zacatecas* (Mexico City, 1963), 3–12.

21. For how the US government retreated from some guest worker program administrative responsibilities, see Cindy Hahamovitch, *No Man's Land: Jamaican Guestworkers in America and the Global History of Deportable Labor* (Princeton, NJ: Princeton University Press, 2011); Don Mitchell, *They Saved the Crops: Labor, Landscape, and the Struggle over Industrial Farming in Bracero-Era California* (Athens: University of Georgia Press, 2012). Hahamovitch focuses primarily on the guest worker initiatives that allowed Caribbean workers, particularly those from Jamaica, to enter the United States, but she also devotes attention to the Bracero Program. While US officials increasingly deferred to the interests of employers during bilateral negotiations and reduced their oversight of work and housing sites, they boosted their immigration enforcement capacity and increasingly prioritized apprehending and deporting undocumented workers. For this, see Calavita, *Inside the State;* Goodman, *The Deportation Machine;* Kang, *The INS on the Line;* and Ngai, *Impossible Subjects*.

22. Harry E. Cross and James A. Sandos, *Across the Border: Rural Development in Mexico and Recent Migration to the United States* (Berkeley: Institute of Governmental Studies, University of California, Berkeley, 1981), 35–48.

23. Perhaps the most notable historical study that advances the "leviathan" interpretation of the post-1940 Mexican state is Enrique Krauze, *La presidencia imperial* (Mexico City: Tusquets Editores, 1997). See also Howard F. Cline, *Mexico: Revolution to Evolution, 1940–1960* (New York: Oxford University Press, 1962); Daniel Cosío Villegas, *El sistema político mexicano: Las posibilidades de cambio* (Mexico City: Editorial J. Mortiz, 1973); Donald J. Mabry, "Changing Models of Mexican Politics: A Review Essay," *New Scholar* 5, no. 1 (1976): 31–37; Octavio Paz, *Posdata* (Mexico City: Siglo XXI, 1970); Luis Reyna and Richard S. Weinert, eds., *Authoritarianism in Mexico* (Philadelphia: Institute for the Study of Human Issues, 1977); Stanley R. Ross, ed., *Is the Mexican Revolution Dead?* (Philadelphia: Temple University Press, 1975); Evelyn P. Stevens, "Mexico's PRI: The Institutionalization of Corporatism?," in *Authoritarianism and Corporatism in Latin America*, ed. James N. Malloy (Pittsburgh: University of Pittsburgh Press, 1977), 227–58.

24. The quotes "considerable cultural, local, and ethnic autonomies" and "salient popular bargaining and veto power" are from Paul Gillingham and Benjamin T.

Smith, "Introduction: The Paradoxes of Revolution," in *Dictablanda: Politics, Work, and Culture in Mexico, 1938–1968*, ed. Paul Gillingham and Benjamin T. Smith (Durham, NC: Duke University Press, 2014), 20–27. The "messiness, ambiguity, contradiction, and diversity" of twentieth-century Mexican state building is from Wil G. Pansters, "Zones and Languages of State-Making: From Pax *Priísta* to Dirty War," in *México beyond 1968: Revolutionaries, Radicals, and Repression during the Global Sixties and Subversive Seventies*, ed. Jaime M. Pensado and Enrique C. Ochoa (Tucson: University of Arizona Press, 2018), 44. See also Gillingham and Smith, *Dictablanda;* Pensado and Ochoa, *México beyond 1968;* Alexander Aviña, *Specters of Revolution: Peasant Guerrillas in the Cold War Mexican Countryside* (New York: Oxford University Press, 2014); A.S. Dillingham, *Oaxaca Resurgent: Indigeneity, Development, and Inequality in Twentieth-Century Mexico* (Stanford, CA: Stanford University Press, 2021); Paul Gillingham, "Maximino's Bulls: Popular Protest after the Mexican Revolution, 1940–1952," *Past & Present* 206, no. 1 (2010): 175–211; Paul Gillingham, *Unrevolutionary Mexico: The Birth of a Strange Dictatorship* (New Haven, CT: Yale University Press, 2021); Rogelio Hernández Rodríguez, *El centro dividido: La nueva autonomía de los gobernadores* (Mexico City: El Colegio de México, Centro de Estudios Internacionales, 2008); Stephen E. Lewis, *Rethinking Mexican Indigenismo: The INI's Coordinating Council in Highland Chiapas and the Fate of a Utopian Project* (Albuquerque: University of New Mexico Press, 2018); Gladys I. McCormick, *The Logic of Compromise in Mexico: How the Countryside Was Key to the Emergence of Authoritarianism* (Chapel Hill: University of North Carolina Press, 2016); Tanalís Padilla, *Rural Resistance in the Land of Zapata: The Jaramillista Movement and the Myth of the Pax Priísta, 1940–1962* (Durham, NC: Duke University Press, 2008); Tanalís Padilla, *Unintended Lessons of Revolution: Student Teachers and Political Radicalism in Twentieth-Century Mexico* (Durham, NC: Duke University Press, 2022); Jaime M. Pensado, *Rebel Mexico: Student Unrest and Authoritarian Political Culture during the Long Sixties* (Stanford, CA: Stanford University Press, 2013); Pablo Piccato, *A History of Infamy: Crime, Truth, and Justice in Mexico* (Oakland: University of California Press, 2017); Thomas Rath, *Myths of Demilitarization in Postrevolutionary Mexico, 1920–1960* (Chapel Hill: University of North Carolina Press, 2013); Benjamin T. Smith, *The Mexican Press and Civil Society, 1940–1976: Stories from the Newsroom, Stories from the Street* (Chapel Hill: University of North Carolina Press, 2018); Eric Zolov, *The Last Good Neighbor: Mexico in the Global Sixties* (Durham, NC: Duke University Press, 2020). For how popular culture reflected the limits of PRI rule during the post-1940 period, see Gilbert M. Joseph, Anne Rubenstein, and Eric Zolov, eds., *Fragments of a Golden Age: The Politics of Culture in Mexico since 1940* (Durham, NC: Duke University Press, 2001); John Mraz, *Looking for Mexico: Modern Visual Culture and National Identity* (Durham, NC: Duke University Press, 2009); Jeffrey M. Pilcher, *Cantinflas and the Chaos of Mexican Modernity* (Wilmington, DE: Scholarly Resources, 2001); Anne Rubenstein, *Bad Language, Naked Ladies, and Other Threats to the Nation: A Political History of Comic Books in Mexico* (Durham, NC: Duke University Press, 1998); Eric Zolov, *Refried Elvis: The Rise of Mexican Counterculture* (Berkeley:

University of California Press, 1999). The studies whose temporal focus extends into the 1970s situate the shift toward an overtly authoritarian governing style in the context of the Cold War. As popular calls for radical revolutionary action that would ameliorate socioeconomic inequalities and generate more democratic forms of governance increased during the 1960s, Mexican officials, like their counterparts in other Latin American nations, violently cracked down on suspected "subversives."

25. Gustavo Arellano, "When The U.S. Government Tried to Replace Migrant Farmworkers with High Schoolers," National Public Radio, August 23, 2018, www.npr.org/sections/thesalt/2018/07/31/634442195/when-the-u-s-government-tried-to-replace-migrant-farmworkers-with-high-schoolers; Alfredo Corchado, "A Former Farmworker on American Hypocrisy," *New York Times,* May 6, 2020, www.nytimes.com/2020/05/06/opinion/sunday/coronavirus-essential-workers.html; Anne Gearan et al., "Biden Meets with Mexican President amid Growing Pressure on Immigration," *Washington Post,* March 1, 2021, www.washingtonpost.com/world/the_americas/biden-lopez-obrador-summit-vaccines-migration/2021/03/01/62e18c02-7a9d-11eb-a976-c028a4215c78_story.html; Kurtis Lee, "Arizona Crowd Welcomes Donald Trump's Tough Stance on Immigration," *Los Angeles Times,* July 11, 2015, www.latimes.com/nation/politics/la-na-trump-arizona-rally-20150710-story.html.

CHAPTER ONE

1. Adolfo Ruiz Cortines to C. Gobernador del Estado, March 3, 1942, AHAG-PEG, SEGOB, PD, 1.19, año 1942, expediente 6.

2. Délano, *Mexico and Its Diaspora in the United States,* 5, 59–82.

3. For the commission's debates and the decision to participate in the Bracero Program, including the initial popular opposition to the Bracero Program and the influence of Manuel Gamio's modernization theories, see Cohen, *Braceros,* 21–42; Craig, *The Bracero Program,* 20–23; Iskander, *Creative State,* 50; Loza, *Defiant Braceros,* 23–60; Rosas, *Abrazando el Espíritu,* 19–23; Snodgrass, "The Bracero Program," 83–88; Torres, *México y el mundo,* 36–39. For Gamio's arguments that Mexican migration to the United States would ultimately benefit Mexico, see Manuel Gamio, *Mexican Immigration to the United States: A Study of Human Migration and Adjustment* (Chicago: University of Chicago Press, 1930). For the nationalization of the oil industry, see Myrna I. Santiago, *The Ecology of Oil: Environment, Labor, and the Mexican Revolution, 1900–1930* (Cambridge: Cambridge University Press, 2006).

4. Manuel Ávila Camacho, "Acuerdo previniendo que se hagan las gestiones necesarias para impartir seguridades a los trabajadores mexicanos que emigren a los Estados Unidos de Norteamérica, July 23, 1942," published August 21, 1942, in *Diario Oficial de la Federación,* vol. 133, no. 45, 1st sec., 1–2.

5. There is a voluminous body of scholarship that examines the uneven centralization efforts of the 1920s and 1930s and the persistence of relatively autonomous regional and local powers during these decades. Notable examples are Thomas

Benjamin and Mark Wasserman, eds., *Provinces of the Revolution: Essays on Regional Mexican History, 1910–1929* (Albuquerque: University of New Mexico Press, 1990); Fallaw, *Cárdenas Compromised;* Nora Hamilton, *The Limits of State Autonomy: Post-Revolutionary Mexico* (Princeton, NJ: Princeton University Press, 1982); Alicia Hernández Chávez, *La mecánica cardenista* (Mexico City: El Colegio de México, 1979); Stephen E. Lewis, *The Ambivalent Revolution: Forging State and Nation in Chiapas, 1910–1945* (Albuquerque: University of New Mexico Press, 2005); Álvaro Matute, *Las dificultades del nuevo estado* (Mexico City: El Colegio de México, Centro de Estudios Históricos, 1995); Jean Meyer, Enrique Krauze, and Cayetano Reyes, *Estado y sociedad con Calles* (Mexico City: El Colegio de México, 1977); Lorenzo Meyer, Rafael Segovia, and Alejandra Lajous, *Los inicios de la institucionalización: La política del Maximato* (Mexico City: El Colegio de México, 1978); Sarah Osten, *The Mexican Revolution's Wake: The Making of a Political System, 1920–1929* (New York: Cambridge University Press, 2018); Alex Saragoza, *The Monterrey Elite and the Mexican State, 1880–1940* (Austin: University of Texas Press, 1988); Benjamin T. Smith, *Pistoleros and Popular Movements: The Politics of State Formation in Postrevolutionary Oaxaca* (Lincoln: University of Nebraska Press, 2009). For the transition to the early postrevolutionary governments, see Alan Knight, "Cardenismo: Juggernaut or Jalopy?" *Journal of Latin American Studies* 26, no. 1 (1994): 73–107; Alan Knight, "The End of the Mexican Revolution? From Cárdenas to Ávila Camacho, 1937–1941," in Gillingham and Smith, *Dictablanda,* 47–69; Luis Medina, *Del cardenismo al avilacamachismo* (Mexico City: El Colegio de México, 1978).

6. The Mexican immigrant population in the United States grew from 103,000 in 1900 to 641,000 in 1930, then fell to 380,000 in 1940 following a series of repatriation campaigns. For early twentieth-century Mexican migratory policy and figures, see Délano, *Mexico and Its Diaspaora in the United States,* 59–82; and FitzGerald, *A Nation of Emigrants,* 39–49. For the informal guest worker initiative of the late 1910s and early 1920s, see Alanís Enciso, *El primer programa bracero y el gobierno de México.* For the repatriation campaigns of the 1930s, when between 500,000 and one million Mexican nationals and their US-born children returned to Mexico, see Fernando Saúl Alanís Enciso, "The Repatriation of Mexicans from the United States and Mexican Nationalism, 1929–1940," in *Beyond la Frontera: The History of Mexico-U.S. Migration,* ed. Mark Overmyer-Velázquez (New York: Oxford University Press, 2011), 51–78; Fernando Saúl Alanís Enciso, *They Should Stay There: The Story of Mexican Migration and Repatriation During the Great Depression,* trans. Russ Davidson (Chapel Hill: University of North Carolina Press, 2017); Francisco E. Balderrama and Raymond Rodríguez, *Decade of Betrayal: Mexican Repatriation in the 1930s,* revised edition (Albuquerque: University of New Mexico Press, 2006). For the lived experiences of Mexican immigrants in both their home communities and the U.S. during this period, see Gamio, *Mexican Immigration to the United States;* Gilbert G. González, "Mexican Labor Migration, 1876–1924," in Overmyer-Velázquez, *Beyond la Frontera,* 28–50; George J. Sánchez, *Becoming Mexican American: Ethnicity, Culture, and Identity in Chicano Los Angeles, 1900–1945* (New York: Oxford University Press, 1993); Paul S. Taylor, *A Spanish-Mexican Peasant Community:*

Arandas in Jalisco, Mexico (Berkeley: University of California Press, 1933); Weise, *Corazón de Dixie*, 14–81; and Julia G. Young, *Mexican Exodus: Emigrants, Exiles, and Refugees of the Cristero War* (New York: Oxford University Press, 2015).

7. Ávila Camacho, "Acuerdo previniendo que se hagan las gestiones necesarias para impartir seguridades a los trabajadores mexicanos que emigren a los Estados Unidos de Norteamérica," 2; Secretaría del Trabajo y Previsión Social, "Los braceros," in *Braceros: Las miradas mexicana y estadounidense: Antología (1945–1964)*, ed. Jorge Durand (Mexico City: Senado de la República, LX Legislatura, Comisión de Biblioteca y Asuntos Editoriales; Porrúa; Zacatecas: Universidad Autónoma de Zacatecas, 2007), 210–11. For the Bracero Savings Fund and its corruption, see Abel Astorga Morales, *Historia de un ahorro sin retorno: Despojo salarial, olvido y reivindicación histórica en el movimiento social de ex braceros, 1942–1964* (Guadalajara: Universidad de Guadalajara, 2017). Former braceros began organizing to demand that federal authorities pay out the moneys that were owed to them from the Bracero Savings Fund during the late twentieth and early twenty-first centuries. For these efforts, see Loza, *Defiant Braceros*, 137–67.

8. Ávila Camacho, "Acuerdo previniendo que se hagan las gestiones necesarias para impartir seguridades a los trabajadores mexicanos que emigren a los Estados Unidos de Norteamérica," 1–2.

9. Adolfo Ruiz Cortines, Circular Número 463, August 21, 1942, AHAGPEG, SEGOB, PD, 1.19, año 1942, expediente 28.

10. Secretaría del Trabajo y Previsión Social, "Los braceros," 171.

11. Ngai, *Impossible Subjects*, 147.

12. Luis L. Mendoza to C. Presidente República, August 24, 1942, AGN, MAC, caja 793, expediente 546.6/120; Alfredo Rodríguez Romo to C. Presidente de la República, August 22, 1942, AGN, MAC, caja 793, expediente 546.6/120. Mendoza wrote from Mexicali on behalf of 400 workers; Rodríguez Romo wrote from Ciudad Juárez on behalf of 900. Neither specified where exactly in Mexico they were from, though Mendoza mentioned having to cross the northern deserts to return home, thus implying that they were from central or southern Mexico.

13. Mariano González to C. General de Div. Dn. Manuel Ávila Camacho, September 23, 1942, AGN, MAC, caja 793 expediente 546.6/120.

14. Anacleto F. Olmos to C. Presidente de la República, September 9, 1942, AGN, MAC, caja 793, expediente 546.6/120.

15. Unknown Foreign Relations Secretariat official to C. Presidente de la República, October 27, 1942, AGN, MAC, caja 793, expediente 546.6/120. The signature page is missing from this document.

16. Lic. Sebastián Ortiz H. to Sr. Matías C. Michel, August 25, 1943, AGN, MAC, caja 793, expediente 546.6/120.

17. Un portavoz to Sr. Presidente de la República, March 17, 1943, AGN, MAC, caja 793, expediente 546.6/120.

18. Salvador Flores Rodríguez to Presidente República, January 14, 1943, AGN, MAC, caja 793, expediente 546.6/120; Francisco Escalante to Presidente de la República, June 7, 1943, AGN, MAC, caja 793, expediente 546.6/120.

19. Lic. Sebastián Ortiz H. to Sres. Adrián González e Ibarra y demás firmantes, July 28, 1943, AGN, MAC, caja 793, expediente 546.6/120.

20. Lic. Luis Fernández del Campo to J. José Terriquez Martínez, September 3, 1943, AGN, MAC, caja 793, expediente 546.6/120.

21. José Terriquez Martínez to Sr. Lic. J. Jesús González Gallo, August 7, 1943, AGN, MAC, caja 793, expediente 546.6/120.

22. Lic. Carlos Herrera Marmolejo to C. Presidente Municipal, June 12, 1943, AGHPEM, SEGOB, TPS, PB, caja 1, expediente 1, fojas 44–45.

23. *Estadísticas históricas de México,* vol. 1, 4th ed., 321.

24. México, Dirección General de Estadística, *Segundo Censo Agrícola Ganadero de los Estados Unidos Mexicanos* (Mexico City, 1951), 32; México, Dirección General de Estadística, *Segundo Censo Ejidal de los Estados Unidos Mexicanos* (Mexico City, 1949), 165, 171. The censuses recorded 2,989,042,083 kilograms of maize and 424,134,108 kilograms of wheat produced in 1940; 1,493,394,678 kilograms of maize and 234,964,208 kilograms of wheat were produced on ejidos.

25. For Gómez's introduction to revolutionary agrarian politics and his Tamaulipas governorship, see Michael A. Ervin, "Marte R. Gómez of Tamaulipas: Governing Agrarian Revolution," in *State Governors of the Mexican Revolution, 1910–1952: Portraits in Conflict, Courage, and Corruption,* ed. Jürgen Buchenau and William H. Beezley (Lanham, MD: Rowman & Littlefield, 2009), 123–38. For his appointment to Ávila Camacho's cabinet, see Olsson, *Agrarian Crossings.*

26. Olsson, *Agrarian Crossings,* 129–58.

27. *Estadísticas históricas de México,* vol. 1, 321.

28. Rubén Jaramillo was a former Zapatista who had supported Lázaro Cárdenas and remained active in Morelos's and Puebla's sugar-growing regions during the post-1940 period. He rebelled against the national government after two failed bids for Morelos's governorship during the 1940s and 1950s but was pardoned both times; government agents ultimately assassinated him in 1962. His brothers Porfirio and Antonio were also active in regional agrarian politics; Porfirio was assassinated in 1955, but Antonio worked within the PRI system. For Rubén's activism and his deteriorating relationship with the federal administrations of the 1940s and 1950s, see Padilla, *Rural Resistance in the Land of Zapata.* For a comparative analysis of all three Jaramillo brothers' political careers, see McCormick, *The Logic of Compromise in Mexico.*

29. Olsson, *Agrarian Crossings,* 135–37. For other instances of post-1940 governments rhetorically linking development initiatives to revolutionary-era projects, see Gilbert M. Joseph, Anne Rubenstein, and Eric Zolov, "Assembling the Fragments: Writing a Cultural History of Mexico since 1940," in *Fragments of a Golden Age: The Politics of Culture in Mexico Since 1940,* ed. Gilbert M. Joseph, Anne Rubenstein, and Eric Zolov (Durham, NC: Duke University Press, 2001), 3–22; Alex Saragoza, "The Selling of Mexico: Tourism and the State, 1929–1952," in Joseph, Rubenstein, and Zolov, *Fragments of a Golden Age,* 91–115; Mary Kay Vaughan, "Transnational Processes and the Rise and Fall of the Mexican Cultural State: Notes from the Past," in Joseph, Rubenstein, and Zolov, *Fragments of a Golden Age,*

471–87; Eric Zolov, "Discovering a Land 'Mysterious and Obvious': The Renarrativizing of Postrevolutionary Mexico," in Joseph, Rubenstein, and Zolov, *Fragments of a Golden Age*, 234–72.

30. Lic. Carlos Herrera Marmolejo to C. Presidente Municipal, June 12, 1943, AGHPEM, SEGOB, TPS, PB, caja 1, expediente 1, fojas 44–45; Lic. Francisco Trujillo Gurría to C. Gobernador del Estado, June 26, 1943, AGHPEM, SEGOB, TPS, PB, caja 1, expediente 1, foja 73. Herrera Marmolejo was a Michoacán state official who forwarded Trujillo Gurría's message regarding the initial evasion of the ejidatario ban to that state's municipal governments.

31. Lic. Crescenciano Aguilera to C. Gobernador del Estado, July 26, 1943, AGHPEM, SEGOB, TPS, PB, caja 1, expediente 1, fojas 42–43.

32. Lic. Luis Marín Pérez to Ciudadano Presidente Municipal, August 9, 1943, AGHPEM, SEGOB, TPS, PB, caja 1, expediente 1, fojas 50, 51, and 54.

33. Lic. Crescenciano Aguilera and Ing. Ramón Castañeda M. to C. Gobernador Constitucional del Estado, July 27, 1943, AGHPEM, SEGOB, TPS, PB, caja 1, expediente 1, fojas 52–53.

34. Lic. Roberto Amorós G. to C. Secretario del Trabajo y Previsión Social, August 10, 1943, AGN, MAC, caja 793, expediente 546.6/120.

35. Gral. Brig. Marcelino García Barragán to C. Presidente Municipal, August 2, 1943, AHEJ, GOB/SC, año 1943, caja 13.

36. Official Mexican figures cited in González Navarro, *Población y sociedad en México (1900–1970)*, vol. 2, chart between pp. 146 and 147; official US figures cited in Ngai, *Impossible Subjects*, 157. According to the figures Ngai cited, a combined 56,301 braceros entered the United States in 1942 and 1943. However, according to González Navarro's figures, the Mexican government selected 80,075 braceros during those years; 42,007 were from Guanajuato, Jalisco, and Michoacán.

37. México, Dirección General de Estadística, *Sexto Censo de Población, 1940: Resumen General*, 1–3.

38. William F. Foshag and Jenaro González R., "Birth and Development of Parícutin Volcano, Mexico," in *Geological Survey Bulletin 965-D* (Washington, DC: US Government Printing Office, 1956), 375–85.

39. Lic. Luis Marín Pérez to Presidente de la República, February 22, 1943, AGN, MAC, caja 892, expediente 561.4/15–13.

40. Foshag and González R., "Birth and Development of Parícutin Volcano," 396.

41. Gral. Félix Ireta V., Memorandum para el señor General de División Manuel Ávila Camacho, Presidente de la República, June 11, 1943, AGN, MAC, caja 892, expediente 561.4/15–13.

42. Mary Lee Nolan, "Impact of Parícutin on Five Communities," in *Volcanic Activity and Human Ecology*, ed. Payson D. Sheets and Donald K. Grayson (New York: Academic Press, 1979), 304.

43. Félix Anguiano Pérez, J. Jesús Orozco T., and Francisco Ramos N. to C. Gral. de División Manuel Ávila Camacho, June 29, 1943, AGHPEM, SEGOB, TPS, PB, caja 1, expediente 1, foja 57.

44. For Cárdenas's lobbying efforts on behalf of Parícutin damnificados, see Christopher R. Boyer, *Political Landscapes: Forests, Conservation, and Community in Mexico* (Durham, NC: Duke University Press, 2015), 156–61.

45. Lic. Luis Marín Pérez to Ciudadano Director de la Oficina de Prevención Social, September 2, 1943, AGHPEM, SEGOB, TPS, PB, caja 1, expediente 1, fojas 64–67.

46. Lic. Luis Padilla Nervo to C. Gobernador del Estado de Michoacán, October 20, 1943, AGHPEM, SEGOB, TPS, PB, caja 1, expediente 1, fojas 108–112.

47. Enrique Bravo Valencia to C. Gral. Félix Ireta Viveros, December 20, 1943, AGHPEM, SEGOB, TPS, PB, caja 1, expediente 1, foja 124.

48. Lic. Luis Marín Pérez to Los Presidentes Municipales de Los Reyes, Peribán, Uruapan, Cotija, and Parangaricutiro, December 23, 1943, AGHPEM, SEGOB, TPS, PB, caja 1, expediente 1, foja 125.

49. Lic. Luis Padilla Nervo to C. Gobernador del Estado de Michoacán, October 6, 1943, AGHPEM, SEGOB, TPS, PB, caja 1, expediente 3, foja 122.

50. El Inspector #67 to C. Jefe del Departamento de Investigaciones Políticas y Sociales, January 5, 1944, AGN, DGIPS, caja 782, expediente 4, foja 2.

51. IPS 38 to C. Jefe del Departamento de Investigación Política y Social, January 18, 1944, AGN, DGIPS, caja 782, expediente 4, foja 23.

52. Carlos A. Madrazo, "La verdad en el 'caso' de los braceros: Origen de esta injusticia y nombre de los verdaderos responsables," in *Braceros: Las miradas mexicana y estadounidense: Antología (1945–1964)*, ed. Jorge Durand (Mexico City: Senado de la República, LX Legislatura, Comisión de Biblioteca y Asuntos Editoriales; Miguel Ángel Porrúa; Zacatecas: Universidad Autónoma de Zacatecas, 2007), 55–84.

53. Carlos Saavedra, PS #2, and Roberto Ramos C. to C. Jefe del Departamento de Investigaciones Políticas y Sociales, AGN, DGIPS, caja 782, expediente 4, fojas 57–58.

54. Lic. Miguel Alemán to C. Gob. del Edo., March 1, 1944, AGHPEM, SEGOB, TPS, PB, caja 1, expediente 2, foja 3.

55. Summary of an April 26, 1944, letter from Estela Merino, Sara Vázquez Batista y demás firmantes to C. Presidente, May 15, 1944, AGN, MAC, caja 793, expediente 546.6/120.

56. Ernesto Hidalgo to C. Presidente Municipal, May 26, 1944, AHAGPEG, SEGOB, PD, 1.19, año 1944, expediente 67; El Inspector Comisionado (37) to C. Lic. Eduardo Ampudia, May 22, 1944, AGN, DGIPS, caja 97, expediente 22, fojas 147–150.

57. Ernesto Hidalgo to C. Presidente Municipal, July 20, 1944, AHAGPEG, SEGOB, PD, 1.03, año 1944, expediente 24.

58. El Inspector Comisionado (37) to C. Lic. Eduardo Ampudia, May 22, 1944, AGN, DGIPS, caja 97, expediente 22, fojas 147–50.

59. Ezequiel Padilla to C. Gobernador Constitucional del Estado, June 7, 1944, AHAGPEG, SEGOB, PD, 1.21.03, año 1944, expediente 18.

60. Gral. Brig. Marcelino García Barragán to C. Gobernador Constl. del Estado, July 29, 1944, AHAGPEG, SEGOB, PD, 1.21.03, año 1944, expediente 17.

61. Lic. Fausto Villagómez to C. Gobernador de Jalisco, August 5, 1944, AHAGPEG, SEGOB, PD, 1.21.03, año 1944, expediente 17.

62. Official figures cited in Ngai, *Impossible Subjects*, 157.

63. Lic. Fausto Villagómez to C. Presidente Municipal, October 10, 1944, AHAGPEG, SEGOB, PD, 1.03, año 1944, expediente 33; Lic. Luis M. Moreno to Ciudadano Presidente Municipal, October 18, 1944, AGHPEM, SEGOB, TPS, PB, caja 1, expediente 2, fojas 13–14.

64. Vicente Cervantes C. to C. Lic. Eduardo Ampudia V., November 21, 1944, AGN, DGIPS, caja 92, expediente 10, foja 134.

65. Lic. Luis Fernández del Campo to C. Gobernador Constitucional del Estado Libre y Soberano de Guanajuato, February 14, 1945, AHAGPEG, SEGOB, PD, 1.19, año 1945, expediente 44; Lic. Luis Fernández del Campo to C. Gobernador del Estado Libre y Soberano de Michoacán, February 14, 1945, AGHPEM, SEGOB, TPS, PB, caja 1, expediente 3, foja 18.

66. Secretaría del Trabajo y Previsión Social, "Aviso a los Braceros," February 8, 1945, AHEJ, GOB/SC, año 1945, caja 44. Although the broadsides are dated earlier than Fernández del Campo's letter, the two documents were sent to the state governments together.

67. Lic. Juan Ignacio Ibáñez to C. Presidente Municipal, February 14, 1945, AHAGPEG, SEGOB, PD, 1.19, año 1945, expediente 20.

68. Lic. Luis M. Moreno to Ciudadano Secretario del Trabajo, February 12, 1945, AGHPEM, SEGOB, TPS, PB, caja 1, expediente 3, fojas 13/14–14/15.

69. Cohen, *Braceros*, 98–103.

70. Summary of a letter from Salvador Guzmán, Felipe Godoy, and others to C. Presidente, June 2, 1945, AGN, MAC, caja 794, expediente 546.6/120–13. The original date of the request is not noted in the summary.

71. Crescenciano Madrigal and others to C. Gral. de Div. Manuel Ávila Camacho, June 18, 1945, AGN, MAC, caja 794, expediente 546.6/120–13.

72. Lic. Benito Coquet to C. Gobernador del Estado, March 5, 1946, AHAGPEG, SEGOB, PD, 1.19, año 1946, expediente 3.

73. Gral. Brig. Marcelino García Barragán to C. Lic. Francisco Trujillo Gurría, March 27, 1946, AHEJ, GOB/SC, año 1946, caja 52.

74. Lic. Francisco Trujillo Gurría to C. Gobernador del Estado, April 27, 1946, AHEJ, GOB/SC, año 1946, caja 52; Summary of a May 18, 1946, letter from Jorge Guerrero Águila, Martín Vázquez Flores, and José Terrones García C. Presidente, May 23, 1946, AGN, MAC, caja 794, expediente 546.6/120–13.

75. Gral. Brig. Marcelino García Barragán to C. Subsecretario del Trabajo y Previsión Social, April 30, 1946, AHEJ, GOB/SC, año 1946, caja 52.

76. Gral. Brig. Marcelino García Barragán to C. Secretario del Trabajo y Previsión Social, May 16, 1946, AHEJ, GOB/SC, año 1946, caja 52.

77. Pablo Hernández to C. Jefe del Departamento del Trabajo y Previsión Social, June 19, 1946, AHEJ, GOB/SC, año 1946, caja 52.

78. Gral. Brig. Marcelino García Barragán to C. Gral. de Div. Manuel Ávila Camacho, June 21, 1946, AGN, MAC, caja 794, expediente 546.6/120–13.

79. Relación de los braceros en la ciudad de Guadalajara el día 24 de junio de 1946 correspondientes a la sección número 3 del Sindicato de Obreros y Campesinos de la Industria Azucarera y Similares de la República Mexicana, June 24, 1946, AHEJ, GOB/SC, año 1946, caja 12.

80. Memorandum sobre la contratación de braceros en Jalisco, undated and unsigned, AHEJ, GOB/SC, año 1946, caja 12. Although undated and unsigned, this memorandum references the events of the 1946 bracero contracting process in Jalisco.

81. Lic. Luis Manuel Moreno to C. Secretario de Trabajo y Previsión Social, March 30, 1946, AGHPEM, SEGOB, TPS, PB, caja 2, expediente sin número, foja 30; Joaquín Bustamante, Aviso Importante a los Aspirantes a Braceros, April 11, 1946, AGHPEM, SEGOB, TPS, PB, caja 2.

82. Michael Snodgrass, "The Golden Age of Charrismo: Workers, Braceros, and the Political Machinery of Postrevolutionary Mexico," in Gillingham and Smith, *Dictablanda*, 189–90; Joaquín Cortés to Lic. Luis M. Moreno, September 25, 1946, AGHPEM, SEGOB, TPS, PB, caja 2, expediente sin número, foja 216; J. Martínez G. and others to Ciudadano Gobernador Constitucional del Estado, October 8, 1946, AGHPEM, SEGOB, TPS, PB, caja 2, expediente sin número, foja 241.

83. Gillingham, *Unrevolutionary Mexico;* Paul Gillingham, "'We Don't Have Arms, But We Do Have Balls': Fraud, Violence, and Popular Agency in Elections," in Gillingham and Smith, *Dictablanda*, 149–72.

84. Jaime Sánchez Susarrey and Ignacio Medina Sánchez, *Jalisco desde la revolución,* vol. 9: *Historia política, 1940–1975* (Guadalajara: Gobierno del Estado de Jalisco; Universidad de Guadalajara, 1987), 27–29, 36–37. For Miguel Henríquez Guzmán's candidacy and his political movement, see Elisa Servín, *Ruptura y oposición: El movimiento henriquista, 1945–1954* (Mexico City: Cal y Arena, 2001).

85. Délano, *Mexico and Its Diaspora in the United States,* 90–92. For more on commercial ties between Mexico and the United States during the postwar period, specifically US-based companies like Sears opening subsidiaries in Mexico, see Julio Moreno, *Yankee Don't Go Home! Mexican Nationalism, American Business Culture, and the Shaping of Modern Mexico, 1920–1950* (Chapel Hill: University of North Carolina Press, 2003).

86. Ngai, *Impossible Subjects,* 157.

87. Craig, *The Bracero Program,* 57–59.

88. Lic. Benito Coquet to C. Secretario de la Presidencia de la República, July 29, 1947, AGN, MAV, caja 594, expediente 546.6/1–32.

89. García y Griego, "The Importation of Mexican Contract Laborers to the United States," 65.

90. Official figures cited in Ngai, *Impossible Subjects,* 157.

91. Lic. Cosme V. Mellado to CC. Presidentes Municipales, Delegados y Subdelegados en el Estado, April 22, 1947, AHEQ, PE, Cronológica, año 1947, caja 6.

92. Héctor Pérez Martínez to C. Gobernador del Estado, April 18, 1947, AGHPEM, SEGOB, TPS, PB, caja 1, expediente 4, foja 237. Bracero contracts were "exclusively" distributed in Guanajuato, Jalisco, Michoacán, and Querétaro in 1947.

93. Official Mexican figures cited in González Navarro, *Población y sociedad en México*, vol. 2, chart between pp. 146 and 147; official U.S. figures cited in Ngai, *Impossible Subjects*, 157. According to Ngai's figures, 598,945 braceros entered the United States from 1948 through 1952. According to González Navarro's figures, the Mexican government documented the home states of 572,333 braceros during that same period; 288,466 were from Aguascalientes, Guanajuato, Jalisco, Michoacán, and Zacatecas.

94. Lic. Nicéforo Guerrero to C. Presidente República, March 26, 1947, AGN, MAV, caja 290, expediente 425.5/2–10.

95. Lic. Carlos G. Guzmán to C. Enrique Rodríguez Cano, July 29, 1950, AHEJ, GOB/SC año 1950, caja 23, expediente 222 (3)/8.

96. Antonio G. Guerra to C. Presidente de la República, September 15, 1947, AGN, MAV, caja 587, expediente 545.3/98; Luis Balderas to Sr. Presidente Miguel Alemán, December 28, 1947, AGN, MAV, caja 587, expediente 545.3/98; Frank A. Martínez to Sr. Presidente Miguel Alemán, May 11, 1948, AGN, MAV, caja 587, expediente 545.3/98.

97. Weise, *Corazón de Dixie*, 82–119. Weise noted that in addition to accepting the Mexican consul's proposed wage levels, Arkansas Delta growers and local governments also exempted braceros from discriminatory Jim Crow laws to avoid being blacklisted.

98. D. D. Esquivel and others to Presidente República, October 16, 1948, AGN, MAV, caja 594, expediente 546.6/1–32; Cohen, *Braceros*, 203.

99. Délano, *Mexico and Its Diaspora in the United States*, 93.

100. Lic. Horacio Terán, Sintesis de los Puntos Básicos Que Contendrá al Acuerdo Internacional Para la Contratación de Braceros Agrícolas Mexicanos Que Vayan a Prestar Sus Servicios a los Estados Unidos de Norteamérica, February 3, 1949, AGN, MAV, caja 594, expediente 546.6/1–32.

101. Lic. J. Jesús González Gallo to C. Presidente Municipal, May 6, 1948, AHEJ, GOB/SC, año 1948, caja 13, expediente 262/8.

102. Lic. Horacio Terán, Sintesis de los Puntos Básicos.

103. José Herrera C. to C. Director General de Investigaciones Políticas y Sociales, August 25, 1949, AGN, DGIPS, caja 802, expediente 8; José F. García and Enrique Martínez to C. Presidente República, October 17, 1949, AGN, MAV, caja 594, expediente 546.6/1–25; Guillermo Jiménez to C. Gobernador Estado Aguascalientes, August 20, 1949, AHEA, SGGOB, caja 573, expediente 348.

104. Lic. Horacio Sobarzo to C. Presidente de la República, February 3, 1949, AGN, MAV, caja 594, expediente 546.6/1–25.

105. Lic. Horacio Sobarzo to Lic. Miguel Alemán, August 6, 1949, AGN, MAV, caja 594, expediente 546.6/1–25; L. O. P., Confidencial, August 20, 1949, AGN, DGIPS, caja 802, expediente 8.

106. Lic. Horacio Sobarzo to C. Adolfo Ruiz Cortines, August 17, 1949, AGN, DGIPS, caja 802, expediente 8.

107. José Herrera C. to C. Director General de Investigaciones Políticas y Sociales, August 25, 1949, AGN, DGIPS, caja 802, expediente 8.

108. José T. Rocha to C. Vicento Ochoa, October 26, 1953, AGN, ARC, caja 301, expediente 404.1/1199; José Lázaro Salinas, *La emigración de braceros: Visión objetiva de un problema mexicano* (Mexico City, 1955), 191.

109. Délano, *Mexico and Its Diaspora in the United States*, 95.

110. Lic. Agustín Yáñez to C. Presidente Municipal, January 19, 1954, AMHTM, caja 379, carpeta 1.

111. Lic. Benito Palomino Dena to C. Corl. De Inf. Jesús Samarrón Flores, February 8, 1954, AHEA, SGGOB, caja 649, expediente 202; Lic. Benito Palomino Dena to C. Prof. y Dip. José Santos Reyna, February 8, 1954, AHEA, SGGOB, caja 649, expediente 202; Lic. Benito Palomino Dena to C. J. Jesús Marmolejo, February 8, 1954, AHEA, SGGOB, caja 649, expediente 202; Lic. Benito Palomino Dena to C. Prof. Faustino Villalobos, February 8, 1954, AHEA, SGGOB, caja 649, expediente 202; Lic. Benito Palomino Dena to C. Lic. Roberto Valadéz Galavíz, February 8, 1954, AHEA, SGGOB, caja 649, expediente 202.

112. Cohen, *Braceros*, 208–11; Kang, *The INS on the Line*, 150–51.

113. García y Griego, "The Importation of Mexican Contract Laborers to the United States," 72–73; Lázaro Salinas, *La emigración de braceros*, 195.

114. Goodman, *The Deportation Machine*, 52–53; Ngai, *Impossible Subjects*, 154–55, official US figures cited on 157.

115. "Audiencia para Investigar el Empleo de los 'Espaldas Mojadas,' por Frank O'Dwyer," *Excélsior*, February 21, 1951; Carlos Violante, "Guadalajara es Puente del Bracerismo Ilegal," *El Universal*, March 2, 1951, 1, 10.

116. Mario Coquet and Carlos Sierra to C. Lamberto Ortega Peregrina, October 19, 1950, AGN, DGIPS, caja 103, expediente 1, foja 270.

117. Goodman, *The Deportation Machine*, 54–71.

118. Calavita, *Inside the State*, 53–55; official US figures cited in Ngai, *Impossible Subjects*, 155–57. Because the number of apprehensions made in 1942 is not available, the average of 356,226 is for the period 1943–54.

119. Official US figures cited in Ngai, *Impossible Subjects*, 156.

120. "II Informe de Gobierno del Presidente Constitucional de los Estados Unidos Mexicanos, Adolfo Ruiz Cortines, 1° de septiembre de 1954," in *Informes Presidenciales: Adolfo Ruiz Cortines* (Mexico City: Dirección de Servicios de Investigación y Análisis, Cámara de Diputados, 2006), 42.

121. Goodman, *The Deportation Machine*, 82–105.

122. Dr. Alfonso Durán V. and Dr. Moisés Mirazo to Señor don Adolfo Ruiz Cortines, October 25, 1954, AGN, ARC, caja 970, expediente 563.3/246.

123. Comerciantes Unidos, S.A., to Sr. don Adolfo Ruiz Cortines, October 22, 1954, AGN, ARC, caja 970, expediente 563.3/246; Asociación de Productores de Cereales de la Región Agrícola de Hermosillo to Sr. don Adolfo Ruiz Cortines, October 22, 1954, AGN, ARC, caja 970, expediente 563.3/246.

124. Alfonso Almada to C. don Adolfo Ruiz Cortines, October 20, 1954, AGN, ARC, caja 970, expediente 563.3/246.

125. Ignacio Soto to Sr. don Adolfo Ruiz Cortines, April 2, 1955, AGN, ARC, caja 970, expediente 563.3/246.

126. Official Mexican figures cited in González Navarro, *Población y sociedad en México*, vol. 2, chart between pp. 146 and 147; official US figures cited in Ngai, *Impossible Subjects,* 157. Per Ngai's figures, 2,223,166 braceros entered the United States during Ruiz Cortines's presidency. According to González Navarro's figures, the Mexican government documented the home states of 1,908,809 braceros during that same period; 874,971 were from Aguascalientes, Guanajuato, Jalisco, Michoacán, and Zacatecas, and only 9,457 were from Sonora.

127. México, Secretaría de Relaciones Exteriores, *Memoria de la Secretaría de Relaciones Exteriores 1° de enero a 31 de diciembre de 1956: Presentada al H. Congreso de la Unión por el C. Lic. Luis Padilla Nervo, secretario del ramo* (Mexico City: Talleres Gráficos de la Nación, 1957), 372–75.

128. Jesús Rodríguez Gaona, Atento memorandum al señor Presidente de la República, poniendo de manifiesto la situación del Municipio de Pénjamo, August 17, 1957, AGN, ARC, caja 1133, expediente 609/659; César Ramírez Miranda, Ramón Vera Salvo, and Pedro Gómez Sánchez, *Historia de la cuestión agraria mexicana: Estado de Zacatecas,* vol. 3 (Mexico City: Juan Pablos Editor; Gobierno del Estado de Zacatecas; Centro de Estudios Históricos del Agrarismo en México, 1990), 102.

129. García y Griego, "The Importation of Mexican Contract Laborers to the United States," 67.

130. Serapión Castañeda P. to H. Gobernador Constitucional del Estado de Aguascalientes, May 15, 1959, AHEA, SGGOB, caja 728, expediente 175; Mario Tapia Ponce to C. Secretario General de Gobierno, June 13, 1959, AHEA, SGGOB, caja 728, expediente 175. For more on this policy and its effects on the agrarian economy of the northern states, see Irina Córdova Ramírez, "Las contrataciones de braceros en el estado de Chihuahua," in *Tras los pasos de los braceros: Entre la teoría y la realidad,* ed. Aidé Grijalva (Mexicali: Universidad Autónoma de Baja California, Instituto de Investigaciones Sociales; Mexico City: Juan Pablos Editor, 2015), 203–25; Aidé Grijalva, "La bracereada que llegó para quedarse: Mexicali y el Programa Bracero," in Grijalva, *Tras los pasos de los braceros,* 227–63.

131. Lic. Rogelio Flores Delgado to C. Presidente del Consejo Político Directivo del P.R.I.-P.N.M., June 22, 1959, AGN, ALM, caja 716, expediente 546.6/101.

132. Official Mexican figures cited in González Navarro, *Población y sociedad en México*, vol. 2, chart between pp. 146 and 147; official US figures cited in Ngai, *Impossible Subjects,* 157. Per the figures Ngai cited, 1,604,488 braceros entered the United States during López Mateos's presidency. However, per the figures González Navarro cited, the Mexican government selected 1,605,957 braceros during that same period; 709,808 were from Aguascalientes, Guanajuato, Jalisco, Michoacán, and Zacatecas.

CHAPTER TWO

1. Ernesto Hidalgo to C. Presidente Municipal, June 5, 1944, AHAGPEG, SEGOB, PD, serie 1.19, año 1944, expediente 67.

2. Lic. Fausto Villagómez to C. Presidente Municipal, June 19, 1944, AHAGPEG, SEGOB, PD, 1.03, año 1944, expediente 16.

3. Rogelio Hernández Rodríguez, "Strongmen and State Weakness," in Gillingham and Smith, *Dictablanda*, 112.

4. El Inspector Comisionado (37) to C. Lic. Eduardo Ampudia, May 22, 1944, AGN, DGIPS, caja 97, expediente 22, fojas 147–50.

5. Lic. Juan Ignacio Ibáñez to Sr. Presidentes Municipales del Estado, February 5, 1945, AHAGPEG, SEGOB, PD, 1.19, año 1945, expediente 20.

6. Carlos Reyes Arroyo to C. Oficial Mayor del Gobierno, February 6, 1945, AHAGPEG, SEGOB, PD, 1.19, año 1945, expediente 20; Lic. Juan Ignacio Ibáñez to C. Presidente Municipal de Pénjamo, February 14, 1945, AHAGPEG, SEGOB, PD, 1.19, año 1945, expediente 20.

7. Luis Briones to Lic. Juan Ignacio Ibáñez, February 8, 1945, AHAGPEG, SEGOB, PD, 1.19, año 1945, expediente 20; Lic. Juan Ignacio Ibáñez to C. Presidente Municipal de Allende, February 14, 1945, AHAGPEG, SEGOB, PD, 1.19, año 1945, expediente 20.

8. Número Aproximado de Trabajadores del Campo Que Pueden Contratarse Como Braceros a los E.U. de A., Según Datos Presidencias Municipales, undated, AHAGPEG, SEGOB, PD, 1.19, año 1945, expediente 20. Though the document is undated, it is included in the file that contains documents pertaining to the February 1945 contracting period. The numbers cited in this document also match those in individual correspondence between municipal and state officials. The document does not cite the numbers from municipalities where the governments did not quickly provide the required information. The correspondence that includes that information is in this same expediente.

9. Lic. Luis M. Moreno to Ciudadano Secretario del Trabajo, February 12, 1945, AGHPEM, SEGOB, TPS, PB, caja 1, expediente 3, fojas 13/14–14/15. Requests are in AGN, MAC, caja 793, expediente 546.6/120; AGN, MAC, caja 794, expediente 546.6/120–15; and AGHPEM, SEGOB, TPS, PB, caja 1, expediente 3.

10. Juan Salceda to C. Lic. José Ma. Mendoza Pardo, March 25, 1945, AGHPEM, SEGOB, TPS, PB, caja 1, expediente 3, foja 237; Verónica Oikión Solano, *Los hombres del poder en Michoacán, 1924–1962* (Zamora: El Colegio de Michoacán; Morelia: Universidad Michoacana de San Nicolás de Hidalgo, Instituto de Investigaciones Históricas, 2004), 314.

11. J. Isabel Galván Ruiz and Higinio Servín Campos to Ciudadano José Garibay Romero, February 21, 1945, AGHPEM, SEGOB, TPS, PB, caja 1, expediente 3, foja 37/38.

12. Abelino Torres Herrera and others to Ciudadano José Garibay Romero, February 21, 1945, AGHPEM, SEGOB, TPS, PB, caja 1, expediente 3, foja 36/37.

13. Procopio Valadéz to Ciudadano Gobernador del Estado, February 21, 1945, AGHPEM, SEGOB, TPS, PB, caja 1, expediente 3, fojas 57/58–58/59.

14. Rubén Silva to Gobernador Constitucional del Estado, March 7, 1945, AGHPEM, SEGOB, TPS, PB, caja 1, expediente 3, foja 103.

15. Pedro Alvarado to Lic. José María Mendoza Pardo, March 5, 1945, AGHPEM, SEGOB, TPS, PB, caja 1, expediente 3, foja 266.

16. Antonio Loera M. to Lic. José María Mendoza Pardo, March 5, 1945, AGHPEM, SEGOB, TPS, PB, caja 1, expediente 3, foja 83/84.

17. Lic. Francisco Trujillo Gurría to Lic. José M. Mendoza Pardo, March 14, 1945, AGHPEM, SEGOB, TPS, PB, caja 1, expediente 3, foja 153.

18. Lic. Roberto Amorós G. to Gobernador Estado, February 22, 1945, AGHPEM, SEGOB, TPS, PB, caja 1, expediente 3, foja 46/47.

19. Lic. Luis M. Moreno to Ciudadano Procurador General de Justicia, February 26, 1945, AGHPEM, SEGOB, TPS, PB, caja 1, expediente 3, foja 59/60; Lic. Francisco Mora Plancarte to Ciudadano Agente del Ministerio Público, February 28, 1945, AGHPEM, SEGOB, TPS, PB, caja 1, expediente 3, foja 60/61.

20. Lic. Víctor Manuel Chávez to Ciudadano Procurador General de Justicia del Estado, March 3, 1945, AGHPEM, Uruapan, caja 1, expediente 7, foja 45/46.

21. Juan Morán and others to C. Comisariado Ejidal, February 8, 1945, AHEA, SGGOB, caja 695, expediente 202.

22. Juan Morán, Itinerario Que se Fija Para la Contratación de Braceros en los Municipios del Estado, Correspondientes al Sector Campesino y Que Son Como Siguen, March 16, 1945, AHEA, SGGOB, caja 695, expediente 202; Juan Morán to C. Ing. Jesús M. Rodríguez, March 28, 1945, AHEA, SGGOB, caja 695, expediente 202.

23. Lic. Benito Coquet to C. Gobernador del Estado, May 30, 1946, AGHPEM, SEGOB, TPS, PB, caja 2, expediente sin número, foja 180.

24. Héctor Pérez Martínez to C. Gobernador del Estado, 18 Apr. 1947, AGHPEM, SEGOB, TPS, PB, caja 1, expediente 4, foja 237.

25. Arcadio Ojeda García to Sr. Lic. José María Mendoza Parra [sic], April 12, 1947, AGHPEM, SEGOB, TPS, PB, caja 1, expediente 4, fojas 328–29.

26. Lic. Luis Manuel Moreno, Instrucciones a la que se sujetará la preselección de braceros: Uruapan, undated, AGHPEM, SEGOB, TPS, PB, caja 1, expediente 4, foja 75. All the bracero selection instructions that Michoacán's government issued in 1947 are undated. However, other documents in the file corroborate that they applied to that year.

27. Miguel Bravo Cortés and Bonifacio Bravo Soto to Ciudadano Presidente de la República, February 28, 1947, AGHPEM, SEGOB, TPS, PB, caja 1, expediente 4, fojas 1–3.

28. Lic. Luis Manuel Moreno to Ciudadano Rafael Hinojosa Torres, April 14, 1947, AGHPEM, SEGOB, TPS, PB, caja 1, expediente 4, foja 70.

29. Oikión Solano, *Los hombres del poder en Michoacán*, 342–46.

30. Lic. Luis Manuel Moreno, Instrucciones a la que se sujetará la preselección de braceros: Pátzcuaro, undated, AGHPEM, SEGOB, TPS, PB, caja 1, expediente 4, foja 72; Lic. Gilberto Vargas López to Ciudadano Presidente Municipal, April 15, 1947, AGHPEM, SEGOB, TPS, PB, caja 1, expediente 4, foja 90.

31. Audén Calvillo to Señor José Ma. Mendoza Pardo, March 13/17, 1947, AGHPEM, SEGOB, TPS, PB, caja 1, expediente 4, fojas 4–7. The letter sent to the governor is dated March 17; the attached list of names is dated March 13.

32. Boyer, *Becoming Campesinos*, 101–03.
33. Loza, *Defiant Braceros*, 8–11, 29–40.
34. Olsson, *Agrarian Crossings*, 182–90.
35. Marco Calderón Mólgora, "Desarrollo integral en las cuencas del Tepalcatepec y del Balsas," in *Las transformaciones de los paisajes culturales en la cuenca del Tepalcatepec*, ed. Juan Ortiz Escamilla (Zamora: El Colegio de Michoacán, 2011), 228–48; Cohen, *Braceros*, 35–42; Loza, *Defiant Braceros*, 92–97; Juan Ortiz Escamilla and Silvia Méndez Maín, "La Ruana: Un modelo de centro ejidal," in *Las transformaciones de los paisajes culturales en la cuenca del Tepalcatepec*, ed. Juan Ortiz Escamilla (Zamora: El Colegio de Michoacán, 2011), 288; Diana E. Sánchez Andrade, "De la tierra fría a la Tierra Caliente: Deterioro ambiental y transformación del paisaje en la microcuenca del Cupatitzio, durante el siglo XX," in Ortiz Escamilla, *Las transformaciones de los paisajes culturales en la cuenca del Tepalcatepec*, 347–52.
36. Guillermo de la Peña, "The End of Revolutionary Anthropology? Notes on Indigenismo," in Gillingham and Smith, *Dictablanda*, 279–98.
37. Loza, *Defiant Braceros*, 23–60.
38. Mary E. Mendoza, "Battling *Aftosa:* North-to-South Migration across the U.S.-Mexico Border, 1947–1954," *Journal of the West* 54, no. 1 (2015): 39.
39. Dip. Enrique Bravo Valencia to Presidente República, March 5, 1947, AGN, MAV, caja 291, expediente 425.5/2–15; Bernabé Macías and Rafael Vega to C. Presidente República, March 26, 1947, AGN, MAV, caja 291, expediente 425.5/2–15.
40. C.J. Alvarez, "The U.S.-Mexico Border and the 1947 Foot-and-Mouth Disease Outbreak in Mexico," *Journal of the Southwest* 61, no. 4 (2019): 691; Mendoza, "Battling *Aftosa*," 39–42.
41. Lic. Nicéforo Guerrero to C. Presidente República, March 26, 1947, AGN, MAV, caja 290, expediente 425.5/2–10.
42. J. Jesús Moreno and others to Ciudadano José Ma. Mendoza Pardo, April 26, 1947, AGHPEM, SEGOB, TPS, PB, caja 1, expediente 4, foja 274.
43. Lic. Luis Manuel Moreno, Instrucciones a la que se sujetará la preselección de braceros: Zamora y Villamar, undated, AGHPEM, SEGOB, TPS, PB, caja 1, expediente 4, foja 98; Lic. Luis Manuel Moreno, Instrucciones a la que se sujetará la preselección de braceros: Cuitzeo, undated, AGHPEM, SEGOB, TPS, PB, caja 1, expediente 4, foja 103.
44. Lic. Gilberto Vargas López to Ciudadano Jefe de Tenencia de Ocampo, April 18, 1947, AGHPEM, SEGOB, TPS, PB, caja 1, expediente 4, foja 166; Gilberto Pizarro Rubio and Benigno Figueroa R., untitled affidavit, April 26, 1947, AGHPEM, SEGOB, TPS, PB, caja 1, expediente 4, foja 288; Rafael Moreno, Isaac Navarrete, and Pedro de la Vega to C. Licenciado Conrado Velázquez Jr., undated, AGHPEM, SEGOB, TPS, PB, caja 1, expediente 4, foja 297. Although the last document cited is undated, it references events that occurred during the 1947 contracting period.
45. "Informe que rindió el C. Lic. Nicéforo Guerrero, el 15 de septiembre de 1947," in *Guanajuato en la voz de sus gobernadores: Compilación de Informes de*

Gobierno, 1917–1991, vol. 1 (Guanajuato: Gobierno del Estado de Guanajuato, 1991), 724–29; Lic. Cosme V. Mellado to CC. Presidentes Municipales, Delegados y Subdelegados en el Estado, April 22, 1947, AHEQ, PE, Cronológica, año 1947, caja 6.

46. Summary of a July 5, 1947, letter from Comités de Lucha Contra la Fiebre Aftosa de Ocotlán, Poncitlán, Zapotlán y Tototlán, Jal., to C. Presidente, July 15, 1947, AGN, MAV, caja 290, expediente 425.5/2–13; Lic. J. Jesús González Gallo to Lic. Rogerio de la Selva, August 5, 1947, AGN, MAV, caja 290, expediente 425.5/2–13.

47. Contratación de Braceros en el Estado, undated, AHEJ, GOB/SC, año 1947, caja 33. Although undated, the figures in this document match those in correspondence between the state government and municipal officials regarding the 1947 contracting period.

48. Dip. Vidal Díaz Muñoz to Presidente República, April 18, 1947, AGN, MAV, caja 593, expediente 546.6/1–13.

49. J. Reyes Tejeda and others, untitled document, May 13, 1936, AHEJ, Trabajo, T-3–936, Movimientos Obreros, caja 3, inventario 7906; Summary of a June 5, 1943, message from Sind. Nal. de Obreros y Campesinos de la Ind. Azucarera y Sim. Secc. 3, June 11, 1943, AGN, MAC, caja 403, expediente 432/551; Fidencio de León R. and others to C. Lic. Miguel Alemán, November 5, 1943, AGN, MAC, caja 403, expediente 432/551.

50. Dip. Heliodoro Hernández Loza to Sr. Presidente de la República, August 14, 1946, AGN, MAC, caja 794, expediente 546.6/120–13. For the labor split in Jalisco, see Jaime E. Tamayo Rodríguez, *La estructura del sindicalismo en Jalisco* (Guadalajara: Instituto de Estudios Sociales, Universidad de Guadalajara, 1985).

51. Francisco F. González, Marcelino Sedano, and J. Refugio Facio to Lic. Miguel Alemán, December 2, 1946, AGN, MAV, caja 296, expediente 432/7; Marcelino Sedano and J. Refugio Facio to C. Presidente República, December 19, 1946, AGN, fondo MAV, caja 296, expediente 432/7.

52. J. Dionisio Ahumada F. to C. Lic. J. Jesús González Gallo, July 3, 1947, AHEJ, GOB/SC, año 1947, caja 24.

53. Zeferino Torres to C. Lic. J. Jesús González Gallo, May 21, 1947, AHEJ, GOB/SC, año 1947, caja 40; Azucareros, undated, AHEJ, GOB/SC, año 1947, caja 40. Torres noted in his correspondence with the governor that Félix Ponce had helped secure the STIASRM's allotment. And although the document is undated, the figures given in the "Azucareros" list match those in correspondence between the state government and union officials regarding the 1947 contracting period.

54. José Ramírez and others to C. Gobernador del Estado, April 25, 1947, AGHPEM, SEGOB, TPS, PB, caja 1, expediente 4, foja 293.

55. Rafael Moreno, Isaac Navarrete, and Pedro de la Vega to C. Lic. Conrado Velázquez, Jr., undated, AGHPEM, SEGOB, TPS, PB, caja 1, expediente 4, foja 297.

56. Francisco González and others to Presidente República, May 26, 1947, AGN, MAV, caja 593, expediente 546.6/1–13.

57. Alfonso Sánchez Castañeda to Sr. Lic. Don Miguel Alemán, April 18, 1947, AGN, MAV, caja 593, expediente 546.6/1–10.

58. "Informe que rindió el C. Lic. Nicéforo Guerrero, el 15 de septiembre de 1947," 727.

59. Official correspondence detailing the number of bracero eligibility cards that Jalisco's government sent to municipal authorities during the May 1948 selection period are in AHEJ, GOB/SC, año 1948, cajas 6–7, 11–14. I was only able to document how 3,178 cards were distributed.

60. Roberto Ramírez to C. Gobernador del Estado, May 27, 1948, AHEJ, GOB/SC, año 1948, caja 14, expediente 240/1.

61. Ezequiel Guardado to C. Srio. General de Gobierno, May 27, 1948, AHEJ, GOB/SC, año 1948, caja 14, expediente 240/1.

62. Diputado Vidal Díaz Muñoz to Sr. Lic. Miguel Alemán Valdés, September 21, 1947, AGN, MAV, caja 593, expediente 546.6/1–13.

63. Sánchez Susarrey and Medina Sánchez, *Jalisco desde la revolución,* vol. 9, 38, 47.

64. Snodgrass, "The Golden Age of Charrismo." The term "charro" was used to describe conservative labor leaders because Jesús Díaz de León, who the Alemán administration installed as the leader of the National Railroad Workers Union in 1948, regularly attended union meetings dressed as a charro (cowboy). Among the other unions that federal authorities intervened in were the Oil Workers Union (1949) and the National Mine and Metal Workers Union (1950), which, along with the National Railroad Workers Union, had attempted to withdraw from the CTM.

65. For the relatively competitive nature of elections during the 1940s, see Gillingham, *Unrevolutionary Mexico;* Gillingham, "'We Don't Have Arms, But We Do Have Balls.'"

66. Lic. Horacio Terán to C. In. Jesús M. Rodríguez, April 22, 1948, AHEA, SGGOB, caja 559, expediente 269.

67. Lic. Juan de Luna Loera to C. Presidente Municipal, May 8, 1948, AHEA, SGGOB, caja 559, expediente 269.

68. Matías Marín L., Padrón de Aspirantes a Braceros Correspondiente al Municipio de Rincón de Romos del Estado de Aguascalientes, May 15, 1948, AHEA, SGGOB, caja 559, expediente 269; José Ma. Martínez Velasco, Relación de aspirantes a Braceros con destino a los Estados Unidos de Norte América, May 14, 1948, AHEA, SGGOB, caja 559, expediente 269; Ing. Luis Ortega Douglas to C. Gobernador Constitucional del Estado, May 21, 1948, AHEA, SGGOB, caja 559, expediente 269; Rafael Reyes Rangel, Lista de los Aspirantes a "Braceros" de las Distintas Comunidades que componen este Municipio, May 17, 1948, AHEA, SGGOB, caja 559, expediente 269; José Rodríguez M., Padrón de los Señores Aspirantes a Braceros que emigrarán a los Estados Unidos de Norte América, May 13, 1948, AHEA, SGGOB, caja 559, expediente 269; Julián Villalobos, Lista de aspirantes a braceros, May 13, 1948, AHEA, SGGOB, caja 559, expediente 269; Padrón de los Aspirantes a Braceros del Sector Popular de los Municipios Siguientes: "Jesús María," unsigned and undated, AHEA, SGGOB, caja 559, expediente 269.

69. Lic. Horacio Terán to C. Ing. Jesús Ma. Rodríguez, April 29, 1948 AHEA, SGGOB, caja 559, expediente 269.

70. Lic. Horacio Terán, Aviso a los Aspirantes a Braceros, March 1948, AHEA, SGGOB, caja 559, expediente 269.

71. Ing. Jesús M. Rodríguez to Sr. Lic. Horacio Terán, May 21, 1948, AHEA, SGGOB, caja 559, expediente 269.

72. Lic. Horacio Terán to C. Jesús M. Rodríguez, May 22, 1948, AHEA, SGGOB, caja 559, expediente 269.

73. Lic. Juan de Luna Loera to C. Lic. Horacio Terán, May 28, 1948, AHEA, SGGOB, caja 559, expediente 269.

74. The records for the April 1952 selection period are the most complete in Irapuato's municipal archive. I was able to document how 17,716 eligibility cards were distributed that month. Of those, 15,726 went to southern Guanajuato municipalities. I should note that I could not document the allocations for eleven of the state's forty-five municipalities, and the correspondence from some municipalities gave only partial allocation figures. These figures are in AHMI, Gobierno, Braceros, caja 38.

75. Florentino Oliva to C. Presidente Municipal, May 18, 1952, AHMI, Gobierno, Braceros, caja 38.

76. Florentino Oliva to C. Justino Lozano Chávez, April 7, 1953, AHMI, Gobierno, Braceros, caja 38; Lic. Ramón Acevedo to C. Presidente Municipal, September 29, 1954, AHMI, Gobierno, Braceros, caja 38; Luis Obregón Santacilia to C. Presidente Municipal, April 13, 1955, AHMI, Gobierno, Braceros, caja 38; J. Jesús Cervantes Reynoso to C. Hilario Carrillo Aguilar, December 14, 1955, AHMI, Gobierno, Braceros, caja 38.

77. José de Anda to C. Secretario Gral. de Gobierno, March 3, 1952, AHEJ, GOB/SC, año 1951, caja 17.

78. José Campos L. to C. Lic. D/ J. Jesús González Gallo, May 6, 1952, AHEJ, GOB/SC, año 1952, caja 17. Campos was the secretary general of STIASRM Local 115, which represented workers in Zapotiltic's El Rincón Mill.

79. Snodgrass, "The Golden Age of Charrismo."

80. The final available eligibility card distribution orders that I consulted during my research were from 1952. However, there are no data available from forty-four Jalisco municipalities, one-third of the state's total at the time, from this year, and the available information from the other municipalities does not cover every selection period that occurred that year. As a result, I do not feel that I have enough information to determine if the number of cards allotted to southern Jalisco municipalities was significant compared to other regions of the state.

81. J. Ascención Hernández Loza to Lic. J. Jesús González Gallo, April 4, 1950, AHEJ, GOB/SC, año 1950, caja 27, expediente 215/12.

82. Anselmo Ramírez Meza to C. Agente del Ministerio Público, April 17, 1950, AHEJ, GOB/SC, año 1950, caja 27, expediente 215/12.

83. J. Dionisio Ahumada F. to Presidente República, May 13, 1947, AGN, MAV, caja 593, expediente 546.6/1–13.

84. Prof. Pascual Romo Conchos to C. Secretario Gral. de Gobierno, July 9, 1955, AHEA, SGGOB, caja 669, expediente 202; Lic. José R. Castañeda Zaragoza

to Ciudadano Presidente Municipal, April 10, 1957, AGHPEM, SEGOB, TPS, PB, caja, caja 3, expediente sin número, foja 112.

85. Melesio Aguilar Ferreira to Ciudadano Presidente Municipal, July 30, 1959, AGHPEM, SEGOB, TPS, PB, caja 4, expediente 6, foja 230.

86. Profr. Manuel López Pérez to Ciudadano Presidente Municipal, July 12, 1963, AGHPEM, SEGOB, TPS, PB, caja 8, expediente 12, foja 14.

87. Alberto Alcalá de Lira to C. Lic. Carlos Salas Calvillo, July 10, 1959, AHEA, SGGOB, caja 728, expediente 175.

88. Lic. Carlos Salas Calvillo to C. Presidente Municipal, May 12, 1959, AHEA, SGGOB, caja 728, expediente 175.

89. Lic. Carlos Salas Calvillo to C. Presidente Municipal, September 18, 1959, AHEA, SGGOB, caja 728, expediente 175.

90. Porfirio Arellano Leos to C. Presidente Municipal, February 23, 1960, AHEA, SGGOB, caja 741, expediente 160; Porfirio Arellano Leos to C. Presidente Municipal, May 28, 1960, AHEA, SGGOB, caja 741, expediente 160; Porfirio Arellano Leos to C. Presidente Municipal, September 29, 1960, AHEA, SGGOB, caja 741, expediente 160.

91. Lic. Carlos Salas Calvillo to C. Presidente Municipal, June 10, 1959, AHEA, SGGOB, caja 728, expediente 175.

92. Amador Guerrero to Lic. Carlos Salas Calvillo, August 11, 1960, AHEA, SGGOB, caja 741, expediente 160.

93. Ing. Luis Ortega Douglas to C. Lic. Rogelio Flores Delgado, August 11, 1960, AHEA, SGGOB, caja 741, expediente 160.

94. Porfirio Arellano Leos to C. Presidente Municipal, February 23, 1960, AHEA, SGGOB, caja 741, expediente 160; Porfirio Arellano Leos to C. Presidente Municipal, September 28, 1960, AHEA, SGGOB, caja 741, expediente 160.

95. I calculated Aguascalientes's bracero eligibility card distribution patterns by consulting AHEA, SGGOB, caja 711, expediente 202; caja 728, expediente 175; and caja 741, expediente 160.

96. I calculated Michoacán's bracero eligibility card distribution patterns by consulting AGHPEM, SEGOB, TPS, PB, caja 4, expedientes 6–7; caja 7, expediente 9; caja 8, expedientes 12–15; caja 9, expedientes 20 and 22; and caja 10, expediente 17.

97. Written contract requests are in the AGHPEM and the AGN. For the AGHPEM, see SEGOB, TPS, PB, caja 4, expedientes 6–7; caja 7, expedientes 8–10; caja 8, expedientes 11–15; caja 9, expedientes 20–22; and caja 10, expedientes 16–19. For the AGN, see ALM, cajas 715–23 and 727.

98. For the course of Parícutin's nine-year eruptive phase, see Foshag and González R., "Birth and Development of Parícutin Volcano."

99. Written contract requests are in the AGHPEM and the AGN. For the AGHPEM, see SEGOB, TPS, PB, caja 4, expedientes 6–7; caja 7, expedientes 8–10; caja 8, expedientes 11–15; caja 9, expedientes 20–22; and caja 10, expedientes 16–19. For the AGN, see ALM, cajas 715–23 and 727. Eligibility card distribution patterns are in AGHPEM, SEGOB, TPS, PB, caja 4, expedientes 6–7; caja 7, expediente 9; caja 8, expedientes 12–15; caja 9, expedientes 20 and 22; and caja 10, expediente 17. It

is not clear if the state government disproportionately favored another region with bracero eligibility cards. Of the 16,128 eligibility cards whose destination I was able to determine during my research, state officials allocated 8 percent to Tierra Caliente municipalities; 7 percent to the Pátzcuaro Basin; 4 percent to the eastern woodlands; and 2 percent to the Sierra de Coalcomán. Of the 813 available written contract requests, at least 7 percent were from the Pátzcuaro Basin; at least 5 percent were from the Tierra Caliente; at least 2 percent were from the eastern forests; and at least 1 percent were from the Sierra de Coalcomán. However, I was unable to determine where 3 percent of the contract requests were sent from, which means that I cannot definitively confirm if the Tierra Caliente, Sierra de Coalcomán, and eastern forest allotments were above popular demand levels.

100. Ignacio Chávez to C. David Franco Rodríguez, May 26, 1962, AGHPEM, SEGOB, TPS, PB, caja 9, expediente 22, foja 89; Ignacio Chávez to Sr. Lic. Don David Franco Rodríguez, June 5, 1962, AGHPEM, SEGOB, TPS, PB, caja 9, expediente 22, foja 91.

101. Juan Rubio to C. Melecio Aguilar Ferreira, February 28, 1962, AGHPEM, SEGOB, TPS, PB, caja 9, expediente 21, fojas 123–24; José Alejo Alejo to C. Gobernador Constitucional del Edo., April 1, 1963, AGHPEM, SEGOB, TPS, PB, caja 7, expediente 9, foja 243.

102. Rubén Ochoa Zambrano to Sr. Oficial Mayor, June 14, 1962, AGHPEM, SEGOB, TPS, PB, caja 9, expediente 22, foja 116.

103. Boyer, *Political Landscapes,* 159–64.

104. For more on the history of these conflicts and how nineteenth-century Liberal and twentieth-century revolutionary agrarian policies affected their course, see Jennie Purnell, "With All Due Respect: Popular Resistance to the Privatization of Communal Lands in Nineteenth-Century Michoacán," *Latin American Research Review* 34, no. 1 (1999): 85–121; Purnell, *Popular Movements and State Formation in Revolutionary Mexico,* 134–62.

105. Lic. Felipe Chávez C. to C. Gobernador Constitucional del Estado, September 20, 1956, AGHPEM, Uruapan, caja 3, expediente 4.

106. Summary of a July 1, 1959, letter from Luiz González Nava to C. Presidente, July 2, 1959, AGN, ALM, caja 717, expediente 546.6/193; Luis González Nava to C. Presidente Constitucional de los Estados Unidos Mexicanos, April 18, 1960, AGN, ALM, caja 719, expediente 546.6/433; Summary of a July 25, 1960, letter from Luis González Nava to an unspecified federal official, August 17, 1960, AGN, ALM, caja 719, expediente 546.6/433.

107. Luis González Nava to C. Don Adolfo Ruiz Cortines, April 1, 1955, AGHPEM, Uruapan, caja 3, expediente 3; Luis González Nava to C. General de División Lázaro Cárdenas del Río, April 6, 1955, AGHPEM, Uruapan, caja 3, expediente 3.

108. J. Jesús Lemus T. to C. Jefe del Departamento Agrario, May 6, 1955, AGHPEM, Uruapan, caja 3, expediente 3.

109. Los Comuneros to C. Gral. Don Dámaso Cárdenas, May 6, 1955, AGHPEM, Uruapan, caja 3, expediente 3. For more on Anguiano and his state-level political activities, see Oikión Solano, *Los hombres del poder en Michoacán.*

110. Alfredo Ortiz Barragán to C. Lic. Emilio Romero Espinosa, September 27, 1955, AGHPEM, Uruapan, caja 3, expediente 3.
111. Mario Tapia Ponce to C. Lic. Carlos Salas Calvillo, April 9, 1957, AHEA, SGGOB, caja 695, expediente 202; Humberto Ramírez Choza to C. Lic. Agustín Arriaga Rivera, April 9, 1964, AGHPEM, SEGOB, TPS, PB, caja 10, expediente 16, foja 163.
112. Interview with Eduardo De Santiago by Mireya Loza, 2005, "Interview no. 1099," Institute of Oral History, University of Texas at El Paso, https://scholarworks.utep.edu/cgi/viewcontent.cgi?article=2118&context=interviews; Interview with Eduardo De Santiago by Myrna Parra-Mantilla, 2003, "Interview No. 1125," Institute of Oral History, University of Texas at El Paso, https://scholarworks.utep.edu/cgi/viewcontent.cgi?article=2145&context=interviews.

CHAPTER THREE

1. José Macías Padilla to C. Jefe del Depto. de Escuelas Rurales, Primarias Foráneas e Incorporación Cultural Indígena, March 11, 1930, AGN, SEP, Dirección General de Educación Primaria, Estados y Territorios, Guanajuato, caja 37746, expediente 20.
2. José Macías Padilla, Informe Sintético de Visita de Inspección, April 23, 1931, AGN, SEP, Dirección General de Educación Primaria, Estados y Territorios, Guanajuato, caja 37746, expediente 20.
3. Roberto Oropeza Nájera, Informe Sintético de Visita de Inspección, February 21, 1933, AGN, SEP, Dirección General de Educación Primaria, Estados y Territorios, Guanajuato, caja 37746, expediente 20. For more on conservative Catholic opposition to secular public education during the 1930s in southern Guanajuato, including the municipality of Salvatierra, see Fallaw, *Religion and State Formation in Postrevolutionary Mexico,* 193–215.
4. Juan Alonso Villagómez and others to C. Don Adolfo Ruiz Cortines, March 2, 1956, AGN, ARC, caja 761, expediente 534.3/1028, foja sin número.
5. For revolutionary anticlericalism, see Adrián A. Bantjes, "Mexican Revolutionary Anticlericalism: Concepts and Typologies," *The Americas* 65, no. 4 (2009): 467–80; Adrián A. Bantjes, "The Regional Dynamics of Anticlericalism and Defanaticization in Revolutionary Mexico," in *Faith and Impiety in Revolutionary Mexico,* ed. Matthew Butler (New York: Palgrave Macmillan, 2007), 111–30; Ben Fallaw, "Varieties of Mexican Revolutionary Anticlericalism: Radicalism, Iconoclasm, and Otherwise, 1914–1935," *The Americas* 65, no. 4 (2009): 481–509; Alan Knight, "The Mentality and Modus Operandi of Revolutionary Anticlericalism," in Butler, *Faith and Impiety in Revolutionary Mexico,* 21–56. For an introduction to the agrarian reform, see Kourí, "La invención del ejido." For the socialist public education curriculum, see Salvador Camacho Sandoval, *Controversia educativa entre la ideología y la fe: Educación socialista en la historia de Aguascalientes, 1876–1940* (Mexico City: Consejo Nacional para la Cultura y las

Artes, 1991); Mary Kay Vaughan, *Cultural Politics in Revolution: Teachers, Peasants, and Schools in Mexico, 1930–1940* (Tucson: University of Arizona Press, 1997); Pablo Yankelevich, *La educación socialista en Jalisco,* 2nd ed. (Zapopan: El Colegio de Jalisco, 2000).

6. Young, *Mexican Exodus.* Young notes that emigration from Greater Bajío states assumed three forms during the Cristero War: labor migrants, many of whom materially and morally supported the Cristeros while they were in the United States; refugees who were seeking to escape the conflict's violence; and clergy members who the Mexican government exiled.

7. For the number of active Cristeros, see Meyer, *The Cristero Rebellion,* 85. For Cristero activity during both the Cristero War and La Segunda, see Bailey, *¡Viva Cristo Rey!;* Butler, *Popular Piety and Political Identity in Mexico's Cristero Rebellion,* 179–212; Curley, *Citizens and Believers,* 235–60; Fallaw, *Religion and State Formation in Postrevolutionary Mexico;* Guerra Manzo, *Del fuego sagrado a la acción cívica;* Meyer, *The Cristero Rebellion;* Olivera Sedano, *La guerra cristera;* Padilla Rangel, *El Catolicismo social y el movimiento Cristero en Aguascalientes;* Purnell, *Popular Movements and State Formation in Revolutionary Mexico.*

8. For the number of active UNS members, see Meyer, *El sinarquismo,* 47. For UNS activity, including its eventual entry into electoral politics, see Meyer, *El sinarquismo, el cardenismo y la iglesia;* Serrano Álvarez, *La batalla del espíritu;* and Zermeño P. and Aguilar V., *Hacia una reinterpretación del sinarquismo actual.* For the attempt to establish a Sinarquista agricultural colony in Baja California Sur, see Jason Dormady, *Primitive Revolution: Restorationist Religion and the Idea of the Mexican Revolution, 1940–1968* (Albuquerque: University of New Mexico Press, 2011), 103–30. For the transnational dimension of the Sinarquista movement, see Nathan Ellstrand, "Reclaiming La Patria: Sinarquismo in the United States, 1937–1946" (PhD diss., Loyola University Chicago, 2022); Julia G. Young, "Fascists, Nazis, or Something Else? Mexico's Unión Nacional Sinarquista in the US Media, 1937–1945," *The Americas* 79, no. 2 (2022): 229–61. For the PAN, see Loaeza, *El Partido Acción Nacional.* For an examination of post–Cristero War conservative Catholic activism in Aguascalientes, including the UNS and the PAN, see Yolanda Padilla Rangel, *Después de la tempestad: La reorganización Católica en Aguascalientes, 1929–1950* (Mexico City: El Colegio de Michoacán, 2000).

9. Roberto Blancarte, "Intransigence, Anticommunism, and Reconciliation: Church/State Relations in Transition," in Gillingham and Smith, *Dictablanda,* 70–88.

10. Smith, *The Roots of Conservatism in Mexico,* 246–93.

11. For how the UNS influenced municipal politics in León, including during the contested 1945–46 electoral cycle, which ended with Governor Hidalgo's removal from office and federal recognition of the Sinarquista victory, see Daniel Newcomer, *Reconciling Modernity: Urban State Formation in 1940s León, Mexico* (Lincoln: University of Nebraska Press, 2004).

12. Jean A. Meyer, "La fiebre aftosa y la Unión Nacional Sinarquista (1947)," trans. María Palomar, *Relaciones* 4, no. 16 (1983): 94.

13. D. A. Brading, *Church and State in Bourbon Mexico: The Diocese of Michoacán, 1749–1810* (Cambridge: Cambridge University Press, 1994); Margaret Chowning, *Rebellious Nuns: The Troubled History of a Mexican Convent, 1752–1863* (New York: Oxford University Press, 2006); Andrés Antonio Fábregas Puig, *La formación histórica de una región: Los Altos de Jalisco* (Mexico City: Centro de Investigaciones y Estudios Superiores en Antropología Social, 1986), 57–104; Óscar Mazín, *Entre dos majestades: El obispo y la iglesia del Gran Michoacán ante las reformas borbónicas, 1758–1772* (Zamora: El Colegio de Michoacán, 1987); John Tutino, *Making a New World: Founding Capitalism in the Bajío and Spanish North America* (Durham, NC: Duke University Press, 2011), 59.

14. Margaret Chowning, "The Catholic Church and the Ladies of the Vela Perpetua: Gender and Devotional Change in Nineteenth-Century Mexico," *Past and Present* 221, no. 1 (2013): 197–237; Brian A. Stauffer, *Victory on Earth or in Heaven: Mexico's Religionero Rebellion* (Albuquerque: University of New Mexico Press, 2019); Jesús Tapia Santamaría, *Campo religioso y evolución política en el Bajío zamorano* (Zamora: El Colegio de Michoacán; Gobierno del Estado de Michoacán, 1986), 129–78.

15. For the number of priests per capita in 1900, see official Mexican figures cited in Purnell, *Popular Movements and State Formation in Revolutionary Mexico*, 95. Jalisco, Aguascalientes, Michoacán, Guanajuato, and Zacatecas ranked fourth, fifth, seventh, eighth, and ninth, respectively, in priests per capita. For the role that parish priests played in rural communities and the social prestige they enjoyed during the early twentieth century, see Butler, *Popular Piety and Political Identity in Mexico's Cristero Rebellion*, 105–45; Luis González y González, *San José de Gracia: Mexican Village in Transition*, trans. John Upton (Austin: University of Texas Press, 1974), 115–45.

16. For anticlerical measures that limited the number of active priests in Jalisco, see Robert Curley, "Anticlericalism and Public Space in Jalisco," *The Americas* 65, no. 4 (2009): 511–33. For President Plutarco Elías Calles's establishment of a national clerical registry, which was the inciting event of the Cristero War, see Meyer, *The Cristero Rebellion*, 41–43; and Olivera Sedano, *La guerra cristera*, 103–8.

17. For how Social Catholicism influenced conservative Catholic religiosity and oppositional politics in the Greater Bajío, see Butler, *Popular Piety and Political Identity in Mexico's Cristero Rebellion*, 15–49, 105–45; Curley, *Citizens and Believers*, 23–74; Padilla Rangel, *El catolicismo social y el movimiento cristero en Aguascalientes*. For a general overview of Social Catholicism in Mexico, see Manuel Ceballos Ramírez, *El catolicismo social: Un tercero en discordia: Rerum novarum, la "cuestión social" y la movilización de los católicos mexicanos (1891–1911)* (Mexico City: El Colegio de México, 1991). For the role that Oaxaca archbishop Eulogio Gillow played in introducing and spreading Social Catholicism in Mexico, see Edward Wright-Ríos, *Revolutions in Mexican Catholicism: Reform and Revelation in Oaxaca, 1887–1934* (Durham, NC: Duke University Press, 2009), 43–72.

18. A rancho is a privately owned estate that is 1,000 hectares or smaller. According to the 1930 Agrarian Census, there were 2,525 privately owned estates in the

municipality of Tepatitlán that were worked directly by their owners and administrators or leased to tenant farmers and sharecroppers. Of these, 2,517 were ranchos; the vast majority of Tepatitlán ranchos, 2,500 of 2,517, were 500 hectares or smaller. For Teptatitlán ranchos in 1930, see México, Dirección General de Estadística, *Primer Censo Agrícola-Ganadero, 1930: Estado de Jalisco* (Mexico City: DAAP, 1938), 146–47. For the development of privately owned haciendas and ranchos during the late colonial period, see D. A. Brading, *Haciendas and Ranchos in the Mexican Bajío: León, 1700–1860* (Cambridge: Cambridge University Press, 1978). For the nineteenth century, see Margaret Chowning, *Wealth and Power in Provincial Mexico: Michoacán from the Late Colony to the Revolution* (Stanford, CA: Stanford University Press, 1999); Jesús Gómez Serrano, *Haciendas y ranchos de Aguascalientes: Estudio regional sobre la tenencia de tierra y el desarrollo agrícola en el siglo XIX* (Aguascaliente: Universidad Autónoma de Aguascalientes, 2012); González y González, *San José de Gracia*, 31–77; John Tutino, "The Revolution in Mexican Independence: Insurgency and the Renegotiation of Property, Production, and Patriarchy in the Bajío, 1800–1855," *Hispanic American Historical Review* 78, no. 3 (1998): 367–418. For the colonial period and the nineteenth century in Zacatecas, see Armando Márquez Herrera, *Historia de la cuestión agraria mexicana: Estado de Zacatecas,* vol. 1 (Mexico City: Gobierno del Estado de Zacatecas; Universidad Autónoma de Zacatecas; Centro de Estudios Históricos del Agrarismo en México, 1990).

19. Butler, *Popular Piety and Political Identity in Mexico's Cristero Rebellion*, 50–79; Curley, *Citizens and Believers,* 141–200; Fábregas Puig, *La formación histórica de una región*, 182–94; González y González, *San José de Gracia*, 146–80; Purnell, *Popular Movements and State Formation in Revolutionary Mexico*, 91–109.

20. Fallaw, *Religion and State Formation in Postrevolutionary Mexico*, 193–215; Ulices Piña, "The Different Roads to Rebellion: Socialist Education and the Second Cristero Rebellion in Jalisco, 1934–1939," *Letras Históricas* 16 (2017): 165–92.

21. Boyer, *Becoming Campesinos*, 16–45; Paul Friedrich, *Agrarian Revolt in a Mexican Village* (Chicago: University of Chicago Press, 1977), 43–77.

22. Boyer, *Becoming Campesinos*, 99–109.

23. Boyer, *Becoming Campesinos*, 154–87; Butler, *Popular Piety and Political Identity in Mexico's Cristero Rebellion*, 146–212; Curley, *Citizens and Believers*, 235–60; González y González, *San José de Gracia*, 146–80; Purnell, *Popular Movements and State Formation in Revolutionary Mexico*, 163–78. For a memoir written by a Guanajuato agrarista, see Alfredo Guerrero Tarquín, *Memorias de un agrarista: Pasajes de la vida de un hombre y de toda una región del Estado de Guanajuato, 1913–1938* (Mexico City: Instituto Nacional de Antropología e Historia, 1987). Though this trend of intracommunity clashes was most evident in Greater Bajío states, it was also present in other central and southern states. For a comparative analysis of religiously influenced political conflicts in the states of Campeche, Guanajuato, Guerrero, and Hidalgo, see Fallaw, *Religion and State Formation in Postrevolutionary Mexico*.

24. For clashes between agraristas and conservative Catholics, including the Cristeros, in Puruándiro during the 1920s, see Héctor Ortiz Ybarra and Vicente

González Méndez, *Puruándiro* (Morelia: Gobierno del Estado de Michoacán, 1980), 239–44. For Múgica's governorship, see Boyer, *Becoming Campesinos,* 80–113.

25. Estanislao Pérez and others to C. Presidente Municipal, January 6, 1944, AGHPEM, Puruándiro, caja 1, expediente 1.

26. José Medrano and others to Ciudadano Gobernador Constitucional del Estado, March 14, 1944, AGHPEM, Puruándiro, caja 1, expediente 1.

27. Lic. Luis Marín Pérez to Ciudadano Comandante de la 21/a. Zona Militar, May 8, 1944, AGHPEM, Puruándiro, caja 1, expediente 1.

28. Lic. José Ma. Mendoza Pardo and Lic. Luis M. Moreno, Acuerdo, November 22, 1944, AGHPEM, Puruándiro, caja 1, expediente 1; Lic. José Ma. Mendoza Pardo and Lic. Luis M. Moreno, Acuerdo, November 27, 1944, AGHPEM, Puruándiro, caja 1, expediente 1; Manuel Jiménez to Gobernador del Estado, November 30, 1944, AGHPEM, Puruándiro, caja 1, expediente 1.

29. January 1, 1945, affidavit signed by J. Refugio Cuevas Anaya, Gregorio Jiménez Pérez, Bernabé Godínez Ruiz, and J. Jesús Ortiz Murillo, AGHPEM, Puruándiro, caja 1, expediente 1.

30. Ortiz Ybarra and González Méndez, *Puruándiro,* 239–44.

31. Lázaro Cárdenas, "Resolución en el expediente de dotación de tierras al poblado San José Huipana, Estado de Michoacán," June 11, 1935, published August 2, 1935, in *Diario Oficial de la Federación,* vol. 91, no. 29, 455–56.

32. Donato Silva to Gobernador del Estado, December 4, 1944, AGHPEM, Puruándiro, caja 1, expediente 1.

33. Summary of a December 1, 1946, letter from Comisariado Ejidal Huipana to C. Presidente, December 9, 1946, AGN, MAV, caja 213, expediente 404.1/26.

34. Summary of a March 5, 1953, letter from Ángel Guevara to C. Secretario, March 10, 1953, AGN, ARC, caja 892, expediente 548.1/91.

35. The requests are all in AGN, ARC, caja 892, expedientes 548.1/76 and 548.1/91. In addition to a bracero contract, Guevara and Ceballos asked for direct financial assistance or for musical instruments that they would give to their children so they could form a performing band.

36. J. Ángel Guevara to C. Precidente [*sic*] de la República, AGN, ARC, caja 892, expediente 548.1/76.

37. J. Ángel Guevara to C. Precidente [*sic*] de la República, undated, marked as received by federal authorities on July 5, 1956, AGN, ARC, caja 892, expediente 548.1/76.

38. J. Ángel Guevara to C. Precidente [*sic*] de la República, May 1957 (exact date not specified), AGN, ARC, caja 892, expediente 548.1/76.

39. Tomás Flores to M.I. Sr. Gobernador del Edo., February 28, 1962, AGHPEM, SEGOB, TPS, PB, caja 9, expediente 22, foja 6.

40. Pablo García Gordillo to C. Gobernador Const. del Estado, November 13, 1963, AGHPEM, Puruándiro, caja 2, expediente 6.

41. A. Obregón, "Resolución en el expediente sobre restitución de tierras, promovido por los vecinos del pueblo Comanja, Michoacán," August 3, 1921, published August 30, 1921, in *Diario Oficial de la Federación,* vol. 18, no. 102, 1,587–89.

42. Lázaro Cárdenas, "Resolución en el expediente de ampliación de ejidos al poblado Comanja, Estado de Michoacán," September 23, 1936, published January 30, 1937, in *Diario Oficial de la Federación,* vol. 100, no. 25, 2nd sec., 2–3.

43. P. Elías Calles, "Acuerdo por el cual se destinan al uso de escuelas, los anexos a los templos de los pueblos de Comanja y Zipiajo, del Municipio de Coeneo, Estado de Michoacán," March 7, 1927, published March 25, 1927, in *Diario Oficial de la Federación,* vol. 41, no. 1, 1st sec., 1.

44. Daniel Torres Gascón to Ciudadano Secretario General de Gobierno, July 6, 1947, AGHEPM, Coeneo, caja 1.

45. Luisa Jiménez to Ciudadano Gobernador Constitucional en el Estado, October 31, 1959, AGHPEM, Coeneo, caja 1.

46. Esteban Arroyo and others to C. Gobernador Constitucional del Estado, November 1, 1950, AGHPEM, Coeneo, caja 1.

47. Antonio Gil Cardona to Ciudadano Secretario General de Gobierno, January 29, 1951, AGHPEM, Coeneo, caja 1.

48. David Herrera Tapia to Ciudadano Gobernador Constitucional del Estado, January 6, 1950 [*sic*], AGHPEM, Coeneo, caja 1; David Herrera Tapia to Ciudadano Secretario General de Gobierno, February 16, 1951, AGHPEM, Coeneo, caja 1. Herrera Tapia mistakenly dated his first letter 1950. The state government's receipt stamp is dated January 9, 1951, and Herrera Tapia refers to events that occurred in fall 1950.

49. J. Jesús Castillo and others to Ciudadano Secretario General de Gobierno, January 11, 1951, AGHPEM, Coeneo, caja 1.

50. Lic. Emilio Romero Espinosa to Ciudadano Comandante de la XXI Zona Militar, February 14, 1951, AGHPEM, Coeneo, caja 1.

51. Aurelio Cervantes Calixto to C. Gral. Dámaso Cárdenas, October 29, 1951, AGHPEM, Coeneo, caja 1.

52. Zeferino Nieves E., Juan Nieves Pedroza, and M. Luisa Jiménez to C. Secretario General de Gobierno, May 23, 1957, AGHPEM, Coeneo, caja 1; Eusebio Nieto Cervantes to Ciudadano Secretario General de Gobierno, October 1, 1957, AGHPEM, Coeneo, caja 1. The Sociedad de Padres de Familia should not be confused with the Unión de Padres de Familia, which is also a PTA-style organization but which was linked to Catholic advocacy groups like Acción Católica. For the Unión, see Valentina Torres Septién, *La educación privada en México (1903–1976)* (Mexico City: El Colegio de México, Universidad Iberoamericana, 1997).

53. Andrés Sandoval Castillo, Lista de Aspirantes a Braceros Para el Vecino País de Norte América, del Pueblo de Comanja del Municipio de Coeneo, Mich., y que se Formula Para su Aprobación en Gobernación, May 2, 1963, AGHPEM, SEGOB, TPS, PB, caja 7, expediente 9, foja 88.

54. Andrés Sandoval Castillo to C. Lic. Agustín Arriaga Rivera, August 14, 1963, AGHPEM, SEGOB, TPS, PB, caja 9, expediente 20, foja 192.

55. Carlos Martínez Aristizábal to Sr. Profr. Leodegario López Ramírez, May 7, 1964, AGHPEM, SEGOB, TPS, PB, caja 10, expediente 16, foja 110. Sandoval Castillo's request, which was dated May 6, is not available. This document is a memo-

randum in which Martínez Aristizábal informs López Ramírez that he will be forwarding Sandoval Castillo's request to him.

56. For the beginning of Cristero conflicts in Guanajuato, see Mónica Blanco, Alma Parra, and Ethelia Ruiz Medrano, *Guanajuato: Historia breve,* 3rd ed. (Mexico City: Fondo de Cultura Económica; El Colegio de México; Fideicomiso Historia de las Américas, 2011), 204; Olivera Sedano, *La guerra cristera,* 131–32, 137–39.

57. Comités Particulares Administrativos Agrarios de El Mármol, Miramar, La Mula, Comalillo, Atarjea, Zapote de Barajas, Rancho Seco, Tepamal y Puerto de Barajas to Ciudadano Gobernador del Estado, November 2, 1931, AHAGPEG, SEGOB, PD, 1.59 (23), año 1931, expediente 3.

58. Juvencio Reyes to C. Llic. Luis Felipe Ordaz Rocha, November 11, 1931, AHAGPEG, SEGOB, PD, 1.59 (23), año 1931, expediente 3.

59. Santiago Guzmán (Por los Jefes de Familia) to Ciudadano Gobernador del Estado, December 14, 1932, AHAGPEG, SEGOB, PD, 1.54 (23), año 1932, expediente 16.

60. Esther Castillo Vda. de Ramos to Ciudadano Gobernador Consitucional del Estado de Guanajuato, April 23, 1942, AHAGPEG, SEGOB, PD, 1.54 (24), año 1942, expediente 5; Santiago Guzmán Molina and Aurelio López Sánchez to C. Presidente de la República, undated, marked as received on October 3, 1958, AGN, ARC, caja 328, expediente 404.1/3667.

61. Prof. Graciano Sánchez to C. Gobernador Constl. del Estado, November 24, 1942, AHAGPEG, SEGOB, PD, 1.54 (24), año 1942, expediente 9.

62. Lic. Fausto Villagómez to C. Presidente Municipal, October 11, 1945, AHAGPEG, SEGOB, PD, 1.54 (24), año 1945, expediente 4.

63. J. Jesús Govea H. to Sr. Lic. D. J. Jesús Castorena, March 6, 1948, AHAGPEG, SEGOB, PD, 1.59 (25), año 1948, expediente 1.

64. Alberto Bello Santana to C. Gobernador Constl. Subst. del Edo., August 10, 1949, AHAGPEG, SEGOB, PD, 1.59 (23), año 1949, expediente 1.

65. Lázaro Cárdenas, "Resolución en el expediente de dotación de tierras al poblado Presa del Aguacate, Estado de Guanajuato," April 22, 1936, published June 13, 1936, in *Diario Oficial de la Federación,* vol. 96, no. 28, 4–6.

66. Summary of a June 1, 1936, letter from Eligio León to C. Presidente, June 6, 1936, AGN, LCR, caja 281, expediente 404.1/5740.

67. Cayetano Quiles to Señor don Enrique Fernández Martínez, October 22, 1936, AHAGPEG, SEGOB, PD, 1.54 (24), año 1936, expediente 16.

68. Florentino Rosas Canchola to C. General de División Manuel Ávila Camacho, August 15, 1942, AGN, MAC, caja 358, expediente 404.1/1249. I was unable to locate an original copy of Acosta's report, which Rosas transcribed into this letter he sent to President Ávila Camacho.

69. Florentino Rosas to Señor Presidente de la República, March 23, 1942, AGN, MAC, caja 358, expediente 404.1/1249.

70. Summary of an April 13, 1944, message from Comisariado Ejidal, Presa del Aguacate to C. Presidente, April 18, 1944, AGN, MAC, caja 358, expediente 404.1/1249. The comisariado ejidal's name is not included in the summary of the

message. Presa del Aguacate's ejidatarios formally requested an ejido expansion in August 1937. Federal authorities did not rule on the request until May 1951, when President Alemán denied it. For the expansion request and its rejection, see Miguel Alemán, "Resolución sobre ampliación de ejido al poblado Presa del Aguacate, en Pénjamo, Gto.," May 16, 1951, published November 1, 1951, in *Diario Oficial de la Federación,* vol. 189, no. 1, 1st sec., 15–16.

71. Cleofas Cervantes Hernández and Alberto Rodríguez to C. Jefe del Departamento Agrario, July 15, 1948, AHAGPEG, SEGOB, PD, 1.54 (25), año 1948, expediente 7. Cervantes Hernández and Rodríguez did not specify if they jointly owned the invaded 27 hectares or if they individually owned holdings that measured a combined 27 hectares.

72. Gabriel Padilla Romo and others to C. Gobernador del Estado, May 1921 [no specific date listed], AHEJ, AG, AG-6-921, Tierras, caja 26, inventario 4117, foja 16; Hilario Núñez and others to C. Gobernador del Estado, May 1921 [no specific date listed], AHEJ, AG, AG-6-921, Tierras, caja 26, inventario 4117, fojas 55–57; Gregorio Orozco and others to C. Gobernador del Estado, June 1921 [no specific date listed], AHEJ, AG, AG-6-921, Tierras, caja 26, inventario 4108, fojas 4–14.

73. Meyer, *The Cristero Rebellion,* 115; José María Muriá, *Jalisco: Historia breve,* 4th ed. (Mexico City: Fondo de Cultura Económica; El Colegio de México; Fideicomiso Historia de las Américas, 2011), 158; Olivera Sedano, *La guerra cristera,* 135–37.

74. V. Álvarez and J. López Estrada to C. Gobernador Constitucional Interino del Estado, April 29, 1927, AHEJ, Gobernación, G-2–927, Guerra, caja 193, inventario 6151.

75. "¡Llamamieno al Pueblo Mexicano!", September 1936, AMHTM, caja 302, expediente 8.

76. "Manifiesto al Pueblo Mexicano", March 10, 1936, AMHTM, caja 302, expediente 8.

77. Lic. Luis F. Canudas Orezza to Gobernador Const. Estado, March 2, 1946, AHEJ, GOB/SC, año 1946, caja 47.

78. Apolonia Hernández Vda. de Flores to C. Presidente de la República, undated, forwarded by Lic. Roberto Amorós G. to C. Gobernador del Estado on July 12, 1945, AHEJ, GOB/SC, año 1945, caja 15. For the establishment of Santa Elena's ejido, see Lázaro Cárdenas, "Resolución en el expediente de dotación de ejidos al poblado Santa Elena, Estado de Jalisco," July 27, 1938, published November 17, 1938, in *Diario Oficial de la Federación,* vol. 109, no. 15, 4–5. The Cárdenas administration allotted 705 hectares to Santa Elena.

79. Lázaro Cárdenas, "Resolución en el expediente de dotación de ejidos al poblado El Alacrán, Estado de Jalisco," September 22, 1937, published December 8, 1937, in *Diario Oficial de la Federación,* vol. 105, no. 32, 3rd sec., 11–13. Two hundred thirty hectares of Manuel Hernández's El Alacrán Rancho were allotted to El Alacrán's ejido, which was allotted a total of 812 hectares.

80. Gral. y Sen. Gabriel Leyva V. to C. General de División Manuel Ávila Camacho, May 8, 1945, AHEJ, GOB/SC, año 1945, caja 33.

81. Pedro Valle to C. Secretario General de Gobierno, June 8, 1945, AHEJ, GOB/SC, año 1945, caja 33. The available evidence does not make clear if the municipal president was related to landowner José Valle Padilla.

82. Lic. Silvano Barba González to C. General Marcelino García Barragán, undated, marked as received by the state government on March 9, 1946, AHEJ, GOB/SC, año 1946, caja 50.

83. Lic. José Andrade González to C. Presidente Municipal de Atotonilco el Alto, March 26, 1946, AHEJ, GOB/SC, año 1946, caja 50; Las Comunidades Agrarias del Municipio de Atotonilco el Alto, Jal. pertenecientes a la Liga de Comunidades Agrarias y Sindicatos Campesinos del Estado (Auténtica) Miembro de la C.N.C., se dirigieron al Señor Presidente de la República, en los términos que siguen, May 14, 1946, AHEJ, GOB/SC, año 1946, caja 6. The ejido leadership councils that signed this declaration represented Margaritas, Milpillas, Mesa del Solorio, Santa Elena, El Refugio, El Maguey, and San Joaquín.

84. Bartolo Lomelí Anguiano to C. Gobernador, May 17, 1946, AHEJ, GOB/SC, año 1946, caja 12.

85. Dip. José Ramírez Muñoz to C. Gral. Miguel Z. Martínez, August 21, 1946, AHEJ, GOB/SC, año 1946, caja 48.

86. Felipe González Gallo to C. Tte. Corl. De Inf. Ismael Ávila Dorantes, May 6, 1947, AHEJ, GOB/SC, año 1947, caja 34. The available evidence does not make clear if the commander was related to Jalisco governor Jesús González Gallo.

87. Rath, *Myths of Demilitarization in Postrevolutionary Mexico,* 116–22.

88. Dr. Manuel González Vargas to C. Gobernador del Estado, October 8, 1947, AHEJ, GOB/SC, año 1947, caja 31.

89. Summary of a January 26, 1950, letter from Comité Ejec. Agrario de S. José de Gracia to C. Presidente, February 3, 1950, AGN, MAV, caja 260, expediente 404.1/4865; J. Jesús Medina to C. Comandante de la 15/a. Zona Militar, February 22, 1950, AHEJ, GOB/SC, año 1950, caja 11.

90. Zenaido González Ruvalcaba to Gobernador Constitucional del Estado, March 11, 1950, AHEJ, GOB/SC, año 1950, caja 25.

91. Padrón e Historial de Núcleos Agrarios, Registro Agrario Nacional, www.ran.gob.mx/ran/index.php/sistemas-de-consulta/phina. The number of Puruándiro ejidos includes seventeen that were transferred to the newly established municipality of José Sixto Verduzco in 1974.

92. Miguel Navarro Castellanos, Lista de los aspirantes a braceros para los campos agrícolas de los Estados Unidos de Norteamérica, inscritos en el Municipio de Tepatitlán de Morelos, Jal., June 3, 1953, AMHTM, caja 374, expediente 59. The municipal president reported that there were 193 aspiring braceros in Tepatitlán; 51 lived in the municipal seat.

93. Mireya Loza, "Pedro Carmona Vera," Bracero History Archive, Item #344, May 20, 2006, http://braceroarchive.org/items/show/344.

94. Pedro Carmona Vera to Sr. Licenciado Adolfo Lópes [sic] Mateos, July 19, 1960, AGN, ALM, caja 719, expediente 546.6/407.

95. Interview with Antonio Nuño Gonzáles by Romelia Richmond, 2008, "Interview no. 1416," Institute of Oral History, University of Texas at El Paso, https://scholarworks.utep.edu/cgi/viewcontent.cgi?article=2747&context=interviews.

96. Colmenares López et al., *Historia de la cuestión agraria mexicana: Estado de Zacatecas,* vol. 2, 134–35, 242–43; Jesús Flores Olague, Mercedes de Vega, Sandra Kuntz Ficker, and Laura del Alizal, *Zacatecas: Historia breve,* 2nd ed. (Mexico City: Fondo de Cultura Económica; El Colegio de México; Fideicomiso Historia de las Américas, 2011), 176–77; Olivera Sedano, *La guerra cristera,* 120–22, 142–43.

97. Ramírez Miranda, Vera Salvo, and Gómez Sánchez, *Historia de la cuestión agraria mexicana: Estado de Zacatecas,* vol. 3, 29–30, 60–62, 67–69.

98. Sandra Lucile Nichols, "Saints, Peaches, and Wine: Mexican Migrants and the Transformation of Los Haro, Zacatecas and Napa, California" (PhD diss., University of California, Berkeley, 2002), 36–39.

99. P. Ortiz Rubio, "Resolución en el expediente de dotación de ejidos a la rancheria El Durazno, Estado de Zacatecas," March 19, 1931, published July 8, 1931, in *Diario Oficial de la Federación,* vol. 67, no. 7, 1st sec., 6–12; Summary of a January 20, 1958, letter from Daniel Bautista García to C. Presidente, January 23, 1958, AGN, ARC, caja 899, expediente 548.1/620.

100. Daniel Bautista García to Sr. Licenciado Sergio L. Benhumea, February 6, 1958, AGN, ARC, caja 899, expediente 548.1/620.

101. These requests are in AGN, MAC, caja 793; AGN, MAV, caja 594; AGN, ARC, cajas 884, 892–900, and 1028; AGN, ALM, cajas 716–24, 727.

102. Summary of a September 1, 1953, letter from Francisco Durán Ortega and others to C. Presidente, September 8, 1953, AGN, ARC, caja 884, expediente 546.6/120; Summary of a February 9, 1959, letter from Francisco Durán Ortega and others to C. Presidente, February 13, 1959, AGN, ALM, caja 716, expediente 546.6/58.

103. Jesús Gómez Serrano and Francisco Javier Delgado, *Aguascalientes: Historia breve,* 2nd ed. (Mexico City: Fondo de Cultura Económica; El Colegio de México; Fideicomiso Historia de las Américas, 2011), 238–39; Rojas, *La destrucción de la hacienda en Aguascalientes,* 82–85.

104. Chávez-García, *Migrant Longing,* 33–66, 99–129, 136.

105. J. Félix de Loera Calvillo to C. Presidente de la República Mexicana, June 22, 1956, AGN, ARC, caja 897, expediente 548.1/450.

106. Alberto Alcalá de Lira to C. Gobernador Constitucional del Edo., August 24, 1957, AHEA, SGGOB, caja 695, expediente 202.

107. Summary of a January 28, 1953, letter from Camilo López Gómez to C. Presidente, February 12, 1953, AGN, ARC, caja 293, expediente 404.1/516.

108. José Esparza Díaz to C. Prof. Edmundo Gámes [sic] Orozco, March 17, 1953, AHEA, SGGOB, caja 632, expediente 224; José Esparza Díaz to C. Prof. Edmundo Gámes [sic] Orozco, April 1, 1953, AHEA, SGGOB, caja 632, expediente 224.

109. Juan Pablo Monreal Buendía to C. Ing. Luis Ortega Douglas, October 31, 1957, AHEA, SGGOB, caja 701, expediente 775.

110. Luis de la Hidalga to C. Delegado Agrario, April 9, 1958, AHEA, SGGOB, caja 705, expediente 4.

111. Summary of an August 8, 1963, letter from Salvador Martínez López to an unnamed federal official, August 16, 1963, AGN, ALM, caja 718, expediente 546.6/296.

112. Summary of an August 16, 1963, letter from Salvador Martínez López to an unnamed federal official, August 20, 1963, AGN, ALM, caja 960, expediente 703.4/2909.

113. Lic. Donato Miranda Fonseca to C. Lic. Gustavo Díaz Ordaz, September 17, 1963, AGN, ALM, caja 960, expediente 703.4/2909.

114. Lázaro Cárdenas, "Resolución en el expediente de dotación de tierras al poblado Romero de Torres, Estado de Michoacán," December 17, 1935, published February 20, 1936, in *Diario Oficial de la Federación,* vol. 94, no. 2, 2nd sec., 5–7.

115. J. Guadalupe Castro to C. Gobernador Constitucional del Estado, March 19, 1945, AGHPEM, SEGOB, TPS, PB, caja 1, expediente 3, fojas 184–185.

116. J. Guadalupe Castro to C. Gobernador Constitucional del Estado, April 15, 1945, AGHPEM, SEGOB, TPS, PB, caja 1, expediente 3, foja 254.

117. Lázaro Cárdenas, "Resolución en el expediente de dotación de ejidos al poblado Changuitiro, Estado de Michoacán," January 6, 1937, published March 11, 1937, in *Diario Oficial de la Federación,* vol. 101, no. 10, 2nd sec., 8–10.

118. Lázaro Cárdenas, "Resolución en el expediente de ampliación de ejidos al poblado Changuitiro, Estado de Michoacán," January 18, 1939, published July 20, 1940, in *Diario Oficial de la Federación,* vol. 121, no. 18, 2nd sec., 4–5.

119. Francisco García Maldonado, interview by author, Winters, CA, May 26, 2020.

120. Humberto Beltrán M., Informe técnico, August 5, 1936. I consulted this document in December 2009 when it was stored in the archive of the Registro Agrario Nacional's branch in Morelia. Shortly thereafter, this document and other relevant ones were transferred to the Archivo General Agrario (AGA) in Mexico City and made unavailable to researchers. The AGA began liberalizing its collections in early 2020. However, the COVID-19 pandemic, which is ongoing as I draft this, has made it impossible for me to travel to the AGA to see if this document is once again available to researchers.

121. Carlos Fuentes Aldama to Ciudadano Gobernador Constitucional del Estado, July 13, 1945, AGHPEM, Churintzio, caja 1, expediente 4, foja 2.

122. Melesio Aguilar Ferreira, Relación de trabajadores emigrantes de Michoacán que salen con destino a Norteamérica por el centro de contratación establecido en ese lugar, July 7, 1959, AGHPEM, SEGOB, TPS, PB, caja 4, expediente 6, foja 77; Bracero contracts issued to David Maldonado Mendoza, personal collection of Bernardina Fuentes Vda. de Maldonado.

123. Boyer, *Becoming Campesinos,* 154–87; Butler, *Popular Piety and Political Identity in Mexico's Cristero Rebellion,* 179–212; Purnell, *Popular Movements and State Formation in Revolutionary Mexico,* 163–78.

124. Amparo Maldonado de García, interview by author, Winters, CA, May 26, 2020.

125. Rafael Morales V. to Ciudadano Presidente Municipal, June 24, 1952, AGHPEM, Churintzio, caja 1, expediente 8, foja 28; Lino Cruz Fuentes, Encargado del Orden de los Poblados y Comunidades de Este Mpio, October 31, 1960, AGHPEM, Churintzio, caja 1, expediente 10, foja 25; Dip. Víctor Cázares Sánchez to C. Lic. Javier Rojo Gómez, August 19, 1964, AGHPEM, Churintzio, caja 1, expediente 14.

126. García Maldonado, interview.

127. Fuentes Aldama to Ciudadano Gobernador Constitucional del Estado.

128. Remigio Arroyo Aviña to Ciudadano Lic. José María Mendoza Pardo, August 10, 1946, AGHPEM, Churintzio, caja 1, expediente 4, foja 6.

129. Gabino Verduzco Galván to Ciudadano Secretario General de Gobierno, October 27, 1947, AGHPEM, Churintzio, caja 1, expediente 4, foja 8.

130. Abelino Heredia Herrera to C. Gral. J. Félix Ireta Viveros, July 7, 1955, AGHPEM, Churintzio, caja 1, expediente 4, foja 14.

131. Maldonado de García, interview.

132. Dip. Víctor Cázares Sánchez to C. Delegado del Depto. de Asuntos Agrarios y Col., January 28, 1963, AGHPEM, Churintzio, caja 1, expediente 12.

133. Dr. Manuel González Vargas to C. Gobernador, June 11, 1947, AHEJ, GOB/SC, año 1947, caja 41.

134. Maldonado de García, interview.

135. Untitled list of braceros selected in the district of La Piedad, February 25, 1945, AGHPEM, SEGOB, TPS, PB, caja 2.

CHAPTER FOUR

1. Miguel Alemán, "Resolución sobre dotación de ejido al poblado Jesús del Monte, en Maravatío, Mich.," November 28, 1951, published August 2, 1952, in *Diario Oficial de la Federación,* vol. 193, no. 29, 6–7. This document is the official resolution to Jesús del Monte's request for ejido lands. It notes that the formal request was dated March 10, 1939.

2. Ángel Sandoval Coronel to Ciudadano Gobernador Constitucional del Estado, March 10, 1945, AGHPEM, SEGOB, TPS, PB, caja 1, expediente 3, foja 106.

3. Alemán, "Resolución sobre dotación de ejido al poblado Jesús del Monte," 6–7.

4. Miguel Alemán, "Resolución sobre dotación de tierras al poblado La Nopalera, en Maravatío, Mich.," March 24, 1948, published June 22, 1948, in *Diario Oficial de la Federación,* vol. 168, no. 43, 5–6.

5. Gledhill, *Casi Nada;* López Castro, *La casa dividida;* Massey et al., *Return to Aztlan.* Gledhill, López Castro, and Massey and his coauthors, including Durand, all note that there was migration from ejidos during the years of the Bracero Program. However, this phenomenon is not the primary focus of their works. López

Castro, Massey, and Durand focus on post–Bracero Program Mexico-US migration, while Gledhill focuses on the agrarian reform's shortcomings.

6. Padrón e Historial de Núcleos Agrarios, Registro Agrario Nacional, www.ran.gob.mx/ran/index.php/sistemas-de-consulta/phina.

7. *Estadísticas históricas de México*, vol. 1, 325, 327. During the period 1915–40, federal administrations redistributed 5.5 million hectares among 399,829 Aguascalientes, Guanajuato, Jalisco, Michoacán, and Zacatecas ejidatarios.

8. A. L. Rodríguez, "Código Agrario de los Estados Unidos Mexicanos," March 22, 1934, published April 12, 1934, in *Diario Oficial de la Federación*, vol. 83, no. 29, 597–618.

9. Padrón e Historial de Núcleos Agrarios, Registro Agrario Nacional.

10. Lázaro Cárdenas, "Código Agrario de los Estados Unidos Mexicanos," September 23, 1940, published October 29, 1940, in *Diario Oficial de la Federación*, vol. 122, no. 48, 2nd sec., 1–56; Manuel Ávila Camacho, "Código Agrario de los Estados Unidos Mexicanos," December 31, 1942, published April 27, 1943, in *Diario Oficial de la Federación*, vol. 137, no. 50, 9–43.

11. Lázaro Cárdenas, "Ley de Crédito Agrícola que reforma la de 24 de enero de 1934," December 19, 1935, published December 20, 1935, in *Diario Oficial de la Federación*, vol. 93, no. 33, 830–32.

12. Padrón e Historial de Núcleos Agrarios, Registro Agrario Nacional.

13. See the following by México, Dirección General de Estadística: *Sexto Censo de Población, 1940: Aguascalientes; Baja California Territorios Norte y Sur*, 15; *Sexto Censo de Población, 1940: Guanajuato*, 13, 49, 85; *Sexto Censo de Población, 1940: Jalisco*, 13, 47, 77, 106, 133, 161; *Sexto Censo de Población, 1940: Michoacán*, 13, 46, 73, 102, 130, 160; *Sexto Censo de Población, 1940: Zacatecas*, 13, 45, 74; *VIII Censo General de Población—1960, 8 de Junio de 1960: Estado de Aguascalientes*, 1–2; *VIII Censo General de Población—1960, 8 de Junio de 1960: Estado de Guanajuato*, 25–34; *VIII Censo General de Población—1960, 8 de Junio de 1960: Estado de Jalisco*, 3–27; *VIII Censo General de Población—1960, 8 de Junio de 1960: Estado de Michoacán*, 3–25; *VIII Censo General de Población—1960, 8 de Junio de 1960: Estado de Zacatecas*, 3–12.

14. There is a voluminous literature on the initial debates on and the eventual implementation and shortcomings of the agrarian reform, in the principal bracero-sending states and in other regions. For the primary bracero-sending states, see Boyer, *Becoming Campesinos;* Colmenares López et al., *Historia de la cuestión agraria mexicana: Estado de Zacatecas*, vol. 2; Craig, *The First Agraristas;* Friedrich, *Agrarian Revolt in a Mexican Village;* Gledhill, *Casi Nada;* Meyer Cosío, *Tradición y progreso;* Moctezuma Longoria, "La otra reforma agraria en Zacatecas"; Rojas, *La destrucción de la hacienda en Aguascalientes*. For a comparative analysis of the Guanajuato Bajío, Michoacán, the Comarca Lagunera, and Tlaxcala, see Iván Restrepo Fernández and José Sánchez Cortés, *La reforma agraria en cuatro regiones: El Bajío, Michoacán, La Laguna y Tlaxcala* (Mexico City: Secretaría de Educación Pública, 1972). For Morelos, see John Womack Jr., *Zapata and the Mexican Revolution* (New York: Vintage Books, 1968). For Chihuahua, see Friedrich Katz, *The Life and Times*

of Pancho Villa (Stanford, CA: Stanford University Press, 1998). For Yucatán, see Fallaw, *Cárdenas Compromised;* and Joseph, *Revolution from Without*. For the Comarca Lagunera, see Wolfe, *Watering the Revolution*.

15. Kourí, "La invención del ejido."

16. For the drafting of the 1917 Constitution and its provisios, see Berta Ulloa, *La constitución de 1917* (Mexico City: El Colegio de México, 1983).

17. For Carrillo Puerto's tenure as Yucatán's governor and his agrarian policies, see Joseph, *Revolution from Without*. For Obregón's and Calles's ideas regarding the agrarian reform, see Hamilton, *The Limits of State Autonomy*.

18. For Cárdenas's Michoacán governorship and how his mentor and predecessor Francisco Múgica influenced his agrarian policies, see Boyer, *Becoming Campesinos*. For the transition to the ejido as the definitive form of land redistribution, see Hamilton, *The Limits of State Autonomy*.

19. For Yucatán, see Fallaw, *Cárdenas Compromised*. For the Comarca Lagunera, see Wolfe, *Watering the Revolution*. These collective ejidos also faltered, though not necessarily because of the strict application of the 1934 Agrarian Code. In the Comarca Lagunera, the construction of dams on the Nazas River affected the aquifers that had been a principal water source for cotton cultivators prior to the agrarian reform. And in Yucatán, state officials and landowners actively pushed back against what they interpreted as unnecessary federal intervention in the regional agrarian economy; this resistance ultimately prompted the Cárdenas administration to turn over the administration of Yucatán's ejido lands to the state government.

20. Rodríguez, "Código Agrario de los Estados Unidos Mexicanos [1934]," 599–605; Cárdenas, "Código Agrario de los Estados Unidos Mexicanos [1940]," 33; Ávila Camacho, "Código Agrario de los Estados Unidos Mexicanos [1942]," 16.

21. See by México, Dirección General de Estadística: *Primer Censo Agrícola-Ganadero, 1930: Estado de Guanajuato* (Mexico City: DAAP, 1937), 12–14; *Primer Censo Agrícola-Ganadero, 1930: Estado de Jalisco*, 146–47; *Primer Censo Agrícola-Ganadero, 1930: Estado de Michoacán* (Mexico City: DAAP, 1937), 20–23.

22. Rodríguez, "Código Agrario de los Estados Unidos Mexicanos [1934]," 605–6.

23. Rodríguez, "Código Agrario de los Estados Unidos Mexicanos [1934]," 606–13; Cárdenas, "Código Agrario de los Estados Unidos Mexicanos [1940]," 19.

24. A. L. Rodríguez, "Resolución en el expediente de dotación de ejidos al poblado Santa Ana Mancera, Estado de Michoacán," July 30, 1934, published October 29, 1934, in *Diario Oficial de la Federación*, vol. 86, no. 41, 1,226–28.

25. Lázaro Cárdenas, "Resolución en el expediente de ampliación de tierras al poblado Isaac Arriaga, Estado de Michoacán," April 1, 1936, published May 6, 1936, in *Diario Oficial de la Federación*, vol. 96, no. 3, 1st sec., 5–6. The exact size of the ejido expansion was 313.60 hectares.

26. Lázaro Cárdenas, "Resolución en el expediente de segunda ampliación de ejidos al poblado Isaac Arriaga, Estado de Michoacán," April 24, 1940, published July 12, 1940, in *Diario Oficial de la Federación*, vol. 121, no. 11, 8–9.

27. Heliodoro Martínez Rangel to C. Gobernador del Estado, February 16, 1945, AGHPEM, SEGOB, TPS, PB, caja 1, expediente 3, foja 30/31.

28. Lázaro Cárdenas, "Resolución en el expediente de dotación de ejidos al poblado Queseras de Cortés, Estado de Guanajuato," January 6, 1937, published February 20, 1937, in *Diario Oficial de la Federación,* vol. 100, no. 42, 3rd sec., 12–14.

29. Miguel Alemán, "Resolución sobre ampliación de ejido al poblado Quesera de Cortés, en Pénjamo, Gto.," July 21, 1948, published September 7, 1948, in *Diario Oficial de la Federación,* vol. 170, no. 6, 2nd sec., 15.

30. José Abundis to C. Gobernador, June 10, 1945, AHAGPEG, SEGOB, PD, 1.19 (24), año 1945, expediente 1.

31. Alemán, "Resolución sobre ampliación de ejido al poblado Quesera de Cortés," 15.

32. Lázaro Cárdenas, "Resolución en el expediente de dotación de tierras al poblado Las Raíces, Estado de Guanajuato," April 29, 1936, published May 16, 1936, in *Diario Oficial de la Federación,* vol. 96, no. 12, 2nd sec., 12–13.

33. Los que subscribimos to Ciudadano Gobernador Constitucional del Estado, December 4, 1944, AHAGPEG, SEGOB, PD, 1.19, año 1944, expediente 151.

34. Lic. Fausto Villagómez to J. Carmen Sierra, December 7, 1944, AHAGPEG, SEGOB, PD, 1.19, año 1944, expediente 151.

35. Los suscritos vecinos de esta comunidad agraria to Lic. D. Ernesto Hidalgo, December 10, 1944, AHAGPEG, SEGOB, PD, 1.19, año 1944, expediente 162; J. Carmen Rodríguez to C. Gobernador, February 4, 1945; José Negrete Ahumada to C. Gobernador, February 14, 1945; Crissóforo Lesso to C. Gobernador, February 19, 1945; Miguel García to C. Gobernador, February 19, 1945; and Ángel Ramírez to C. Gobernador, February 19, 1945. All the 1945 requests are in AHAGPEG, SEGOB, PD, 1.19 (40), año 1945, expediente 1.

36. Lázaro Cárdenas, "Resolución en el expediente de dotación de ejidos al poblado Presa de San Andrés, Estado de Guanajuato," April 29, 1936, published May 19, 1936, in *Diario Oficial de la Federación,* vol. 96, no. 14, 9–11; Lázaro Cárdenas, "Resolución en el expediente de dotación de ejidos al poblado El Salitre, Estado de Gunajuato," April 29, 1936, published June 1, 1936, in *Diario Oficial de la Federación,* vol. 96, no. 17,, 4–6; Lázaro Cárdenas, "Resolución en el expediente de dotación de ejidos al poblado Sanabria, Estado de Guanajuato," August 4, 1936, published October 23, 1936, in *Diario Oficial de la Federación,* vol. 98, no. 44, 3rd sec., 1–3; Lázaro Cárdenas, "Resolución en el expediente de dotación de ejidos al poblado Las Jicamas, Estado de Guanajuato," August 4, 1936, published October 24, 1936, in *Diario Oficial de la Federación,* vol. 98, no. 45, 3rd sec., 15–16; Lázaro Cárdenas, "Resolución en el expediente de dotación de ejidos al poblado San Antonio de Pantoja, Estado de Guanajuato," September 16, 1936, published October 22, 1936, in *Diario Oficial de la Federación,* vol. 98, no. 43, 3rd sec., 6–7; Lázaro Cárdenas, "Resolución en el expediente de dotación de ejidos al poblado Santa Catarina, Estado de Guanajuato," September 30, 1936, published December 23, 1936, in *Diario Oficial de la Federación,* vol. 99, no. 35, 2nd sec., 5–7. The precise sizes of the ejidos were 138.91 hectares (Santa Catarina); 210.58 hectares (San Antonio de Pantoja); 270.09 hectares (Sanabria); 488

hectares (Presa de San Andrés); 787 hectares (Las Jicamas); and 1,862 hectares (El Salitre).

37. Boyer, *Political Landscapes*, 111, 160.

38. Lázaro Cárdenas, "Resolución en el expediente de dotación de tierras al poblado Pretoria, Estado de Michoacán," August 12, 1936, published September 28, 1936, in *Diario Oficial de la Federación,* vol. 98, no. 23, 1st sec., 8–9.

39. Juventino Ruiz to Ciudadano Gobernador Constitucional del Estado, February 1, 1945, AGHPEM, SEGOB, TPS, PB, caja 1, expediente 3, foja 29/30.

40. José Rentería to C. Gobernador, January 26, 1944 (sic), AHAGPEG, SEGOB, PD, 1.19 (40), año 1945, expediente 1. The state government marked this request as received in January 1945, and it is included in the file that has other bracero contract requests that aspiring Valle de Santiago braceros sent to state officials that year.

41. Lázaro Cárdenas, "Resolución en el expediente de dotación de ejidos al poblado Mogotes o Rancho Nuevo de San Andrés, Estado de Guanajuato," April 29, 1936, published June 4, 1936, in *Diario Oficial de la Federación,* vol. 96, no. 20, 1st sec., 7–9. The ejido was allotted a total 1,338 hectares. The noncultivable lands were earmarked for communal-use livestock grazing.

42. José Rentería to C. Gobernador, February 18, 1945, AHAGPEG, SEGOB, PD, 1.19 (40), año 1945, expediente 1.

43. A. L. Rodríguez, "Resolución en el expediente de dotación de ejidos al poblado Laredo, Estado de Michoacán," September 3, 1934, published October 31, 1934, in *Diario Oficial de la Federación,* vol. 86, no. 43, 2nd sec., 1,283–85.

44. Gregorio Morales to Ciudadano Gobernador Constitucional del Estado, March 1, 1945, AGHPEM, SEGOB, TPS, PB, caja 1, expediente 3, foja 73/74.

45. Mateo Rubalcava Juárez to C. Ing. Don Luis Ortega Douglas, August 18, 1957, AHEA, SGGOB, caja 695, expediente 202.

46. Summary of an August 1, 1960, message from Manuel Berúmen Ortiz to an unidentified federal official, August 9, 1960, AGN, ALM, caja 720, expediente 546.6/533.

47. Manuel Ávila Camacho, "Resolución en el expediente de dotación de ejidos al poblado Centro de Arriba, Estado de Aguascalientes," March 15, 1944, published August 24, 1944, in *Diario Oficial de la Federación,* vol. 145, no. 47, 12–14.

48. P. Ortiz Rubio, "Resolución en el expediente de dotación de ejidos a la ranchería Ermita de Guadalupe, Estado de Zacatecas," August 19, 1932, published December 15, 1932, in *Diario Oficial de la Federación,* vol. 75, no. 39, 3rd sec., 12–15. For the statutes that structured the establishment of Ermita de Guadalupe's ejido, see Plutarco Elías Calles, Ley que reforma la de Dotaciones y Restituciones de Tierras y Aguas, reglamentaria del Artículo 27 Constitucional, de 23 de abril de 1927, August 11, 1927, published August 18, 1927, in *Diario Oficial de la Federación,* vol. 43, no. 41, 1st sec., 3–13.

49. Lázaro Cárdenas, "Resolución en el expediente de dotación de ejidos al poblado La Luz, Estado de Zacatecas," April 3, 1940, published July 20, 1940, in *Diario Oficial de la Federación,* vol. 121, no. 18, 1st sec., 4–6.

50. Adolfo Ruiz Cortines, "Resolución sobre dotación de tierras al poblado Presa de los Serna, en Calvillo, Ags.," March 6, 1957, published May 17, 1957, in *Diario Oficial de la Federación*, vol. 222, no. 14, 10–12.

51. J. Encarnación Flores to C. Ing. Luis Ortega Douglas, September 7, 1957, AHEA, SGGOB, caja 695, expediente 202.

52. Adolfo de la Serna and others to Sr. Ing. Luis Ortega Douglas, August 28, 1957, AHEA, SGGOB, caja 701, expediente 664. Adolfo, the lead signatory of the letter, was the only one who signed his last name as "de la Serna."

53. Ing. Ricardo Becerríl López to C. Gobernador Constitucional del Estado, October 25, 1957, AHEA, SGGOB, caja 701, expediente 664.

54. Aureliano Guzmán Elías, Rinde informe de comisión, October 17, 1957, AHEA, SGGOB, caja 701, expediente 664.

55. Lic. Carlos Salas Calvillo to CC. Adolfo, Cipriano, Arturo, Jesús y Rogelio de la Serna, November 9, 1957, AHEA, SGGOB, caja 701, expediente 664.

56. J. Encarnación Flores to Señor Ingeniero Luis Ortega Douglas, July 5, 1960, AHEA, SGGOB, caja 741, expediente 160.

57. For the shift to new high-yield maize varieties and a comparative analysis of the Papaloapan and Tepalcatepec River Commissions, see Olsson, *Agrarian Crossings*, 129–90. Olsson notes that there was a key difference in the high-yield maize varieties that the Ávila Camacho and Alemán administrations promoted. The former government promoted "synthetic" varieties that were a cross of varieties that had been inbred for one or two generations; these varieties could produce similar yields if they were planted in consecutive seasons. The Alemán administration embraced "hybrid" varieties that had been inbred for multiple generations; these varieties' yields declined if they were planted in consecutive seasons, which required the purchase of the latest "hybrid" varieties every year. For studies that focus exclusively on the river basin commissions, see David Barkin and Timothy King, *Regional Economic Development: The River Basin Approach in Mexico* (Cambridge: Cambridge University Press, 1970); Calderón Mólgora, "Desarrollo integral en las cuencas del Tepalcatepec y del Balsas"; Thomas T. Poleman, *The Papaloapan Project: Agricultural Development in the Mexican Tropics* (Stanford, CA: Stanford University Press, 1964).

58. Gregorio Cervantes to C. Gobernador Constitucional del Estado, December 25, 1944, AHAGPEG, SEGOB, PD, 1.19, año 1944, expediente 160.

59. Lázaro Cárdenas, "Resolución en el expediente de dotación de ejidos al poblado San Cristóbal de Ayala, Estado de Guanajuato," November 30, 1938, published July 8, 1939, in *Diario Oficial de la Federación*, vol. 115, no. 7, 3rd sec., 7–10.

60. México, Dirección General de Estadística, *Sexto Censo de Población, 1940: Guanajuato*, 129.

61. J. C. Chávez and others to C. D. Adolfo Ruiz Cortines, April 16, 1953, AGN, ARC, caja 301, expediente 404.1/1199.

62. J. C. Chávez to C. Presidente de la República, June 26, 1953, AGN, ARC, caja 301, expediente 404.1/1199.

63. A. L. Rodríguez, "Resolución en el expediente de dotación de tierras al poblado San Antonio, Estado de Jalisco," November 19, 1934, published February 26, 1935, in *Diario Oficial de la Federación*, vol. 88, no. 48, 4–5; Lázaro Cárdenas, "Resolución en el expediente de dotación de tierras al poblado El Gobernador, Estado de Jalisco," July 2, 1935, published August 12, 1935, in *Diario Oficial de la Federación*, vol. 91, no. 37, 616–18; Lázaro Cárdenas, "Resolución en el expediente de dotación de tierras al poblado San Ramón, Estado de Jalisco," August 13, 1935, published September 20, 1935, in *Diario Oficial de la Federación*, vol. 92, no. 16, 277–79; Lázaro Cárdenas, "Resolución en el expediente de dotación de ejidos al poblado La Paz de Ordaz, Estado de Jalisco," November 4, 1936, published December 29, 1936, in *Diario Oficial de la Federación*, vol. 99, no. 40, 1st sec., 6–8; Lázaro Cárdenas, "Resolución en el expediente de dotación de ejidos al poblado Salamea, Estado de Jalisco," November 4, 1936, published December 30, 1936, in *Diario Oficial de la Federación*, vol. 99, no. 41, 2nd sec., 31–32; Lázaro Cárdenas, "Resolución en el expediente de dotación de ejidos al poblado San Francisco y anexas, Estado de Jalisco," November 4, 1936, published January 6, 1937, in *Diario Oficial de la Federación*, vol. 100, no. 4, 11–13; Lázaro Cárdenas, "Resolución en el expediente de dotación de tierras al poblado El Portezuelo, Estado de Jalisco," November 13, 1936, published January 29, 1937, in *Diario Oficial de la Federación*, vol. 100, no. 24, 2nd sec., 9–12; Lázaro Cárdenas, "Resolución en el expediente de dotación de tierras al poblado Loreto Occidente, Estado de Jalisco," April 20, 1938, published June 8, 1938, in *Diario Oficial de la Federación*, vol. 108, no. 25, 6–7.

64. Lázaro Cárdenas, "Resolución en el expediente de ampliación de ejidos al poblado de La Paz de Ordaz, Estado de Jalisco," May 4, 1938, published June 11, 1938, in *Diario Oficial de la Federación*, vol. 108, no. 28, 2nd sec., 15–16.

65. Manuel Ávila Camacho, "Resolución en el expediente de segunda ampliación de ejidos al poblado El Gobernador, Estado de Jalisco," June 25, 1941, published August 1, 1941, in *Diario Oficial de la Federación*, vol. 127, no. 28, 3rd sec., 12–13.

66. Miguel Alemán, "Resolución sobre tercera ampliación de ejido al poblado El Gobernador, en La Barca, Jal.," December 21, 1949, published March 2, 1950, in *Diario Oficial de la Federación*, vol. 179, no. 2, 2nd sec., 15–16.

67. Miguel Alemán, "Resolución sobre ampliación de ejido al poblado Salamea en la [sic] Barca, Jal.," November 9, 1949, published February 3, 1950, in *Diario Oficial de la Federación*, vol. 178, no. 29, 2nd sec., 11–12.

68. Adolfo López Mateos, "Resolución sobre segunda ampliación de ejido al poblado San Antonio, en La Barca, Jal.," October 20, 1964, published January 19, 1965, in *Diario Oficial de la Federación*, vol. 268, no. 15, 15–16.

69. See by México, Dirección General de Estadística: *Sexto Censo de Población, 1940: Jalisco*, 208; *Integración Territorial de los Estados Unidos Mexicanos: Séptimo Censo General de Población, 1950: Estado de Jalisco* (Mexico City, 1952), 18.

70. For Tapia's career and how late nineteenth- and early twentieth-century agrarian conditions in Zacapu influenced his support of land redistribution, see Friedrich, *Agrarian Revolt in a Mexican Village*.

71. Padrón e Historial de Núcleos Agrarios, Registro Agrario Nacional.

72. Padrón e Historial de Núcleos Agrarios, Registro Agrario Nacional. According to the Registro Agrario Nacional's (National Agrarian Registry's) online database, Alemán's administration approved the expansion of Las Canoas's ejido on February 22, 1950, and the official decision was published in the March 21, 1950, issue of the *Diario Oficial de la Federación*. However, I have not been able to find that issue of the newspaper in any archival collection, and it is not available in the newspaper's electronic collection.

73. "Solicitud de los vecinos del poblado Cantabría, en Zacapu, Mich., para la creación de un centro de población agrícola," November 11, 1950, published March 13, 1951, in *Diario Oficial de la Federación*, vol. 185, no. 11, 1st sec., 8; "Solicitud de vecinos radicados en el poblado de Cantabría, en Zacapu, Mich., para la creación de un centro de población agrícola que se denominará Melchor Ocampo," March 18, 1961, published July 20, 1961, in *Diario Oficial de la Federación*, vol. 247, no. 17, 11.

74. See by México, Dirección General de Estadística: *Sexto Censo de Población, 1940: Michoacán*, 130; *VIII Censo General de Población—1960, 8 de Junio de 1960: Estado de Michoacán*, 25.

75. Requests are in AGHPEM, SEGOB, TPS, PB, caja 7, expedientes 9, 10; caja 8, expedientes 11–13, 15; caja 9, expedientes 20, 22; and caja 10, expedientes 16, 18.

76. P. Elías Calles, "Resolución en el expediente de restitución de tierras promovida por vecinos de la Villa de Zacapu de Mier, Estado de Michoacán," October 8, 1925, published October 17, 1925, in *Diario Oficial de la Federación*, vol. 32, no. 39, 674–82; Lázaro Cárdenas, "Resolución en el expediente de ampliación automática de ejidos al poblado Zacapu de Mier, Estado de Michoacán," February 6, 1935, published March 8, 1935, in *Diario Oficial de la Federación*, vol. 89, no. 7, 79–80. The initial grant redistributed 1,600 hectares among 371 ejidatarios; the expansion redistributed 114 hectares among 38 ejidatarios.

77. Mateo Ambrís Constantino to C. Gobernador del Estado, February 27, 1964, AGHPEM, SEGOB, TPS, PB, caja 9, expediente 22, fojas 129–30.

78. Olsson, *Agrarian Crossings*, 171–72.

79. Requests are in AGHPEM, SEGOB, TPS, PB, caja 7, expedientes 8–10; caja 8, expedientes 13–15.

80. José Arroyo R. to C. Lic. Don., Agustín Arriaga Rivera, August 9, 1963, AGHPEM, SEGOB, TPS, PB, caja 7, expediente 9, foja 11.

81. Lázaro Cárdenas, "Resolución en el expediente de dotación de ejidos al poblado Monteleón, Estado de Michoacán," February 3, 1937, published June 11, 1937, in *Diario Oficial de la Federación*, vol. 102, no. 29, 2nd sec., 10–12.

82. Aurelio Vázquez Razo to C. Gobernador Constitucional del Estado de Mich., August 15, 1963, AGHPEM, SEGOB, TPS, PB, caja 7, expediente 10, fojas 148–50; Lázaro Cárdenas, "Resolución en el expediente de dotación de tierras al poblado La Sauceda, Estado de Michoacán," April 30, 1935, published July 4, 1935, in *Diario Oficial de la Federación*, vol. 91, no. 4 42–43.

83. López Mateos, "Resolución sobre segunda ampliación de ejido al poblado San Antonio," 15–16.

CHAPTER FIVE

1. Anonymous to Señor Lic. J. Jesús González Gallo, May 12, 1947, AHEJ, Gobernación, G-1-947, PEN, caja 161, inventario 3527.
2. Benjamin T. Smith, "Building a State on the Cheap: Taxation, Social Movements, and Politics," in Gillingham and Smith, *Dictablanda,* 255–75.
3. María Teresa Fernández Aceves, "Advocate or *Cacica*? Guadalupe Urzúa Flores: Modernizer and Peasant Political Leader in Jalisco," in Gillingham and Smith, *Dictablanda,* 236–54. Urzúa Flores was an active leader in Jalisco's Regional Agrarian Committee and the Confederación Nacional Campesina during the 1930s and 1940s. In 1955, she became the first woman elected to represent Jalisco in the federal Chamber of Deputies. Throughout her career she lobbied and secured funding for public health and education facilities in San Martín de Hidalgo, where she was raised, and she also advocated for increased women's participation in the land redistribution process.
4. El Inspector Comisionado (37) to C. Lic. Eduardo Ampudia, May 22, 1944, AGN, DGIPS, caja 97, expediente 22, fojas 147–50.
5. Lic. Luis Fernández del Campo to C. Gobernador del Estado de Guanajuato, August 15, 1944, AHAGPEG, SEGOB, PD, 1.19, año 1944, expediente 90; Lic. Juan Ignacio Ibáñez to Director Luis Fernández del Campo, August 22, 1944, AHAGPEG, SEGOB, PD, 1.19, año 1944, expediente 90. Puente sent his complaint to President Ávila Camacho on July 28, 1944. I could not find the original in the archive, but a federal Labor Secretariat official, Luis Fernández del Campo, transcribed it in full in his August 15 letter to Guanajuato's governor.
6. Affidavit signed by Luis Moreno Llinas, Ramón Cedeño Rodríguez, and Manuel Hernández, August 9, 1944, AHAGPEG, SEGOB, PD, 1.19, año 1944, expediente 91.
7. Carlos Luna Rodríguez, Zeferino Reyes Padilla, and Ignacio Rodríguez Ramos to C. Gobernador Constitucional del Estado, August 22, 1944, AHAGPEG, SEGOB, PD, 1.19, año 1944, expediente 92.
8. Ernesto Hidalgo to C. Presidente Municipal, August 4, 1944, AHAGPEG, SEGOB, PD, 1.19, año 1944, expediente 67; Lic. Juan Ignacio Ibáñez to C. Presidente Municipal de Romita, August 26, 1944, AHAGPEG, SEGOB, PD, 1.19, año 1944, expediente 92.
9. Lic. Juan Ignacio Ibáñez, Memorandum, September 18, 1944, AHAGPEG, SEGOB, PD, 1.19, año 1944, expediente 92.
10. Lic. Juan Ignacio Ibáñez to C. Presidente Municipal de Dolores Hidalgo, February 14, 1945, AHAGPEG, SEGOB, PD, 1.19, año 1945, expediente 20.
11. Sebastián Balderas and others to C. Secretario del Trabajo y Previsión Social, February 26, 1945, AHAGPEG, SEGOB, PD, 1.19 (14), expediente 2.
12. Domingo Álvarez to Sr. Lic. Don Carlos G. Guzmán, May 24, 1948, AHEJ, GOB/SC, año 1948, caja 12, expediente 50.
13. Domingo Álvarez to C. Lic. J. Jesús González Gallo, June 2, 1948, AHEJ, GOB/SC, año 1948, caja 12, expediente 50.

14. Rosas, *Abrazando el Espíritu*, 19–27.

15. Jesús de Ávila, Jesús Alvarado, and Alfonso Lamas to Manuel Ávila Camacho, April 29, 1946, AGN, MAC, caja 796, expediente 546.6/120-32.

16. México, Dirección General de Estadística, *Sexto Censo de Población, 1940: Resumen General*, 8. For President Ávila Camacho's comments, see Cecilia Greaves L., *Del radicalismo a la unidad nacional: Una visión de la educación en el México contemporáneo (1940–1964)* (Mexico City: El Colegio de México, 2008), 127.

17. Greaves L., *Del radicalismo a la unidad nacional*, 127–35.

18. Prof. Edmundo Gámes [sic] Orozco to C. Prof. Luis de la Fuente, April 3, 1945, AHMZAC, Ayuntamiento II, Alfabetización, caja 1, expediente 3–30-Abril-1945.

19. Prof. Luis de la Fuente to C. Comisario Municipal, San Blas, Zac., April 6, 1945, AHMZAC, Ayuntamiento II, Alfabetización, caja 1, expediente 3–30-Abril-1945; Prof. Luis de la Fuente to C. Comisario Municipal, Miguel Hidalgo, Zac. (antes San Miguel), April 6, 1945, AHMZAC, Ayuntamiento II, Alfabetización, caja 1, expediente 3–30-Abril-1945.

20. Prof. Luis de la Fuente to C. Comisario Municipal, July 3, 1945, AHMZAC, Ayuntamiento II, Alfabetización, caja 1, expediente 2–31-Julio-1945.

21. Prof. Edmundo Gámes [sic] Orozco to CC. Presidentes Municipales de las Juntas de Alfabetización en el Estado, October 3, 1935, AHMZAC, Ayuntamiento II, Alfabetización, caja 1, expediente 5–29-Octubre-1945; Prof. Edmundo Gámes [sic] Orozco to CC. Presidentes Municipales y de las Juntas de Alfabetización en el Edo., November 1, 1945, AHMZAC, Ayuntamiento II, Alfabatización, caja 1, expediente 1–30-Noviembre 1945.

22. Prof. Edmundo Gámes [sic] Orozco to C. Prof. Luis de la Fuente, April 3, 1945, AHMZAC, Ayuntamiento II, Alfabetización, caja 1, expediente 3–30-Abril-1945.

23. Juan Morán Sánchez to C. Magdaleno Robledo, May 13, 1948, AHEA, SGGOB, caja 559, expediente 269.

24. Aquiles Rodríguez Nava and Francisco Contreras to Banco Nacional de Crédito Ejidal, S.A. de C.V., April 24, 1953, AHEA, SGGOB, caja 632, expediente 224.

25. Prisciliano Pérez G. and Antonio Cervantes C. to C. Dip. y Lic. Julio Torres R., March 22, 1945, AGHPEM, SEGOB, TPS, PB, caja 1, expediente 3, foja 174.

26. Blanco, Parra, and Ruiz Medrano, *Guanajuato*, 204–06.

27. Serrano Álvarez, *La batalla del espíritu*, vol. 1, 316.

28. Ing. Roberto Vargas Cienfuegos to Sr. Gobernador Estado, May 23, 1942, AHAGPEG, SEGOB, PD, 1.54 (17), año 1942, expediente 2; Martín Zuloaga V. to Lic. Carlos Herrera Marmolejo, May 25, 1942, AHAGPEG, SEGOB, PD, 1.54 (17), año 1942, expediente 2.

29. Agapito Vázquez to C. Lic. Crescenciano Aguilera, July 10, 1943, AHAGPEG, SEGOB, PD, 1.54 (17), año 1943, expediente 2.

30. Ángela Contreras de Bustamante to C. Presidente de la República, February 2, 1944, AHAGPEG, SEGOB, PD, 1.54 (17), año 1944, expediente 3.

31. Martín Zuloaga Vargas to C. Licenciado Carlos Herrera Marmolejo, June 25, 1942, AHAGPEG, SEGOB, PD, 1.54 (17), año 1942, expediente 6.

32. Higinio Bonilla to C. Lic. José Aguilar y Maya, October 27, 1949, AHAGPEG, SEGOB, PD, 1.58 (16), año 1949, expediente 2.

33. Higinio Bonilla to C. Antonio Ramírez, November 10, 1949, AHAGPEG, SEGOB, PD, 1.58 (16), año 1949, expediente 2.

34. Lic. Francisco Salcedo Casas to C. Gobernador del Estado, January 23, 1950, AHAGPEG, SEGOB, PD, 1.58 (16), año 1950, expediente 1. Salcedo Casas was a federal official, and he transcribed the anonymous complaint that was initially sent to federal authorities.

35. Lic. Francisco Salcedo Casas to C. Gobernador del Estado, AHAGPEG, SEGOB, PD, 1.58 (16), año 1950, expediente 1. The documents detailing the disputes between El Carmen's agraristas and the Furber family are in AHAGPEG, SEGOB, PD, 1.54 (18), año 1937, expediente 5; and AHAGPEG, SEGOB, PD, 1.54 (18), año 1938, expediente 1.

36. Antonio Ramírez M. to C. Secretario Gral. de Gobierno, February 17, 1950, AHAGPEG, SEGOB, PD, 1.58 (16), año 1950, expediente 1; Antonio Ramírez to C. Secretario General de Gobierno, March 4, 1950, AHAGPEG, SEGOB, PD, 1.58 (16), año 1950, expediente 1.

37. Anonymous to C. Adolfo Ruiz Cortines, August 2, 1952, AHAGPEG, SEGOB, PD, 1.59 (17), año 1952, expediente 1; Florentino Oliva to C. Secretario General del Gobierno, September 27, 1952, AHAGPEG, SEGOB, PD, 1.59 (17), año 1952, expediente 1.

38. Manuel Ríos Thivol to C. Lic. Alejandro Ortega Romero, June 21, 1952, AGN, DGIPS, caja 84, expediente 2, fojas 326–329.

39. Anonymous to Ciudadano Adolfo Ruiz Cortines, August 13, 1952, AHAGPEG, SEGOB, PD, 1.59 (17), año 1952, expediente 1.

40. Florentino Oliva to C. Secretario General de Gobierno, September 27, 1952, AHAGPEG, SEGOB, PD, 1.59 (17), año 1952, expediente 1.

41. Manuel Ríos Thivol to C. Lic. Alejandro Ortega Romero, June 21, 1952, AGN, DGIPS, caja 84, expediente 2, fojas 326–329.

42. Florentino Oliva to Ciudadano Delegados Municipales, April 13, 1953, AHMI, Gobierno, Braceros, caja 38.

43. Florentino Oliva, "A Los Aspirantes a Braceros," February 29, 1952, AHMI, Gobierno, Braceros, caja 38.

44. Enrique Aranda Jr. to Sr. Florentino Oliva, April 5, 1952, AHMI, Gobierno, Braceros, caja 38; José Chaurand Concha to C. Presidente Municipal, April 5, 1952, AHMI, Gobierno, Braceros, caja 38; Alfonso Morales Herrera to Presidente Municipal Florentino Oliva, April 4, 1952, AHMI, Gobierno, Braceros, caja 38.

45. Florentino Oliva to C. Lic. Enrique Mendoza Ortiz, February 8, 1954, AHAGPEG, SEGOB, PD, 1.54 "B,", año 1954, expediente 4.

46. J. Cruz Vargas, Cecilio Reyes, and Jaime Rodríguez to C. Secretario de Gobierno, February 15, 1955, AHAGPEG, SEGOB, PD, 1.50 (17), año 1955, expediente 1.

47. J. Jesús Cervantes Reynoso to C. Secretario General del Gobierno, March 7, 1955, AHAGPEG, SEGOB, PD, 1.50 (17), año 1955, expediente 1.

48. Acta Constitutiva de la "Alianza de Braceros Nacionales de México, en los Estados Unidos de Norteamérica," October 2, 1943, AGN, MAC, caja 446, expediente 437.1/340.

49. José Hernández S. to Sr. Presidente de la República, October 18, 1943, AGN, MAC, caja 446, expediente 437.1/340.

50. José Hernández Serrano to C. Gobernador, June 14, 1945, AHAGPEG, SEGOB, PD, 1.19 (2), año 1945, expediente 3; José Hernández Serrano and Reynaldo Aguirre Miranda to Ciudadano General de División Manuel Ávila Camacho, July 2, 1945, AGN, MAC, caja 793, expediente 546.6/120. Mireya Loza notes that the Alianza shifted its focus to lobbying for improved wages and working conditions after World War II. In 1951, the Alianza's secretary general, Hernández Serrano, and the Mexican American labor organizer Ernesto Galarza launched an attempt to forge a partnership between the Alianza and US-based farmworkers' unions, but the initiative faltered due to the US growers' hostility and the Alianza's lack of official support in Mexico. For this transnational labor organizing effort, see Loza, *Defiant Braceros*, 97–133.

51. Lic Juan Ignacio Ibáñez to C. Presidente Municipal de Tarimoro, June 18, 1945, AHAGPEG, SEGOB, PD, 1.19 (37), año 1945, expediente 1.

52. José Hernández Serrano to Secretario General del Comité Regional Pro-Braceros del Pueblo de Tarimoro, Gto., July 21, 1945, AHAGPEG, SEGOB, PD, 1.19 (37), año 1945, expediente 1.

53. Ernesto Santa Cruz García to Ciudadano Secretario General de la Alianza de Braceros Nacionales de México en los Estados Unidos de Norteamérica, July 24, 1945, AHAGPEG, SEGOB, PD, 1.19 (37), año 1945, expediente 1.

54. José Hernández Serrano to C. Presidente Municipal de Tarimoro, July 28, 1945, AHAGPEG, SEGOB, PD, 1.19 (37), año 1945, expediente 1.

55. Ernesto Santa Cruz García to Ciudadano Srio. General de Alianza de Braceros Nacionales de México en los Estados Unidos de Norteamérica, August 15, 1945, AHAGPEG, SEGOB, PD, 1.19 (37), año 1945, expediente 2.

56. José Hernández Serrano to C. Gobernador de Guanajuato, August 17, 1945, AHAGPEG, SEGOB, PD, 1.19 (37), año 1945, expediente 2.

57. Loza, *Defiant Braceros,* 127–28.

58. Rodolfo Mendoza D. to C. Ing. Luis Ortega Douglas, April 8, 1960, AHEA, SGGOB, caja 741, expediente 160.

59. Lic. Carlos Salas Calvillo to C. Presidente Municipal, April 12, 1960, AHEA, SGGOB, caja 741, expediente 160; Gonzalo de la Torre D. to C. Lic. Carlos Salas Calvillo, April 16, 1960, AHEA, SGGOB, caja 741, expediente 160.

60. Octavio Briseño and others to C. Presidente de la República, September 28, 1959, AGN, ALM, caja 718, expediente 546.6/276.

61. Ernesto Robles and others to Sr. Presidente Adolfo López Mateos, May 18, 1960, AGN, ALM, caja 716, expediente 546.6/76.

62. Rafael Velderrain to C. Ernesto Robles, June 30, 1960, AGN, ALM, caja 716, expediente 546.6/76.

63. Amador Magaña V. and others to C. Gobernador Constitucional del Estado, May 7, 1964, AGHPEM, SEGOB, TPS, PB, caja 10, expediente 16, foja 141.

64. Leopoldo Gómez M., "$1,000.00 por 'Bracero' en Puruándiro," *El Informador,* September 23, 1964, 3–4.

65. José Díaz Delgado, J. Guadalupe Molina Villacaña, Ubaldo Lara López, and Francisco Ceballos Flores to C. Lic. Agustín Arriag Rivera, October 5, 1964, AGHPEM, Puruándiro, caja 3, expediente 1; José Vargas Rivera to C. Lic. Agustín Arriaga Rivera, November 12, 1964, AGHPEM, Puruándiro, caja 3, expediente 1.

66. Rosas, *Abrazando el Espíritu,* 23–27. Rosas shows that in addition to attending town hall meetings, women in bracero-sending communities like San Martín de Hidalgo and Acámbaro, Guanajuato, formed support networks to alleviate the emotional strain of being separated from their husbands and other male relatives for months at a time. For these support networks, see Rosas, *Abrazando el Espíritu,* 147–84.

67. Juana Dimas Sosa Vda. de Téllez to C. Lic. Agustín Arriaga R., April 15, 1964, AGHPEM, SEGOB, TPS, PB, caja 10, expediente 16, foja 71.

68. Juana Dimas Sosa Vda. de Téllez to C. Gobernador, April 29, 1964, AGHPEM, SEGOB, TPS, PB, caja 10, expediente 16, fojas 79–80.

69. Ma. Guadalupe Gómez to C. Oficial Mayor de Gobierno, June 6, 1964, AGHPEM, SEGOB, TPS, PB, caja 10, expediente 18, foja 107.

70. FitzGerald, *A Nation of Emigrants,* 51–52.

71. Abundio Medina Piñón to C. Profr. Manuel Chávez Campos, October 16, 1963, AGHPEM, SEGOB, TPS, PB, caja 7, expediente 10, foja 169.

72. Profr. Manuel López Pérez to Ciudadano Presidente Municipal, July 12, 1963, AGHPEM, SEGOB, TPS, PB, caja 8, expediente 12, foja 14.

73. Manuel Cárdenas Mejorada to Ciudadano Secretario General de Gobierno, May 8, 1964, AGHPEM, SEGOB, TPS, PB, caja 10, expediente 18, fojas 124–126.

74. Manuel Cárdenas Mejorada to Ciudadano Secretario General de Gobierno, May 8, 1964, AGHPEM, SEGOB, TPS, PB, caja 10, expediente 18, fojas 124–126.

75. Fernández Aceves, "Advocate or *Cacica*?," 236–54.

76. These requests are in AGHPEM, SEGOB, TPS, PB, caja 4, expediente 6; caja 7, expedientes 8–10; caja 8, expedientes 11–15; caja 9, expedientes 20–22; and caja 10, expedientes 16–19.

77. Delfino Loya to C. Presidente, February 21, 1944, AGN, MAC, caja 793, expediente 546.6/120; J. Jesús Ávila García to Ciudadano Gobernador del Estado, August 2, 1945, AGHPEM, SEGOB, TPS, PB, caja 1, expediente 3, foja 360; and Antonio Leyva to C. Presidente, April 10, 1948, AGN, MAV, caja 593, expediente 546.6/120-15.

78. Dr. Humberto Cerda Pimentel to C. Secretario General de Gobierno, February 10, 1962, AGHPEM, SEGOB, TPS, PB, caja 9, expediente 21, foja 85; Juan Chávez Magaña, Lista de Aspirantes a Braceros, February 10, 1962, AGHPEM, SEGOB, TPS, PB, caja 9, expediente 21, fojas 86–87. Chávez Magaña was Tangancícuaro's comisariado ejidal, and he certified that the aspiring braceros were not ejidatarios.

79. Carlos Tamayo Valladolid to Ciudadano Gobernador Constitucional del Estado, August 18, 1963, AGHPEM, SEGOB, TPS, PB, caja 7, expediente 9, foja 25; Carlos Tamayo Valladolid to C. Gobernador del Estado, August 12, 1963, AGHPEM, SEGOB, TPS, PB, caja 8, expediente 13, foja 176; Carlos Tamayo Valladolid to Cidudadano Gobernador Constitucional del Estado, August 19, 1963, AGHPEM, SEGOB, TPS, PB, caja 8, expediente 14, fojas 12–13; and Carlos Tamayo Valladolid to Ciudadano Gobernador Constitucional del Estado, August 14, 1963, AGHPEM, SEGOB, TPS, PB, caja 8, expediente 14, foja 101.

80. Roberto Ángeles to C. Lic. D. David Franco Rodríguez, March 16, 1962, AGHPEM, SEGOB, TPS, PB, caja 9, expediente 22, foja 15.

81. David López Manríquez to Ciudadano Secretario General de Gobierno, May 4, 1963, AGHPEM, SEGOB, TPS, PB, caja 7, expediente 9, foja 240.

82. J. Jesús Aguilar Naranjo to Oficial Mayor Gobierno, June 28, 1963, AGHPEM, SEGOB, TPS, PB, caja 8, expediente 11, foja 104.

83. Benjamín García Guzmán to C. Profr. Leodegario López Ramírez, August 16, 1963, AGHPEM, SEGOB, TPS, PB, caja 8, expediente 14, foja 130.

84. These requests are in AGHPEM, SEGOB, TPS, PB, caja 4, expediente 6; caja 7, expedientes 8–10; caja 8, expedientes 11–15; caja 9, expedientes 20–22; caja 10, expedientes 16–19; and AGN, ALM, caja 716, expediente 546.6/36; caja 717, expediente 546.6/228; caja 718, expediente 546.6/344.

85. These requests are in AGHPEM, SEGOB, TPS, PB, caja 1, expedientes 1, 3, and 4; AGN, MAC, caja 793, expediente 546.6/120; caja 794, expediente 546.6/120-15; and AGN, ARC, caja 881, expediente 546.4/28; caja 892, expediente 548.1/107; caja 896, expediente 548.1/362; caja 897, expediente 548.1/504; caja 899, expedientes 548.1/655, 548.1/657, and 548.1/670.

86. Cornelio Maldonado Pulido to Ciudadano Profesor Manuel López Pérez, May 20, 1963, AGHPEM, SEGOB, TPS, PB, caja 7, expediente 9, foja 76.

87. Carlos Esqueda to Ciudadano Gobernador Constitucional del Estado, August 28, 1963, AGHPEM, SEGOB, TPS, PB, caja 8, expediente 14, foja 126.

88. Ramón Vargas Mondragón to C. Lic. José L. Flores, February 21, 1964, AGHPEM, SEGOB, TPS, PB, caja 9, expediente 20, foja 169.

89. Luis Aboites Aguilar, *Excepciones y privilegios: Modernización tributaria y centralización en México, 1922-1972* (Mexico City: El Colegio de México, Centro de Estudios Históricos, 2003), 39, 191–224, 227–59.

90. Smith, "Building a State on the Cheap," 262–68.

91. Ing. Emilio Díaz Carreón to C. Comisariado Ejidal de San Nicolás, December 19, 1962, AGHPEM, Puruándiro, caja 1, expediente 11.

92. J.J. Múgica and José López to C. Lic. Agustín Arriaga Rivera, May 10, 1964, AGHPEM, SEGOB, TPS, PB, caja 10, expediente 16, foja 147.

93. María Pimentel to Sr. Agustín Arriaga Rivera, May 15, 1964, AGHPEM, SEGOB, TPS, PB, caja 10, expediente 19, foja 58.

94. Smith, "Building a State on the Cheap," 268.

95. Eduardo Chaparro Plata to Ciudadano Gobernador Constitucional del Estado, June 18, 1957, AGHPEM, SEGOB, TPS, PB, caja 3, expediente sin número,

foja 150; Eduardo Chaparro Plata, Con el objeto de evitar malas interpretaciones propaladas oficiosamente, May 28, 1957, AGHPEM, SEGOB, TPS, PB, caja 3, expediente sin número, foja 151.

96. Juan Hernández H. and others to C. Gobernador Constitucional Substituto del Estado, undated, marked as received by the state government on March 25, 1954, AHEA, SGGOB, caja 649, expediente 202.

97. Francisco Hernández Mota to C. Don Adolfo Ruiz Cortines, August 29, 1957, AGN, ARC, caja 616, expediente 508.1/372.

98. Summary of a March 13, 1962, letter from Marcelino Hernández Díaz to an unnamed federal official, March 16, 1962, AGN, ALM, caja 718, expediente 546.6/296.

99. Anonymous to C. Don Adolfo López Mateos, September 30, 1960, AGN, ALM, caja 720, expediente 546.6/553.

100. Juan Hernández H. and others to C. Gobernador Constitucional Substituto del Estado, undated, marked as received by the state government on March 25, 1954, AHEA, SGGOB, caja 649, expediente 202.

101. Ing. Jorge L. Tamayo to Sr. Ruiz Silva, April 7, 1953, AHEA, SGGOB, caja 613, expediente 120; Salvador Guzmán to C.D. Alfonso Bernal S., April 10, 1953, AHEA, SGGOB, caja 613, expediente 120; Ildefonso Eguía Cortés to Gobierno del Estado de Aguascalientes, April 15, 1953, AHEA, SGGOB, caja 613, expediente 120; Enrique Macías de Lara to C. Roberto Serna, July 6, 1957, AHEA, SGGOB, caja 700, expediente 564.

102. Francisco Hernández Mota to C. Don Adolfo Ruiz Cortines, August 29, 1957, AGN, ARC, caja 616, expediente 508.1/372.

103. Summary of a March 13, 1962, letter from Marcelino Hernández Díaz to an unnamed federal official, March 16, 1962, AGN, ALM, caja 718, expediente 546.6/296.

104. Anonymous to C. Don Adolfo López Mateos, September 30, 1960, AGN, ALM, caja 720, expediente 546.6/553.

105. Ezequiel Víctor R., Luis Oseguera H., and Mariano Martínez C. to C. Lic. Agustín Arriaga Rivera, May 23, 1963, AGHPEM, SEGOB, TPS, PB, caja 8, expediente 11, fojas 26–27; Lic. José L. Flores to Ciudadano Presidente Municipal, June 22, 1963, AGHPEM, SEGOB, TPS, PB, caja 8, expediente 11, foja 24. The copy of the original letter stored in the archive is incomplete. Flores's June 22 letter is a complete transcription of the original May 23 letter.

CONCLUSION

1. Craig, *The Bracero Program,* 150–97; Flores, *Grounds for Dreaming,* 75–134; Flores, "A Town Full of Dead Mexicans"; Ronald L. Mize, "The State Management of Guest Workers: The Decline of the Bracero Program, The Rise of Temporary Worker Visas," in *A Nation of Immigrants Reconsidered: US Society in an Age of Restriction,* ed. Maddalena Marinari, Madeline Y. Hsu, and María Cristina García

(Urbana: University of Illinois Press, 2019), 135–36; Ngai, *Impossible Subjects*, 158–66. Farmworkers' unions that represented Mexican Americans had opposed the Bracero Program since its inception because they argued that employers used braceros to depress the wages of US-born workers and break strikes. Organized labor's opposition returned to the spotlight during the program's later years after investigative journalists cast new light on employer abuses of braceros. These exposés, as well as incidents like a September 1963 automobile accident in California's Salinas Valley that led to the death of thirty-one braceros, spurred civil rights organizations to denounce the Bracero Program.

2. David FitzGerald and David Cook-Martín, "The Geopolitical Origins of the 1965 Immigration Act," in Marinari, Hsu, and García, *A Nation of Immigrants Reconsidered*, 92–95; Ngai, *Impossible Subjects*, 254–58; Kunal M. Parker, *Making Foreigners: Immigration and Citizenship Law in America, 1600–2000* (New York: Cambridge University Press, 2015), 206–8. The 1965 Immigration and Nationality Act's hemispheric entry quotas replaced the national-origin entry quotas that restricted immigration from European nations with significant Catholic and Jewish populations, as well as Asian nations. The 1965 legislation allowed for 170,000 annual entries from the eastern hemisphere (defined as Africa, Asia, and Europe) and capped the number of entry visas that could be allotted to any individual eastern hemisphere nation at 20,000 per year. Because legislators simultaneously believed that quotas needed to be applied fairly to both hemispheres and that demographic expansion in Latin America would lead to unchecked migration from that region to the United States, an annual entry quota of 120,000 was applied to the western hemisphere (defined as North America, Central America, South America, and the Caribbean). Although the cap of 20,000 visas per nation did not apply to the western hemisphere when the 1965 Immigration and Nationality Act first became law, the hemispheric quota marked the first time that a fixed ceiling had been placed on the number of people who could migrate from Mexico to the United States. In 1976, Congress amended the act so that the 20,000 per nation maximum was also applied to the western hemisphere.

3. The H2 visa category was created by the 1952 McCarran-Walter Act, and it was initially designed to replace a World War II–era bilateral US-British initiative that allowed seasonal farmworkers from Caribbean colonies like the Bahamas and Jamaica to work in southeastern states like Florida and Georgia. For the development of the H2 visa category, see Hahamovitch, *No Man's Land*, 117–20; Mize, "The State Management of Guest Workers," 124–30. For how Georgia farm owners began using H2 visas to hire Mexican workers during the decades following the Bracero Program's termination, see Weise, *Corazón de Dixie*, 120–78.

4. Hahamovitch, *No Man's Land*, 55.

5. Jennifer A. Miller, *Turkish Guest Workers in Germany: Hidden Lives and Contested Borders, 1960s to 1980s* (Toronto: University of Toronto Press, 2018), 31–56.

6. For Mexico's late twentieth-century economic crisis and liberalizing macroeconomic reforms, see Sarah Babb, *Managing Mexico: Economists from Nationalism to Neoliberalism* (Princeton, NJ: Princeton University Press, 2001), 137–98; Jorge G.

Castañeda, *The Mexican Shock: Its Meaning for the United States* (New York: New Press, 1995); Stephen Haber, Herbert S. Klein, Noel Maurer, and Kevin J. Middlebrok, *Mexico since 1980* (New York: Cambridge University Press, 2008); Judith Adler Hellman, *Mexican Lives* (New York: New Press, 1995); Judith Adler Hellman, *Mexico in Crisis* (New York: Holmes and Meier, 1983); Louise E. Walker, *Waking from the Dream: Mexico's Middle Class after 1968* (Stanford, CA: Stanford University Press, 2013); Heather L. Williams, *Social Movements and Economic Transition: Markets and Distributive Conflict in Mexico* (New York: Cambridge University Press, 2001). For how transnational social networks created during the years of the Bracero Program, the economic crises of the post-Bracero Program years, and economic liberalization influenced migration patterns, see Massey et al., *Return to Aztlan*, 44–79, 139–71; Massey, Durand, and Malone, *Beyond Smoke and Mirrors*, 18–21, 41–42, 74–83.

7. Campbell Gibson and Kay Jung, "Historical Census Statistics on the Foreign-Born Population of the United States" (Washington, DC: US Census Bureau, 2006), 30. For the state of origin of post–Bracero Program Mexican immigrants, see survey figures cited in Durand, Massey, and Zenteno, "Mexican Immigration to the United States," 110–12. The low figure of 39 percent comes from survey data collected by the Mexican government from 1991 to 1992; the high figure of 51 percent comes from survey data collected by the Mexican government from 1978 to 1979. A 1984 survey administered by the Mexican government indicated that 44 percent of Mexican immigrants were from the principal bracero-sending states.

8. For analyses of post–Bracero Program undocumented migration patterns and the lived experiences of undocumented immigrants and their families, see Durand and Massey, *Crossing the Border;* Manuel García y Griego and Mónica Verea Campos, eds., *México y Estados Unidos frente a la migración de los indocumentados* (Mexico City: Coordinación de Humanidades; Porrúa, 1988); Richard C. Jones, ed., *Patterns of Undocumented Migration: Mexico and the United States* (Totowa, NJ: Rowman and Allanheld, 1984); Massey, Durand, and Malone, *Beyond Smoke and Mirrors;* Douglas S. Massey and Audrey Singer, "New Estimates of Undocumented Mexican Migration and the Probability of Apprehension," *Demography* 32, no. 2 (1995): 203–13; Ana Raquel Minian, *Undocumented Lives: The Untold Story of Mexican Migration* (Cambridge, MA: Harvard University Press, 2018); Audrey Singer and Douglas S. Massey, "The Social Process of Undocumented Border Crossing among Mexican Migrants," *International Migration Review* 32, no. 3 (1998): 561–92. For the escalation of punitive immigration enforcement policies during the late twentieth and early twenty-first centuries, see Goodman, *The Deportation Machine*, 169–83; Douglas S. Massey, "What Were the Paradoxical Consequences of Militarizing the Border with Mexico?," in *The Trump Paradox: Migration, Trade, and Racial Politics in US-Mexico Integration,* ed. Raúl Hinojosa-Ojeda and Edward Telles (Oakland: University of California Press, 2021), 32–46; Massey, Durand, and Malone, *Beyond Smoke and Mirrors,* 93–98, 105–12. The Border Patrol launched blockades in El Paso and San Diego in 1993 and 1994, respectively. Among the late twentieth-century laws that aimed to restrict undocumented migration were the

1986 Immigration Reform and Control Act—which increased the Border Patrol's budget allocation and enacted civil penalties for employers who knowingly hired undocumented workers—the 1996 Illegal Immigration Reform and Immigrant Responsibility Act—which authorized the hiring of 1,000 new Border Patrol agents and the construction of new fencing on the border, increased the number of felony offenses that would result in mandatory detention and deportation, mandated multiyear reentry bans for undocumented immigrants who were apprehended more than once, and allowed state and local law enforcement officers to act as immigration enforcement agents in cooperation with federal personnel—and the 1996 Personal Responsibility and Work Opportunity Reconciliation Act, which declared undocumented immigrants ineligible for federal social benefits. In the early twenty-first century, the 2006 Secure Fences Act authorized the construction of 700 miles of fencing on the border, as well as the installation of electronic surveillance equipment, and the Border Patrol's budget increased 167 percent between 2000 and 2010.

9. Massey and Singer, "New Estimates of Undocumented Mexican Migration and the Probability of Apprehension," 209–11.

10. For the passage of the Immigration Reform and Control Act, see Durand, Massey, and Zenteno, "Mexican Immigration to the United States," 108–12; Massey, Durand, and Malone, *Beyond Smoke and Mirrors*, 47–50; Minian, *Undocumented Lives*, 183–207. For INS estimates regarding the number of undocumented Mexican immigrants living in the United States in 2000, see Office of Policy and Planning, US Immigration and Naturalization Service, "Estimates of the Unauthorized Immigrant Population Residing in the United States," 9.

11. Massey, "What Were the Paradoxical Consequences of Militarizing the Border with Mexico?," 44; René Zenteno and Roberto Suro, "Recessions versus Removals: Which Finished Mexican Unauthorized Migration?," in Hinojosa-Ojeda and Telles, *The Trump Paradox*, 69–70.

12. All figures are from Zenteno and Suro, "Recessions versus Removals," 65–67.

13. César Silva Rojas, "Braceros: Echeverría buscará con los E.U. otro convenio," *La Prensa*, May 16, 1972, 2.

14. Alberto Cañas G., "Manifesto Echeverría: Firmar un Compromiso Sería Reconocer que la Inmigración de Braceros es Necesaria," *Ovaciones*, October 23, 1974, 3.

15. Alejandro Iñigo, "El Bracerismo, por Falta de Agua y Tierra, Dijo," *Excélsior*, October 23, 1974, 1; Julio Pomar, "México no Aceptará una Cuota Sobre Braceros: LE," *El Día*, October 23, 1974, 1.

16. For Echeverría's economic policies, including how they influenced Mexican foreign relations during his presidency, see A. S. Dillingham, "Mexico's Turn Toward the Third World: Rural Development under President Luis Echeverría," in *México Beyond 1968: Revolutionaries, Radicals, and Repression during the Global Sixties and Subversive Seventies*, ed. Jaime M. Pensado and Enrique C. Ochoa (Tucson: University of Arizona Press, 2018), 113–32; Gabriela Soto Laveaga, *Jungle Laboratories: Mexican Peasants, National Projects, and the Making of the Pill* (Durham, NC: Duke University Press, 2009), 113–50; Christy Thornton, *Revolution in*

Development: Mexico and the Governance of the Global Economy (Oakland: University of California Press, 2021), 166–89.

17. Minian, *Undocumented Lives,* 38–39, 41.

18. For a summary and analysis of Fox's campaign statements and the 2001 negotiations, see Délano, *Mexico and Its Diaspora in the United States,* 165–81. Fox made his declarations regarding a negotiation deadline one week before the September 11, 2001, terrorist attacks against the United States. Délano acknowledges that US foreign policy was reoriented after the attacks, but she also notes that Bush administration officials began expressing reservations about the negotiations as soon as Fox made his statements.

19. For Trump's immigration policies and rhetoric, see Raúl Hinojosa-Ojeda and Edward Telles, "How Do We Explain Trump's Paradoxical Yet Electorally Successful Use of a False US-Mexico Narrative?," in Hinojosa-Ojeda and Telles, *The Trump Paradox,* 15–31; David Montejano, "What Is the Historical and Political Context for Trump's Nativist Appeal?," in Hinojosa-Ojeda and Telles, *The Trump Paradox,* 191–203.

20. For Central American migration to the United States, see Sarah Blanchard, Erin R. Hamilton, Néstor Rodríguez, and Hirotoshi Yoshioka, "Shifting Trends in Central American Migration: A Demographic Examination of Increasing Honduran-U.S. Immigration and Deportation," *Latin Americanist* 55, no. 4 (2011): 61–84; María Cristina García, "Central American Migration and the Shaping of Refugee Policy," in *Migrants and Migration in Modern North America: Cross-Border Lives, Labor Markets, and Politics,* ed. Dirk Hoerder and Nora Faires (Durham, NC: Duke University Press, 2011), 347–63; Susanne Jonas and Néstor Rodríguez, *Guatemala-U.S. Migration: Transforming Regions* (Austin: University of Texas Press, 2014); Cecilia Menjívar, *Fragmented Ties: Salvadoran Immigrant Networks in America* (Berkeley: University of California Press, 2000).

21. For López Obrador's February 2021 visit to Zacatecas and his comments there, see Gerardo Romo, "AMLO propondrá a Biden una nueva versión del Programa Bracero," *Proceso,* February 27, 2021, www.proceso.com.mx/nacional/2021/2/27/amlo-propondra-biden-una-nueva-version-del-programa-bracero-259164.html.

22. Gearan et al., "Biden Meets with Mexican President amid Growing Pressure on Immigration."

BIBLIOGRAPHY

ARCHIVES AND LIBRARIES

Archivo General e Histórico del Poder Ejecutivo de Michoacán, Morelia
    Fondo Secretaría de Gobierno
        Sección Trabajo y Previsión Social
            Serie Programa Braceros
    Serie Churintzio
    Serie Coeneo
    Serie Puruándiro
    Serie Uruapan
Archivo General de la Nación, Mexico City
    Fondo Adolfo López Mateos
    Fondo Adolfo Ruiz Cortines
    Fondo Dirección General de Investigaciones Políticas y Sociales
    Fondo Lázaro Cárdenas del Río
    Fondo Manuel Ávila Camacho
    Fondo Miguel Alemán Valdés
    Fondo Secretaría de Educación Pública
Archivo Histórico del Archivo General del Poder Ejecutivo de Guanajuato, Guanajuato City
    Fondo Secretaría de Gobierno
        Sección Municipios
            Serie C-1
        Sección Primer Departamento
            Serie 1.03
            Serie 1.19
            Serie 1.19 (2)
            Serie 1.19 (14)
            Serie 1.19 (24)

        Serie 1.19 (37)
        Serie 1.19 (40)
        Serie 1.21.03
        Serie 1.50 (17)
        Serie 1.54 (17)
        Serie 1.54 (18)
        Serie 1.54 (23)
        Serie 1.54 (24)
        Serie 1.54 (25)
        Serie 1.54 "B"
        Serie 1.58 (16)
        Serie 1.59 (17)
        Serie 1.59 (23)
        Serie 1.59 (25)
Archivo Histórico del Estado de Aguascalientes, Aguascalientes City
    Fondo Secretaría General de Gobierno
Archivo Histórico del Estado de Jalisco, Guadalajara
    Fondo Agricultura y Ganadería
        Clasificación AG-6-921
            Serie Tierras
    Fondo Gobernación
        Clasificación G-1-947
            Serie Política Estatal y Nacional
        Clasificación G-2-927
            Serie Guerra
    Fondo Gobernación sin Clasificar
    Fondo Trabajo
        Clasificación T-3-396
            Serie Movimientos Obreros
Archivo Histórico del Estado de Querétaro, Santiago de Querétaro
    Fondo Poder Ejecutivo
        Sección Cronológica
Archivo Histórico Municipal de Irapuato, Irapuato
    Sección Gobierno
        Serie Braceros
Archivo Histórico del Municipio de Zacatecas, Zacatecas City
    Fondo Ayuntamiento II
        Serie Alfabetización
Archivo Municipal e Histórico de Tepatitlán de Morelos, Tepatitlán de Morelos
Bancroft Library, University of California, Berkeley
Nettie Lee Benson Latin American Collection, University of Texas at Austin

PERIODICALS

El Día, Mexico City
Diario Oficial de la Federación, Mexico City
Excélsior, Mexico City
El Informador, Morelia
Los Angeles Times, Los Angeles
New York Times, New York City
Ovaciones, Mexico City
La Prensa, Mexico City
Proceso, Mexico City
El Universal, Mexico City
Washington Post, Washington, DC

PUBLISHED PRIMARY SOURCES

Estadísticas históricas de México, vol. 1, 4th ed. Aguascalientes: INEGI, Instituto Nacional de Estadística, Geografía e Informática, 1999.
"Informe que rindió el C. Lic. Nicéforo Guerrero, el 15 de septiembre de 1947." In *Guanajuato en la voz de sus gobernadores: Compilación de Informes de Gobierno, 1917–1991,* vol. 1, 693–744. Guanajuato: Gobierno del Estado de Guanajuato, 1991.
"II Informe de Gobierno del Presidente Constitucional de los Estados Unidos Mexicanos, Adolfo Ruiz Cortines, 1º de Septiembre de 1954." In *Informes Presidenciales: Adolfo Ruiz Cortines,* 40–80. Mexico City: Dirección de Servicios de Investigación y Análisis, Cámara de Diputados, 2006.
Lázaro Salinas, José. *La emigración de braceros: Visión objetiva de un problema mexicano.* Mexico City, 1955.
Madrazo, Carlos A. "La verdad en el 'caso' de los braceros: Origen de esta injusticia y nombre de los verdaderos responsables." In *Braceros: Las miradas mexicana y estadounidense: Antología (1945–1964),* edited by Jorge Durand, 55–84. Mexico City: Senado de la República, LX Legislatura, Comisión de Biblioteca y Asuntos Editoriales; Miguel Ángel Porrúa; Zacatecas: Universidad Autónoma de Zacatecas, 2007.
México, Dirección General de Estadística. *VIII Censo General de Población—1960, 8 de Junio de 1960: Estado de Aguascalientes.* Mexico City, 1963.
———. *VIII Censo General de Población—1960, 8 de Junio de 1960: Estado de Guanajuato.* Mexico City, 1963.
———. *VIII Censo General de Población—1960, 8 de Junio de 1960: Estado de Jalisco.* Mexico City, 1963.
———. *VIII Censo General de Población—1960, 8 de Junio de 1960: Estado de Michoacán.* Mexico City, 1963.

———. *VIII Censo General de Población—1960, 8 de Junio de 1960: Estado de Zacatecas.* Mexico City, 1963.
———. *VIII Censo General de Población—1960, 8 de Junio de 1960: Resumen General.* Mexico City, 1962.
———. *Integración Territorial de los Estados Unidos Mexicanos: Séptimo Censo General de Población, 1950: Estado de Jalisco.* Mexico City, 1952.
———. *Primer Censo Agrícola-Ganadero, 1930: Estado de Guanajuato.* Mexico City: DAAP, 1937.
———. *Primer Censo Agrícola-Ganadero, 1930: Estado de Jalisco.* Mexico City: DAAP, 1938.
———. *Primer Censo Agrícola-Ganadero, 1930: Estado de Michoacán.* Mexico City: DAAP, 1937.
———. *Segundo Censo Agrícola Ganadero de los Estados Unidos Mexicanos, 1940: Resumen General.* Mexico City, 1951.
———. *Segundo Censo Ejidal de los Estados Unidos Mexicanos, 1940: Resumen General.* Mexico City, 1949.
———. *Sexto Censo de Población, 1940: Aguascalientes; Baja California Territorios Norte y Sur.* Mexico City, 1943.
———. *Sexto Censo de Población, 1940: Guanajuato.* Mexico City, 1943.
———. *Sexto Censo de Población, 1940: Jalisco.* Mexico City, 1943.
———. *Sexto Censo de Población, 1940: Michoacán.* Mexico City, 1943.
———. *Sexto Censo de Población, 1940: Resumen General.* Mexico City, 1943.
———. *Sexto Censo de Población, 1940: Zacatecas.* Mexico City, 1943.
México, Secretaría de Relaciones Exteriores. *Memoria de la Secretaría de Relaciones Exteriores 1° de enero a 31 de diciembre de 1956: Presentada al H. Congreso de la Unión por el C. Lic. Luis Padilla Nervo, secretario del ramo.* Mexico City: Talleres Gráficos de la Nación, 1957.
Office of Policy and Planning, US Immigration and Naturalization Service. "Estimates of the Unauthorized Immigrant Population Residing in the United States: 1990 to 2000." www.dhs.gov/xlibrary/assets/statistics/publications/Ill_Report_1211.pdf.
Secretaría del Trabajo y Previsión Social. "Los braceros." In *Braceros: Las miradas mexicana y estadounidense: Antología (1945–1964)*, edited by Jorge Durand, 155–230. Mexico City: Senado de la República, LX Legislatura, Comisión de Biblioteca y Asuntos Editoriales; Miguel Ángel Porrúa; Zacatecas: Universidad Autónoma de Zacatecas, 2007.

SECONDARY SOURCES

Aboites Aguilar, Luis. *Excepciones y privilegios: Modernización tributaria y centralización en México, 1922–1972.* Mexico City: El Colegio de México, Centro de Estudios Históricos, 2003.
Alanís Enciso, Fernando Saúl. *El primer programa bracero y el gobierno de México, 1917–1918.* San Luis Potosí: El Colegio de San Luis, 1999.

———. "The Repatriation of Mexicans from the United States and Mexican Nationalism, 1929–1940." In *Beyond la Frontera: The History of Mexico-U.S. Migration,* edited by Mark Overmyer-Velázquez, 51–78. New York: Oxford University Press, 2011.

———. *They Should Stay There: The Story of Mexican Migration and Repatriation during the Great Depression.* Translated by Russ Davidson. Chapel Hill: University of North Carolina Press, 2017.

Alvarez, C. J. "The U.S.-Mexico Border and the 1947 Foot-and-Mouth Disease Outbreak in Mexico." *Journal of the Southwest* 61, no. 4 (2019): 691–724.

Arroyo Alejandre, Jesús, Adrián de León Arias, and M. Basilia Valenzuela. *Migración rural hacia Estados Unidos: Un estudio regional en Jalisco.* Mexico City: Consejo Nacional para la Cultura y las Artes, 1991.

Astorga Morales, Abel. *Historia de un ahorro sin retorno: Despojo salarial, olvido y reivindicación histórica en el movimiento social de ex braceros, 1942–1964.* Guadalajara: Universidad de Guadalajara, 2017.

Aviña, Alexander. *Specters of Revolution: Peasant Guerrillas in the Cold War Mexican Countryside.* New York: Oxford University Press, 2014.

Babb, Sarah. *Managing Mexico: Economists from Nationalism to Neoliberalism.* Princeton, NJ: Princeton University Press, 2001.

Bailey, David C. *¡Viva Cristo Rey! The Cristero Rebellion and the Church-State Conflict in Mexico.* Austin: University of Texas Press, 1974.

Balderrama, Francisco E., and Raymond Rodríguez. *Decade of Betrayal: Mexican Repatriation in the 1930s.* Rev. ed. Albuquerque: University of New Mexico Press, 2006.

Bantjes, Adrián A. *As If Jesus Walked on Earth: Cardenismo, Sonora, and the Mexican Revolution.* Wilmington, DE: Scholarly Resources, 1998.

———. "Mexican Revolutionary Anticlericalism: Concepts and Typologies." *The Americas* 65, no. 4 (2009): 467–80.

———. "The Regional Dynamics of Anticlericalism and Defanaticization in Revolutionary Mexico." In *Faith and Impiety in Revolutionary Mexico,* edited by Matthew Butler, 111–30. New York: Palgrave Macmillan, 2007.

Barkin, David, and Timothy King. *Regional Economic Development: The River Basin Approach in Mexico.* Cambridge: Cambridge University Press, 1970.

Benjamin, Thomas, and Mark Wasserman, eds. *Provinces of the Revolution: Essays on Regional Mexican History, 1910–1929.* Albuquerque: University of New Mexico Press, 1990.

Betanzos, Óscar, ed. *Historia de la cuestión agraria mexicana.* Vol. 3: *Campesinos, terratenientes y revolucionarios, 1910–1920.* Mexico City: Siglo XXI, 1988.

Blancarte, Roberto. "Intransigence, Anticommunism, and Reconciliation: Church/State Relations in Transition." In *Dictablanda: Politics, Work, and Culture in Mexico, 1938–1968,* edited by Paul Gillingham and Benjamin T. Smith, 70–88. Durham, NC: Duke University Press, 2014.

Blanchard, Sarah, Erin R. Hamilton, Néstor Rodríguez, and Hirotoshi Yoshioka. "Shifting Trends in Central American Migration: A Demographic Examination of Increasing Honduran-U.S. Immigration and Deportation." *Latin Americanist* 55, no. 4 (2011): 61–84.

Blanco, Mónica, Alma Parra, and Ethelia Ruiz Medrano. *Guanajuato: Historia breve*. 3rd ed. Mexico City: Fondo de Cultura Económica; El Colegio de México; Fideicomiso Historia de las Américas, 2011.

Boyer, Christopher R. *Becoming Campesinos: Politics, Identity, and Agrarian Struggle in Postrevolutionary Michoacán, 1920–1935*. Stanford, CA: Stanford University Press, 2003.

———. *Political Landscapes: Forests, Conservation, and Community in Mexico*. Durham, NC: Duke University Press, 2015.

Brading, D. A. *Church and State in Bourbon Mexico: The Diocese of Michoacán, 1749–1810*. Cambridge: Cambridge University Press, 1994.

———. *Haciendas and Ranchos in the Mexican Bajío: León, 1700–1860*. Cambridge: Cambridge University Press, 1978.

Brilliant, Mark. *The Color of America Has Changed: How Racial Diversity Shaped Civil Rights Reform in California, 1941–1978*. New York: Oxford University Press, 2010.

Butler, Matthew. *Popular Piety and Political Identity in Mexico's Cristero Rebellion: Michoacán, 1927–29*. Oxford: Published for the British Academy by Oxford University Press, 2004.

Calavita, Kitty. *Inside the State: The Bracero Program, Immigration, and the I.N.S.* New York: Routledge, 1992.

Calderón Mólgora, Marco. "Desarrollo integral en las cuencas del Tepalcatepec y del Balsas." In *Las transformaciones de los paisajes culturales en la cuenca del Tepalcatepec*, edited by Juan Ortiz Escamilla, 227–58. Zamora: El Colegio de Michoacán, 2011.

Camacho Sandoval, Salvador. *Controversia educativa entre la ideología y la fe: Educación socialista en la historia de Aguascalientes, 1876–1940*. Mexico City: Consejo Nacional para la Cultura y las Artes, 1991.

Cámara, Fernando, and Robert Van Kemper, eds. *Migration across Frontiers: Mexico and the United States*. Albany: Institute of Mesoamerican Studies, State University of New York, 1979.

Castañeda, Jorge G. *The Mexican Shock: Its Meaning for the United States*. New York: New Press, 1995.

Cebada, María del Carmen. "La migración hacia Estados Unidos y dos comunidades de origen en el estado de Guanajuato." *Regiones* 1, no. 1 (1993): 73–87.

Ceballos Ramírez, Manuel. *El catolicismo social: Un tercero en discordia: Rerum novarum, la "cuestión social" y la movilización de los católicos mexicanos (1891–1911)*. Mexico City: El Colegio de México, 1991.

Chávez-García, Miroslava. *Migrant Longing: Letter Writing across the U.S.-Mexico Borderlands*. Chapel Hill: University of North Carolina Press, 2018.

Chowning, Margaret. "The Catholic Church and the Ladies of the Vela Perpetua: Gender and Devotional Change in Nineteenth-Century Mexico." *Past & Present* 221, no. 1 (November 2013): 197–237.

———. *Rebellious Nuns: The Troubled History of a Mexican Convent, 1752–1863*. New York: Oxford University Press, 2006.

———. *Wealth and Power in Provincial Mexico: Michoacán from the Late Colony to the Revolution*. Stanford, CA: Stanford University Press, 1999.

Cline, Howard F. *Mexico: Revolution to Evolution, 1940–1960*. New York: Oxford University Press, 1962.

Cohen, Deborah. *Braceros: Migrant Citizens and Transnational Subjects in the Postwar United States and Mexico*. Chapel Hill: University of North Carolina Press, 2011.

Colmenares López, Javier, Ma. Ruth López Ruiz, Soledad Sotelo Belmontes, Pedro Gómez Sánchez, and Guillermo Guzmán Flores. *Historia de la cuestión agraria mexicana: Estado de Zacatecas*. Vol. 2. Mexico City: Juan Pablos Editor, Gobierno del Estado de Zacatecas, Universidad Autónoma de Zacatecas, Centro de Estudios Históricos del Agrarismo en México, 1992.

Córdova Ramírez, Irina. "Las contrataciones de braceros en el estado de Chihuahua." In *Tras los pasos de los braceros: Entre la teoría y la realidad*, edited by Aidé Grijalva, 203–25. Mexicali: Universidad Autónoma de Baja California, Instituto de Investigaciones Sociales; Mexico City: Juan Pablos Editor, 2015.

Cornelius, Wayne A., and Jorge A. Bustamante, eds. *Mexican Migration to the United States: Origins, Consequences, and Policy Options*. San Diego: Center for U.S.-Mexican Studies, University of California, San Diego, 1989.

Cosío Villegas, Daniel. *El sistema político mexicano: Las posibilidades de cambio*. Mexico City: Editorial J. Mortiz, 1973.

Craig, Ann L. *The First Agraristas: An Oral History of a Mexican Agrarian Reform Movement*. Berkeley: University of California Press, 1983.

Craig, Richard B. *The Bracero Program: Interest Groups and Foreign Policy*. Austin: University of Texas Press, 1971.

Cross, Harry E., and James A. Sandos. *Across the Border: Rural Development in Mexico and Recent Migration to the United States*. Berkeley: Institute of Governmental Studies, University of California, Berkeley, 1981.

Curley, Robert. "Anticlericalism and Public Space in Revolutionary Jalisco." *The Americas* 65, no. 4 (April 2009): 511–33.

———. *Citizens and Believers: Religion and Politics in Revolutionary Jalisco, 1900–1930*. Albuquerque: University of New Mexico Press, 2018.

De la Peña, Guillermo. "The End of Revolutionary Anthropology? Notes on Indigenismo." In *Dictablanda: Politics, Work, and Culture in Mexico, 1938–1968*, edited by Paul Gillingham and Benjamin T. Smith, 279–98. Durham, NC: Duke University Press, 2014.

De la Peña, Sergio, ed. *Historia de la cuestión agraria mexicana*. Vol. 6: *El agrarismo y la industrialización de México, 1940–1950*. Mexico City: Siglo XXI, 1989.

Délano, Alexandra. *Mexico and Its Diaspora in the United States: Policies of Emigration since 1848*. New York: Cambridge University Press, 2011.

Dillingham, A. S. "Mexico's Turn Toward the Third World: Rural Development under President Luis Echeverría." In *México Beyond 1968: Revolutionaries,*

Radicals, and Repression during the Global Sixties and Subversive Seventies, edited by Jaime M. Pensado and Enrique C. Ochoa, 113–32. Tucson: University of Arizona Press, 2018.

———. *Oaxaca Resurgent: Indigeneity, Development, and Inequality in Twentieth-Century Mexico*. Stanford, CA: Stanford University Press, 2021.

Dinerman, Ina R. *Migrants and Stay-at-Homes: A Comparative Study of Rural Migration from Michoacán, Mexico*. La Jolla: Center for U.S.-Mexican Studies, University of California, San Diego, 1982.

Dormady, Jason. *Primitive Revolution: Restorationist Religion and the Idea of the Mexican Revolution, 1940-1968*. Albuquerque: University of New Mexico Press, 2011.

Durand, Jorge. "Guanajuato, cantera de migrantes." *Encuentro* 4, no. 4 (1990): 49–62.

Durand, Jorge, and Douglas S. Massey, eds. *Crossing the Border: Research from the Mexican Migration Project*. New York: Russell Sage Foundation, 2004.

Durand, Jorge, Douglas S. Massey, and René M. Zenteno. "Mexican Immigration to the United States: Continuities and Changes." *Latin American Research Review* 36, no. 1 (2001): 107–27.

Ellstrand, Nathan. "Reclaiming La Patria: Sinarquismo in the United States, 1937–1946." PhD diss., Loyola University Chicago, 2022.

Ervin, Michael A. "Marte R. Gómez of Tamaulipas: Governing Agrarian Revolution." In *State Governors of the Mexican Revolution, 1910–1952: Portraits in Conflict, Courage, and Corruption*, edited by Jürgen Buchenau and William H. Beezley, 123–38. Lanham, MD: Rowman & Littlefield, 2009.

Escárcega López, Everardo, ed. *Historia de la cuestión agraria mexicana*. Vol. 5: *El cardenismo, un parteaguas histórico en el proceso agrario nacional, 1934–1940*. Mexico City: Siglo XXI, 1990.

Fábregas Puig, Andrés Antonio. *La formación histórica de una región: Los Altos de Jalisco*. Mexico City: Centro de Investigaciones y Estudios Superiores en Antropología Social, 1986.

Fallaw, Ben. *Cárdenas Compromised: The Failure of Reform in Postrevolutionary Yucatán*. Durham, NC: Duke University Press, 2001.

———. *Religion and State Formation in Postrevolutionary Mexico*. Durham, NC: Duke University Press, 2013.

———. "Varieties of Mexican Revolutionary Anticlericalism: Radicalism, Iconoclasm, and Otherwise, 1914–1935." *The Americas* 65, no. 4 (April 2009): 481–509.

Fernández Aceves, María Teresa. "Advocate or *Cacica*? Guadalupe Urzúa Flores: Modernizer and Peasant Political Leader in Jalisco." In *Dictablanda: Politics, Work, and Culture in Mexico, 1938–1968*, edited by Paul Gillingham and Benjamin T. Smith, 236–54. Durham, NC: Duke University Press, 2014.

FitzGerald, David. *A Nation of Emigrants: How Mexico Manages Its Migration*. Berkeley: University of California Press, 2009.

FitzGerald, David, and David Cook-Martín. "The Geopolitical Origins of the 1965 Immigration Act." In *A Nation of Immigrants Reconsidered: US Society in an Age of Restriction, 1924–1965,* edited by Maddalena Marinari, Madeline Y. Hsu, and María Cristina García, 83–102. Urbana: University of Illinois Press, 2018.

Flores, Lori A. *Grounds for Dreaming: Mexican Americans, Mexican Immigrants, and the California Farmworker Movement.* New Haven, CT: Yale University Press, 2016.

———. "A Town Full of Dead Mexicans: The Salinas Valley Bracero Tragedy of 1963, the End of the Bracero Program, and the Evolution of California's Chicano Movement." *Western Historical Quarterly* 44, no. 2 (2013): 124–43.

Flores Olague, Jesús, Mercedes de Vega, Sandra Kuntz Ficker, and Laura del Alizal. *Zacatecas: Historia breve.* 2nd ed. Mexico City: Fondo de Cultura Económica; El Colegio de México; Fideicomiso Historia de las Américas, 2011.

Foshag, William F., and Jenaro Gonzáles R. "Birth and Development of Parícutin Volcano, Mexico." In *Geological Survey Bulletin 965-D,* 355–488. Washington, DC: US Government Printing Office, 1956.

Fowler Salamini, Heather. *Agrarian Radicalism in Veracruz, 1920–38.* Lincoln: University of Nebraska Press, 1978.

Friedrich, Paul. *Agrarian Revolt in a Mexican Village.* Chicago: University of Chicago Press, 1977.

Galarza, Ernesto. *Merchants of Labor: The Mexican Bracero Story: An Account of the Managed Migration of Mexican Farm Workers in California, 1942–1960.* Santa Barbara, CA: McNally and Loftin, 1964.

Gamboa, Erasmo. *Bracero Railroaders: The Forgotten World War II Story of Mexican Workers in the U.S. West.* Seattle: University of Washington Press, 2016.

———. *Mexican Labor and World War II: Braceros in the Pacific Northwest, 1942–1947.* Seattle: University of Washington Press, 2000.

Gamio, Manuel. *Mexican Immigration to the United States: A Study of Human Migration and Adjustment.* Chicago: University of Chicago Press, 1930.

García, Alberto. "The Politics of Bracero Migration." PhD diss., University of California, Berkeley, 2016.

———. "Regulating Bracero Migration: How National, Regional, and Local Political Considerations Shaped the Bracero Program." *Hispanic American Historical Review* 101, no. 3 (2021): 433–60.

García, María Cristina. "Central American Migration and the Shaping of Refugee Policy." In *Migrants and Migration in Modern North America: Cross-Border Lives, Labor, and Markets,* edited by Dirk Hoerder and Nora Faires, 347–63. Durham, NC: Duke University Press, 2011.

García y Griego, Manuel. "El comienzo y el final: La interdependencia estructural y dos negociaciones sobre braceros." In *Interdependencia: Un enfoque útil para el análisis de las relaciones México–Estados Unidos,* edited by Blanca Torres, 87–117. Mexico City: El Colegio de México, Centro de Estudios Internacionales, 1990.

———. "The Importation of Mexican Contract Laborers to the United States, 1942–1964: Antecedents, Operation, and Legacy." In *The Border That Joins: Mexican Migrants and U.S. Responsibility,* edited by Peter G. Brown and Henry Shue, 49–98. Totowa, NJ: Rowman & Littlefield, 1983.

García y Griego, Manuel, and Mónica Verea Campos, eds. *México y Estados Unidos frente a la migración de los indocumentados*. Mexico City: Coordinación de Humanidades; Porrúa, 1988.

Gibson, Campbell, and Kay Jung. "Historical Statistics on the Foreign-Born Population of the United States: 1850 to 2000." Washington, DC: US Census Bureau, 2006.

Gillingham, Paul. "Maximino's Bulls: Popular Protest after the Mexican Revolution, 1940–1952." *Past & Present* 206, no. 1 (February 2010): 175–211.

———. *Unrevolutionary Mexico: The Birth of a Strange Dictatorship*. New Haven, CT: Yale University Press, 2021.

———. "'We Don't Have Arms, But We Do Have Balls': Fraud, Violence, and Popular Agency in Elections." In *Dictablanda: Politics, Work, and Culture in Mexico, 1938–1968*, edited by Paul Gillingham and Benjamin T. Smith, 149–72. Durham, NC: Duke University Press, 2014.

Gillingham, Paul, and Benjamin T. Smith, "Introduction: The Paradoxes of Revolution." In *Dictablanda: Politics, Work, and Culture in Mexico, 1938–1968*, edited by Paul Gillingham and Benjamin T. Smith, 1–43. Durham, NC: Duke University Press, 2014.

Gledhill, John. *Casi Nada: A Study of Agrarian Reform in the Homeland of Cardenismo*. Albany: Institute for Mesoamerican Studies, University at Albany, State University of New York; Distributed by University of Texas Press, 1991.

Gómez Serrano, Jesús. *Haciendas y ranchos de Aguascalientes: Estudio regional sobre la tendencia de la tierra y el desarrollo agrícola en el siglo XIX*. Aguascalientes: Universidad Autónoma de Aguascalientes, 2012.

Gómez Serrano, Jesús, and Francisco Javier Delgado. *Aguascalientes: Historia breve*. 2nd ed. Mexico City: Fondo de Cultura Económica; El Colegio de México; Fideicomiso Historia de las Américas, 2011.

González, Gilbert G. "Mexican Labor Migration, 1876–1924." In *Beyond la Frontera: The History of Mexico-U.S. Migration*, edited by Mark Overmyer-Velázquez, 28–50. New York: Oxford University Press, 2011.

González Navarro, Moisés. *Población y sociedad en México (1900–1970)*. Vol. 2. Mexico City: Universidad Nacional Autónoma, 1974.

González y González, Luis. *San José de Gracia: Mexican Village in Transition*. Translated by John Upton. Austin: University of Texas Press, 1974.

Goodman, Adam. *The Deportation Machine: America's Long History of Expelling Immigrants*. Princeton, NJ: Princeton University Press, 2020.

Greaves L., Cecilia. *Del radicalismo a la unidad nacional: Una visión de la educación en el México contemporáneo (1940–1964)*. Mexico City: El Colegio de México, 2008.

Grijalva, Aidé. "La bracereada que llegó para quedarse: Mexicali y el Programa Bracero." In *Tras los pasos de los braceros: Entre la teoría y la realidad*, edited by Aidé Grijalva, 227–63. Mexicali: Universidad Autónoma de Baja California, Instituto de Investigaciones Sociales; Mexico City: Juan Pablos Editor, 2015.

Guerra Manzo, Enrique. *Del fuego sagrado a la acción cívica: Los católicos frente al estado en Michoacán, 1920–1940*. Zamora: El Colegio de Michoacán; Mexico City: Universidad Autónoma Metropolitana, Unidad Xochimilco; Itaca, 2015.

Guerrero Tarquín, Alfredo. *Memorias de un agrarista: Pasajes de la vida de un hombre y de toda una región del Estado de Guanajuato, 1913–1938*. Mexico City: Instituto Nacional de Antropología e Historia, 1987.

Gutiérrez, David G. *Walls and Mirrors: Mexican Americans, Mexican Immigrants, and the Politics of Ethnicity*. Berkeley: University of California Press, 1995.

Gutiérrez, Laura D. "A Constant Threat: Deportation and Return Migration to Northern Mexico, 1918–1965." PhD diss., University of California, San Diego, 2016.

Haber, Stephen, Herbert S. Klein, Noel Maurer, and Kevin J. Middlebrok. *Mexico since 1980*. New York: Cambridge University Press, 2008.

Hahamovitch, Cindy. *No Man's Land: Jamaican Guestworkers in America and the Global History of Deportable Labor*. Princeton, NJ: Princeton University Press, 2011.

Hamilton, Nora. *The Limits of State Autonomy: Post-Revolutionary Mexico*. Princeton, NJ: Princeton University Press, 1982.

Hellman, Judith Adler. *Mexican Lives*. New York: New Press, 1995.

———. *Mexico in Crisis*. New York: Holmes and Meier, 1983.

Henderson, Timothy J. *The Worm in the Wheat: Rosalie Evans and Agrarian Struggle in the Puebla-Tlaxcala Valley, 1906–1927*. Durham, NC: Duke University Press, 1998.

Hernández, Kelly Lytle. *Migra! A History of the U.S. Border Patrol*. Berkeley: University of California Press, 2010.

Hernández Chávez, Alicia. *La mecánica cardenista*. Mexico City: El Colegio de México, 1979.

Hernández Rodríguez, Rogelio. *El centro dividido: La nueva autonomía de los gobernadores*. Mexico City: El Colegio de México, Centro de Estudios Internacionales, 2008.

———. "Strongmen and State Weakness." In *Dictablanda: Politics, Work, and Culture in Mexico, 1938–1968*, edited by Paul Gillingham and Benjamin T. Smith, 108–25. Durham, NC: Duke University Press, 2014.

Hinojosa-Ojeda, Raúl, and Edward Telles. "How Do We Explain Trump's Paradoxical Yet Electorally Successful Use of a False US-Mexico Narrative?" In *The Trump Paradox: Migration, Trade, and Racial Politics in Mexico-US Integration*, edited by Raúl Hinojosa-Ojeda and Edward Telles, 15–31. Oakland: University of California Press, 2021.

Iskander, Natasha. *Creative State: Forty Years of Migration and Development Policy in Morocco and Mexico*. Ithaca, NY: ILR Press, 2010.

Jonas, Susanne, and Néstor Rodríguez. *Guatemala-U.S. Migration: Transforming Regions*. Austin: University of Texas Press, 2014.

Jones, Richard C., ed. *Patterns of Undocumented Migration: Mexico and the United States*. Totowa, NJ: Rowman and Allanheld, 1984.

Joseph, G. M. *Revolution from Without: Yucatán, Mexico, and the United States, 1880–1924*. New York: Cambridge University Press, 1982.

Joseph, Gilbert M., Anne Rubenstein, and Eric Zolov. "Assembling the Fragments: Writing a Cultural History of Mexico since 1940." In *Fragments of a Golden Age: The Politics of Culture in Mexico since 1940*, edited by Gilbert M. Joseph, Anne Rubenstein, and Eric Zolov, 3–22. Durham, NC: Duke University Press, 2001.

———, eds. *Fragments of a Golden Age: The Politics of Culture in Mexico since 1940.* Durham, NC: Duke University Press, 2001.

Kang, S. Deborah. *The INS on the Line: Making Immigration Law on the US-Mexico Border, 1917–1954.* New York: Oxford University Press, 2017.

Katz, Friedrich. *The Life and Times of Pancho Villa.* Stanford, CA: Stanford University Press, 1998.

Kloppe-Santamaría, Gema. *In the Vortex of Violence: Lynching, Extralegal Justice, and the State in Post-Revolutionary Mexico.* Oakland: University of California Press, 2020.

Knight, Alan. "Cardenismo: Juggernaut or Jalopy?" *Journal of Latin American Studies* 26, no. 1 (February 1994): 73–107.

———. "The End of the Mexican Revolution? From Cárdenas to Ávila Camacho, 1937–1941." In *Dictablanda: Politics, Work, and Culture in Mexico, 1938–1968*, edited by Paul Gillingham and Benjamin T. Smith, 47–69. Durham, NC: Duke University Press, 2014.

———. "The Mentality and Modus Operandi of Revolutionary Anticlericalism." In *Faith and Impiety in Revolutionary Mexico,* edited by Matthew Butler, 21–56. New York: Palgrave Macmillan, 2007.

Kourí, Emilio. "La invención del ejido." *Nexos* 37, no. 445 (January 2015): 54–61.

Krauze, Enrique. *La presidencia imperial.* Mexico City: Tusquets Editores, 1997.

Lewis, Stephen E. *The Ambivalent Revolution: Forging State and Nation in Chiapas, 1910–1945.* Albuquerque: University of New Mexico Press, 2005.

———. *Rethinking Mexican Indigenismo: The INI's Coordinating Council in Highland Chiapas and the Fate of a Utopian Project.* Albuquerque: University of New Mexico Press, 2018.

Loaeza, Soledad. *El Partido Acción Nacional: La larga marcha, 1939–1994: Oposición leal y partido de protesta.* Mexico City: Fondo de Cultura Económica, 1999.

López Castro, Gustavo. *La casa dividida: Un estudio de caso sobre la migración a Estados Unidos en un pueblo michoacano.* Zamora: El Colegio de Michoacán; Asociación Mexicana de Población, 1986.

———, ed. *Migración en el occidente de México.* Zamora: El Colegio de Michoacán, 1988.

Loza, Mireya. *Defiant Braceros: How Migrant Workers Fought for Racial, Sexual, and Political Freedom.* Chapel Hill: University of North Carolina Press, 2016.

Mabry, Donald J. "Changing Models of Mexican Politics: A Review Essay." *New Scholar* 5, no. 1 (1976): 31–37.

Márquez Herrera, Armando. *Historia de la cuestión agraria mexicana: Estado de Zacatecas.* Vol. 1. Mexico City: Gobierno del Estado de Zacatecas; Universidad Autónoma de Zacatecas; Centro de Estudios Históricos del Agrarismo en México, 1990.

Massey, Douglas S. "What Were the Paradoxical Consequences of Militarizing the Border with Mexico?" In *The Trump Paradox: Migration, Trade, and Racial Politics in US-Mexico Integration,* edited by Raúl Hinojosa-Ojeda and Edward Telles, 32–46. Oakland: University of California Press, 2021.

Massey, Douglas S., Rafael Alarcón, Jorge Durand, and Humberto González. *Return to Aztlan: The Social Process of International Migration from Western Mexico.* Berkeley: University of California Press, 1987.

Massey, Douglas S., Joaquín Arango, Graeme Hugo, Ali Kouaouci, Adela Pellegrino, and J. Edward Taylor. "Theories of International Migration: A Review and Appraisal." *Population and Development Review* 19, no. 3 (September 1993): 431–66.

Massey, Douglas S., Jorge Durand, and Nolan J. Malone. *Beyond Smoke and Mirrors: Mexican Immigration in an Era of Economic Integration.* New York: Russell Sage Foundation, 2002.

Massey, Douglas S., and Audrey Singer. "New Estimates of Undocumented Mexican Migration and the Probability of Apprehension." *Demography* 32, no. 2 (1995): 203–13.

Matute, Álvaro. *Las dificultades del nuevo estado.* Mexico City: El Colegio de México, Centro de Estudios Históricos, 1995.

Mazín, Óscar. *Entre dos majestades: El obispo y la iglesia del Gran Michoacán ante las reformas borbónicas, 1758–1772.* Zamora: El Colegio de Michoacán, 1987.

McCormick, Gladys I. *The Logic of Compromise in Mexico: How the Countryside Was Key to the Emergence of Authoritarianism.* Chapel Hill: University of North Carolina Press, 2016.

Medina, Luis. *Del cardenismo al avilacamachismo.* Mexico City: El Colegio de México, 1978.

Mendoza, Mary E. "Battling *Aftosa:* North-to-South Migration across the U.S.-Mexico Border, 1947–1954." *Journal of the West* 54, no. 1 (2015): 39–50.

Menjívar, Cecilia. *Fragmented Ties: Salvadoran Immigrant Networks in America.* Berkeley: University of California Press, 2000.

Meyer, Jean A. *The Cristero Rebellion: The Mexican People between Church and State, 1926–1929.* Translated by Richard Southern. Cambridge: Cambridge University Press, 1976.

———. "La fiebre aftosa y la Unión Nacional Sinarquista (1947)." Translated by María Palomar. *Relaciones* 4, no. 16 (1983): 93–112.

———. *El sinarquismo, el cardenismo, y la iglesia: 1937–1947.* Mexico City: Tusquets Editores, 2003.

———. *El sinarquismo: ¿Un fascismo mexicano?* Mexico City: Editorial J. Mortiz, 1979.

Meyer, Jean, Enrique Krauze, and Cayetano Reyes. *Estado y sociedad con Calles.* Mexico City: El Colegio de México, 1977.

Meyer, Lorenzo, Rafael Segovia, and Alejandra Lajous. *Los inicios de la institucionalización: La política del Maximato.* Mexico City: El Colegio de México, 1978.

Meyer Cosío, Francisco Javier. *Tradición y progreso: La reforma agraria en Acámbaro, Guanajuato (1917–1941).* Mexico City: Instituto Nacional de Estudios Históricos de la Revolución Mexicana, Secretaría de Gobernación, 1993.

Miller, Jennifer A. *Turkish Guest Workers in Germany: Hidden Lives and Contested Borders, 1960s to 1980s.* Toronto: University of Toronto Press, 2018.

Minian, Ana Raquel. *Undocumented Lives: The Untold Story of Mexican Migration.* Cambridge, MA: Harvard University Press, 2018.

Mitchell, Don. *They Saved the Crops: Labor, Landscape, and the Struggle over Industrial Farming in Bracero-Era California.* Athens: University of Georgia Press, 2012.

Mize, Ronald L. "The State Management of Guest Workers: The Decline of the Bracero Program, the Rise of Temporary Worker Visas." In *A Nation of Immigrants Reconsidered: US Society in an Age of Restriction, 1924–1965,* edited by Maddalena Marinari, Madeline Y. Hsu, and María Cristina García, 123–43. Urbana: University of Illinois Press, 2018.

Moctezuma Longoria, Miguel. "La otra reforma agraria en Zacatecas (1917–1934)." In *Temas de historia, sociedad, política y cultura en Zacatecas,* edited by Alicia Bazarte Martínez and Eligio Meza Padilla, 73–94. Zacatecas: Maestría en Ciencia Política, Universidad Autónoma de Zacatecas, 1998.

Moguel, Julio, ed. *Historia de la cuestión agraria mexicana.* Vol. 7: *La época de oro y el principio de la crisis de la agricultura mexicana, 1950–1970.* Mexico City: Siglo XXI, 1988.

Montalvo, Enrique, ed. *Historia de la cuestión agraria mexicana.* Vol. 4: *Modernización, lucha agraria y poder político, 1920–1934.* Mexico City: Siglo XXI, 1988.

Montejano, David. "What Is the Historical and Political Context for Trump's Nativist Appeal?" In *The Trump Paradox: Migration, Trade, and Racial Politics in Mexico-US Integration,* edited by Raúl Hinojosa-Ojeda and Edward Telles, 191–203. Oakland: University of California Press, 2021.

Moreno, Julio. *Yankee Don't Go Home! Mexican Nationalism, American Business Culture, and the Shaping of Modern Mexico, 1920–1950.* Chapel Hill: University of North Carolina Press, 2003.

Mraz, John. *Looking for Mexico: Modern Visual Culture and National Identity.* Durham, NC: Duke University Press, 2009.

Muriá, José Maria. *Jalisco: Historia breve.* 4th ed. Mexico City: Fondo de Cultura Económica; El Colegio de México; Fideicomiso Historia de las Américas, 2011.

Newcomer, Daniel. *Reconciling Modernity: Urban State Formation in 1940s León, Mexico.* Lincoln: University of Nebraska Press, 2004.

Ngai, Mae M. *Impossible Subjects: Illegal Aliens in the Making of Modern America.* Princeton, NJ: Princeton University Press, 2004.

Nichols, Sandra Lucile. "Saints, Peaches, and Wine: Mexican Migrants and the Transformation of Los Haro, Zacatecas and Napa, California." PhD diss., University of California, Berkeley, 2002.

Nolan, Mary Lee. "Impact of Parícutin on Five Communities." In *Volcanic Activity and Human Ecology,* edited by Payson D. Sheets and Donald K. Grayson, 293–338. New York: Academic Press, 1979.

Ochoa Serrano, Álvaro, and Gerardo Sánchez Díaz. *Michoacán: Historia breve*. 2nd ed. Mexico City: Fondo de Cultura Económica; El Colegio de México; Fideicomiso Historia de las Américas, 2011.

Oikión Solano, Verónica. *Los hombres del poder en Michoacán, 1924–1962*. Zamora: El Colegio de Michoacán; Morelia: Universidad Michoacana de San Nicolás de Hidalgo, Instituto de Investigaciones Históricas, 2004.

Olivera Sedano, Alicia. *La guerra cristera: Aspectos del conflicto religioso de 1926 a 1929*. Mexico City: Fondo de Cultura Económica, 2019.

Olsson, Tore C. *Agrarian Crossings: Reformers and the Remaking of the US and Mexican Countryside*. Princeton, NJ: Princeton University Press, 2017.

Ortiz Escamilla, Juan, and Silvia Méndez Maín. "La Ruana: Un modelo de centro ejidal." In *Las transformaciones de los paisajes culturales en la cuenca del Tepalcatepec*, edited by Juan Ortiz Escamilla, 259–302. Zamora: El Colegio de Michoacán, 2011.

Ortiz Ybarra, Héctor, and Vicente González Méndez. *Puruándiro*. Morelia: Gobierno del Estado de Michoacán, 1980.

Osten, Sarah. *The Mexican Revolution's Wake: The Making of a Political System, 1920–1929*. New York: Cambridge University Press, 2018.

Overmyer-Velázquez, Mark, ed. *Beyond la Frontera: The History of Mexico-U.S. Migration*. New York: Oxford University Press, 2011.

Padilla, Tanalís. *Rural Resistance in the Land of Zapata: The Jaramillista Movement and the Myth of the Pax Priísta, 1940–1962*. Durham, NC: Duke University Press, 2008.

———. *Unintended Lessons of Revolution: Student Teachers and Political Radicalism in Twentieth-Century Mexico*. Durham, NC: Duke University Press, 2022.

Padilla Rangel, Yolanda. *Después de la tempestad: La reorganización Católica en Aguascalientes, 1929–1950*. Mexico City: El Colegio de Michoacán, 2001.

———. *El Catolicismo social y el movimiento Cristero en Aguascalientes*. Aguascalientes: Instituto Cultural de Aguascalientes, 1992.

Pansters, Wil G. "Zones and Languages of State-Making: From Pax *Priísta* to Dirty War." In *México Beyond 1968: Revolutionaries, Radicals, and Repression during the Global Sixties and Subversive Seventies*, edited by Jaime M. Pensado and Enrique C. Ochoa, 33–50. Tucson: University of Arizona Press, 2018.

Parker, Kunal M. *Making Foreigners: Immigration and Citizenship Law in America, 1600–2000*. New York: Cambridge University Press, 2015.

Paz, Octavio. *Posdata*. Mexico City: Siglo XXI, 1970.

Pensado, Jaime M. *Rebel Mexico: Student Unrest and Authoritarian Political Culture during the Long Sixties*. Stanford, CA: Stanford University Press, 2013.

Pensado, Jaime M., and Enrique C. Ochoa, eds. *México Beyond 1968: Revolutionaries, Radicals, and Repression during the Global Sixties and Subversive Seventies*. Tucson: University of Arizona Press, 2018.

Piccato, Pablo. *A History of Infamy: Crime, Truth, and Justice in Mexico*. Oakland: University of California Press, 2017.

Pilcher, Jeffrey M. *Cantinflas and the Chaos of Mexican Modernity*. Wilmington, DE: Scholarly Resources, 2001.

Piña, Ulices. "The Different Roads to Rebellion: Socialist Education and the Second Cristero Rebellion in Jalisco, 1934–1939." *Letras Históricas* 16 (2017): 165–92.

Poleman, Thomas T. *The Papaloapan Project: Agricultural Development in the Mexican Tropics*. Stanford, CA: Stanford University Press, 1964.

Purnell, Jennie. *Popular Movements and State Formation in Revolutionary Mexico: The Agraristas and Cristeros of Michoacán*. Durham, NC: Duke University Press, 1999.

———. "With All Due Respect: Popular Resistance to the Privatization of Communal Lands in Nineteenth-Century Michoacán." *Latin American Research Review* 34, no. 1 (1999): 85–121.

Ramírez Miranda, César, Ramón Vera Salvo, and Pedro Gómez Sánchez. *Historia de la cuestión agraria mexicana: Estado de Zacatecas*. Vol. 3. Mexico City: Juan Pablos Editor; Gobierno del Estado de Zacatecas; Universidad Autónoma de Zacatecas; Centro de Estudios Históricos del Agrarismo en México, 1990.

Rath, Thomas. *Myths of Demilitarization in Postrevolutionary Mexico, 1920–1960*. Chapel Hill: University of North Carolina Press, 2013.

Reichert, Joshua S. "A Town Divided: Economic Stratification and Social Relations in a Mexican Migrant Community." *Social Problems* 29, no. 4 (1982): 411–23.

Restrepo Fernández, Iván, and José Sánchez Cortés. *La reforma agraria en cuatro regiones: El Bajío, Michoacán, La Laguna y Tlaxcala*. Mexico City: Secretaría de Educación Pública, 1972.

Reyna, Luis, and Richard S. Weinert, eds. *Authoritarianism in Mexico*. Philadelphia: Institute for the Study of Human Issues, 1977.

Roberts, Kenneth D. "Agrarian Structures and Labor Mobility in Rural Mexico." *Population and Development Review* 8, no. 2 (1982): 299–322.

Rodríguez, Chantel Renee. "Health on the Line: The Politics of Citizenship and the Railroad Bracero Program of World War II." PhD diss., University of Minnesota, 2013.

Rojas, Beatriz. *La destrucción de la hacienda en Aguascalientes, 1910–1931*. Zamora: El Colegio de Michoacán, 1981.

Rosas, Ana Elizabeth. *Abrazando el Espíritu: Bracero Families Confront the US-Mexico Border*. Berkeley: University of California Press, 2014.

Ross, Stanley R. *Is the Mexican Revolution Dead?* Philadelphia: Temple University Press, 1975.

Rubenstein, Anne. *Bad Language, Naked Ladies, and Other Threats to the Nation: A Political History of Comic Books in Mexico*. Durham, NC: Duke University Press, 1998.

Sánchez, George J. *Becoming Mexican American: Ethnicity, Culture, and Identity in Chicano Los Angeles, 1900–1945*. New York: Oxford University Press, 1993.

Sánchez Andrade, Diana E. "De la tierra fría a la Tierra Caliente: Deterioro ambiental y transformación del paisaje en la microcuenca del Cupatitzio, durante el siglo XX." In *Las transformaciones de los paisajes culturales en la cuenca del Tepalcatepec*, edited by Juan Ortiz Escamilla, 323–74. Zamora: El Colegio de Michoacán, 2011.

Sánchez Susarrey, Jaime, and Ignacio Medina Sánchez. *Jalisco desde la revolución*. Vol. 9: *Historia política, 1940–1975*. Guadalajara: Gobierno del Estado de Jalisco; Universidad de Guadalajara, 1987.

Saragoza, Alex. *The Monterrey Elite and the Mexican State, 1880–1940*. Austin: University of Texas Press, 1988.

———. "The Selling of Mexico: Tourism and the State, 1929–1952." In *Fragments of a Golden Age: The Politics of Culture in Mexico since 1940*, edited by Gilbert M. Joseph, Anne Rubenstein, and Eric Zolov, 91–115. Durham, NC: Duke University Press, 2001.

Santiago, Myrna I. *The Ecology of Oil: Environment, Labor, and the Mexican Revolution, 1900–1938*. Cambridge: Cambridge University Press, 2006.

Serrano Álvarez, Pablo. *La batalla del espíritu: El movimiento sinarquista en el Bajío (1932–1951)*. 2 vols. Mexico City: Consejo Nacional para la Cultura y las Artes, 1992.

Servín, Elisa. *Ruptura y oposición: El movimiento henriquista, 1945–1954*. Mexico City: Cal y Arena, 2001.

Sifuentez, Mario Jiménez. *Of Forests and Fields: Mexican Labor in the Pacific Northwest*. New Brunswick, NJ: Rutgers University Press, 2016.

Singer, Audrey, and Douglas S. Massey. "The Social Process of Undocumented Border Crossing among Mexican Migrants." *International Migration Review* 32, no. 3 (1998): 561–92.

Smith, Benjamin T. "Building a State on the Cheap: Taxation, Social Moments, and Politics." In *Dictablanda: Politics, Work, and Culture in Mexico, 1938–1968*, edited by Paul Gillingham and Benjamin T. Smith, 255–75. Durham, NC: Duke University Press, 2014.

———. *The Mexican Press and Civil Society, 1940–1976: Stories from the Newsroom, Stories from the Street*. Chapel Hill: University of North Carolina Press, 2018.

———. *Pistoleros and Popular Movements: The Politics of State Formation in Postrevolutionary Oaxaca*. Lincoln: University of Nebraska Press, 2009.

———. *The Roots of Conservatism in Mexico: Catholicism, Society, and Politics in the Mixteca Baja, 1750–1962*. Albuquerque: University of New Mexico Press, 2012.

Snodgrass, Michael. "The Bracero Program, 1942–1964." In *Beyond la Frontera: The History of Mexico-U.S. Migration*, edited by Mark Overmyer-Velázquez, 79–102. New York: Oxford University Press, 2011.

———. "The Golden Age of Charrismo: Workers, Braceros, and the Political Machinery of Postrevolutionary Mexico." In *Dictablanda: Politics, Work, and Culture in Mexico, 1938–1968*, edited by Paul Gillingham and Benjamin T. Smith, 175–95. Durham, NC: Duke University Press, 2014.

———. "Patronage and Progress: The Bracero Program from the Perspective of Mexico." In *Workers across the Americas: The Transnational Turn in Labor History*, edited by Leon Fink, 245–66. New York: Oxford University Press, 2011.

Soto Laveaga, Gabriela. *Jungle Laboratories: Mexican Peasants, National Projects, and the Making of the Pill*. Durham, NC: Duke University Press, 2009.

Stauffer, Brian A. *Victory on Earth or in Heaven: Mexico's Religionero Rebellion.* Albuquerque: University of New Mexico Press, 2019.

Stevens, Evelyn P. "Mexico's PRI: The Institutionalization of Corporatism?" In *Authoritarianism and Corporatism in Latin America,* edited by James N. Malloy, 227–58. Pittsburgh, PA: University of Pittsburgh Press, 1977.

Tamayo Rodríguez, Jaime E. *La estructura del sindicalismo en Jalisco.* Guadalajara: Instituto de Estudios Sociales, Universidad de Guadalajara, 1985.

Tapia Santamaría, Jesús. *Campo religioso y evolución política en el Bajío zamorano.* Zamora: El Colegio de Michoacán; Gobierno del Estado de Michoacán, 1986.

Taylor, Paul S. *A Spanish-Mexican Community: Arandas in Jalisco, Mexico.* Berkeley: University of California Press, 1933.

Thornton, Christy. *Revolution in Development: Mexico and the Governance of the Global Economy.* Oakland: University of California Press, 2021.

Torres, Blanca. *México y el mundo: Historia de sus relaciones exteriores: De la guerra al mundo bipolar.* Mexico City: El Colegio de México, 2010.

Torres Septién, Valentina. *La educación privada en México (1903–1976).* Mexico City: El Colegio de México; Universidad Iberoamericana, 1997.

Tutino, John. *Making a New World: Founding Capitalism in the Bajío and Spanish North America.* Durham, NC: Duke University Press, 2011.

———. "The Revolution in Mexican Independence: Insurgency and the Renegotiation of Property, Production, and Patriarchy in the Bajío, 1800–1855." *Hispanic American Historical Review* 78, no. 3 (August 1998): 367–418.

Ulloa, Berta. *La constitución de 1917.* Mexico City: El Colegio de México, 1983.

Vaughan, Mary Kay. *Cultural Politics in Revolution: Teachers, Peasants, and Schools in Mexico, 1930–1940.* Tucson: University of Arizona Press, 1997.

———. "Transnational Processes and the Rise and Fall of the Mexican Cultural State: Notes from the Past." In *Fragments of a Golden Age: The Politics of Culture in Mexico since 1940,* edited by Gilbert M. Joseph, Anne Rubenstein, and Eric Zolov, 471–87. Durham, NC: Duke University Press, 2001.

Vézina, Catherine. *Diplomacia migratoria: Una historia transnacional del Programa Bracero, 1947–1952.* Mexico City: CIDE; Acervo Histórico Diplomático, Estados Unidos Mexicanos, Secretaría de Relaciones Exteriores, 2017.

Walker, Louise E. *Waking from the Dream: Mexico's Middle Classes after 1968.* Stanford, CA: Stanford University Press, 2013.

Weise, Julie M. *Corazón de Dixie: Mexicanos in the U.S. South since 1910.* Chapel Hill: University of North Carolina Press, 2015.

Williams, Heather L. *Social Movements and Economic Transition: Markets and Distributive Conflict in Mexico.* New York: Cambridge University Press, 2001.

Wolfe, Mikael D. *Watering the Revolution: An Environmental and Technological History of Agrarian Reform in Mexico.* Durham, NC: Duke University Press, 2017.

Womack, John, Jr. *Zapata and the Mexican Revolution.* New York: Vintage Books, 1968.

Wright-Ríos, Edward. *Revolutions in Mexican Catholicism: Reform and Revelation in Oaxaca, 1887–1934.* Durham, NC: Duke University Press, 2009.

Yankelevich, Pablo. *La educación socialista en Jalisco*. 2nd ed. Zapopan: El Colegio de Jalisco, 2000.

Young, Julia G. "Fascists, Nazis, or Something Else? Mexico's Unión Nacional Sinarquista in the US Media, 1937–1945." *The Americas* 79, no. 2 (2022): 229–61.

———. *Mexican Exodus: Emigrants, Exiles, and Refugees of the Cristero War*. New York: Oxford University Press, 2015.

Zenteno, René, and Roberto Suro. "Recessions versus Removals: Which Finished Unauthorized Migration?" In *The Trump Paradox: Migration, Trade, and Racial Politics in US-Mexico Integration*, edited by Raúl Hinojosa-Ojeda and Edward Telles, 63–77. Oakland: University of California Press, 2021.

Zermeño P., Guillermo, and Rubén Aguilar V. *Hacia una reinterpretación del sinarquismo actual: Notas y materiales para su estudio*. Mexico City: Universidad Iberoamericana, Departamento de Historia, 1988.

Zolov, Eric. "Discovering a Land 'Mysterious and Obvious': The Renarrativizing of Postrevolutionary Mexico." In *Fragments of a Golden Age: The Politics of Culture in Mexico since 1940*, edited by Gibert M. Joseph, Anne Rubenstein, and Eric Zolov, 234–72. Durham, NC: Duke University Press, 2001.

———. *The Last Good Neighbor: Mexico in the Global Sixties*. Durham, NC: Duke University Press, 2020.

———. *Refried Elvis: The Rise of the Mexican Counterculture*. Berkeley: University of California Press, 1999.

INDEX

Aboites Aguilar, Luis, 143
Abundis, José, 108
Acosta, Ricardo, 80
advocacy requests, 141–143
aftosa outbreak, 51–53, 70
Agrarian and Ejido Censuses (1940), 20, 115
Agrarian Census (1930), 187n18
Agrarian Code (1934), 99, 100–104, 105, 106–108, 109, 114, 118–120, 198n19
Agrarian Code (1940), 99–100, 114
Agrarian Code (1942), 99–100, 102
Agrarian Commission, 115
agrarian reform, 7–8, 98–100, 119–120; background and provisions of, 100–104; Banco Ejidal and, 110–111, 128–129; conservative shift in policy pf, 114–119; contested boundaries and, 111–114; ejidatario restrictions, 20–21; insufficient lands and, 105–108; poor quality land and, 108–110; religious-political conflicts on, 73–74, 77, 88–89, 129. *See also* land redistribution
agricultural production: cotton, 39, 40, 51, 101, 198n19; maize, 20, 114, 119, 169n24; wheat, 20, 169n24
Aguado, Ricardo, 134–135
Aguascalientes state, 2*map*; bracero migration from, 3, 41; Calvillo, 69, 88–91, 96, 112, 120, 144–146; religious-political conflict in, 5–6, 88–91; San José del Río, 135. *See also* state administration of the Bracero Program
Aguilar, Ramón, 73, 93

Aguilar Naranjo, Jesús, 142
Ahumada, Dionisio, 59–60
Alcalá de Lira, Alberto, 60, 89
Aldama, Juan, 136
Alemán, Miguel: administration of the Bracero Program by, 26, 31, 32–33, 35; foot-and-mouth disease and, 52; on potential guest worker program, 15
Alianza de Braceros Nacionales de México en los Estados Unidos de Norteamérica, 133–135, 207n50
Almada, Alfonso, 39
Alvarez, C. J., 51
Álvarez, Domingo, 126
Ambrís Constantino, Mateo, 118
Ángeles, Roberto, 142, 147
Anguiano, Victoriano, 65
Anguiano Pérez, Félix, 23–24
Arandas, Jalisco, 81, 139
Arellano, Miguel, 147
Arkansas, US, 18, 34, 160n8, 174n97
Arriaga Rivera, Agustín, 78, 118, 137
Arroyo, Agustín, 68
Arroyo, Martín, 129
Atotonilco el Alto, Jalisco, 81–84
author's positionality, 3
Avalos Osorio, Filemón, 53
Avaytua González, Ángel, 26
Ávila Camacho, Manuel: administration of Bracero Program by, 22–23, 29–32; emigration policies of, 14; establishment of Bracero Program and, 15, 16–18, 150; land redistribution by, 21;

235

Ávila Camacho, Manuel *(continued)*
as president, 10; religious-political conflicts and, 70

Bahamas, 151–152
Balderas, Sebastián, 125–126
Banco Nacional de Crédito Agrícola, 17
Banco Nacional de Crédito Ejidal (Banco Ejidal), 100, 110–111, 129
Bañuelos, Antonio, 145–146
La Barca, Jalisco, 115–116, 120, 121
Bautista García, Daniel, 96
Becerríl López, Ricardo, 112
Beltrán, Humberto, 93
Bonilla, Higinio, 130
border policing, 2
Boyer, Christopher, 24, 50, 63, 72, 93, 109
Bracero Program, overview, 1–11, 149–156
Bracero Savings Fund, 17, 168n7
Bravo Cortés, Miguel, 49
Bravo Valencia, Enrique, 54
bribery, 121–125; in Aguascalientes, 144–146; in Guanajuato, 54, 55, 121; in Jalisco, 139; for López Gómez, 91; at Mexico City Contracting Center, 25, 41; in Michoacán, 137; in Zacatecas, 136
Briseño, Octavio, 136
Bush, George W., 155
Butler, Matthew, 72, 93

Calles, Plutarco Elías, 101
Calvillo, Aguascalientes, 69, 88–91, 96, 112, 120, 144–146
Campesino Union, 47
Cañada de Corralejo, 79–80
Cárdenas, Dámaso, 77
Cárdenas del Río, Lázaro: agrarian reform by, 99–103, 106–109, 114–117; bracero migration during presidency, 69; land distribution by, 21, 198n19; as president, 10
Cárdenas Mejorada, Manuel, 140–141
Caribbean Farmworker Program, 151–152
Carmona Vera, Pedro, 86, 96
Carrillo Puerto, Felipe, 101
Castorena, Jesús, 79
Castro, J. Guadalupe, 91–92

Catholicism: Greater Bajío roots in, 71–73; opposition groups of, 10, 69, 129. *See also* Cristero War (1926–29); religious-political conflicts and Bracero migration
Ceballos, Teresa, 74
Centro de Arriba, Zacatecas, 111
Cerda Pimentel, Humberto, 141
Cervantes, Gregorio, 115
Cervantes Calixto, Aurelio, 77
Cervantes Calixto, Emigdio, 76–77
Cervantes Hernández, Cleofas, 81, 96
Cervantes Reynoso, Jesús, 133
CFE (Comisión Federal de Electricidad), 143–144
Changuitiro, Michoacán, 3, 70, 92–95, 96, 142
Chaparro Plata, Eduardo, 144
charro, as term, 181n64
Chávez, Felipe, 63–64
Chávez, Vicente, 54
Chávez-García, Miroslava, 88
Chávez Magaña, Juan, 208n78
Chihuahua City Contracting Center, 35, 36, 65
Chowning, Margaret, 71
Churintzio, Michoacán, 92–93, 95, 142
CNC (Confederación Nacional Campesina), 83
Coeneo, Michoacán, 76–77, 78, 85, 109–110, 138–139
coercion, 133–141
Cohen, Deborah, 50, 109
Confederación de Trabajadores de México (CTM), 29, 181n64
Confederación Nacional Campesina (CNC), 83
contracting centers: in central Mexican states, 25–28, 32–35, 36, 58, 124–125; in Mexico City, 16, 19–25, 45, 148; in northern Mexican states, 40–42. *See also* municipal administration of the Bracero Program; *names of individual contract centers;* precontracting centers
Contreras de Bustamante, Ángela, 130
Coquet, Benito, 49
corruption. *See* bribery; coercion
Cosgaya, Carmen, 127

cotton production, 39, 40, 51, 101, 198n19. *See also* agricultural production
coyotes (smugglers), 139, 140, 147. *See also* undocumented migration
Craig, Richard, 32
Cristero War (1926–29), 5–6, 69, 72–73, 81–82, 88, 93, 129. *See also* Catholicism
Cristóbal Ruiz, Francisco, 54–55
Cross, Harry, 10
CTM (Confederación de Trabajadores de México), 29, 181n64

decentralization of the Bracero Program, 9–10, 12, 24–29, 33, 41–43, 46, 150
De la Fuente, Luis, 127
Délano, Alexandra, 14, 32
De la Peña, Guillermo, 51
De la Torre, Gonzalo, 135–136
De Loera, Félix, 89
Departamento de Investigaciones Políticas y Sociales. *See* DIPS
De Santiago, Eduardo, 65, 66
Diario Oficial de la Federación (publication), 17
Díaz Muñoz, Vidal, 53, 56
Díaz Ordaz, Gustavo, 10
Dimas Sosa, Juana, 138
DIPS (Departamento de Investigaciones Políticas y Sociales), 5, 25, 28, 37, 45, 123, 131
disease outbreak, 51–53, 70
Dolores Hidalgo, Guanajuato, 125
Domínguez, Juan, 68
Durand, Jorge, 99
Durán Ortega, Francisco, 88

Echeverría, Luis, 10–11, 154, 156
ejidatarios, 6, 20–21, 99. *See also* agrarian reform; ejidos; land redistribution
ejidos, 6, 20. *See also* agrarian reform; land redistribution; *names of specific ejidos*
electrification, 123, 143–144, 146. *See also* hydroelectric infrastructure
Ermita de Guadalupe, Zacatecas, 111
La Escondido, Zacatecas, 127–128
Esparza Díaz, José, 90
Esqueda, Carlos, 142
Excélsior (publication), 37

federal administration of the Bracero Program, 10–11; decentralization of program, 9–10, 12, 24–29, 33, 41–43, 46, 150; establishment of program, 14–18; Jalisco ban by, 29–31; mass deportation from US and, 36–42; Mexico City Contracting Center for, 16, 19–25; undocumented migration and, 32–35. See also *names of specific presidents;* state administration of the Bracero Program
Fernández del Campo, Luis, 20, 28–29
FitzGerald, David, 139
Flores, Encarnación, 112
Flores, Eulalio, 126
foot-and-mouth disease, 51–53, 70
Fox, Vicente, 154–155, 156, 214n18
fraccionamiento process, 79–80
Franco Rodríguez, David, 63, 64
Friedrich, Paul, 72
Las Fuentes, Michoacán, 146–147
Fuentes Aguilar, David, 96, 97
Fuentes Aldama, Carlos, 95
Fuentes Fajardo, Ladislao, 93, 96
Fuentes Fajardo, Porfirio, 93, 95, 96, 97
Fuentes Fajardo, Teófilo, 93
Furber, Roberto, 130

Gámez Orozco, Edmundo, 127, 128
Gamio, Manuel, 15
García Barragán, Marcelino, 27–28, 30–31, 84
García Guzmán, Benjamín, 142
García y Griego, Manuel, 33
Garibay Romero, José, 46–47, 54
Gastarbeiter initiatives, 152
Gillingham, Paul, 31
Gledhill, John, 99
El Gobernador, Jalisco, 115, 116, 117
Gómez, María Guadalupe, 138–139
Gómez, Marte R., 15, 20–21, 114
Gómez Sánchez, Pedro, 87
González, Francisco, 53, 55
González, Mariano, 18
González Gallo, Felipe, 84, 126
González Gallo, Jesús, 53, 56, 59, 95, 121
González Hernández, Miguel, 145
González Nava, Luis, 64–65
González Ruvalcaba, Zenaido, 85

González Vargas, Manuel, 84–85, 95–96
Goodman, Adam, 36–37, 38
Govea, Jesús, 79
Great Depression, 16
Greaves, Cecilia, 127
Guanajuato state, 2*map;* bracero migration from, 3, 22, 27–28, 39, 41; foot-and-mouth disease outbreak in, 52; La Quesera de Cortés, 107–108; Pénjamo, 7, 22, 78–81, 103, 124; Purísima del Rincón, 123–124; Las Raíces, 108–109; Rancho Nuevo de San Andrés, 110; religious-political conflicts in, 5–6, 78–81, 132; Romita, 125; San Diego de Alejandría, 27–28; San Francisco del Rincón, 123–124; Valle de Santiago, 109–110, 137. *See also under* Irapuato; state administration of the Bracero Program
Guerrero, Amador, 61
Guerrero, Nicéforo, 34, 52, 55
guest worker initiatives, 151–153, 164n21
Guevara, Ángel, 74, 96
Guzmán, Carlos, 34, 126
Guzmán Elías, Aureliano, 112

H2 visa program, 149, 211n3. *See also* US immigration policies
Hahamovitch, Cindy, 152, 164n21
health examinations, 17, 24
Henríquez Guzmán, Miguel, 31, 133
Heredia Herrera, Abelino, 95
Hermosillo Contracting Center, 35, 39
Hermosillo Medical Association, 39–40
Hernández, Alfredo, 77–78
Hernández, Juan, 145, 146
Hernández, Manuel, 26
Hernández Díaz, Marcelino, 145
Hernández Mota, Francisco, 145, 146
Hernández Rodríguez, Rogelio, 44
Hernández Serrano, José, 133–135
Herrera Tapia, David, 77
Hidalgo, Ernesto, 43, 70, 107–109
Hinojosa Torres, Rafael, 49–50, 54
hunger strike, 58
Hurtado, Benigno, 87
hydroelectric infrastructure, 51, 115, 118. *See also* electrification

Ibarra, Salvador, 65
Illegal Immigration Reform and Immigrant Responsibility Act (1996), 213n8
Immigration and Nationality Act (US; 1965), 149, 211n2
Immigration Reform and Control Act (US; 1986), 153, 213n8
Indigenous bracero workers, 23, 50–51, 109, 62–65, 124
INS (Immigration and Naturalization Service; US), 28, 32, 33, 36–37, 150, 153. *See also* US immigration policies
Institutional Revolutionary Party. *See* PRI
Irapuato Contracting Center, 29, 35, 36, 58, 124–125
Irapuato Precontracting Center, 26, 43, 123, 125
Irapuato Sinarquistas, 129–132
Ireta, Félix, 22, 24–25, 73
Isaac Arriaga, Michoacán, 105–107, 108

Jalisco state, 2*map;* Arandas, 81, 139; bracero migration from, 3, 27–28, 39, 41; ejidos of, 115–121; federal ban on braceros from, 29–31; Jesús María, 126; La Paz de Ordaz, 115–116, 117; religious-political conflict in, 5–6, 81–86; San Antonio, 115, 116, 117, 119; San Francisco, 115, 117; San José de Gracia, 85–86; San Martín de Hidalgo, 126, 138; San Ramón, 115, 117; Santa Elena, 70, 82–84; Tepatitlán, 7, 81–82, 85. *See also* state administration of the Bracero Program
Jamaica, 151–152
Jaramillo, Antonio, 169n28
Jaramillo, Porfirio, 169n28
Jaramillo, Rubén, 21, 169n28
Jerez, Zacatecas, 65, 87–88, 111, 120
Jesús del Monte, Michoacán, 98
Jesús María, Jalisco, 126
Juárez, Melecio, 77–78

Kissinger, Henry, 154
Kourí, Emilio, 101

labor unions: contract allotments and, 44; cooperation with, 16, 17, 31; intraunion conflict of, 53–54; lobbying efforts by, 4,

5, 9; Mexican American leaders on, 211n1. *See also* SNOCIAS; STIASRM; UNS
Land and Water Grants Law (1927), 111
landlessness, 81–86, 105–108
land redistribution, 6, 20–21, 87–88, 99–104, 128–129. *See also* agrarian reform
Lazcano, Luis Ortiz, 50
Lemus, José, 144
León, Eligio, 80
Lerma River, 118
Liévanos Ríos, Abdías, 137
Liga de Comunidades Agrarias (League of Agrarian Communities), 44, 48, 60–61, 89, 117
literacy program, 127–128
livestock disease outbreak, 51–53
Lomelí Anguiano, Bartolo, 84
López, Jacinto, 35
López Castro, Gustavo, 99
López Gómez, Camilo, 89, 90, 91
López Manriquez, David, 142
López Martínez, Leodegario, 138–139
López Mateos, Adolfo, 10, 41, 86, 91, 119, 136, 141
López Obrador, Andrés Manuel, 155–156
Loreto Occidental, Jalisco, 115, 116, 117
Loza, Mireya, 50, 51
Luis Moya, Zacatecas, 136
Luna Rodríguez, Carlos, 125
La Luz, Zacatecas, 112–113

Macías Padilla, José, 68
Madrazo, Carlos, 25
Magaña Valdovinos, Amador, 137
maize production, 20, 114, 119, 169n24. *See also* agricultural production
Maldonado, Félix, 93
Maldonado Corral, Sergio, 140
Maldonado Mendoza, David, 93, 94*fig.*, 96
Maldonado Pulido, Cornelio, 142
maps, 2, 7, 8, 40
Marín Pérez, Luis, 23, 73
Martínez, José María "Chema," 59
Martínez, Mariano, 146–147
Martínez López, Salvador, 91
Martínez Rangel, Heliodoro, 106

Marxism, 71–72
mass deportation from US, 28, 36–42, 175n118
Massey, Douglas, 99
Medellín, Jorge, 26
Medina Piñón, Abundio, 139–140
Medina Sánchez, Ignacio, 31, 56
Medrano, José, 73
Mejía, J. J., 144
Mendoza, Josefa, 93
Mendoza, Luis L., 168n12
Mendoza, Mary, 51
Mendoza, Rodolfo, 135–136
Mendoza Pardo, José María, 46–52, 54, 91, 98, 106, 110
Mexicali Contracting Center, 36
Mexico City Contracting Center, 16, 19–25, 45, 148
Mexico–United States Commission for the Eradication of Foot-and-Mouth Disease, 51–52
Meyer, Jean, 5–6
Michel, Matías, 19
Michoacán state, 2*map*; bracero migration from, 3, 23–24, 39, 41; Changuitiro, 3, 70, 92–95, 96, 142; Coeneo, 76–77, 78, 85, 109–110, 138–139; foot-and-mouth disease outbreak in, 52; Las Fuentes, 146–147; Isaac Arriaga, 105–107, 108; Jesús del Monte, 98; Monteleón, 119; La Nopalera, 98–99; Pátzcuaro Basin, 50–51, 139–140, 184n99; La Piedad, 103; Puruándiro, 73–75, 85, 105, 120, 129, 137, 143–144, 193n91; religious-political conflicts in, 5–6, 73–78, 91–95; Romero de Torres, 91–92; San José Huipana, 74, 96, 105; San Nicolás, 143–144; Santa Ana Mancera, 105; Zacapu, 111, 117, 118, 120, 142; Zamora, 47–48, 52, 54–55, 69, 91, 119, 142. *See also* state administration of the Bracero Program
Minero Roque, José, 39
Minian, Ana, 154
Monreal Buendía, Juan Pablo, 90
Monteleón, Michoacán, 119
Monterrey Contracting Center, 35, 36, 61
Morán, Juan, 48, 128
Mora Plancarte, Francisco, 47–48

Morelos state, 123–124, 169n28
Moreno, Luis, 47–48
Movimiento de Regeneración Nacional, 155
Múgica, Francisco, 72, 73
municipal administration of the Bracero Program, 10, 121–123, 146–148; advocacy, public works, and taxation by, 141–146; bracero selection as political tool of, 125–133; control and coercion by, 133–141; at precontracting centers, 26–27, 43–45, 123; state's reliance on, 56–60, 150. *See also* contracting centers

Natera, Pánfilo, 27, 45, 87, 123
National Action Party. *See* PAN
National Chamber of Industry, 39
National Stadium, Mexico City, 19, 24–26, 29. *See also* Mexico City Contracting Center
National Synarchist Union. *See* UNS
Navarro Castellanos, Miguel, 85–86
Ngai, Mae, 36–37
Nichols, Sandra, 87
La Nopalera, Michoacán, 98–99
Nuño Gonzáles, Antonio, 86

Ochoa Zambrano, Rubén, 62
Oficina de Estudios Especiales, 114
Oikión Solano, Verónica, 50
Ojeda García, Arcadio, 49
Oliva, Florentino, 58, 130–133
Olmos, Anacleto, 18
Olsson, Tore, 21
Operation Wetback, 37
Oropeza Nájera, Roberto, 68
Ortega Douglas, Luis, 61, 89, 112
Ortega Ramíres, Natividad, 124–125
Ortiz, Sebastián, 19, 20
Ortiz Lazcano, Luis, 50
Oseguera, Luis, 146–147

Padilla, Ezequiel, 27
Padilla Nervo, Luis, 24–25
Palomino Dena, Benito, 36, 145, 146
PAN (Partido Acción Nacional): bracero program and, 122, 154; Cristeros and, 6, 76, 81; demonstrations by, 95; electoral politics by, 69–70, 130, 137; eligibility cards and political alignment of, 122. *See also* Panistas
Panistas, 130–131, 132. *See also* PAN (Partido Acción Nacional); religious-political conflicts and Bracero migration
Papaloapan River, 115, 118
Papaloapan River Commission, 120
Parícutin Volcano eruption and *damnificados*, 9, 23–24, 46, 63, 151
Partido Acción Nacional. *See* PAN
Partido Popular (Popular Party), 35
Partido Revolucionario Institucional. *See* PRI
Pátzcuaro Basin, Michoacán, 50–51, 139–140, 184n99
La Paz de Ordaz, Jalisco, 115–116, 117
Pénjamo, Guanajuato, 7, 22, 78–81, 103, 124. *See also* Guanajuato state
Pérez, Prisciliano, 129
Personal Responsibility and Work Opportunity Reconciliation Act (1996), 213n8
La Piedad, Michoacán, 103
Pimentel, María, 144
Political and Social Investigations Department. *See* DIPS
political conflicts. *See* religious-political conflicts and Bracero migration
Ponce, Félix, 54, 59
population statistics, 8, 23, 153, 159n5, 170n36, 176n132
postrevolutionary Mexican state (1940–76), 4
precontracting centers, 26–27, 43–45, 123. *See also* contracting centers; municipal administration of the Bracero Program
Presa del Aguacate ejido, 70, 79–81, 192n70
Presa de los Serna, Zacatecas, 112–113
PRI (Partido Revolucionario Institucional): bracero program and, 147; electoral politics of, 29, 31, 65, 70, 129–131, 169n28; political control by, 4, 10–11; union cooperation of, 83
Protestantism, 15
public works, 142–146
Puente, Ignacio, 123–124
Purísima del Rincón, Guanajuato, 123–124

Purnell, Jennie, 72, 93
Puruándiro, Michoacán, 73–75, 85, 105, 120, 129, 137, 143–144, 193n91

quarantine, 51–52
La Quesera de Cortés, Guanajuato, 107–108
Quiles, Cayetano, 80
Quiroz Ramírez, Ignacio, 124

Las Raíces, Guanajuato, 108–109
Ramírez, Antonio, 130
Ramírez Miranda, César, 87
rancho, as term, 187n18
Rancho Nuevo de San Andrés, Guanajuato, 110
Rath, Thomas, 84
Refrigerated Maritime Transports (TMR), 38
Regional Cereal Producers Association, 39
religious-political conflicts and Bracero migration, 5–8, 68–71, 95–97, 151; Catholic roots of Greater Bajío, 71–73; Cristero War, 5–6, 69, 70, 72–73, 81–82, 88, 93, 129; in northeastern Jalisco, 81–86; in northern Michoacán, 73–78, 91–95; in southern Guanajuato, 78–81, 132; in southern Zacatecas, 86–88; in southwestern Aguascalientes, 88–91. *See also* Catholicism
remittances, 15, 155
Rentería, José, 110
research method, 4–5
Reyes, Juvencio, 78–79
Reyes Padilla, Zeferino, 125
Reynoso, Leobardo, 87
rifle sanitario strategy, 52
Ríos Thivol, Manuel, 131, 132
river basin commissions, 63, 64, 118, 120
Robles, Ernesto, 136
Rocha, David, 125
Rocha, José, 38
Rockefeller Foundation, 114
Rodríguez, Abelardo, 105
Rodríguez, Alberto, 81, 96
Rodríguez Gaona, Jesús, 39, 48–49, 57–58
Rodríguez Ramos, Ignacio, 125
Rojas Segura, Manuel, 140–141

Romero de Torres, Michoacán, 91–92
Romita, Guanajuato, 125
Rosas, Ana Elizabeth, 126, 138, 208n66
Rosas, Florentino, 80
Ruiz Cortines, Adolfo, 14, 17, 35–39, 74, 131

Salamea, Jalisco, 115, 116, 117
Salas Calvillo, Carlos, 60, 135
San Antonio, Jalisco, 115, 116, 117, 119
San Antonio de Aceves, 79
San Blas, Zacatecas, 127–128
Sánchez Susarrey, Jaime, 31, 56
San Diego de Alejandría, Guanajuato, 27–28
Sandos, James, 10
Sandoval Castillo, Andrés, 78, 96
Sandoval Coronel, Ángel, 98
San Francisco, Jalisco, 115, 117
San Francisco del Rincón, Guanajuato, 123–124
San Francisco Mill, 53
San José de Gracia, Jalisco, 85–86
San José del Río, Aquacalientes, 135
San José Huipana, Michoacán, 74, 96, 105
San Martín de Hidalgo, Jalisco, 126, 138
San Miguel, Zacatecas, 127–128
San Nicolás, Michoacán, 143–144
San Ramón, Jalisco, 115, 117
Santa Ana Mancera, Michoacán, 105
Santa Cruz García, Ernesto, 134–135
Santa Cruz Mill, 29
Santa Elena, Jalisco, 70, 82–84
Secretaría de Educación Pública. *See* SEP
Secure Fences Act (2006), 213n8
selection process as political tool, 125–133
SEP (Secretaría de Educación Pública), 68, 127, 128
Serna, Adolfo, 112
Serna, Arturo, 112
Serna, Cipriano, 112
Serna, Jesús, 112
Serna, Rogelio, 112
Serrano Álvarez, Pablo, 129
Sierra Purépecha, 23, 50–51, 62–65, 109, 124
Sinarquistas, 70, 73–74, 95, 129–132. *See also* religious-political conflicts and Bracero migration

Sindicato de Trabajadores de la Industria Azucarera y Similares de la República Mexicana. *See* STIASRM
Sindicato Nacional de Obreros y Campesinos de la Industria Azucarera y Similares (SNOCIAS), 30, 31
Smith, Benjamin, 70, 143
SNOCIAS (Sindicato Nacional de Obreros y Campesinos de la Industria Azucarera y Similares), 30, 31
Snodgrass, Michael, 31
Sobarzo, Horacio, 35
Social Catholicism, 71–72. *See also* Catholicism
Sociedad de Padres de Familia, 78
SS *Mercurio*, 38
state administration of the Bracero Program, 43–45, 65–67; 1947 distributions in, 49–55; conclusion of, 60–65; contracting centers processing, 45–49; reliance on municipal governments by, 56–60. *See also* federal administration of the Bracero Program; *names of specific Mexican states*
Stauffer, Brian, 71
STIASRM (Sindicato de Trabajadores de la Industria Azucarera y Similares de la República Mexicana), 29–31, 53–57, 59–60, 182n78
strategic tightrope, 21
Swing, Joseph, 36, 37

Talamantes, Epimenio, 145–146
Tamayo Valladolid, Carlos, 141
Tapia, Primo, 117
taxation, 60, 122, 140–141, 143
Tepalcatepec River, 115
Tepalcatepec River Commission, 63, 64, 120
Tepatitlán, Jalisco, 7, 81–82, 85. *See also* Jalisco state
Terán, Horacio, 57
Terriquez Martínez, José, 20
Tlaquepaque Contracting Center, 35, 36
Torreón Contracting Center, 35
Torres, Julio, 129
Torres Bodet, Jaime, 15

Torres Espinosa, Ignacio, 47–48, 55
Torres Hernández, Leopoldo, 124–125
Torres Herrera, Abelino, 47
Transportes Marítimos Refrigerados (TMR), 38
Tres Mezquites, Michoacán, 129
Trujillo, Carlos, 83–84
Trujillo Gurría, Francisco, 22, 25, 30
Truman, Harry, 34
Trump, Donald, 155
Turkey, 152

UCC (Unión Cívica Calvillense), 90–91
undocumented migration, 28, 32–35, 139, 140, 147, 152–153
Unión Cívica Calvillense (UCC), 90–91
Unión Nacional Sinarquista. *See* UNS
United Merchants Corporation, 39
El Universal (publication), 37
UNS (Unión Nacional Sinarquista), 6, 10, 69–70, 73, 81, 82, 122, 129, 131–132, 147
Uribe, Dolores, 127
Uruapan Contracting Center, 29
Urzúa Flores, Guadalupe, 123, 204n3
US immigration policies, 28, 32–42, 149, 151–156, 175n118, 211nn2–3, 213n8. *See also* INS (Immigration and Naturalization Service; US)

Valadéz, Procopio, 47
Valle de Santiago, Guanajuato, 109–110, 137
Valle Padilla, José, 82
Vargas Cienfuegos, Roberto, 130
Vargas Mondragón, Ramón, 142
Vargas Reyes, Santiago, 64–65
Vargas Rivera, José, 137
Vázquez, Daniel, 125
Vázquez Cerda, Fidencio, 83–84
Vela Perpetua, 71
Velderrain, Rafael, 137
Vera Salvo, Ramón, 87
Vergara, Eusebio, 79, 80
Víctor, Ezequiel, 146–147
Villagómez, Fausto, 28, 43
Viudas de Oriente, 128
volcanic eruption. *See* Parícutin Volcano eruption and *damnificados*

wage discrimination, 17
Weise, Julie, 34, 174n97
wheat production, 20, 169n24. *See also* agricultural production
Women's League, 78

Xoconoxtle el Grande, Guanajuato, 126

Yáñez Delgadillo, Agustín, 36

Zacapu, Michoacán, 111, 117, 118, 120, 142
Zacatecas City Precontracting Center, 26–27, 45, 123, 127
Zacatecas state, 2*map,* 39; bracero migration from, 3, 27, 41, 127–128; Ermita de Guadalupe, 111; La Escondido, 127–128; La Luz, 112–113; precontracting center in, 26–27, 45, 123; Presa de los Serna, 112–113; religious-political conflicts in, 5–6, 86–88; San Blas, 127–128; San Miguel, 127–128. *See also* state administration of the Bracero Program
Zamora, Michoacán, 7, 47–48, 52, 54–55, 69, 91, 119, 142. *See also* Michoacán state
Zarza, Eduardo, 68

Founded in 1893,
UNIVERSITY OF CALIFORNIA PRESS
publishes bold, progressive books and journals
on topics in the arts, humanities, social sciences,
and natural sciences—with a focus on social
justice issues—that inspire thought and action
among readers worldwide.

The UC PRESS FOUNDATION
raises funds to uphold the press's vital role
as an independent, nonprofit publisher, and
receives philanthropic support from a wide
range of individuals and institutions—and from
committed readers like you. To learn more, visit
ucpress.edu/supportus.

www.ingramcontent.com/pod-product-compliance
Lightning Source LLC
Chambersburg PA
CBHW020757230426
43666CB00007B/737